Patoka River
National Wildlife Refuge & Management Area
Comprehensive Conservation Plan

Patoka River
National Wildlife Refuge and Management Area

Comprehensive Conservation Plan Approval

Submitted by:

_____William McCoy_____ Aug. 21, 2008
William McCoy   Date
Refuge Manager

Concur:

_____Rick Frietsche_____ 08/26/2008
Rick Frietsche   Date
Acting Refuge Supervisor, Area 2

_____Nita M. Fuller_____ 8.29.2008
Nita M. Fuller   Date
Regional Chief, National Wildlife Refuge System

Approve:

_____Charlie Wooley_____ 9/2/08
Charles M. Wooley   Date
Acting Regional Director
for Robyn Thorson
Regional Director

Patoka River
National Wildlife Refuge & Management Area

Comprehensive Conservation Plan

Chapter 1: Introduction and Background 1
    Introduction 1
    Purpose and Need for Plan 1
    Establishment of the Refuge 3
    Refuge Purposes 4
    Refuge Vision 4
    The U.S. Fish and Wildlife Service 4
    The National Wildlife Refuge System 4
    Legal and Policy Guidance 6
        Compatibility Policy 6
        Biological Integrity, Diversity, and Environmental Health Policy 7
        Other Guidance 7
    Existing Partnerships 7
    Volunteers and Friends Group 8
    Museums and Repositories 8

Chapter 2: The Planning Process 9
    Public Scoping 9
        The Comments 9
        Internal Scoping 10
    Preparation, Publishing, Finalization and Implementation of the CCP 11
    Summary of Issues, Concerns and Opportunities 11

Chapter 3: Refuge Environment and Management 14
    Introduction 14
    Wetland Loss in Indiana 14
    The Ohio River Valley Ecosystem 16
    Other Units Administered 20
    Migratory Bird Conservation Initiatives 20
        North American Waterfowl Management Plan 20
        Partners In Flight 21
        U.S. Shorebird Conservation Plan 21
        Waterbird Conservation for the Americas 22
        North American Bird Conservation Initiative 23
    Region 3 Fish and Wildlife Conservation Priorities 24
    Indiana Comprehensive Wildlife Strategy 24
    Other Recreation and Conservation Lands in the Area 24
        Sugar Ridge Fish & Wildlife Area 24
        Glendale Fish & Wildlife Area 24

- Pike State Forest 24
- Ferdinand State Forest 26
- Other Recreation and Conservation Lands 26
- Socioeconomic Setting 26
  - Population 26
  - Employment 26
  - Income and Education 27
  - Potential Refuge Visitors 27
- Climate 27
- Climate Change 28
  - Observed Climate Trends 29
  - Scenarios of Future Climate 29
  - Midwest Key Issues 29
    - Reduction in Lake and River Levels 29
    - Agricultural Shifts 30
    - Changes in Semi-natural and Natural Ecosystems 30
- Air Quality 31
- Geology and Soils 32
  - Geology 32
  - Minerals 32
    - Oil 32
    - Gas 32
    - Coal 33
- Soils 33
  - Bottomland Soil Associations 33
  - Upland Soil Associations 34
- Water and Hydrology 35
- Refuge Resources 37
  - Plant Communities 37
    - Wetlands 37
    - Open Water 38
    - Uplands 38
    - Invasive Plant Species 38
    - Threatened and Endangered Plants 39
  - Fish and Wildlife Communities 39
    - Birds 39
  - Mammals 41
    - Game Mammals 41
    - Furbearers 42
    - Nongame mammals 43
    - Amphibians and Reptiles 43
  - Fish 44
  - Invertebrates 45
    - Insects 45
    - Molluscs 45
- Threatened and Endangered Species 46
  - Threatened and Endangered Flora 46
  - Threatened and Endangered Fauna 46
    - Whooping Crane (Grus Americana) 46

    Bald Eagle (Haliaeetus leucocephalus) 46
    Least Tern (Sterna antillarum) (Interior Population) 48
    Fat Pocketbook (Potamilus capax) 48
    Indiana Bat (Myotis sodalist) 48
    Copperbelly Water Snake (Nerodia erythrogaster neglecta) 49
Threats to Resources 49
  Invasive Species 49
  Contaminants 52
Interstate 69 55
Administrative Facilities 56
Archeological and Cultural Values 56
Current Management 57
  Habitat Management 57
    Forested Wetlands (Bottomland Forest) 57
    Emergent Wetlands 60
    Lakes and Ponds 60
    Patoka River, Oxbows, and Patoka Tributaries 60
    Water Quality 60
    Moist Soil Units 60
    Grasslands 60
    Upland Forests 60
    Cropland 61
    Upland Openings 61
    Invasive Plant Species 61
    Interior Least Tern Nesting Habitat 61
    Private Lands and Watershed Management 61
    Farm Services Administration Conservation Easements 61
    Land Acquisition 62
  Wildlife Management 62
    Threatened and Endangered Species 62
    Migratory and Resident Birds 62
    Native Resident Wildlife 62
    Fish and Other Aquatic Species 62
    Interior Least Terns 62
    Pest Management 62
  Fish and Wildlife Monitoring 62
  Visitor Services 63
    Hunting 63
    Fishing 63
    Wildlife Observation and Photography 65
    Interpretation 65
    Environmental Education 65
    Friends and Volunteers 65
    Outreach 65
  Archeological and Cultural Values 65
    Special Management Areas 65
Wilderness Review 65

Chapter 4: Management Direction **66**
    Goals, Objectives and Strategies 66

Chapter 5: Plan Implementation **82**
    New and Existing Projects 82
        Construct Visitor Parking Lots 82
        Completion of Observation Deck 82
        Reconnect Oxbows on Patoka River 82
        Maintenance and Construction of Storage Facilities 82
        Macrotopography Wetlands 82
    Future Staffing Requirements 83
    Partnership Opportunities 83
    Step-down Management Plans 84
    Archeological and Cultural Values 84
    Monitoring and Evaluation 85
    Plan Review and Revision 85

Appendix A: Finding of No Significant Impact **87**
Appendix B: Glossary **91**
Appendix C: Species Lists **97**
Appendix D: Resource Conservation Priorities, Ohio River Valley Ecosystem **119**
Appendix E: Compliance Requirements **125**
Appendix F: Mailing List **131**
Appendix G: Compatibility Determinations **137**
Appendix H: List of Preparers **139**
Appendix I: Literature Cited **143**
Appendix J: Priority Refuge Operational and Maintenance Needs **151**
Appendix K: Response to Comments on the Draft CCP **155**

List of Figures

Figure 1: Location of Patoka River NWR & MA 2
Figure 2: Patoka River NWR & MA Delineations 5
Figure 3: Acquisition Authority, Patoka River NWR & MA 15
Figure 4: Ohio River Valley Ecosystem 17
Figure 5: Bird Conservation Region in Which Patoka River NWR & MA is Located 23
Figure 6: Other Conservation Lands in the Area of Patoka River NWR & MA 25
Figure 7: Hydrology at Patoka River NWR & MA 36
Figure 8: Projected Route of Interstate 69 56
Figure 9: Current Landcover (West), Patoka River NWR & MA 58
Figure 10: Current Landcover (East), Patoka River NWR & MA 59
Figure 11: Current Visitor Facilities, Patoka River NWR & MA 64
Figure 12: Long-term (100 Years) Landcover, Patoka River NWR & MA (East) 67
Figure 13: Long-term (100 Years) Landcover, Patoka River NWR & MA (West) 68
Figure 14: Current and Future Concept of Patoka River Channel 69
Figure 15: Current Staffing Chart, Patoka River NWR 83
Figure 16: Staffing Required to Fully Implement Plan 83

List of Tables

Table 1: Status of Land Acquisition, Patoka River NWR & MA 16
Table 2: Endangered, Threatened, or Rare Vascular Plants in Gibson and Pike Counties, Indiana, as of 2005 47
Table 3: Endangered, Threatened, or Rare Fauna in Gibson and Pike Counties, Indiana, as of 2005 50
Table 4: Invasive Plants and Animals at Patoka NWR/MA 53
Table 5: Step-down Management Plan Schedule 84

Chapter 1: Introduction and Background

Introduction

Patoka River National Wildlife Refuge and Management Area (NWR & MA) is a work in progress. Established in 1994, approximately one-fourth of the total area approved for acquisition is presently part of the Refuge. Acquiring additional lands within the approved boundary is an ongoing effort. The Refuge is the 502nd refuge within the National Wildlife Refuge System and second refuge established in the State of Indiana.

The Patoka River had long been recognized for its wetland and wildlife values on a local, statewide and regional basis. In the late 1980s and early 1990s, the Service proposed establishing a national wildlife refuge/wildlife management area along the Patoka River in Pike and Gibson Counties of southwestern Indiana (see Figure 1). The portion of the river included in the proposal contains one of the few remaining expanses of bottomland hardwood forest wetlands in Indiana and the midwestern United States.

The area provides some of the best Wood Duck production habitat in all of Indiana. In all there are more than 380 species of wildlife on the Refuge, including the federally-listed endangered Indiana bat.

The area's natural resources face considerable challenges. Along the Patoka River, ditching, diking and channelization dating back to the early 1900s contributed to wetland losses. Water quality in the Patoka River drainage was diminished by over 20,000 acres of abandoned coal mine lands, oil well development activities, intensive agricultural operations, and community effluent.

Migrating Trumpeter Swans. Patoka River NWR & MA. Photo credit: USFWS

Purpose and Need for Plan

This Comprehensive Conservation Plan (CCP) articulates the management direction for Patoka River NWR & MA for the next 15 years. Through the development of goals, objectives, and strategies, the CCP describes how the Refuge contributes to the overall mission of the National Wildlife Refuge System. Several legislative mandates within the National Wildlife Refuge System Improvement Act of 1997 have guided the development of this plan. These mandates include:

- Wildlife has first priority in the management of refuges.
- Wildlife-dependent recreation activities: namely hunting, fishing, wildlife observation, wildlife photography, environmental education and interpretation are priority public uses of refuges. We will facilitate these activities when they do not interfere with our ability to fulfill the refuges' purpose or the mission of the Refuge System.

Figure 1: Location of Patoka River NWR & MA

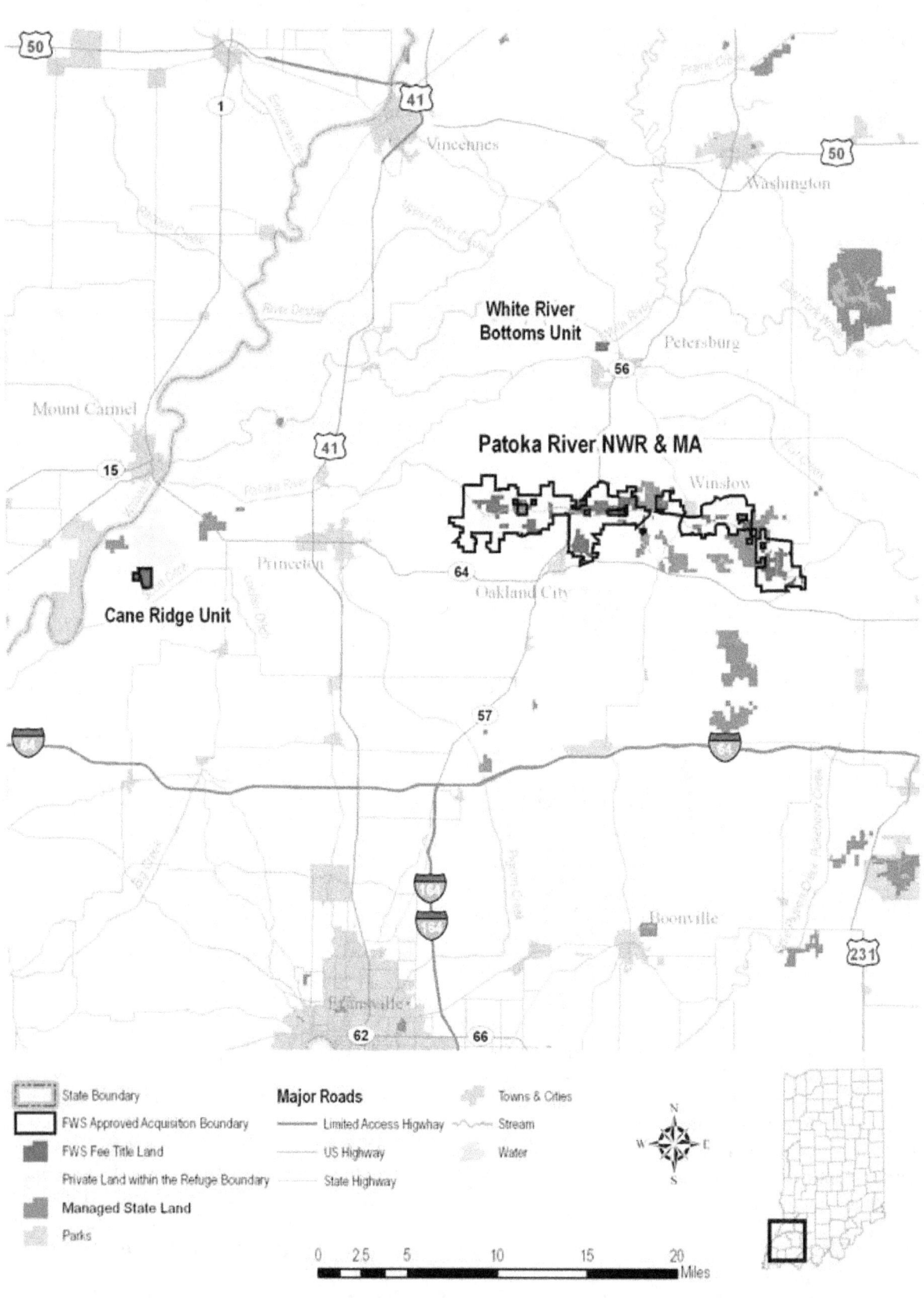

- Other uses of the Refuge will only be allowed when determined appropriate and compatible with Refuge purposes and mission of the Refuge System.

The plan will guide the management of Patoka River NWR & MA by:

- Providing a clear statement of direction for the future management of the Refuge.
- Making a strong connection between Refuge activities and conservation activities that occur in the surrounding area.
- Providing Refuge neighbors, users, and the general public with an understanding of the Service's land acquisition and management actions on and around the Refuge.
- Ensuring the Refuge actions and programs are consistent with the mandates of the National Wildlife Refuge System.
- Ensuring that Refuge management considers federal, state, and county plans.
- Ensuring that Refuge management considers the preservation of historic properties.
- Establishing long-term continuity in Refuge management.
- Providing a basis for the development of budget requests on the Refuge's operational, maintenance, and capital improvement needs.

Establishment of the Refuge

In 1986, the Emergency Wetlands Resources Act (Act) was enacted by Congress to promote the conservation of America's wetlands by intensifying cooperative efforts among federal agencies, states, local governments, and private interests for conservation, management, and acquisition of wetlands.

The Department of the Interior developed a National Wetlands Priority Conservation Plan as directed by Section 301 of the Act, and in the Midwest Region a Regional Wetlands Concept Plan (USFWS, 1990) was prepared to provide a framework for protecting priority wetlands in the eight states states that make up the Region: Illinois, Indiana, Iowa, Michigan, Minnesota, Missouri, Ohio and Wisconsin. The Regional Wetlands Concept Plan provided the focus for acquisition, restoration and renewal of valuable wetlands, emphasizing those areas where losses are highest.

The stretch of the Patoka River running through Pike and Gibson Counties in southern Indiana was identified as a focus area within the 1990 Regional Wetlands Concept Plan. The area is part of the middle Mississippi River and lower Ohio River drainage and is characterized by rich bottomland hardwood wetlands that historically provided prime breeding and wintering habitat for species such as Wood Ducks, Mallards and Bald Eagles.

Patoka River NWR & MA was established in 1994. The authorized boundary (also known as the "acquisition boundary") – which delineates where the Service can acquire property from willing sellers – encompasses 23,743 acres of wetlands, floodplain forest, and upland buffer along 30 miles of the Patoka River corridor. Management objectives are identical for the National Wildlife Refuge, authorized at 6,970 acres, and the Management Area (MA), authorized for the remaining 15,847 acres. The separate designations avoid legal conflicts with the Surface Mining Control and Reclamation Act (SMCRA) of 1977.

SMCRA prohibits surface mining within national wildlife refuges. Legally, this was interpreted to apply to all lands within the authorized boundary of a national wildlife refuge regardless of ownership. Much of the land along the Patoka River corridor is privately owned and underlain by surface and/or underground minable coal reserves. Designating the entire area within the boundary as a National Wildlife Refuge would have prohibited surface mining and required compensating land owners for the value of this property right.

To find a solution to this dilemma, the U.S. Office of Surface Mining was contracted to complete a coal study to determine which lands within the acquisition boundary were underlain by potentially min-

Mallard nest, Patoka River NWR & MA. Photo credit: USFWS

able coal reserves. The areas with coal deposits were delineated and identified as a "selection area" for the acquisition of Wildlife Management Areas instead of being identified as an acquisition area for the National Wildlife Refuge. Figure 2 shows the distribution of these areas within the Refuge boundary. This naming convention was done to avert a conflict with the SMCRA and to avoid the unintentional taking of surface minable coal rights of private land owners. It has no implications for the management of these areas.

Refuge Purposes

Refuge purposes are specified or derived from the law, proclamation, Executive Order, agreement, public land order, donation document, or administrative memorandum establishing, authorizing, or expanding a refuge, refuge unit, or refuge subunit. Patoka River NWR & MA has the following refuge purposes:

> "... the conservation of the wetlands of the Nation in order to maintain the public benefits they provide and to help fulfill international obligations contained in various migratory bird treaties and conventions ...Ó 16 U.S.C. 3901(b) (Emergency Wetlands Resources Act of 1986)

> "... particular value in carrying out the national migratory bird management program. 16 U.S.C. 667b (An Act Authorizing the Transfer of Certain Real Property for Wildlife)

> "... (1) to protect, enhance, restore, and manage an appropriate distribution and diversity of wetland ecosystems and other habitats for migratory birds and other fish and wildlife in North America; (2) to maintain current or improved distributions of migratory bird populations; and (3) to sustain an abundance of waterfowl and other migratory birds consistent with the goals of the North American Waterfowl Management Plan and the international obligations contained in the migratory bird treaties and conventions and other agreements with Canada, Mexico, and other countries." 16 U.S.C. 4401-4413 (North American Wetlands Conservation Act)

Refuge Vision

The Patoka River National Wildlife Refuge and Management Area restores, protects and manages a diverse bottomland hardwood forest ecosystem and associated habitats for migratory birds, threatened and endangered species, and indigenous fish and wildlife, while striving to develop citizen understanding and support for the protection of natural resources by providing wildlife-related education and recreation opportunities.

The U.S. Fish and Wildlife Service

The U.S. Fish and Wildlife Service (Service) is the primary federal agency responsible for conserving, protecting, and enhancing the nation's fish and wildlife populations and their habitats. The Service administers the lands of the National Wildlife Refuge System, oversees the enforcement of federal wildlife laws, management and protection of migratory bird populations, restoration of nationally significant fisheries, administration of the Endangered Species Act, and the restoration of wildlife habitat such as wetlands.

The National Wildlife Refuge System

Refuge lands are part of the National Wildlife Refuge System, which was founded in 1903 when President Theodore Roosevelt designated Pelican Island in Florida as a sanctuary for brown pelicans. Today, the System is a network of more than 540 refuges covering more than 93 million acres of public lands and waters. Most of these lands (82 percent) are in Alaska, with approximately 16 million acres located in the lower 48 states and several island territories. The National Wildlife Refuge System is the world's largest collection of lands specifically managed for fish and wildlife. Overall, it provides habitat for more than 5,000 species of birds, mammals, fish, and insects. As a result of international treaties for migratory bird conservation as well as other legislation, such as the Migratory Bird Conservation Act of 1929, many refuges have been established to protect migratory waterfowl and their migratory flyways from their northern nesting grounds to southern wintering areas. Refuges also play a vital role in preserving endangered and threatened species. Among the most notable is Aransas National Wildlife Refuge in Texas, which provides winter habitat for the Whooping Crane. Likewise, the Florida Panther NWR protects one of the nation's most

Chapter 1: Introduction and Background

Figure 2: Patoka River NWR & MA Delineations

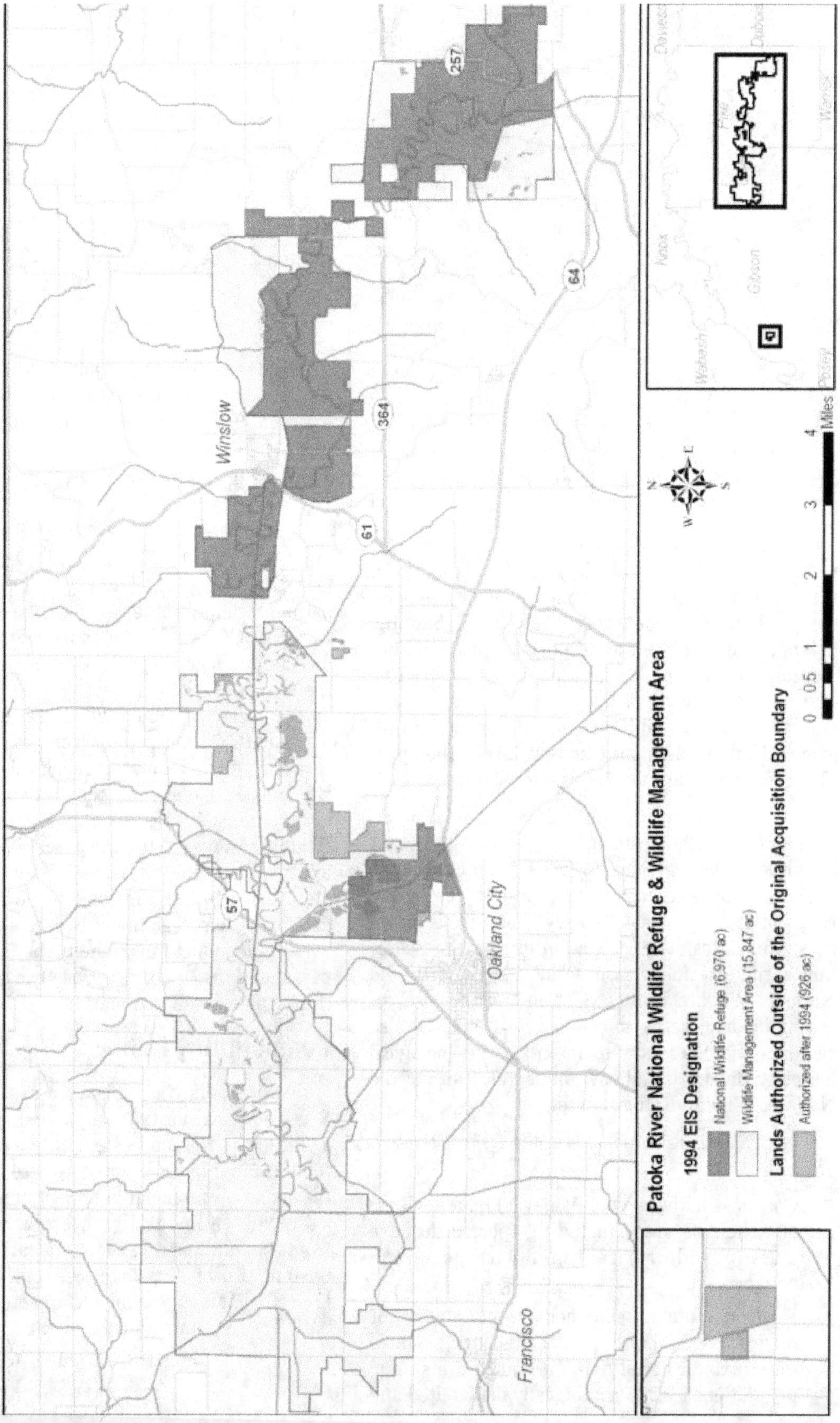

Patoka River National Wildlife Refuge and Management Area / Comprehensive Conservation Plan

Snakey Point fishing pier, Patoka River NWR & MA. Photo credit: USFWS

endangered predators, and the Mississippi Sandhill Crane NWR an endangered, non-migratory species of the Sandhill Crane.

Refuges also provide unique opportunities for people. When it is compatible with wildlife and habitat conservation, they are places where people can enjoy wildlife-dependent recreation such as hunting, fishing, wildlife observation, photography, environmental education, and environmental interpretation. Many refuges have visitor centers, wildlife trails, automobile tours, and environmental education programs. Nationwide, approximately 39.5 million people visited national wildlife refuges in 2003.

The National Wildlife Refuge System Improvement Act of 1997 established several important mandates aimed at making the management of national wildlife refuges more cohesive. The preparation of comprehensive conservation plans is one of those mandates. The legislation directs the Secretary of the Interior to ensure that the mission of the National Wildlife Refuge System and purposes of the individual refuges are carried out. It also requires the Secretary to maintain the biological integrity, diversity, and environmental health of the National Wildlife Refuge System.

The goals of the National Wildlife Refuge System are to:

- Conserve a diversity of fish, wildlife, and plants and their habitats, including species that are endangered or threatened with becoming endangered.
- Develop and maintain a network of habitats for migratory birds, anadromous and interjurisdictional fish, and marine mammal populations that is strategically distributed and carefully managed to meet important life history needs of these species across their ranges.
- Conserve those ecosystems, plant communities, wetlands of national or international significance, and landscapes and seascapes that are unique, rare, declining, or underrepresented in existing protection efforts.
- Provide and enhance opportunities to participate in compatible wildlife-dependent recreation (hunting, fishing, wildlife observation and photography, and environmental education and interpretation).
- Foster understanding and instill appreciation of the diversity and interconnectedness of fish, wildlife, and plants and their habitats.

Legal and Policy Guidance

The National Wildlife Refuge System Improvement Act of 1997 established several important mandates aimed at making the management of national wildlife refuges more cohesive. The preparation of CCPs is one of those mandates. The Act directs the Secretary of the Interior to ensure that the mission of the National Wildlife Refuge System and purposes of the individual refuges are carried out. The 1997 Refuge Improvement Act requires the Secretary to maintain the biological integrity, diversity, and environmental health and to identify the archeological and cultural values of the National Wildlife Refuge System. The Act deals with compatibility of uses on refuges and directs the Secretary of Interior to issue regulations for compatibility determinations. The Act also directs that compatible wildlife-dependent uses should be facilitated. Since passage of the Act, the Service has adopted policies that implement direction of the Act.

Compatibility Policy

Service policy says that no uses for which the Service has authority to regulate may be allowed on a unit of the Refuge System unless it is determined to be compatible. A compatible use is a use that, in the sound professional judgment of the refuge manager, will not materially interfere with or detract from the fulfillment of the National Wildlife Refuge System mission or the purposes of the national wildlife refuge. Managers must complete a written compatibility determination for each use, or collection of

Chapter 1: Introduction and Background

Foxglove beard-tongue, Patoka River NWR & MA. Photo credit: USFWS

like uses, that is signed by the manager and the Regional Chief of Refuges in the respective Service region.

Biological Integrity, Diversity, and Environmental Health Policy

The Service is directed in the Refuge Improvement Act to "ensure that the biological integrity, diversity, and environmental health of the Refuge System are maintained for the benefit of present and future generations of Americans…" The biological integrity policy helps define and clarify this directive by providing guidance on what conditions constitute biological integrity, diversity, and environmental health; guidelines for maintaining existing levels; guidelines for determining how and when it is appropriate to restore lost elements; and guidelines in dealing with external threats to biological integrity, diversity and health.

Other Guidance

In addition to the Refuge's establishing executive orders, authorizing legislation, and the National Wildlife Refuge System Improvement Act of 1997, several Federal laws, executive orders, and regulations govern administration of the Refuge. Appendix E contains a partial list of the legal mandates that guided the preparation of this plan and those that pertain to Refuge management activities.

Existing Partnerships

Working with others through intra- and inter-agency partnerships is essential to accomplishing the mission of the Fish and Wildlife Service as well as assisting Patoka River NWR & MA in achieving its purposes and vision. Partnerships with other federal and state agencies and with a diversity of public and private organizations are increasingly important. Other agencies can provide invaluable assistance in research and maintenance. Private groups and non-profit organizations greatly enhance public involvement in the Refuge, building enthusiasm and support for its mission.

Within the Ohio River Valley ecosystem in which Patoka River NWR is located, the Service partners with a number of other agencies and institutions, both governmental and non-governmental. These include:

- State conservation and natural resources agencies, including the Indiana Department of Natural Resources (Indiana Wildlife and Fisheries);
- Federal agencies, including the U.S. Forest Service, U.S. Environmental Protection Agency, National Park Service, U.S. Geological Survey Biological Resources Division, and Natural Resources Conservation Service;
- Local governments;
- Institutions of higher learning;
- Local landowners and businesses
- Non-governmental conservation organizations

Besides the partnerships that the Fish and Wildlife Service holds on the national and regional (ecosystem) level, Patoka River NWR maintains formal and informal working partnerships with the following agencies, non-governmental conservation organizations, and businesses:

- Indiana Department of Natural Resources
- Division of Fish and Wildlife
- Division of Mining and Reclamation
- Division of Oil and Gas
- Division of Nature Preserves

- Indiana Heritage Trust
- Indiana Department of Transportation
- USDA Natural Resources Conservation Service (NRCS)
- Gibson County Coal
- Duke Energy (an electric utility operating the Gibson Generating Station)
- Ducks Unlimited
- Evansville Chapter of the National Audubon Society
- Waterfowl U.S.A.
- Quail Unlimited
- National Wild Turkey Federation
- National Fish and Wildlife Foundation
- PRIDE – Refuge Friends
- Izaak Walton League
- U.S. Army Corps of Engineers- Louisville
- U.S. Office of Surface Mining and Reclamation

Volunteers and Friends Group

The Refuge also relies on the selfless dedication of volunteers to extend the efforts of staff. Volunteers play an important role in the management and maintenance of the fish and wildlife resources on Patoka River Wildlife Refuge. In an era of flat or declining budgets, it is more important now than ever that volunteers step forward to help protect and preserve our natural resource heritage for present and future generations to enjoy.

Patoka River NWR also has an informal Friends group that has helped implement projects like construction of the fishing pier and trail at Snakey Point and the South Fork Fishermans Trail.

Museums and Repositories

The Refuge has no reported museum property on- or off-site; no natural history specimens, no artwork, nor historic documents or photographs nor any other kind of historical material. The several cultural resources surveys conducted on the Refuge have produced no archeological collections.

Chapter 2: The Planning Process

Patoka River NWR's CCP has been written with input and assistance from citizens, non-governmental conservation organizations (NGOs), and other government agencies. The participation of these stakeholders is vital and all of their ideas have been valuable in determining the future direction of the three refuges. Refuge and regional staff – indeed, the entire U.S. Fish and Wildlife Service – are grateful to all of those who have contributed time, expertise and ideas throughout the comprehensive conservation planning process. We appreciated the enthusiasm and commitment expressed by many for the lands and living resources administered by Patoka River NWR.

Public Scoping

Work on the comprehensive conservation plan began with a public scoping meeting held on October 14, 2004 at the Indiana Department of Natural Resources' Sugar Ridge Fish and Wildlife Area Office, south of Winslow, Indiana. More than 30 people attended the meeting to offer their ideas for the Refuge's management.

People attending the meeting were offered a variety of ways to submit their comments. Refuge staff and regional planners were available to talk about issues, and staff used a computer to write a short summary of the conversation so that it would be recorded. Attendees could also use a survey form or index card to submit written comments. In addition, staff prepared questions about Refuge management to post throughout the room, and people attending the meeting were invited to use red or green stickers to indicate whether they supported a given idea or not.

Staff also invited people to record their experiences on Patoka River NWR on a timeline.

Canada Geese, Patoka River NWR & MA. Photo credit: USFWS

The Comments

There were a number of comments about land acquisition. Most were supportive of additional land acquisition with some noting frustration with the land appraisal process. Others mentioned that insufficient funds were hampering acquisition efforts. Two comments opposed additional funding for land acquisition.

Some comments expressed concern about management of lands presently owned by the Refuge citing the need for additional money and staff to carry out proper management. Trespassing from Refuge lands onto adjoining private lands was seen as a problem by some, and a number supported increased law enforcement presence.

Opinion on hunting was mixed, with some people supporting additional hunting opportunities. Others said that hunting should not be allowed on some portions of the Refuge; some were interested in limiting hunting to encourage wildlife and others were interested in preserving portions of the Refuge for wildlife observation even during hunting seasons. There was support and some opposition to establishing sanctuary areas where no hunting would occur.

A number of individual comments supported allowing a variety of uses including night fishing, harvesting nuts, berries, and mushrooms, and trapping.

There was strong support for a visitor center. Additional trails as well as user fees were supported by some and opposed by others.

A number of people expressed concern about the potential construction of Interstate 69 and the effect it may have on the Refuge.

Another survey question asked whether there should be more trails on the Refuge. Most of the comments supported additional trails, with one person saying he or she supported more trails except where they might inhibit wildlife. One commenter said the Refuge does not need additional trails, and another said that the existing trails need greater visibility in the community.

Concern about the effect the Interstate 69 project might have on the Refuge was expressed in responses to a survey question asking what changes might help or challenge the Refuge. Two people expressed reservations about the project's effect on the Refuge and a third person said that depending on how it's done the highway project could have either a good or bad effect on the Refuge.

Problems facing the Refuge were described as funding for acquisition, funding in general, all-terrain vehicles, and visibility.

Nine people attending the meeting supported an entrance or user fee while two people indicated that they did not support a fee.

Internal Scoping

On April 19, 2005 the Regional Office held an internal scoping meeting on the development of the Patoka River NWR Comprehensive Conservation Plan. People attending the meeting included the Deputy Regional Director, the Deputy Chief of Refuges, the Chief of Engineering, and staff from the Division of Conservation Planning, the Division of Migratory Birds, the Division of Ecological Services, the Division of Visitor Services, the Division of Realty, and the North American Waterfowl Management Plan.

Flooded river oxbow, Patoka River NWR & MA. Photo credit: USFWS

Regional Office staff idenfitied several issues that should be addressed in the comprehensive conservation plan:

- How will the Interstate 69 project affect the Refuge? The location of exits, a rest stop and a pull off all have positive and negative aspects for the Refuge.
- What is a reasonable acquisition goal for next 15 years?
- Land acquisition is difficult for the Service right now because of funding issues.
- Is there potential for increasing the number of accesses to the Refuge?
- Are there opportunities for moving the Refuge's Headquarters to property owned by the Service or other government agency instead of continuing to lease space?
- More law enforcement presence is needed. Is there any potential for an agreement with the State Conservation Officers?
- The Refuge needs greater local visibility.
- Are there funding sources available that would help the Region get enough money to buy larger properties?
- There is potential for improving fishery habitat in a variety of ways, including connecting oxbows, increasing the hydrology of the oxbows, possibly cleaning out some of the oxbows that are filling in. The Refuge currently cannot afford these projects, but staff should develop a fisheries management plan in the event that the Service is able to acquire necessary tracts.

- Increasing fishing opportunities is of considerable local interest.
- There are several endangered species in the area, including the copperbelly watersnake. The copperbelly watersnake conservation agreement area encompasses a large part of the Refuge area; nine coal companies signed this agreement; it kept the Service from listing the copperbelly watersnake if the areas in the conservation area are not mined.

Preparation, Publishing, Finalization and Implementation of the CCP

The Draft CCP and Draft Environmental Assessment (EA) for Patoka River NWR & MA were prepared by a contractor with a great deal of input, review and support from Refuge staff and the Service's Regional Office. The Draft CCP/EA was published in two phases and in accordance with the National Environmental Policy Act (NEPA). The Draft EA (Appendix A of the Draft CCP) presented a range of alternatives for future management and identified the preferred alternative, which formed the basis of the Draft CCP. A 30-day public review period, which included a public meeting, followed release of the draft CCP. Verbal and written comments received by the Service have been incorporated where appropriate.

The alternative that was ultimately selected has become the basis of the ensuing Final CCP.

Channelized section, Patoka River, Patoka River NWR & MA. Photo credit: USFWS

This document then, becomes the basis for guiding management on the Refuges and the management areas over the coming 15-year period. It will guide the development of more detailed step-down management plans for specific resource areas; it will underpin the annual budgeting process through project submittals to the Service Asset and Maintenance Management System (SAMMS). Most importantly, it lays out the general approach to managing habitat, wildlife, and people at Patoka River NWR and Wildlife Management Area that will direct day-to-day decision-making and actions.

The Draft CCP/EA was released for public review and comment on October 17, 2007. A Draft CCP/EA or a summary of the document was sent to more than 416 individuals, organizations, and local, state, and federal agencies and elected officials. An open house event was held on November 7, 2007, at the Sugar Ridge Fish and Wildlife Area headquarters following release of the draft document. We received a total of 18 comment letters and e-mails during the 45-day review period. Appendix K of the CCP summarizes these comments and our responses. Several of the comments resulted in changes in the CCP.

Summary of Issues, Concerns and Opportunities

Issue Statement

The Service often cannot compete with other buyers for properties within the Refuge's acquisition boundary due to lack of funds. This makes it difficult to grow the Refuge at a time when interest in and demand for public land is increasing.

Background: Since the Refuge was established in 1994, the Service has acquired 6,162 out 23,743 acres within the acquisition boundary. The Land Protection Plan groups land parcels within the acquisition boundary into four priority classes:

- Bottomlands supporting natural habitat and parcels essential to the restoration of a woodland corridor along the length of the Patoka River within the Project boundary;
- Bottomland farmland in the floodplain;
- Upland forest and reclaimed land; and
- Upland farmland and other lands, such as abandoned mine lands.

There are more willing sellers than funds available, and acquisition budgets are declining as land values around the Refuge rise. Economic growth and the potential construction of Interstate 69 are likely to continue to drive up land values. Many scoping respondents supported additional land acquisition. The Refuge continues to work with partners such as Ducks Unlimited to acquire property.

Issue Statement

Local public support of the Refuge has been closely tied to hunting and fishing. There is demand to provide areas for other wildlife-dependent uses and for wildlife sanctuary, which could reduce the amount of the Refuge open to hunting and fishing.

Community involvement, Patoka River NWR & MA. Photo credit: USFWS

Background: All but 606 acres of the 6,162 acres of Refuge lands are open to hunting and fishing consistent with Indiana DNR regulations. Hunting is prohibited on about 5 acres surrounding a trail and boat launch, and within a single 113-acre block of reclaimed mine land. This block will be open to hunting when the lands meet reclamation criteria and the bond collected from the mining company is released. Hunting also is prohibited on the 488-acre Cane Ridge Wildlife Management area 24 miles west of the Refuge office. The number of other wildlife-dependent uses is growing and facilities constructed to support these uses are popular with visitors. During scoping, respondents suggested providing additional trails and other facilities as well as designating a portion of the Refuge as a waterfowl sanctuary free of hunting. Others opposed any reduction of lands open to hunting and fishing.

Issue Statement

There is demand for additional public use on the Refuge. Some of the uses are not wildlife-dependent.

Background: Local residents grew accustomed to recreating on private lands because absentee landowners, usually coal companies, did little to enforce against trespass. Today, these landowners are leasing the land and more aggressively enforcing trespassing laws. With fewer places to recreate, use has shifted to Refuge lands. Also, economic prosperity within the region has drawn more people to the area. Some of these newcomers also recreate on Refuge lands. The Refuge is open to the priority wildlife-dependent uses noted in the 1997 Refuge Improvement Act (hunting, fishing, wildlife observation, wildlife photography, environmental education, and environmental interpretation). Other uses have been authorized through a special use permit system at the discretion of the Refuge Manager. A number of scoping comments suggested that recreation opportunities on the Refuge could make it a tourist destination. Others requested specific uses of Refuge lands.

Issue Statement

Refuge habitats are at risk from a number of threats such as agricultural runoff, coal mining, potential construction of Interstate 69, illegal uses such as All-Terrain Vehicles (ATV's), and development of lands not yet acquired.

Background: Most of these threats to land and resources in the area preceded establishment of the Refuge in the 1990s. They are long-term threats to the quality and quantity of terrestrial and aquatic wildlife habitat in the area. Water quality impairment from agricultural runoff and coal mining may have improved somewhat since the Refuge's establishment. Construction of Interstate 69 has not yet occurred, but continues to loom ever closer. Land development – both residential and commercial, and to some extent industrial – has accelerated in recent years as the area's amenities (accessible outdoors, semi-rural/small town lifestyle, low housing prices and cost of living) have attracted outsiders and returning native-born residents alike.

Issue Statement

The patchwork of public and private lands within the Refuge boundary can be confusing to visitors and may lead to conflicts with adjoining private land owners.

American lotus, Patoka River NWR & MA. Photo credit: USFWS

Background: Approximately 75 percent of the lands within the Refuge's acquisition boundary are not owned by the Service. The Refuge has a small scale map showing ownership, but Refuge boundaries are not posted and the patchwork of public and private lands within the acquisition boundary could easily confuse visitors. One scoping respondent expressed concern about trespass from neighboring Refuge lands.

Issue Statement

Demand for visitor services, facilities, information, and environmental education exceeds existing supply and/or the capacity of existing staff and budgets.

Background: Refuge visitation continues to climb and is currently estimated at 21,221 visitors per year. Presently, the Refuge has maps and fact sheets available during business hours at the Refuge office. The staff and volunteers deliver off-Refuge environmental education programs several times per year, but there is additional demand that is not being met. A number of scoping respondents requested additional Refuge information, environmental education, or facilities.

Issue Statement

Some Visitor Services facilities do not meet U.S. Fish and Wildlife Service standards.

Background: As a relatively new Refuge with no park ranger or public use/visitor services specialist on site, Patoka River NWR has not yet developed facilities or visitor services on a par with many older refuges. During scoping, many participants called attention to a need for greater information about the Refuge and what it has to offer to be made available to the public via e-mail, the Internet, newsletters, signage, and so forth. Respondents expressed unawareness of the existence of trails for wildlife observation, for example. There is no visitor center on the Refuge to provide information, interpretation, and environmental education.

Issue Statement

Refuge ecosystems and the effects of management activities (including public use) are not well understood.

Background: Sustaining wildlife populations is central to the mission of the National Wildlife Refuge System, but in many cases information is lacking regarding the success of management activities or the effect of public uses on Refuge wildlife. This hampers managers' ability to adapt habitat management practices or modify public uses in ways that best sustain wildlife numbers. Presently, the Refuge monitors the Least Terns at Cane Ridge WMA, conducts seasonal waterfowl, shorebird and breeding songbird counts, bands Wood Ducks, and contributes to the Indiana DNR's annual turkey call survey. Monitoring of uses as well as management activities is necessary to determine success or thresholds.

Issue Statement

Productivity (fishery) is declining in some oxbow lakes along the channelized portion of the Patoka River.

Background: In the 1920s area residents channelized a portion of the Patoka River in an attempt to drain nearly 100,000 acres of forested wetlands for farming. Known as Houchin's Ditch and beginning at the town of Winslow, the project replaced 36 miles of natural, meandering river with about 17 miles of dredged, straight ditch. The dredged spoil deposited on both sides of the ditch cut off 19 miles of natural river meanders on the north and south sides of the new ditch main channel. Water exchange within these cut off oxbows is now limited to periods of high water. Heavy sediment loads during these periods result in increased deposition in the oxbows. Consequently, the oxbows are becoming shallower and hold water for a shorter duration. Although this process occurs in all natural riverine systems, new oxbows are continually being created as river meanders are severed from the main channel. In the case of Houchins's Ditch, these oxbows are not being replaced and the associated wetland habitat is being lost.

Chapter 3: Refuge Environment and Management

Introduction

Established in 1994, the Patoka River National Wildlife Refuge and Management Area is located in Pike and Gibson counties in southwestern Indiana. It was created under authority of the Emergency Wetlands Resources Act in part to protect one of two remaining intact floodplain forest systems within Indiana. The river corridor project encompasses 30 miles of the Patoka River and 19 miles of oxbows with a total of 12,700 acres of existing wetlands.

Presently, the acquisition boundary for the NWR & MA includes 23,743 acres. This differs from the 22,083 acres included in the Record of Decision for the 1994 Environmental Impact Statement (EIS) that established the Refuge & MA. There are two reasons for this difference. The first is that past methods of calculating acres (e.g. summing acres found in tax records or plat books) have given way to computerized Geographic Information Systems (GIS) that rely on standardized data which provide greater uniformity of acreage values. It is important to note that for legal transactions deed acres remain the legal standard, but habitat acreage figures throughout this document are based on GIS generated values. In the EIS the area within the acquisition boundary was stated at 22,083 acres. The same boundary is calculated to contain 22,817 acres using GIS protocols. The second reason for the acreage difference is that an additional 926 acres have been authorized for acquisition since the original boundary was established, bringing the total area authorized for acquisition to the present figure of 23,743 acres. The Refuge also administers a 219-acre parcel transferred to the Service from the Farm Ser-

Great Horned Owl nest, Patoka River NWR & MA. Photo credit: USFWS

vices Agency now known as White River Bottoms. Although managed by Refuge staff, and part of the National Wildlife Refuge System it is not included as part of the Patoka River NWR & MA and does not figure in the total acreage. See Figure 3 and Table 1.

Most of the information in this chapter comes from the Environmental Impact Statement (EIS) prepared in conjunction with the establishment of the Patoka River National Wetlands Project (USFWS, 1994). The wetlands project led to the creation of Patoka River National Wildlife Refuge and Management Area.

Wetland Loss in Indiana

The 20th century witnessed a dramatic decline in the acreage of America's wetland habitat that is so critical to maintaining migratory bird and other

Chapter 3: Refuge Environment and Management

Figure 3: Acquisition Authority, Patoka River NWR & MA

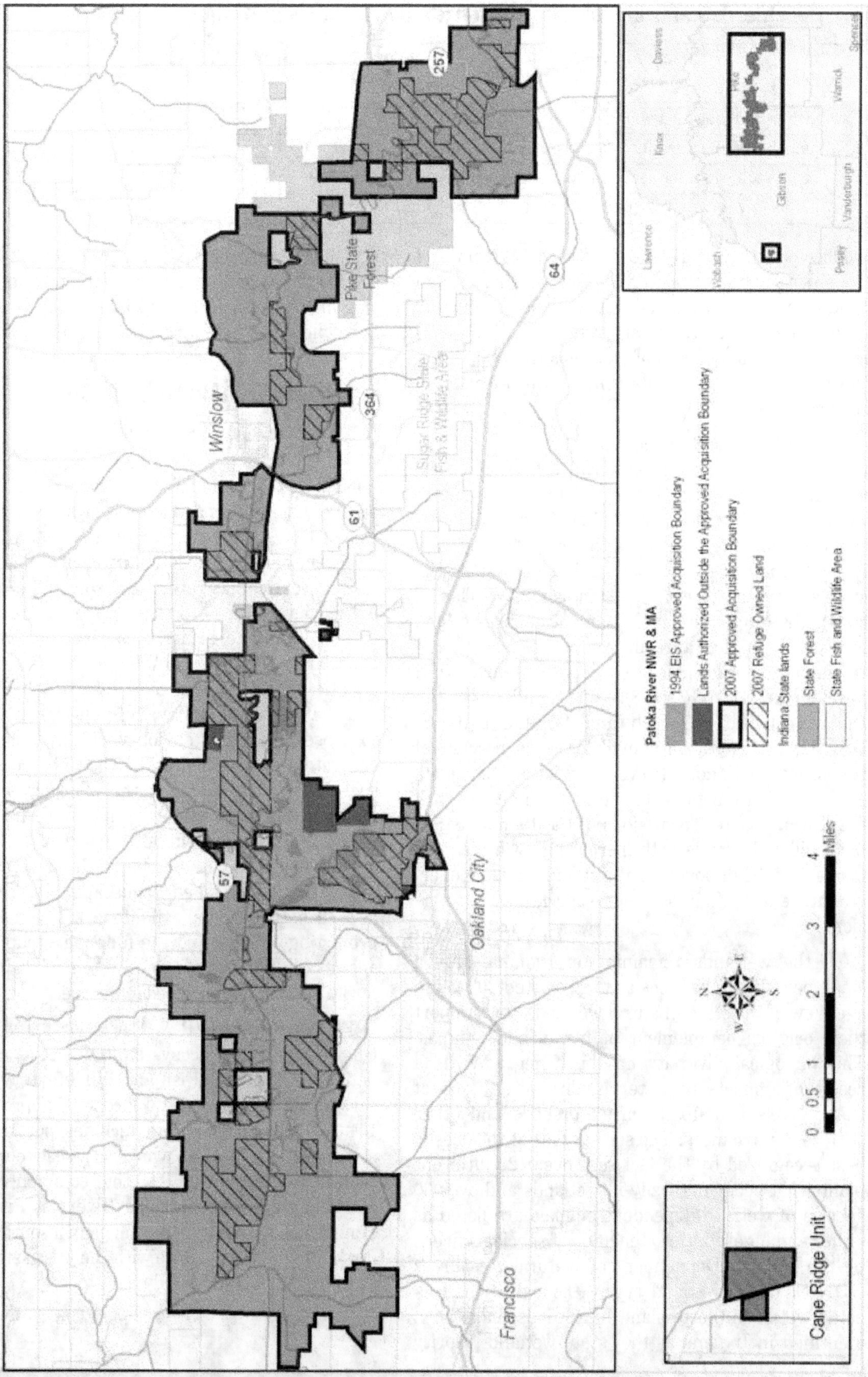

Patoka River National Wildlife Refuge and Management Area / Comprehensive Conservation Plan

Table 1: Status of Land Acquisition, Patoka River NWR & MA

Description	Acres Cited in 1994 EIS	Current GIS Acres
Establishment acquisition boundary	22,083	22,817
Additional lands approved for acquisition	--	926
Total acres authorized for acquisition	--	23,743
FSA Lands (White River Bottoms)	--	219

wildlife populations. By the close of the century and the dawn of the new millennium, the U.S. Fish and Wildlife Service estimated that nationally, only 103 million acres (less than half) remained of the estimated 221 million acres of wetlands that existed in the lower 48 states at the time of Euro-American settlement.

In the State of Indiana, long-term wetland loss has been even more dramatic. Of the estimated 5.5 million acres of wetlands that existed in Indiana at the time of settlement, only 813,000 acres (15 percent) remained by the 1990s (Rolley, 1991), according to the most recent and complete analysis of the state's wetland resources (Indiana WETlands, 2004). Historically, about 85 percent of this wetland loss has been for agricultural purposes with the remainder attributable to urban and industrial development (IDNR, 1988). In the mid-1990s, the Indiana Division of Fish and Wildlife and the USFWS estimated an annual loss of 5 percent of remaining wetlands. However, wildlife biologists and conservationists held hope that compliance with the "Swampbuster" provisions of the 1985 and 1990 farm bills, alongside with increasing awareness by farmers of the importance of wetlands, could moderate future wetland losses due to agricultural conversion.

Of the wetlands remaining in Indiana, only a small percentage remains as they existed 200 years ago. Few of the state's natural wetlands now support their original complement of plants and animals. This biological diversity has been degraded as a result of impacts to water quality, alterations of water levels and upstream watersheds and other surface disturbances. The seriousness of this loss is best recognized by the fact that over 120 different plants that occur naturally in wetlands and over 60 species of wetland-dependent animals are listed as either endangered, threatened or of special concern by the Indiana Department of Natural Resources (IDNR). Of all wetland types, the palustrine forested wetlands (bottomland hardwoods) have been identified in Indiana as the "state wetland priority type." This means priority for protection is based on the historical pattern of loss and alterations occurring in Indiana and the multiple values they have to fish, wildlife and plant resources (IDNR, 1988).

The Ohio River Valley Ecosystem

The U.S. Fish and Wildlife Service has adopted an ecosystem approach to conservation because we cannot look just at an individual animal, species, or fragment of land in isolation from all that surrounds it. The Service has recognized some 53 ecosystems in the conterminous 48 states. We recognize that we are not going to achieve conservation within the boundaries of a National Wildlife Refuge, or restore aquatic resources with a National Fish Hatchery, and that listing an endangered species is not going to conserve the system on which it depends. The ecosystem approach thus strives to be comprehensive. It is based on all of the biological resources within a watershed (the total land area from which water drains into a single stream, lake, or ocean) and it considers the economic health of communities within that watershed landscape. An ecosystem approach to fish and wildlife conservation means protecting or restoring the function, structure, and species composition of an ecosystem while providing for its sustainable socioeconomic use.

Patoka River NWR & MA is located within the Ohio River Valley Ecosystem (ORVE) as currently defined by the U.S. Fish and Wildlife Service. This ecosystem drains a total area of approximately 141,000 square miles and includes portions of 10 states. The Ohio River, which is the backbone of this ecosystem, is formed by the confluence of the Allegheny and Monongahela Rivers at Pittsburgh, Pennsylvania and flows 981 miles in a southwesterly direction to its confluence with the Mississippi River at Cairo, Illinois (ORVET, no date).

Figure 4: Ohio River Valley Ecosystem

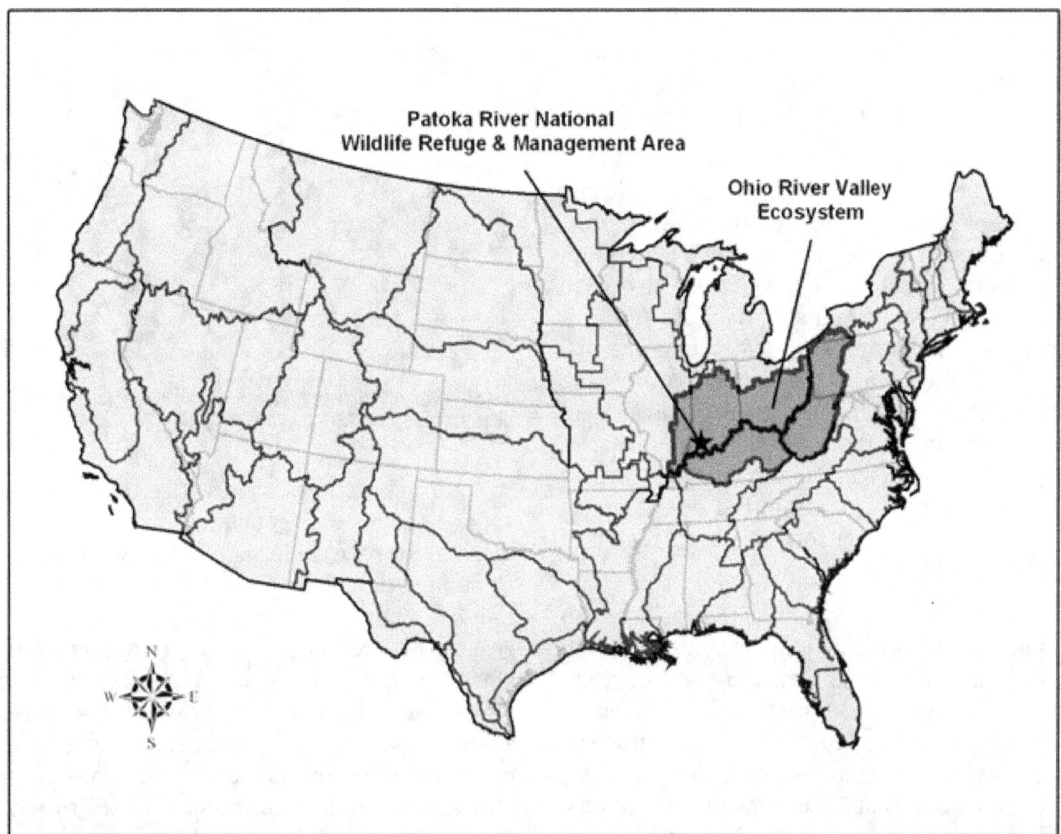

The Ohio River ecosystem bisects three regions of the Deciduous Forest Formation of eastern North America: the Mixed Mesophytic Forest Region (upper basin, roughly upstream of Portsmouth, Ohio), the Western Mesophytic Forest Region (lower basin from Portsmouth, Ohio, to Paducah, Kentucky), and the Mississippi Alluvial Plain Section of the Southeastern Evergreen Forest Region (lowermost portion of the basin from Paducah, Kentucky, to Cairo, Illinois (USFWS, 1999). (See Figure 4)

The mixed mesophytic and western mesophytic forests have been classified broadly as a tulip poplar-oak region. The dense, mixed mesophytic forest contains a fair abundance of two indicator species, white basswood and yellow buckeye, in a total group of 15 to 20 dominant species. The western mesophytic forest is marked by a transition from extensive mixed mesophytic communities in the east to extensive oak and oak-hickory communities in the west. The western mesophytic forest is less dense, has few dominants, and usually lacks the two indicator species of the mixed mesophytic forest.

In the lower, downstream portion of the ecosystem, near Paducah, Kentucky, the Ohio River enters the northernmost extension of the Mississippi Alluvial Plain. In this alluvial region, three subdivisions of "bottomland forest" (i.e., palustrine forested wetland) are recognized: swamp forest, hardwood bottoms, and ridge bottoms. The swamp forest, consisting principally of cypress and tupelo gum, occupies land on which water stands throughout the year except during periods of extreme drought. The hardwood bottoms contain a large number of species, frequently flood, and generally remain covered with water through the late winter and spring. Ridge bottoms contain some of the tree species of hardwood bottoms, but have a larger number of oaks and hickories; occurring at slightly higher elevations than hardwood bottoms, these areas are covered by water only during floods (USFWS, 1999).

The rich flora and fauna of the ORVE reflect its diverse physiography and unique geologic past. Numerous Service trust resources occur in the ecosystem, including many federally listed endangered/threatened plants, mussels, fishes, birds and mammals; waterfowl and other migratory water birds; and neotropical migratory land birds.

The unusually rich and diverse fauna found in the ecosystem is the product of a multitude of biotic and abiotic factors which have evolved over time. Throughout geologic time, changes in such factors as topography, climate, and geomorphology have formed, modified, and eliminated habitats and consequently have had a profound effect upon the distribution of the faunal assemblages in the ecosystem. Due to the ecosystem's central geographical location in the eastern United States, some species with northern affinities and others with southern affinities occur in the ecosystem in addition to those common to the central region of the country (USFWS, 1999).

Over the past few centuries of Euro-American settlement and industrialization, the Ohio River Valley ecosystem has been subjected to many environmental stresses which have diminished the bounty of its living resources. Much of the region's economic activity – agriculture, lumbering, mining, energy production, manufacturing, and recreation – is based on the watershed's natural resources. Sustaining most of these activities requires maintenance of a healthy ecosystem. Stress from human activities has adversely affected the ecological integrity of the ORVE, and there are indications that this stress is increasing.

Environmental alteration and degradation are continuing challenges to the maintenance of a productive and healthy ORVE. Resources of the area are threatened by land conversion, poor land-use practices, direct and indirect physical alteration of the area's rivers and streams, acid mine drainage and acid precipitation, destruction of wetland habitats, and both point- and nonpoint-source discharges of pollutants. Herbicides, insecticides, nutrients, and sediment are significant components of the agricultural runoff that adversely affect aquatic systems throughout the area. Acid precipitation from sulfur dioxide and nitrous oxides from power plants and other airborne pollutants are having dramatic effects on aquatic and terrestrial communities, particularly at high elevations (USFWS, 1999).

Restoring habitat through partnerships Patoka River NWR & MA. Photo credit: USFWS

Natural resources are further threatened by an expanding human population and its increased demand for renewable and nonrenewable resources. Contamination of both aquatic and terrestrial systems through acid mine drainage and the accidental release of toxic chemicals is a continuing threat. Operation and maintenance of the inland navigation system and the recent invasion of the non-native zebra mussel are having significant adverse impacts on native flora and fauna of the area's rivers and streams. Other non-native species are threatening native components of aquatic and terrestrial systems throughout the area. The expansion of urban and suburban areas within the ecosystem and the concurrent loss of forest, wetlands, agricultural lands, and other types of open space associated with this expansion have reduced the quantity and quality of natural habitats available to fish and wildlife.

The Service published a strategic plan on conserving the trust resources of the ORVE in 1999 (USFWS, 1999). The plan set forth four goals:

1. Protect, restore and enhance habitats and essential processes necessary to maintain healthy native animal and plant populations.

2. Protect, restore and enhance diversity of native flora and fauna.

3. Promote and support compatible and sustainable uses of the ecosystem's resources and utilize existing laws, regulations, and influence to control incompatible and unsustainable uses of these resources.

4. Develop public awareness and support for ecosystem resource issues.

The strategic plan also identified seven resource priorities:

Resource Priority 1: In cooperation with partners, reverse the decline of native aquatic mollusks within the Ohio River Valley Ecosystem with emphasis on endangered, threatened and candidate species and species of concern.

Resource Priority #2: In cooperation with partners, reverse the decline and achieve stable, viable populations of migratory landbirds and other bird species of concern.

Resource Priority 3: In cooperation with partners, reverse the decline of native fishes with emphasis on interjurisdictional listed and candidate species and species of concern.

Resource Priority 4: In cooperation with partners, protect and restore karst/cave habitat supporting listed and candidate species and species of concern.

Resource Priority 5: In cooperation with partners, protect and restore wetland, riverine and riparian habitat in the Ohio River watershed for the protection and enhancement of migratory waterbirds and other wetland dependant species of concern.

Resource Priority 6: In cooperation with partners, reduce the decline and promote the recovery of rare resources identified as listed/proposed threatened and endangered species, candidate species and species of concern not otherwise addressed in Resource Priorities 1- 5 (e.g. plants, reptiles, amphibians, etc.).

Resource Priority 7: In cooperation with partners, achieve the necessary level of protection for those high priority areas within the Ohio River Valley Ecosystem that would help meet the goals of the ORVE Team. In particular, emphasis will be placed on the objectives of Resource Priorities 1 through 6 and Public Use Priority 1.

A number of action strategies accompanied these resource priorities in the strategic plan. In addition, the plan contained one public use priority:

Public Use Priority 1: In cooperation with partners, promote and support sustainable fish and wildlife-oriented recreational uses while maintaining the long-term health of the ecosystem and the Service's trust resources.

The Service's ORVE Team has several important roles. Primary among them is serving as an advocate at the field level for federal trust fish and wildlife resources within the Ohio River watershed. This includes reviewing the Team's resource priorities and charting a direction for the Team to ensure it addresses the highest priority resource needs. To facilitate accomplishment of the Team's on-the-ground efforts, the Team actively seeks funding, explores expansion of existing partnerships and establishment of new ones, and seeks ways to involve all interested stakeholders (USFWS, 1999).

The ORVE Team is comprised of representatives of each of the Service's field offices located within the Region 3 (Midwest), 4 (Southeast), and 5 (Northeast) portions of the Ohio River Valley watershed. In addition, representatives from the respective Service regional offices, as well as several state fish and wildlife agencies, participate as Team members. Typically, the Team meets three times per year at various locations within the ecosystem.

Snowy Egret. Photo credit: USFWS

The Team's seven Sub-groups are the primary mechanisms for conducting activities on the ground. The Sub-groups correspond to the Team's resource priorities, i.e., fish and wildlife and associated habitats, and its public use priority. They are, in no priority order: native aquatic mollusks; migratory land birds and other bird species of concern; native fishes; karst/cave habitat; wetland, riverine, and riparian habitat; declining and rare species; and fish and wildlife-oriented recreational use. In addition to the Sub-groups, the Team has established four Standing Committees to conduct activities that generally cut across all priority resources. The Standing Committees address GIS needs and activities, outreach, acid mine drainage and valley fills, and land protection (USFWS, 1999).

Other Units Administered

The staff of Patoka River NWR & MA administers two units apart from the main body of the Refuge: Cane Ridge and White River Bottoms. Both units are part of the National Wildlife Refuge System, but White River Bottoms is not officially included as part of the total acreage comprising the Patoka River Refuge & MA.

The 488-acre Cane Ridge Wildlife Management Area lies 24 miles west of the Refuge headquarters near the confluence of the White, Patoka, and Wabash Rivers, a traditional waterfowl migration and wintering area. Acquired by a coalition of conservation partners, the property became part of Patoka River NWR & MA in 1999. The area includes 193 acres of moist soil wetlands in four management units, 180 acres of reforested bottomland hardwoods, and a 59-acre deep water impoundment with nesting islands that provide habitat for the federally endangered Least Tern. Cane Ridge WMA is a Globally Important Bird Area.

The 219-acre White River Bottoms Wildlife Management Area lies 9 miles to the north of Oakland City. This WMA lies just to the northwest of Petersburg on the south side of the White River. Although not officially included as part of Patoka River NWR & MA, White River Bottoms became part of the National Wildlife Refuge System when control of the land was transferred to the Service in 1994 from the Farm Services Agency. It has been restored from agricultural fields by being planted to bottomland hardwood trees.

Migratory Bird Conservation Initiatives

Over the last decade, bird conservation planning has become increasingly exciting as it has evolved from a largely local, site-based focus to a more regional, landscape-oriented perspective. Significant challenges include locating areas of high-quality habitat for the conservation of particular guilds and priority bird species, making sure no species are inadvertently left out of the regional planning process, avoiding unnecessary duplication of effort, and identifying unique landscape and habitat elements of particular tracts targeted for protection, management and restoration. Several migratory bird conservation initiatives have emerged to help guide the planning and implementation process. Collectively, they comprise a tremendous resource as Patoka River National Wildlife Refuge and Management Area engages in comprehensive conservation planning and its translation into effective on-the-ground management.

North American Waterfowl Management Plan

Signed in 1986, the North American Waterfowl Management Plan (NAWMP) outlines a broad framework for waterfowl management strategies and conservation efforts in the United States, Canada, and Mexico. The goal of the NAWMP is to restore waterfowl populations to historic levels throughout the continent. The NAWMP is designed to reach its objectives through key joint venture areas, species joint ventures, and state implementation plans within these joint ventures.

Patoka River NWR & MA is in the Upper Mississippi River-Great Lakes Joint Venture. The boundaries of this joint venture extend across Minnesota, Iowa, Missouri, Wisconsin, Illinois, Indiana, and Michigan. They include important migration and staging areas that were converted to agriculture. The purpose of the Upper Mississippi River-Great Lakes Joint Venture is to increase populations of waterfowl and other wetland wildlife by protecting, restoring, creating, and enhancing wetlands and associated upland habitats. Joint venture partners include private landowners, the National Fish and Wildlife Foundation, state agencies, and the U.S. Fish and Wildlife Service. Partners are endeavoring

Nesting Interior Least Tern. Photo credit: USFWS

to increase public awareness through information and education and are providing incentives to private landowners (Graziano and Cross, 1993).

The 1998 NAWMP Update established a habitat objective for the Upper Mississippi – Great Lakes Joint Venture of protecting 1,329,000 acres of waterfowl and wetland habitat and restoring or enhancing another 605,200 acres (NAWMP, 1998).

A 2004 update to the NAWMP set a target of conserving 758,572 additional acres of waterfowl and wetland habitat in the Upper Mississippi – Great Lakes Joint Venture through a combination of securement, protection, restoration, enhancement, and management (NAWMP, 2004).

Partners In Flight

Formed in 1990, Partners in Flight (PIF) is concerned primarily with landbirds and has developed Bird Conservation Plans for numerous *Physiographic Areas* across the U. S. (see http://www.partnersinflight.org). These plans include priority species lists, associated habitats, and management strategies. Patoka River NWR lies within PIF Physiographic Area 14, the Interior Low Plateaus Area.

The Interior Low Plateaus form a diverse landscape consisting of six distinct subregions that extends from north Alabama across central Tennessee and Kentucky into southern Illinois, Indiana, and Ohio. Its hilly topography sets it apart from the Coastal Plain to the south and Prairie Peninsula to the north. To the west, the Mississippi River valley separates the Interior Low Plateaus from the Ozark Highlands. Western mesophytic, oak-hickory, and beech-maple forests were historically the most abundant cover types. There were also tallgrass prairie elements in the north and northwest, oak savannahs in the Bluegrass and other northern sections, barrens and glades in central regions, and forested wetlands along major waterways (PIF, no date).

Habitat loss through conversion to agriculture and other uses and the fragmentation and reduced quality of what remains are the biggest conservation challenges in this area. Grasslands and savannahs have been converted to cool season pasture. Many glades and barrens have become urban areas, and others have been overtaken by woody vegetation due to fire suppression. Floodplain forests have largely been either inundated by reservoirs or converted to row crops. Conservation objectives vary by subregion, but in general, in order to perpetuate existing high priority species and to create an opportunity to re-establish two extirpated species (Greater Prairie-Chicken and Swallow-tailed Kite), the following actions should be implemented:

- Sustain existing forested acreage, with about 80 percent in hardwoods and the remainder in short-rotation pine management;
- Manage about 400,000 ha of that hardwood forest in long rotation patches of about 4,000 ha each;
- Consolidate an additional 90,000 ha of forested wetland;
- Additionally, restore 40,000 ha of native warm season grass and oak savannah habitat; and
- Incorporate bird conservation into ongoing barren and glade conservation projects.

U.S. Shorebird Conservation Plan

Partners from state and federal agencies and NGOs from across the country combined their resources and expertise to develop a conservation strategy for migratory shorebirds and their habitats. The plan provides a scientific framework to determine species, sites, and habitats that most urgently need conservation action. Main goals of the U.S. Shorebird Conservation Plan, which was completed in 2000, are to ensure that adequate quantity and quality of shorebird habitat is maintained at the local level and to maintain or restore shorebird populations at the continental and hemispheric levels. Separate technical reports were developed for a conservation assessment, research needs, a comprehensive monitoring strategy, and education and outreach. These national assessments were used to step down goals and objectives into 11 regional conservation plans. Although some outreach, education, research, monitoring, and habitat conservation programs are being implemented, accomplishment of conservation objectives for all shorebird species will require a coordinated effort among traditional and new partners. The U. S. Shorebird Conservation Plan Council serves as the steering committee for the U. S. Shorebird Conservation Plan and oversees the implementation of the regional, national, and international goals of the Plan. Meetings of the Council are held twice a year (USFWS, no date).

Under the Shorebird Conservation Plan, Patoka River NWR is located in the Upper Mississippi Valley/Great Lakes Region (UMVGL), which is covered by a regional plan prepared in 2000 and updated in 2006 (de Szalay et al., 2006). The UMVGL region is a diverse area that includes five Bird Conservation Regions and provides important habitat for shorebirds, especially migrants. Thirty-two shorebird species occur in the region, with 25 being common or abundant. Twenty-three species are of moderate or higher concern in the region. High-priority species include: greater yellowlegs, whimbrel, buff-breasted sandpiper, short-billed dowitcher, marbled godwit, Wilson's phalarope, upland sandpiper, American woodcock, and the Federally-listed piping plover; the latter five species breed in the region.

Various habitats within the region, including natural and managed wetlands, river floodplains, lake shoreline, sand and gravel bars, reservoirs, and flooded agricultural fields, provide the shallow water and sparsely-vegetated conditions required by foraging shorebirds. However, like other interior areas, the UMVGL region experiences dynamic climatic conditions, making habitat conditions for shorebirds unpredictable. Moreover, loss of wetlands from urban development, river dredging and diking, and agriculture has reduced the amount of habitat in the region. A primary goal of this UMVGL regional shorebird plan is to ensure the availability of shorebird foraging and nesting sites over a range of climatic conditions by protecting, restoring, and managing a variety of habitat types throughout the UMVGL region.

Waterbird Conservation for the Americas

Formerly known as the North American Waterbird Conservation Plan, Waterbird Conservation for the Americas (WCA) is an independent, international, broad-based, and voluntary partnership created to link the work of individuals and institutions having interest and responsibility for conservation of waterbirds and their habitats in the Americas (WCA, 2005a). WCA's vision is that the distribution, diversity, and abundance of populations and habitats of breeding, migratory, and nonbreeding waterbirds are sustained or restored throughout the lands and waters of North America, Central America, and the Caribbean. The geographic extent of the WCA initiative includes North America, Central America, the islands and waters of the Caribbean, the Pacific Ocean including the U.S.-associated Pacific Islands, and the western Atlantic Ocean including Bermuda. The WCA includes the interests of 29 nations.

The term "waterbird" refers to bird species dependent on aquatic habitats to complete portions of their life cycles. It includes seabirds, coastal waterbirds, wading birds, and marsh birds. The WCA focuses these groups. Shorebirds and waterfowl, while indeed waterbirds, are the subject of their own initiatives (discussed above).

Under WCA, planning regions were created to allow planning at a scale that is practical yet provides landscape-level perspective. Regional boundaries are based on a combination of both political and ecological considerations. Patoka River NWR is situated in the Upper Mississippi Valley/Great Lakes (UMVGL) Region, within a subregion known as Bird Conservation Region (BCR) 24, the Central Hardwoods. Like the NAWMP, WCA has also established joint ventures, and that of BCR 24 is called the Central Hardwoods Joint Venture (CHJV).

The UMVGL Region provides a wide variety of waterbird nesting, roosting and foraging habitats, including marshes, ponds, creeks, streams, sloughs, lake shorelines, islands (especially in the Great Lakes), shoals, river floodplains (especially along the Mississippi, Illinois, Missouri, and Ohio Rivers), and reservoirs. Forty-six waterbird species regularly occur in the region during at least one portion of the year, including loons, grebes, pelicans, cormorants, herons, night-herons, egrets, bitterns, rails, moorhens, coots, cranes, gulls and terns, and 19 of these species are of high conservation, stewardship or management concern. In the context of the continental, the region is extremely important for many of these waterbird species. Though the UMVGL Region has experienced major declines in wetland habitat over the last 200 years, the northern portion of the UMVGL Region still contains large amounts of wetlands and the Great Lakes are a stronghold for island breeders (WCA, 2005b).

Figure 5: Bird Conservation Region in Which Patoka River NWR & MA is Located

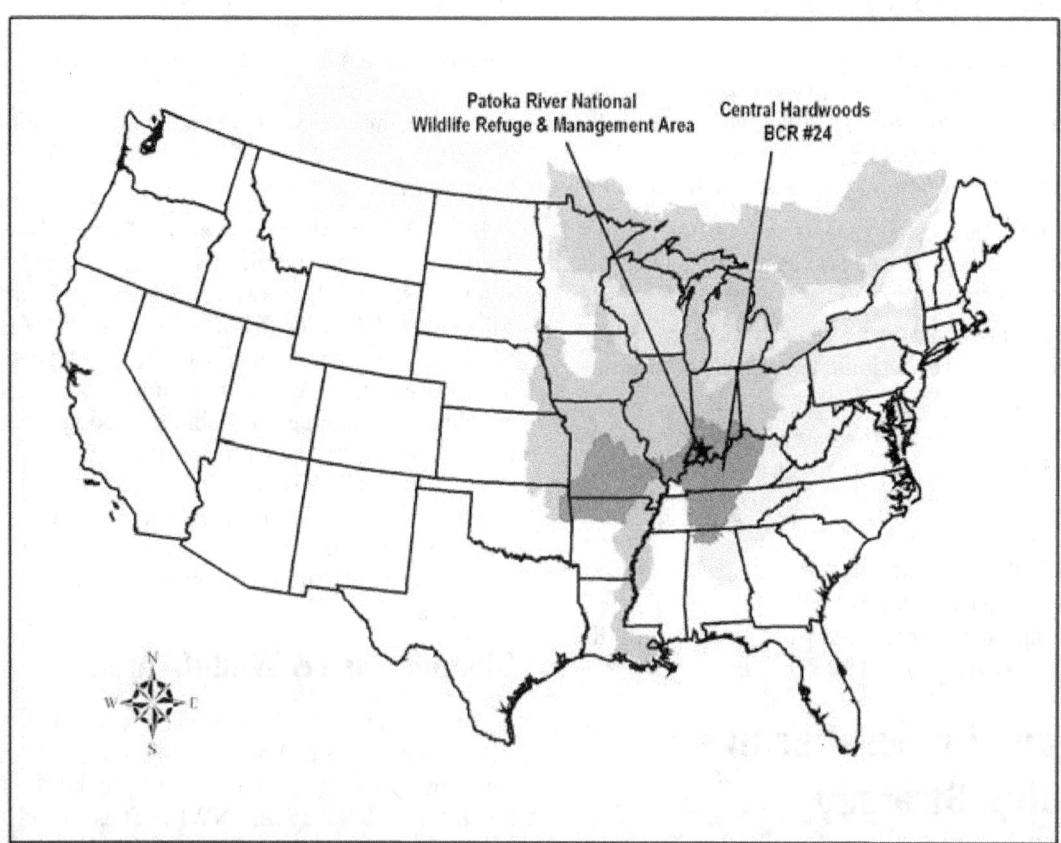

A Regional Plan for waterbird management and conservation is currently being prepared and Patoka River National Wildlife Refuge figures in that plan, which described the Refuge as, "one of the most significant bottomland hardwood forests remaining in the Midwest."

North American Bird Conservation Initiative

In a continental effort, the North American Waterfowl Management Plan, Partners in Flight, U.S. Shorebird Conservation Plan, and Waterbird Conservation for the Americas planning efforts are being integrated under the umbrella of the North American Bird Conservation Initiative (NABCI). The goal of NABCI is to facilitate the delivery of the full spectrum of bird conservation through regionally-based, biologically-driven, landscape-oriented partnerships (see http://www.dodpif.org/nabci/index.htm). The NABCI strives to integrate the conservation objectives for all birds in order to optimize the effectiveness of management strategies.

NABCI also uses BCRs as its planning units. BCRs are becoming increasingly common as the unit of choice for regional bird conservation efforts; as it does for the WCA initiative, Patoka River NWR lies within BCR 24, the Central Hardwoods for the purposes of the NABCI (see Figure 5).

Each of the above four bird conservation initiatives has a process for designating conservation priority species, modeled to a large extent on the PIF method of calculating scores based on independent assessments of global relative abundance, breeding and wintering distribution, vulnerability to threats, area importance (at a particular scale, e.g. PA or BCR), and population trend. These scores are often used by agencies in developing lists of bird species of concern; e.g., the U. S. Fish and Wildlife Service based its assessments for its 2001 list of nongame Birds of Conservation Concern primarily on the PIF, shorebird, and waterbird status assessment scores.

Region 3 Fish and Wildlife Conservation Priorities

Every species is important. But the number of species in need of attention exceeds the resources of the Service. To focus effort effectively, Region 3 of the Fish and Wildlife Service compiled a list of Resource Conservation Priorities. The list includes:

- all federally listed threatened and endangered species and proposed and candidate species that occur in the Region
- migratory bird species derived from Service wide and international conservation planning efforts
- rare and declining terrestrial and aquatic plants and animals that represent an abbreviation of the Endangered Species program's preliminary draft "Species of Concern" list for the Region.

Appendix D includes 116 Resource Conservation Priority species within the Ohio River Valley Ecosystem and notes those known to occur on the Refuge.

Indiana Comprehensive Wildlife Strategy

The Indiana Comprehensive Wildlife Strategy completed in 2006 identifies conservation priorities within Indiana. Patoka River NWR & MA staff contributed to the plan and the Refuge provides habitat for more than 50 of the birds, mammals, reptiles, and amphibians listed in the Strategy as conservation priorities (see Appendix C: Species Lists).

Other Recreation and Conservation Lands in the Area

Sugar Ridge Fish & Wildlife Area

Sugar Ridge Fish & Wildlife Area, owned and managed by the Indiana Department of Natural Resources (IDNR), is unique in that much of the land has been strip-mined for coal and since reclaimed. Sugar Ridge (Figure 6) is made up of six separate areas, totaling approximately 8,100 acres, interspersed with the USFWS's Patoka River NWR holdings. The strip-mined land now features about 100 pits and lakes, along with rows of overburden from the mining operation. The land that has not been mined is mostly rough and rolling. A large part of the land which is now Sugar Ridge Fish and Wildlife Area (Areas I, II and III) was once leased from Amax Coal Company. Leasing began in 1964 and continued until 1980 when most of the land was donated to the Division of Fish and Wildlife (IDNR, no date-a).

Sugar Ridge is open to various forms of outdoor recreation by the public, including hunting (deer, squirrel, and wild turkey are common); fishing on 145 acres in 24 major fishing pits for such sport fish as bluegill, redear, channel catfish, and largemouth bass; trapping (by drawing only); and wildlife watching on upland game habitat, wooded reclaimed mine areas and stripper pits which attract a wide variety of song birds, woodpeckers, hawks, and waterfowl. In addition, mushrooms, berries and nuts may be gathered. A written permit is required to remove plants, animals, rocks and fossils (IDNR, no date-a).

Glendale Fish & Wildlife Area

The Indiana DNR's Glendale Fish & Wildlife Area maintains 8,060 acres of land and over 1,400 acres of lakes and impoundments about 12 miles north of Patoka River NWR. These lands and waters provide quality hunting and fishing opportunities for the public, as well as wildlife watching and camping in designated areas. Wetland trapping is available by drawing only (IDNR, no date-b).

Acquisition began in 1956, and land purchases were made through the 1960s. Several minor purchases were made in the 1970s. The construction of the dam that formed Dogwood Lake began in 1963 and was completed in 1965. The lake, with an average depth of eight feet, was renovated in 1978 and restocked with fish in 1979 (IDNR, no date-b).

Pike State Forest

Pike State Forest, owned and operated by Indiana DNR's Division of Forestry, sits astride the Patoka River adjacent to Patoka River NWR toward its eastern side. The State Forest (SF) consists of 3,889 acres which vary from hilly uplands to the low bottomlands of the river. Due to its diverse habitats, a wide variety of plant and animal life make their homes at Pike SF. Several recreational opportunities are available on the SF, including hunting, horseback riding, picnicking, bird watching

Figure 6: Other Conservation Lands in the Area of Patoka River NWR & MA

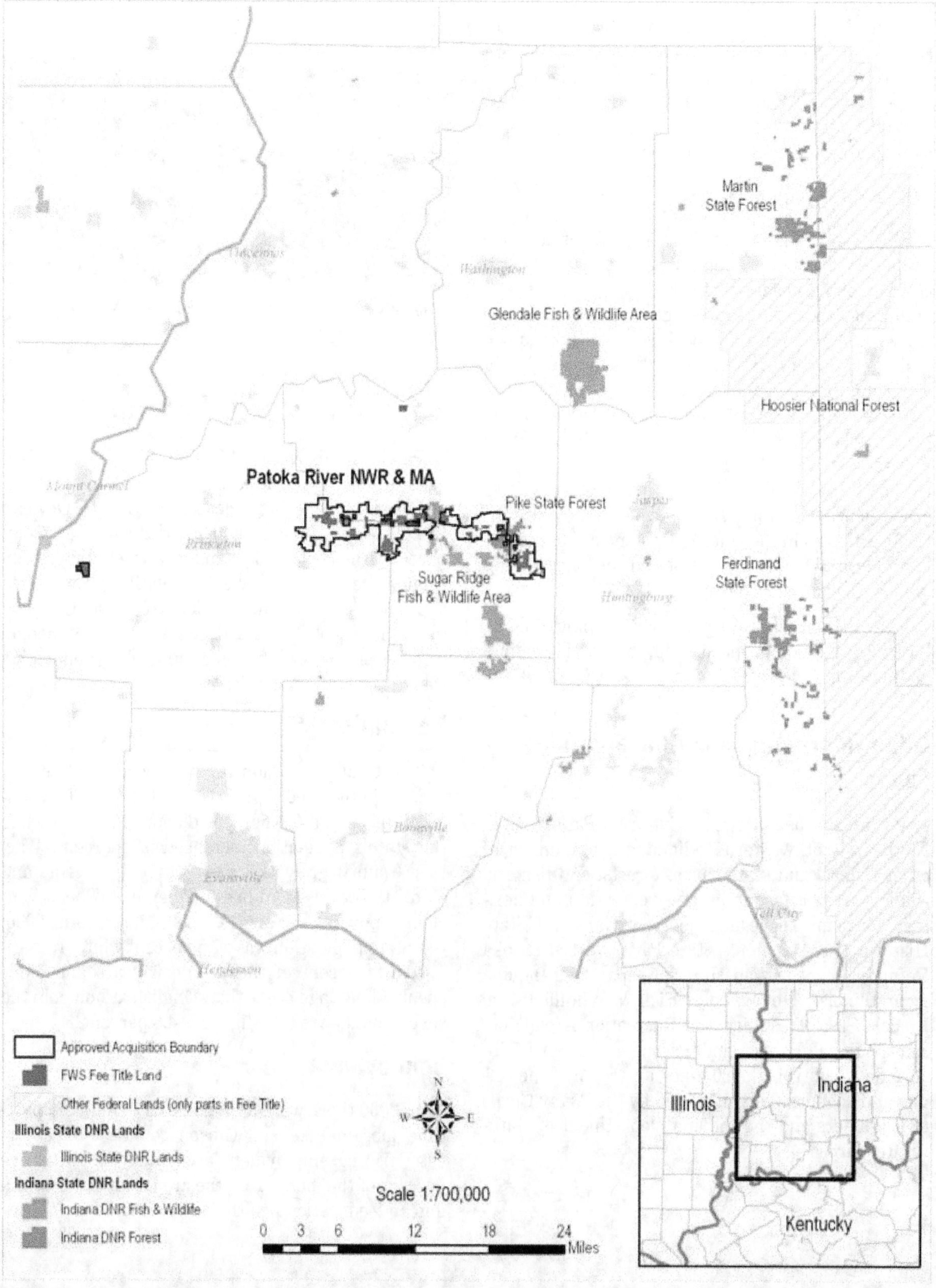

and hiking. Visitors can also camp for a fee, with sites available on a first come, first serve basis (IDNR, 2005a).

Acquisition of the land that makes up Pike State Forest began in the 1930s, and continues through the present day. Most of the historic buildings on the property were constructed by the Works Progress Administration (WPA) during the Great Depression, using material cut from local timber stands.

Ferdinand State Forest

Ferdinand State Forest is located about 20 miles southeast of Patoka River NWR. This State Forest consists of 7,700-acres with limited acquisition still occurring. In 1933, the 900 acres that became the SF were purchased by a local conservation club to build a lake and establish an area to hunt and fish. The club offered management of the project to the Indiana Department of Conservation the following year, marking the establishment of Ferdinand State Forest (IDNR, 2005b). In 1934, the Civilian Conservation Corps (CCC) built a camp there, as well as roads, service buildings, and one of the most beautiful forest lakes in the state. Ferdinand SF has excellent deer and squirrel hunting and the surrounding area is rich in German heritage.

The state forest offers primitive camping, fishing, boating, swimming, picnicking, mountain biking, and hunting for whitetail deer, turkey, squirrel, fox and raccoon.

Other Recreation and Conservation Lands

Within an hour or two's drive from Patoka River NWR in southwestern Indiana are a number of other federal and state parks, forests, and fish and wildlife areas offering outdoor recreation and heritage tourism. These include New Harmony State Historic Site, Harmonie State Park (west of Patoka Refuge, along the Wabash River separating Indiana from Illinois), Hovey Lake Fish & Wildlife Area, Lincoln State Park, Jackson Recreation Area, Hoosier National Forest, and Patoka Lake, an 8,800-acre flood control lake 60 miles upstream of the refuge and cooperatively managed by the Army Corps of Engineers and the Indiana Department of Natural Resources.

Grey wood/beaver flooding, Patoka River NWR & MA. Photo credit: USFWS

Socioeconomic Setting

Patoka River National Wildlife Refuge and Management Area is located in Pike and Gibson Counties, Indiana, and is in close proximity to Daviess, Dubois, Knox, Spencer, and Warrick Counties. Compared to the State of Indiana as a whole this seven-county area has a smaller population growth rate and is less racially and ethnically diverse. On average, the area's population has a lower median income, and less high school and college education than the state's population.

Population

The total population of the seven counties was 226,861 in the 2000 Census (USCB, 2006). The population increased 6.9 percent during the 1990s while the state's population increased 9.7 percent. Warrick County grew the most at 16.6 percent, and Knox the least at minus 1.6 percent. The seven-county population was 97.3 percent white in 2000; the State population was 87.5 percent white. In Indiana, 6.4 percent of the people 5 years and older speak a language other than English at home; in the seven-county area the figure is 4.6 percent.

Employment

In 2000 there were a total of 21,744 full- and part-time jobs in Pike and Gibson counties. Farm/forestry/fishing employment accounted for about five percent of the jobs across the area. The manufacturing and education/health/social services industries were and are the largest economic and employment sectors in these counties (USCB, 2000a; USCB, 2000b).

Income and Education

Average per-capita income in the seven-county area was $18,619 in 1999; in Indiana it was $20,397. The median household income in the seven-county area was $40,057 in 1999; in the state it was $41,567 (USCB, 2006).

In the seven-county area, 14.8 percent of persons over 25 years of age hold a bachelor's degree or higher. The comparable figure in the state is 19.4 percent. This discrepancy is typical of the difference between largely rural areas like these seven counties and entire state populations which include large numbers of more urban residents who are professionals and have higher educational attainment on average (USCB, 2006).

Potential Refuge Visitors

In order to estimate the potential market for visitors to the Refuge, we looked at 1998 consumer behavior data for an area within an approximate 60 mile radius. The data were organized by zip code areas. We used a 60 mile radius because we thought this was an approximation of a reasonable drive to the Refuge for an outing.

The consumer behavior data that we used in the analysis is derived from Mediamark Research Inc. data. The company collects and analyzes data on consumer demographics, product and brand usage, and exposure to all forms of advertising media. The consumer behavior data were projected by Tetrad Computer Applications Inc. to new populations using Mosaic data. Mosaic is a methodology that classifies neighborhoods into segments based on their demographic and socioeconomic composition. The basic assumption in the analysis is that people in demographically similar neighborhoods will tend to have similar consumption, ownership, and lifestyle preferences. Because of the assumptions made in the analysis, the data should be considered as relative indicators of potential, not actual participation.

We looked at potential participants in birdwatching, photography, freshwater fishing, hunting, and hiking. In order to estimate the general environmental orientation of the population we also looked at the number of people who potentially might hold a membership in an environmental organization.

Winter scenery, Patoka River NWR & MA. Photo credit: USFWS

The consumer behavior data apply to persons greater than 18 years old. For the area that we included in our analysis, out of a total population of 1,233,654 the population of persons greater than 18 years old was 925,980. The estimated maximum participants in the 60 mile radius for each activity are: birdwatching (72,351), photography (99,570), hunting (82,727), freshwater fishing (146,610), and hiking (86,325). The number of persons who might hold a membership in an environmental organization is estimated at about 19,941. The projections represent the core audience for repeated trips to the Refuge. On days with special events or major attractions such as when large numbers of birds are at the Refuge, visitors can be expected to travel longer distances.

Climate

The Refuge lies in the path of moisture-bearing low pressure formations that move from the western Gulf region, northeastward over the Mississippi and Ohio Valleys to the Great Lakes and northern Atlantic Coast. Much of the area's precipitation results from these storm systems, especially in the cooler part of the year. The average annual precipitation totals 44.2 inches. Of this total, about 23 inches, or nearly 52 percent, falls during the growing season of April to September. The highest and lowest annual precipitation totals for the period of record are 64.8 inches in 1945 and 28.0 inches in 1887, respectively. Maximum monthly precipitation is 15.1 inches while the minimum is 0.05 inches. The average seasonal snowfall is about 13.5 inches. On the average, 3 days out of the year have at least 1 inch of snow on the ground (NOAA, 1991).

Convective thunderstorms developing in the maritime tropical air from the Gulf of Mexico and squall line activity seem to be the factors which combine to supply summer rainfall. Severe storms are rather infrequent, but high winds and hail often accompany these storms and can cause isolated property damage. The area is in "tornado alley," with the potential for tornados highest in early spring and late fall. The tornado frequency is probably less than one every 10 years.

In winter the average temperature is 34 degrees Fahrenheit, with an average daily minimum of 25 degrees. The lowest temperature on record (January 17, 1977) is minus 18 degrees. In summer the average temperature is 76 degrees, and the average daily maximum is 87 degrees. The highest recorded temperature (September 2, 1953) is 104 degrees (NOAA, 1991). Based on the average dates the first and last killing frosts, the area normally has 180 to 190 frost free days per year (SCS, 1989).

Prevailing wind direction is from the south-southwest. Strong and cold north to northwest winds occur from late autumn to early spring as large domes of arctic high pressure move into the Midwest. The strongest winds occur during a deep winter storm passage through the Lower Ohio Valley.

The average relative humidity is mid-afternoon is roughly 60 percent. Humidity is higher at night and the average at dawn is about 85 percent.

Climate Change

The U.S. Department of the Interior issued an order in January 2001 requiring federal agencies, under its direction, that have land management responsibilities to consider potential climate change impacts as part of long range planning endeavors.

The increase of carbon dioxide (CO_2) within the earth's atmosphere has been linked to the gradual rise in surface temperature commonly referred to as global warming. In relation to comprehensive conservation planning for national wildlife refuges, carbon sequestration constitutes the primary climate-related impact that refuges can affect in a small way. The U.S. Department of Energy's "*Carbon Sequestration Research and Development*" defines carbon sequestration as "...the capture and secure storage of carbon that would otherwise be emitted to or remain in the atmosphere."

Vegetated land is a tremendous factor in carbon sequestration. Terrestrial biomes of all sorts – grasslands, forests, wetlands, tundra, and desert – are effective both in preventing carbon emission and acting as a biological "scrubber" of atmospheric CO_2. The Department of Energy report's conclusions noted that ecosystem protection is important to carbon sequestration and may reduce or prevent loss of carbon currently stored in the terrestrial biosphere.

Conserving natural habitat for wildlife is the heart of any long-range plan for national wildlife refuges. The actions proposed in this CCP would conserve or restore land and habitat, and would thus retain existing carbon sequestration on the Refuge. This in turn contributes positively to efforts to mitigate human-induced global climate change.

One Service activity in particular – prescribed burning – releases CO_2 directly to the atmosphere from the biomass consumed during combustion. However, there is actually no net loss of carbon, since new vegetation quickly germinates and sprouts to replace the burned-up biomass and sequesters or assimilates an approximately equal amount of carbon as was lost to the air (Boutton et al. 2006). Overall, there should be little or no net change in the amount of carbon sequestered at Patoka NWR from any of the proposed management alternatives.

Several impacts of climate change have been identified that may need to be considered and addressed in the future:

- Habitat available for cold water fish such as trout and salmon in lakes and streams could be reduced.
- Forests may change, with some species shifting their range northward or dying out, and other trees moving in to take their place.
- Ducks and other waterfowl could lose breeding habitat due to stronger and more frequent droughts.
- Changes in the timing of migration and nesting could put some birds out of sync with the life cycles of their prey species.
- Animal and insect Species historically found farther south may colonize new areas to the north as winter climatic conditions moderate

The managers and resource specialists on the Refuge need to be aware of the possibility of change due to global warming. When feasible, documenting long-term vegetation, species, and hydrologic changes should become a part of research and monitoring programs on the Refuge. Adjustments in refuge management direction may be necessary over the course of time to adapt to a changing climate.

The following paragraphs are excerpts from the 2000 report, *Climate Change Impacts on the United States: The Potential Consequences of Climate Variability and Change*, produced by the National Assessment Synthesis Team, an advisory committee chartered under the Federal Advisory Committee Act to help the US Global Change Research Program fulfill its mandate under the Global Change Research Act of 1990. These excerpts are from the section of the report focused upon the eight-state Midwest region.

Observed Climate Trends

Over the 20th century, the northern portion of the Midwest, including the upper Great Lakes, has warmed by almost 4°F (2°C), while the southern portion, along the Ohio River valley, has cooled by about 1°F (0.5°C). Annual precipitation has increased, with many of the changes quite substantial, including as much as 10 to 20% increases over the 20th century. Much of the precipitation has resulted from an increased rise in the number of days with heavy and very heavy precipitation events. There have been moderate to very large increases in the number of days with excessive moisture in the eastern portion of the basin.

Scenarios of Future Climate

During the 21st century, models project that temperatures will increase throughout the Midwest, and at a greater rate than has been observed in the 20th century. Even over the northern portion of the region, where warming has been the largest, an accelerated warming trend is projected for the 21st century, with temperatures increasing by 5 to 10 degrees Fahrenheit (3 degrees to 6 degrees Celsius). The average minimum temperature is likely to increase as much as 1 degree to 2 degrees Fahrenheit (0.5 to 1 degree Celsius) more than the maximum temperature. Precipitation is likely to continue its upward trend, at a slightly accelerated rate; 10 to 30 percent increases are projected across much of the region. Despite the increases in precipitation, increases in temperature and other meteorological factors are likely to lead to a substantial increase in evaporation, causing a soil moisture deficit, reduction in lake and river levels, and more drought-like conditions in much of the region. In addition, increases in the proportion of precipitation coming from heavy and extreme precipitation are very likely.

Midwest Key Issues

Reduction in Lake and River Levels

Water levels, supply, quality, and water-based transportation and recreation are all climate-sensitive issues affecting the region. Despite the projected increase in precipitation, increased evaporation due to higher summer air temperatures is likely to lead to reduced levels in the Great Lakes. Of 12 models used to assess this question, 11 suggest significant decreases in lake levels while one suggests a small increase. The total range of the 11 models' projections is less than a 1-foot increase to more than a 5-foot decrease. A 5-foot (1.5- meter) reduction would lead to a 20 to 40 percent reduction in outflow to the St. Lawrence Seaway. Lower lake levels cause reduced hydropower generation downstream, with reductions of up to 15 percent by 2050. An increase in demand for water across the region at the same time as net flows decrease is of particular concern. There is a possibility of increased national and international tension related to increased pressure for water diversions from the Lakes as demands for water increase. For smaller lakes and rivers, reduced flows are likely to cause water quality issues to become more acute. In addition, the projected increase in very heavy precipitation events will likely lead to increased flash flooding and worsen agricultural and other non-point source pollution as more frequent heavy rains wash pollutants into rivers and lakes. Lower water levels are likely to make water-based transportation more difficult with increases in the costs of navigation of 5 to 40 percent. Some of this increase will likely be offset as reduced ice cover extends the navigation season. Shoreline damage due to high lake levels is likely to decrease 40 to 80 percent due to reduced water levels.

Adaptations: A reduction in lake and river levels would require adaptations such as re-engineering of ship docks and locks for transportation and recreation. If flows decrease while demand increases, international commissions focusing on Great Lakes water issues are likely to become even more important in the future. Improved forecasts and warnings of extreme precipitation events could help reduce some related impacts.

Agricultural Shifts

Agriculture is of vital importance to this region, the nation, and the world. It has exhibited a capacity to adapt to moderate differences in growing season climate, and it is likely that agriculture would be able to continue to adapt. With an increase in the length of the growing season, double cropping, the practice of planting a second crop after the first is harvested, is likely to become more prevalent. The CO2 fertilization effect is likely to enhance plant growth and contribute to generally higher yields. The largest increases are projected to occur in the northern areas of the region, where crop yields are currently temperature limited. However, yields are not likely to increase in all parts of the region. For example, in the southern portions of Indiana and Illinois, corn yields are likely to decline, with 10-20 percent decreases projected in some locations. Consumers are likely to pay lower prices due to generally increased yields, while most producers are likely to suffer reduced profits due to declining prices. Increased use of pesticides and herbicides are very likely to be required and to present new challenges.

Adaptations: Plant breeding programs can use skilled climate predictions to aid in breeding new varieties for the new growing conditions. Farmers can then choose varieties that are better attuned to the expected climate. It is likely that plant breeders will need to use all the tools of plant breeding, including genetic engineering, in adapting to climate change. Changing planting and harvest dates and planting densities, and using integrated pest management, conservation tillage, and new farm technologies are additional options. There is also the potential for shifting or expanding the area where certain crops are grown if climate conditions become more favorable. Weather conditions during the growing season are the primary factor in year-to-year differences in corn and soybean yields. Droughts and floods result in large yield reductions; severe droughts, like the drought of 1988, cause yield reductions of over 30 percent. Reliable seasonal forecasts are likely to help farmers adjust their practices from year to year to respond to such events.

Changes in Semi-natural and Natural Ecosystems

The Upper Midwest has a unique combination of soil and climate that allows for abundant coniferous tree growth. Higher temperatures and increased evaporation will likely reduce boreal forest acreage, and make current forestlands more susceptible to

Wood Duck pair, Patoka River NWR & MA. Photo credit: USFWS

pests and diseases. It is likely that the southern transition zone of the boreal forest will be susceptible to expansion of temperate forests, which in turn will have to compete with other land use pressures. However, warmer weather (coupled with beneficial effects of increased CO2),are likely to lead to an increase in tree growth rates on marginal forestlands that are currently temperature-limited. Most climate models indicate that higher air temperatures will cause greater evaporation and hence reduced soil moisture, a situation conducive to forest fires. As the 21st century progresses, there will be an increased likelihood of greater environmental stress on both deciduous and coniferous trees, making them susceptible to disease and pest infestation, likely resulting in increased tree mortality.

As water temperatures in lakes increase, major changes in freshwater ecosystems will very likely occur, such as a shift from cold water fish species, such as trout, to warmer water species, such as bass and catfish. Warmer water is also likely to create an environment more susceptible to invasions by non-native species. Runoff of excess nutrients (such as nitrogen and phosphorus from fertilizer) into lakes and rivers is likely to increase due to the increase in heavy precipitation events. This, coupled with warmer lake temperatures, is likely to stimulate the growth of algae, depleting the water of oxygen to the detriment of other living things. Declining lake levels are likely to cause large impacts to the current distribution of wetlands. There is some chance that some wetlands could gradually migrate, but in areas where their migration is limited by the topography, they would disappear. Changes in bird populations and other native wildlife have already been linked to increasing temperatures and more changes are likely in the future. Wildlife populations are particularly susceptible to climate extremes due to the effects of drought on their food sources.

Air Quality

The U. S. Environmental Protection agency has established National Ambient Air Quality Standards (NAAQS) to protect public health and welfare from the detrimental effects of air pollution. Acquired lands of the Refuge and MA are located in areas designated as Nonattainment for Fine Particulate Matter PM-2.5. These areas include Cane Ridge WMA in Montgomery Township, Gibson County and the White River Bottoms WMA in Washington Township, Pike County. Air pollution concentrations for fine particulate matter is above the NAAQS levels for this "criteria pollutant" regulated by the Clean Air Act.

Southwest Indiana is in the Illinois Coal Basin and is blessed with rivers and large quantities of coal. These natural resources have resulted in the concentration of many coal-fired power plants. In fact, southwest Indiana has the highest concentration of coal-fired power plants per given area of anywhere on earth. As such, air pollution associated with these power plants is at a high level which explains why six of the seven counties in southwest Indiana are all or partially in Nonattainment for Fine Particulate Matter (PM- 2.5).

The "criteria pollutants" identified by the EPA as part of the Clean Air Act include carbon monoxide(CO), ozone(O3), nitrogen oxides(NOx), sulfur dioxide(SO2), lead(Pb) and particulate matter(PM). The Clean Air Act's Prevention of Significant Deterioration(PSD) program sets strict standards to limit the amount of additional pollutants(SO2), nitogen dioxide(NO2) and total suspended particulate concentrations) that can be released into the air within designated Attainment Areas. Under this program, Attainment Areas are divided into three classes, each allowing different levels of additional pollutants. The Refuge and MA as well as most of Indiana, is currently a Class II Attainment Area. A Class II designation allows moderate additional deterioration of air quality unless the area comes under Nonattainment status. Nonattainment status means any new source or proposed modifications to existing sources of air pollutants must provide for offset reductions in existing pollution so that the air quality does not deteriorate even further.

Primary pollutants affecting the area's air quality are fine particulate matter, SO2 and NO2, all of which are associated with coal-burning power plants. Nitrogen oxide is a major component of ozone smog and fine particulate matter. these pollutants are known to cause premature mortality and aggravate respiratory and cardiovascular disease, lung disease and asthma. Most vulnerable to these air pollutants are older adults, people with heart and lung disease, children and pregnant women.

Of the many coal-fired power plants in southwest Indiana, several contribute more concentrated pollutants to the air shed of the Refuge and MA based on their closer proximity and location considering prevailing winds. To the west is Duke Energy's Gibson Generating Station (third largest in world based on 3,250 megawatts), to the north is Indianapolis Power and Light and the Frank E. Ratts Generating Station of Hoosier Energy Division and to the south is the Alcoa Generating Plant in Warrick County and the American Electric Power - Indiana Michigan Power Plant at Rockport.

These and other coal -fired plants are all making major investments in pollution control devices to reduce emissions. However, their emissions are still increasing due to an increase in the amount of coal being burned to produce more power and changes in the blends of coal being burned. Atmospheric concentrations of these EPA "criteria pollutants" can only improve with offset reductions of existing pollution sources.

At the beginning of this 21st century, private industry is being spurred on to construct new ethanol refineries and biofuel power plants with offers of Federal subsidies, relaxation of air pollution standards for ethanol refineries and new regulations requiring energy production from renewable fuel sources. In recognition of the increasing demand for more electric power sources and the Federal mandate to increase the use of fuels made from renewable resources, the Indiana Department of Environmental Management (IDEM) is preparing a new Air Monitoring Station Plan to increase the number of air monitoring stations across the State. The location of these new Air Monitoring Stations will better document existing air pollution Nonattainment locations and serve as a guide for locating new sources of pollution away from existing Nonattainment Areas.

Construction of the new-terrain I-69 Interstate highway crossing through the Refuge and MA will make this a high growth potential area. For the long

Chapter 3: Refuge Environment and Management

Wintering waterfowl, Patoka River NWR & MA. Photo credit: USFWS

term protection and management of the biological resources of the Refuge and MA and enjoyment of these resources by the visiting public, a cooperative effort between the Service and IDEM is being made to establish an Air Monitoring Station on or near the refuge. This is the best way to allow for wise decision making related to permitting new-source industrial developments with inherent pollution outputs.

Geology and Soils

This section of Chapter 3 draws heavily on the Patoka River National Wetlands Project EIS, pages 75-88 (USFWS, 1994).

Geology

The Refuge is located on the eastern shelf of the Illinois River Basin, a prominent regional downwarp (bowl) centered in southeastern Illinois. During the Paleozoic Era this basin underwent repeated cycles of subsidence and uplift with accompanying sedimentation and erosion. The cycles stopped in late Pennsylvanian time when the basin was uplifted and subjected to a final episode of degradation (IDGNR, 1898). The remaining thickness of Pennsylvanian rocks in the area is about 1,200 to 1,900 feet. These rocks are composed of cyclical sequences of shale, siltstone and sandstone intermixed with thin, widespread beds of coal, clay, limestone and black shale. In general, these intermixed layers are dipping 1 to 2 degrees west towards the center of the basin.

Within the Pennsylvanian-age rocks, five distinct formations are exposed within the Refuge & MA boundaries:

- *Staunton Formation:* Composed primarily of sandstone and sandy shale, this 75 to 100 feet thick layer is the oldest (deepest) formation and crops out near the eastern boundary of the Refuge & MA.
- *Linton Formation:* Above the Staunton is the 80-feet thick Linton formation. Composed primarily of sandstone, and shale, this formation is found in the eastern and central areas of the Refuge & MA.
- *Petersburg Formation:* This formation lies above the Linton and crops out in the east and central portions of the Refuge & MA. Approximately 100 feet thick, the formation is a sequence of shale, limestone and sandstone.
- *Dugger Formation:* Above the Petersburg lies a 70 to 100-feet thick sequence of sandstone, siltstone, limestone, shale, coal, and underclay comprising the Dugger formation. This formation occurs in the higher elevations of the western portion of the Refuge & MA.
- *Shelburn Formation:* Composed primarily of sandstone and shale, this formation caps the highest sites in the western part of the Refuge & MA.

In addition to these rock formations, most of the area is covered by a mantle of unconsolidated material. During the Pleistocene period, till, outwash and loess was deposited during successive cycles of continental glaciation, ending about 8,000 years ago with the withdrawal of the Wisconsinian glaciers from Indiana. These deposits range from only several feet to nearly 100 feet thick, with the deepest deposits occurring in the western portion of the Refuge & MA (IDNR, 1990).

Minerals

Oil

Small oil production wells are common within and adjacent to the Refuge & MA with the majority on the western end near Oatsville.

Gas

In the past, any natural gas produced incidental to oil production was vented or burned off at the wellhead. In the past two years, interest has been building in producing natural gas from a deeper geological seam known as the New Albany Shale. This is a complex unconventional reservoir with low volume but low decline production found at about 4,000 feet deep in Gibson County. To date, only a few of these wells have been drilled in southwest Indiana. Coalbed methane gas (CBM) is also being explored as a possible new source of energy especially if coal production continues to decline because of the high sulfur content of most Illinois Basin coals. Methane gas is also being produced from old underground mine voids with one mine gas well in Gibson County.

Coal

The Refuge & MA lies on the eastern edge of the Illinois Coal Basin and is in the heart of Indiana's coal producing region. Most of the coal is of moderate to high sulfur content, which means the coal has to be cleaned and the sulfur scrubbed out of emissions when used in steam electric power plants. Although coal mining has been continuous in and near the Refuge & MA for nearly a century, substantial deposits of coal remain unmined. Recent coal industry statistics indicate that approximately 3,670 million tons of recoverable coal (surface and underground minable) remain in Pike and Gibson counties (ICC, 1992). The Office of Surface Mining (OSM) estimated a total coal reserve base of 105 million tons within the Refuge & MA alone, of which 40.5 million tons are accessible by underground mining and 65.5 million tons accessible by surface mining methods.

Over 20,000 acres of Pike County were surface mined for coal prior to the passage of the Surface Mining Control and Reclamation Act of 1977 (SMCRA). Many of the remaining ungraded spoil ridges and final-cut lakes provide excellent wildlife habitat. Nevertheless, some old overburden spoil ridges and abandoned coal preparation sites contain low grade coal, shale and sandstone laced with natural pyrites. Rainfall leaches out high levels of acid-forming substances such as sulfates and metals such as magnesium, iron, aluminum and manganese. As these metals dissolve in the acid water, the total acid salts reach toxic concentration levels. Toxic runoff from such areas impairs water quality in streams and lakes, devastating aquatic life.

Today, all water from mining sites must pass through sediment ponds to improve water quality; mined areas are graded back to approximate original contours and covered with topsoil; pyritic bearing rock is buried deep in the mine pit out of contact with surface water flows and the site is revegetated according to approved reclamation plans. The array of problems long associated with the area's surface mining activities are not a result of today's mining methods, but rather from strip mining prior to SMCRA. Within the Refuge & MA boundaries there

Impacts of strip mining on adjacent lands, Patoka River NWR & MA. Photo credit: USFWS

are approximately 150 acres of old strip mines. Most of the acid producing abandoned mine lands are located outside the Refuge but within the watershed. Most of these have been or are being reclaimed by Indiana Department of Natural Resources' Abandoned Mine Land Program.

Soils

Lying in the valley's floor and subject to periodic flooding, bottomland soil associations make up the majority of Refuge soils. Upland soil associations are located above the flood-zone on valley sideslopes and ridges.

Bottomland Soil Associations

Found on the floodplains of the Patoka River and its major tributaries, these soils were formed in the sand, silt and clay deposited during flood events. Soils within these associations are nearly level, deep, and poorly drained. Soils can also be classified based on hydric (wetness) characteristics, which in turn influence the type of plants that will grow there. Hydric soils are soils that are wet long enough to periodically produce anaerobic conditions. Hydric soils or soils with hydric inclusions comprise the majority of the soil types found in the bottomland.

Nearly 75 percent (16,970 acres) of the Refuge & MA is composed of three such soil associations:

- *Belknap-Bonnie-Wakeland Association:* While it makes up only 13 percent of Pike County, this association represents 46 percent of the Refuge & MA. With adequate drainage, these soils are used mainly for cultivated crops. Some areas are used for hay and pasture while other areas

Chapter 3: Refuge Environment and Management

South Fork Patoka River, Patoka River NWR & MA. Photo credit: USFWS

are wooded. Flooding and wetness are the principle problems.

- *Stendal-Bonnie-Birds Association:* This soil association represents about 7 percent of Gibson County and 12 percent of the Refuge. The soils are used mainly as cropland, but flooding, wetness, and ponding are problems. They are well-suited for woodland, and used as such along stream channels and in undrained areas.
- *Petrolia Association:* Approximately 3 percent of Gibson County and 17 percent of the Refuge & MA is comprised of this soil association. Flooding and wetness can hinder crop production, but the soils are well-suited for woodland.

Upland Soil Associations

These associations are found on ridge tops and side slopes adjacent to the above floodplain soils. Having formed in loess, material weathered from sandstone, siltstone, shale, and regolith in surface-mined areas, these soils are generally formed on gently to severely sloping sites and are well-drained.

About 25 percent of the Refuge & MA is composed of five upland soil associations:

- *Zanesville-Hosmer Association:* This soil association represents nearly 17 percent of Pike County and seven percent of the Refuge & MA. These soils are fairly well suited for cultivated crops, woodland and recreational uses. Erosion is a hazard, and Hosmer soil's fragipan restricts rooting depth and permeability. Wetness is a problem associated with perched water tables.
- *Zanesville-Gilpin Association:* Soils in this association make up 14 percent of Pike County and five percent of the Refuge & MA. The hazard of erosion, the slope, a fragipan in the Zanesville soils and the moderate depth to bedrock in the Gilpin soils make the association better suited to woodlands, hay and pasture than to cultivated crops.
- *Hosmer Association:* This soil association comprises 16 percent of Pike and Gibson counties and five percent of the Refuge & MA. These soils are used mainly for cultivated crops, hay, and pasture. Some areas are wooded. Erosion is the primary hazard. Hosmer's fragipan restricts rooting depth and can create localized wetness due to perched water tables.
- *Fairpoint-Bethesda Association:* Soils in this association make up about 16 percent of Pike County and nearly four percent of the Refuge & MA. These soils are found in very steep areas where overburden was cast during surface mining, and in nearly level to strongly sloping areas where overburden was smoothed and shaped. This soil association is mainly suited for woodland, hay and pasture because of the slope, erosion hazard, low available water capacity and scattered rock fragments.
- *Alford-Sylvan Association:* This soil association accounts for approximately 19 percent of Pike and Gibson counties and roughly four percent of the Refuge & MA. These soils are well suited to woodland. The steeper areas of this association are used for hay and pasture while the flatter sites are generally suited to cropland. Slope and the hazard of erosion are the primary problems.

Although there are 73 recognized soil types within the 23,743-acre Refuge & MA, over 70 percent of the Refuge is comprised of soils from just six soil series. These include:

- Belknap series (4,144 acres)
- Bonnie series (3,744 acres)

- Petrolia series (3,230 acres)
- Hosmer series (1,835 acres)
- Zanesville series (1,441 acres)
- Steff series (1386 acres).

The majority of these soil series represent soils that are either hydric or contain hydric inclusions, and are located in the Patoka River floodplain. Fifteen soil types are considered hydric and an additional 15 soil types contain pockets of hydric soil. Combined, these 30 soil types account for over 15,000 acres, or 68 percent of the Refuge. Of the remaining 7,000-plus Refuge acres, approximately 5,300 acres are prone to erosion and are classified highly erodible.

Water and Hydrology

This section was reproduced or modified from the Patoka River National Wetlands Project EIS, pages 88 to 101 (USFWS, 1994).

The drainage area of the Patoka River watershed includes 862 square miles in eight counties. At the upper eastern end of the watershed, the Patoka flows rapidly within a relatively narrow floodplain through deeply incised uplands, dropping at the rate of 12 feet per mile. Much of the uplands in this segment of the watershed are forested, with relatively small farms interspersed throughout. As the river enters the flat land created by Glacial Lake Patoka near Jasper, flow slows dramatically as the river's gradient decreases to 1 foot per mile. The predominant land use in the uplands changes from forestland to farmland.

The Refuge is located within this slow, meandering stretch of river with its wide floodplain, numerous oxbows and low rolling uplands. A total of 30 miles of river channel, 16 miles of natural meanders plus 14 miles on the western end that were channelized in the 1920s, are included in the Refuge & MA boundaries. In addition there are 19 miles of oxbow lakes and three miles of the South Fork, a major tributary entering the Patoka River just north of Oakland City (Figure 7).

Two notable events influence the present water regime of the Patoka River. The first was an attempt to drain nearly 100,000 acres of forested wetlands for farming in the 1920s. Known as Houchin's Ditch and beginning at the town of Winslow, the project replaced 36 miles of natural, meandering river with about 17 miles of dredged, straight ditch. The assumption was that by straightening and deepening the channel, high water would flush through the area more quickly and adjoining lands could be more easily drained. Although some subsequent drainage and clearing of adjacent forested wetlands occurred, overall the project was a failure because of the bowl-shaped topography of this section of the floodplain, the river's low gradient, and the hydrologic relationship between the Patoka and Wabash Rivers.

Nearly 19 miles of natural river meanders were cut off and isolated from the main channel. Water exchange within these man-made oxbows is now limited to periods of high water. Unfortunately, heavy sediment loads are carried during these periods and results in increased deposition in the oxbows. Consequently, these important ecological units are becoming shallower and hold water for a shorter duration. Although this process occurs in all natural riverine systems, new oxbows are continually being created as river meanders are severed from the main channel. In the case of Houchins's Ditch, these oxbows are not being replaced and the associated wetland habitat is being lost.

The second major event affecting the river's flow regime was the Corps of Engineers' construction in the late 1970s of Patoka Lake. Located approximately 63 miles above the Refuge, this 8,000-acre impoundment was designed to provide flood control as well as recreation and water supply. Since the lake was built, flow regulation by it has reduced flood stages in the lower segment of the river usually several times a year.

During the initial start-up of Patoka Lake in 1979, the month of July received an all time high record one month rainfall. The lake behind the dam rose rapidly forcing summer releases of stored water. This resulted in flooding of much of the floodplain crop fields, particularly within the present Refuge and MA boundaries. Farmers blamed the new dam for creating the problem and demanded that something be done. Subsequently, in an effort to lessen the possibilities of summer flooding, a special federal appropriation of $1.3 million was provided to the Corps to remove all channel obstructions and most leaning trees on both sides of the river from the Patoka Lake Dam to the Wabash River, a length of 121 miles. This was completed in 1981. It reduced localized flooding immediately upstream of drift piles, but largely eliminated in-stream cover and the overhead tree canopy, negatively affecting the river's fish and wildlife resources. The project also

Chapter 3: Refuge Environment and Management

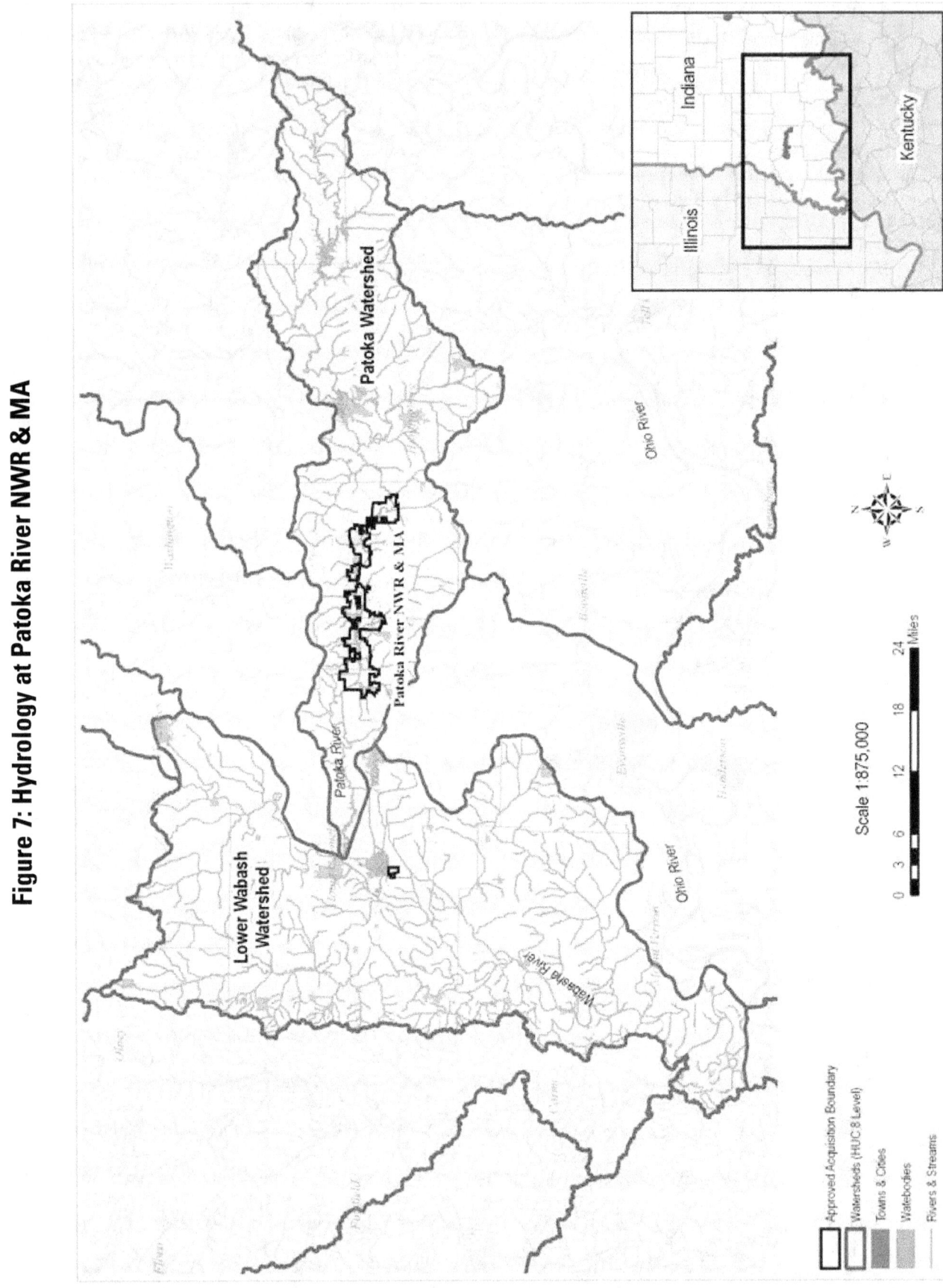

Figure 7: Hydrology at Patoka River NWR & MA

increased the rate and extent of streambank erosion by removing many of the tree roots which had stabilized the river bank.

Agriculture (and associated land clearing, ditching and drain tiles), surface coal mining, and to a lesser extent urban development affect the Patoka River and its watershed. These activities contribute to rapid runoff of precipitation, increased soil erosion, and heavy sediment loads in streams. After any substantial rain event, the Patoka River and its tributaries are characterized by turbid, sediment-laden water.

Ditching, damming, and channelization efforts dating back to the early 1900s are largely responsible for the loss of wetlands throughout the area. Oil well developments, over 20,000 acres of abandoned coal mine lands, intensive agricultural and logging operations as well as runoff or discharges of industrial, community, and farming effluents degrade water quality within the watershed.

Refuge Resources

The sections under this heading draw heavily upon the Patoka River National Wetlands Project EIS (USFWS, 1994).

Plant Communities

Wetlands

Within the Refuge & MA are 12,700 acres of forested wetlands, emergent wetlands, scrub-shrub wetlands, agriculturally modified wetlands, and open water habitat.

American lotus, Snakey Point Marsh, Patoka River NWR & MA. Photo credit: USFWS

Forested Wetland

The majority (55 percent) of wetlands within the Refuge & MA fall in this category. Characterized by woody vegetation that is 20 feet or taller, forested wetlands are found within the floodplain of the Patoka River and its tributaries where the terrain is relatively flat and soils are poorly drained. Soils may remain saturated for most of the growing season on some sites and only a week or two during the growing season on other sites. Most areas of forested wetland experience some degree of annual flooding. Tree species composition often reflects the hydrology of the site. On the wettest areas, the mature forested wetland supports black willow, sweetgum and river birch. Areas frequently or seasonally flooded are dominated by silver maple, cottonwood, sycamore, pin oak, Shumard oak, swamp chestnut oak, overcup oak, swamp white oak, green ash, and red maple. On drier bottomland sites that are infrequently flooded for short durations, the dominant canopy trees include American beech, pecan, black walnut, American elm, and cherrybark and other oaks. For a more complete list of plants common to the Refuge's bottomland forested wetlands see Appendix C.

Forested wetlands transformed by flooding as a result of beaver activity cover hundreds of acres within the Refuge. Depending on when they were created, these areas may contain stumps as well as dead and/or dying trees. They are typically covered by a growth of duckweed, with coontail and bladderwort under the surface. Buttonbush, whitegrass, common arrowhead, and knotweed commonly dominate the borders.

Scrub-shrub Wetland

These freshwater, vegetated wetlands are dominated by woody vegetation less than 20 feet tall. Scrub-shrub wetlands may represent a successional stage leading to forested wetland, or they may be relatively self-maintaining, stable communities. They are more or less permanently inundated. Plant species found in shrub-shrub wetlands include true shrubs such as buttonbush, red-osier dogwood and swamp privet, as well as young trees, or trees and shrubs that are small or stunted because of environmental conditions. Some of these include pumpkin ash, red maple, and willows.

Within the Refuge, scrub-shrub wetlands are found exclusively around the fringes of beaver flooded areas and in many of the numerous river oxbows created either through natural river meandering or as a result of river channelization in the

American Coot, Patoka River NWR & MA. Photo credit: USFWS

1920s. A total of 1,053 acres (4.7 percent) of Refuge lands are scrub-shrub wetlands, which represents eight percent of the Refuge's total wetland acreage.

Emergent Wetland

Emergent wetlands, commonly referred to as marshes and sloughs, are characterized by erect, rooted water plants that are present for most of the growing season in most years. These wetlands normally contain standing water, though at times they will dry up. Common perennial plants found in emergent wetlands include cattail, bulrushes, sedges, dock, and smartweeds. For a more complete list of plants found in this wetland type within the Refuge see Appendix C.

The Refuge contains about a thousand acres of emergent wetlands. This represents about 4.5 percent of the Refuge and 8 percent of the Refuge's total wetland acreage.

Agriculturally Modified Wetland

Lands in this category, although disturbed annually by agricultural activities, still possess the hydrologic characteristics and hydric soils necessary to perform many of the natural functions of undisturbed wetlands. These functions include absorbing rain and flood waters and recharging local groundwater and aquifers. Because of their location in the floodplain, winter flooding makes waste grain as well as natural foods available to migrating and wintering waterfowl. The majority of waterfowl use within the Refuge is currently associated with these agricultural lands. Approximately 22 percent of the Refuge wetlands fall into this category, and nearly all are located at the western end of the Refuge & MA.

Open Water

The 837 acres of Refuge in this category include upland lakes and ponds, oxbows associated with the Patoka River and the waters of the Patoka River and its various tributaries.

Uplands

The principal natural community found in the Refuge is classified upland forest. As with the bottomland forests, upland forest resources have been heavily utilized by the area's timber industry. Mature upland forests are extremely limited in the Refuge; they occur at higher elevations where terrain is steeper and soils are well-drained. On southwest-facing slopes, these forests would typically contain both white and black oaks, hickory, and blackgum. On more mesic (wetter) sites, such as northeast aspects and valleys, the tree species composition would include red oaks, yellow poplar, beech, sugar maple, walnut, hickory, and cherry. Some pines are present in upland forest, but they are not indigenous to this part of Indiana. Although upland forest can be found in most areas of the Refuge, the majority is located in Pike County. This natural community type represents 15 percent of the total Refuge & MA.

Invasive Plant Species

Some exotic (also known as non-native or alien) plants greatly alter the plant communities of natural areas while others more commonly affect already disturbed or agricultural areas. Left unchecked, noxious plant species can seriously degrade the productivity and wildlife value of invaded habitats.

Fortunately, most of the Refuge & MA's wetlands are relatively free of noxious plants. Those in the area possessing the greatest potential for serious impacts include common reed grass, reed canary grass, and moneywort. The first two are a greater threat in open wetland sites, whereas moneywort can carpet large areas of floodplain forests (as well as open areas). Purple loosestrife was found in the Refuge in 2006 and eliminated. Both purple loosestrife and common reed grass have been observed to form monocultures, completely overrunning wetlands to the exclusion of almost all other plant species. Monitoring will be necessary to assure prompt action is taken to control these plants before they become a problem in the future.

On upland sites and agricultural communities, the most troublesome noxious plant is Johnson grass. Owing to its hardiness, growth and reproductive mechanisms, and its close relationship to domestic corn, this introduced species is widespread and difficult to control in both Pike and Gibson counties. As a result of seed dispersal during flood events, bottomland agricultural fields are particularly prone to infestation making it common to see this plant in those areas.

Other plants classified as noxious weeds in the area include Canadian thistle, bur cucumber and shatter cane. Although locally significant, these species do not represent as pervasive a problem as Johnson grass.

Threatened and Endangered Plants

The Indiana Natural Heritage Data Center is a continuously updated data management system which contains locations of all rare plant species in Indiana. Based on this information, which includes both historical collections and recent discoveries, the Indiana Division of Nature Preserves (IDNP) compiled a list of 55 potential rare plants which could occur within the Refuge & MA. IDNP personnel then conducted field investigations to confirm the presence of any of these rare plant species. In 1991, 17 individual areas within the Refuge & MA were inventoried. A total of 20 state-listed plant species were verified during the survey (Homoya, et al., 1992). No federally-listed threatened or endangered plants are known to occur within the Patoka River NWR/NWA.

Two of the 20 state-listed plant species are particularly noteworthy. The discovery of sickle pod (Cassis obtusifolia) represents the first documented occurrence of this species in the state. Also, three populations of buttonweed (*Diodia virginiana*) were found in the Project area. These finds represent the second, third and fourth occurrences of this species documented in Indiana. The vast majority of rare plants found during IDNP'S survey are associated with forested and emergent wetlands. Although a few species were found in disturbed habitat, most were growing in relatively stable wetland communities, and were scattered rather evenly throughout the inventoried area of the Patoka River floodplain.

Fish and Wildlife Communities

Birds

The Patoka River and surrounding wetland and upland areas provide an array of habitat types which fulfill the necessary breeding, feeding, migration and wintering requirements for a variety of avian species. Scientific surveys, organized bird counts and casual observations have recorded over 231 species of waterfowl, wading and shore birds, songbirds, game birds and others within the Refuge & MA.

Waterfowl

The Patoka River bottoms, particularly during periods of high water in late fall and early spring, is an important waterfowl migration stop-over in the eastern portion of the Mississippi flyway, and one of the more important sites in the state. Average fall/winter duck populations in the Refuge & MA are conservatively estimated at 5,000-8,000 birds during years with good available water, i.e., sufficient rainfall to provide lowland flooding. Data available for waterfowl use during spring migration shows a minimum of 15,000 ducks, utilizing the area on their journey north. Most of this use occurs in the Oatsville, Wirth and Wheeling Bottoms, historically high-use areas, although birds are also found on the other numerous wetlands throughout the Refuge & MA. Cane Ridge Wildlife Management Area, west of the main body of the Refuge and along the Wabash River, seasonally attracts waterfowl populations estimated at 10,000 ducks and 8,000 Snow Geese annually.

The Patoka River valley contains some of the best Wood Duck nesting and brood rearing habitat in the State. Beaver activity is largely responsible, although other factors such as rising water tables

Drake Wood Duck. Photo credit: USFWS

and erosion-related sedimentation of area ditches also have contributed to the increase in wetlands. Although Wood Duck is the major species breeding on the Refuge & MA, adjacent lands, particularly strip-mined areas reclaimed since 1977, also support nesting by several other waterfowl species, including Mallards, Blue-wing Teal and Northern Shoveler. Local nesting by Giant Canada Geese has been documented since the early 1980s. Most nesting is found on reclaimed strip mine lands.

Shorebirds and Wading Birds

The Patoka River NWR & MA provides an abundant source of food and high quality nesting and roosting sites for resident and migrating shorebirds and wading birds. Although approximately 40 species have been observed in the Refuge & MA, the majority are transitory, utilizing the emergent wetlands, shallow flood waters and temporary mudflats for resting and to obtain protein (in the form of invertebrates) essential for continued migration and successful reproduction.

The Refuge & MA hosts numerous species of plovers, sandpipers, dowitchers, and rails, among others. One notable migrant is the Sandhill Crane. Each fall, thousands of cranes stage at the Jasper-Pulaski Fish and Wildlife area in northern Indiana. Their journey to wintering grounds in Florida takes them over the Patoka River bottomlands. When habitat conditions are suitable, flocks of 50 to 100 birds have been observed resting and feeding before continuing south.

Several species of wading birds, notably the Great Blue Heron, Black-Crowned Night-Heron and Yellow-Crowned Night-Heron, are known to nest within the Refuge & MA. Several other species, including the American and Least Bitterns, Green-Backed Heron, Piping Plover, Killdeer, and Common Snipe have breeding ranges which encompass the Refuge & MA, and it is reasonable to assume that many or most of these species nest here. Wilson's Phalarope and Black-necked Stilt are documented nesters at Cane Ridge Wildlife Management Area, located west of the main body of the Refuge along the Wabash River.

Raptors

The Refuge area supports permanent or seasonal populations of at least 14 species of birds of prey. Open fields and emergent wetlands provide essential habitat for Northern Harriers, American Kestrels, Short-eared Owls, Barn Owls, and Broad-Winged, Rough-Legged, and Red-Tailed Hawks. Forested wetlands and upland forests support Cooper's and Sharp-Shinned Hawks, Great Horned Owls, Barred Owls and Eastern Screech Owls. In addition, the state-listed Red-Shouldered Hawk currently nests within the Refuge & MA. The Patoka River area probably has the largest expanse of nesting habitat for this species remaining in the state.

The Osprey, a state-listed endangered species, as well as a species of management concern to the Service, has been observed utilizing Patoka River wetlands during migration. The Mississippi Kite, extremely rare in Indiana, has also been observed on the Refuge.

Upland Game Birds

Resident populations of Bobwhite Quail, Ruffed Grouse and eastern Wild Turkey occur within Patoka River NWR & MA. Resident and migrant populations of Mourning Dove and American Woodcock also occur locally.

In general, quail require a diversity of habitats, including forests, brush, grass and cultivated lands. Successional zones between forest and field (edge or ecotone) is particularly important.

Few quail inhabit the interior of large tracts of bottomland or upland forests. Quail populations in the area are considered fair, with annual recruitment determined generally by winter and spring weather and the availability of suitable nesting/brood habitat.

Ruffed Grouse is a woodland species that generally prefers early stages of forest succession. Hardwood thickets characterized by dense stands of young saplings and vine tangles, old fields reverting to trees and young pine plantations are important habitat components. Historically, Ruffed Grouse populations in Indiana were declining in the early 1960s and their distribution was restricted to a small area in the south-central part of the state. An intense trapping and transplanting effort by the Indiana DNR was undertaken to reverse this trend. As Indiana forests have matured, the amount of young forest preferred by Ruffed Grouse has declined, resulting in lower grouse numbers in recent years.

Generally speaking, the Wild Turkey is a forest dweller, favoring mature mast-producing hardwoods (mainly oaks) with a mixture of understory plants like dogwood, sassafras, and greenbriar. Turkeys also make use of green plants (clover, wheat) and seeds (grasses, wheat, agricultural crops) found in pastures, crop fields, roadsides and disturbed or

Opossum and young, Patoka River NWR & MA. Photo credit: USFWS

abandoned areas. These more open areas provide the insects needed by poults for the protein necessary for rapid growth and development, and the forest/field interface is often preferred by nesting hens. The Refuge & MA contains these essential habitat components, and consequently the area supports a good turkey population.

Although migratory, Mourning Doves are present on the Refuge year round. Winter birds are principally migrants from northern areas utilizing the area after the local breeding population has migrated south. Heaviest concentrations of Mourning Doves occur in late summer as breeding birds and young of the year stage in large flocks prior to moving south. Most local birds are gone by early November. Because of their adaptability and high reproductive capacity, Mourning Doves are the most abundant upland game bird in the area as well as in the state. Strictly ground-feeding seed eaters, doves find abundant foods at Patoka River NWR & MA. Principal foods include waste grain in winter wheat, corn, milo and silage fields, annual weeds (foxtail, spurge, crabgrass, ragweed) in abandoned or disturbed area, and both planted and volunteer vegetation in large areas of newly-reclaimed strip mining lands.

Although limited nesting is known to occur, American Woodcock primarily utilize the area during spring and fall migrations. During these seasons they occur in fairly dense coverts of regenerating woodlands in the early stages of succession. Because the woodcock relies almost exclusively on earthworms as a food source, favored sites are in rich, moist bottomlands or upland riparian areas. Although never abundant on the Refuge, large flights during migration, particularly in the fall, can result in temporarily high populations in small, isolated areas offering good habitat with plenty of worms.

Passerines (Perching Birds)

Detailed information on the abundance of some non-game bird species is not available, but it is known that well over 100 species of passerines and other species utilize the Refuge & MA at some time each year. Prior to settlement, the larger, unbroken tracts of bottomland forest were undoubtedly important habitat for many neotropical migrants, that is, species that summer and breed in North America and winter in Latin America. Neotropical migrants include most of our forest and grassland songbirds. Subsequent forest fragmentation, both in southern Indiana and nationally for agricultural expansion, roadways, urbanization, utility (pipeline and transmission line) corridors, and timber production has had serious impacts on many of these birds and population declines have been noted for many species. However, counts of singing male Cerulean Warblers noted while canoeing the Patoka River in the eastern third of the Refuge, showed some of the highest count totals recorded in Indiana. The large number of Prothonotary Warbler pairs recorded in the bottoms during a 1997-98 Breeding Bird Research Study by Hurley was significant enough to justify listing the Patoka River NWR as an Important Bird Area by the National Audubon Society.

At the time of the NWR/MA's establishment in the early 1990s, forestland within the area, both upland and bottomland, had been reduced in extent and quality. Yet it still offered the best habitat in the area and has been utilized for nesting and migration by a variety of warblers, thrushes, vireos, woodpeckers, flycatchers and sparrows. The Refuge's reforestation efforts over the past decade have been beneficial to shrub-scrub and forest-dwelling passerines.

Mammals

Indiana is home to 54 species of mammals, of which 41 species occur on the Patoka River NWR & MA. These include an array of game, non-game and furbearing mammals.

Game Mammals

The Refuge provides excellent habitat for Indiana's only big game species, the white-tailed deer. Interspersed bottomland forest, agricultural fields, idle/scrub lands, wetlands and upland forest provides the habitat diversity necessary for abundant food, protective cover, and reproductive activities. Population density estimates in the 1990s by the Indiana DNR indicate 33 deer per square mile of suitable habitat in Pike County and 22 deer per square mile of deer habitat in Gibson County. In terms of county-wide averages for all types of land and habitat types, Pike County supports 15 deer per square mile while Gibson County is estimated at six per square mile. With the exception of open water and some emergent wetlands, the Refuge & MA is considered to be suitable deer habitat, and supports approximately 25 to 30 deer per square mile. Deer are present in sufficient abundance to cause agricultural depredation in isolated locations. Because of the area's deer abundance, deer hunting is an extremely popular activity for local and visiting sportsmen.

Patoka River woodlands and adjacent uplands provide habitat for both fox and gray squirrels, the most sought after small game mammals in the state. Productive squirrel habitat contains adequate den trees for escape, protection and reproduction, and dependable food sources in all seasons. Squirrel reproduction and survival fluctuates with changing yields of heavy-seeded mast, particularly acorns. Other fruits and berries, floral parts, buds, bark, roots, fungi and animal matter provide foods when heavy mast is unavailable. A variety of hardwood tree species is essential to a balanced habitat, but the stocking of heavy-seeded species – oak, hickory, beech, walnut – determines carrying capacity.

Much of the bottomland forest within the proposed Project area has been continually harvested for the heavy-seeded tree species, i.e., oak and hickory. Subsequently, these woodlands do not contain optimum stands of these important squirrel foods, and populations are considered fair. Upland forests, particularly those managed by the Indiana DNR, are characterized by more tree species diversity; their squirrel populations are generally considered good.

The other major small game mammal within the Refuge & MA is the eastern cottontail rabbit. They require early successional vegetation, and rabbits are found in good numbers in and around abandoned fields, fence rows, pasture borders and reclaimed strip mine lands. As strict herbivores, the cottontail favors new growth grasses, succulent forbs and some agricultural grains. During severe winter weather, the bark of young woody growth can sustain rabbits for short periods.

Furbearers

Furbearers generally include those animals harvested by hunting or trapping primarily for the commercial value of their pelts. Because most of these animals are closely associated with wetland/aquatic sites, Patoka River NWR & MA provides excellent habitat for furbearers such as muskrats, beaver, coyotes, foxes, and others.

Marshes are the preferred habitats of muskrats, but the species also occurs along streams and ditches as well as in lakes and ponds. Areas such as Snakey Point provide excellent muskrat habitat. Although somewhat cyclical, muskrat populations in area marshes, ponds, oxbows, and the Patoka River itself are considered good.

Beaver are thought to have been extirpated in Indiana by 1900. Natural range expansion by way of the extensive river systems and relocating some beavers to wild areas away from human habitations have resulted in a nearly state-wide distribution today. Within the Refuge & MA, nearly all suitable habitat is currently occupied by beaver. Beaver activity is responsible for the shallow water and standing dead timber in several large areas, most notably west of Line Road and north of Snakey Point. Beavers impound areas adjacent to water courses to provide access to food and other essential habitat needs; these areas are later abandoned when food supplies are depleted and the animals move to new territory. Although significant in short-term impacts, these activities are a natural phenomenon in the Patoka's bottomland forests and increase the diversity of wetland types and the wildlife that utilize them. This cycle (bottomland timber beaver impoundment emergent marsh scrub-shrub wetland bottomland timber) has occurred historically in the Patoka bottoms.

Unfortunately, the beaver's habit of impounding waters frequently brings it in direct conflict with man. Beaver activity results in plugged road culverts and flooded roadways, water encroachment on railroad grades, reduced drainage and flooding of agricultural lands, and loss of timber resources. Beaver can be trapped and dams can be removed, but as long as suitable habitat is available these remedies are at best temporary because beaver will quickly re-colonize the site. Refuge management policy is to remove nuisance beavers whenever their works on the refuge are impacting private lands off the refuge.

Coyotes and red and gray foxes are relatively common on the Refuge & MA. Over the last few decades, the coyote population has gradually increased in areas of suitable habitat, primarily upland brushy, grassy and abandoned fields. Abandoned strip-mined lands as well as newly reclaimed areas provide ideal habitat for coyotes. Red foxes occur in similar habitat and it is believed that the coyote often displaces some red fox from these areas, thus depressing red fox populations. Gray foxes are found more commonly in bushy and wooded habitats both in uplands and bottomlands. Food habits of coyotes and foxes are similar and include primarily small rodents and occasional birds. When present in sufficient numbers coyotes are known to prey heavily on white-tailed deer fawns. Occasionally, coyotes impact livestock producers (sheep and pigs).

Mink, otters, weasels, skunks, opossum, and raccoons are also relatively abundant in the area. Food habits range from the carnivorous behavior of minks, otters, and weasels to the omnivorous habits of raccoons, opossum, and skunks. Mink, otters, weasels and raccoon are closely associated with wetland habitats, streams and ponds; opossum and skunks are more often found in the uplands. Because they are all considered predators, they occasionally cause damage to domestic animals, i.e., prey on poultry and other tended animals. Otters were reintroduced into the Patoka River by the Indiana Department of Natural Resources over a period of several years in the late 1990s. This popular reintroduction effort has resulted in otters dispersing throughout the Patoka River Watershed and beyond.

Nongame mammals

Numerous small nongame mammals find suitable habitat on the Refuge & MA. Included in this group are shrews, moles, bats, chipmunks, mice and voles. Although there are little specific data regarding population sizes, the interspersion of woodlands, wetlands, abandoned fields, agricultural lands, creeks, ponds and river make it reasonable to assume that these species are faring well. Although rarely observed, and frequently underappreciated, nongame mammals are critically important as a food source for the larger, predatory mammals as well as most of the area's hawks and owls.

Amphibians and Reptiles

The Patoka River valley is within the range of at least 60 species of herptiles, that is, snakes, turtles, lizards, skinks, salamanders, newts, sirens, toads and frogs (Conant, 1958). A diverse assortment of reptiles and amphibians occur on the Refuge and fill

Five-lined skink, Patoka River NWR & MA. Photo credit: USFWS

many important niches in the ecosystem's natural food chain. Patoka's herpefauna include the northern copperbelly water snake, a species of concern which has been found to inhabit the buttonbush swamps of the bottoms in large numbers, and spring's tiny harbinger, the spring peeper, a small frog whose persistent, shrill mating call pierces March nights in an ancient rite of spring.

Because the majority of these species require moist woodlands, ponds, streams, marshes, swamps or quiet backwaters, Patoka River NWR & MA provides excellent herptilian habitat. Many species of reptiles and amphibians are nocturnal or secretive in nature which makes it difficult to adequately determine population status. And although there are no current data on population levels, it is assumed that numbers are adequate to maintain existing herptile communities. However, it is reasonable to assume that, as has been noted with other aquatic organisms, populations of reptiles and amphibians have been negatively impacted by the long-term degradation of water quality in the Patoka River watershed. As the acid mine water drainage is eliminated in the watershed and refuge bottomland fields are purchased and restored to hardwood forests, water quality is constantly improving. The South Fork Patoka River is an outstanding example of watershed restoration efforts leading to the reestablishment of a stream fishery which now supports nesting Bald Eagles and public fishing opportunities where none existed for 50 years prior to Refuge establishment.

Fish

Most of the Refuge's fishery resources are associated with the Patoka River and its wetlands. Two fisheries surveys of the Patoka River and many of its tributaries in the late 1980s and early 1990s revealed that fish populations were surprisingly diverse and abundant, especially considering the environmental abuses this river has endured over the past 70 years (Stefanavage, 1993; U.S. Fish and Wildlife Service, 1989). A total of 66 species of fish representing 15 families were found to inhabit these waters. Although not usually considered prime fish habitat, overall species diversity in the Patoka River in 1991 compared favorably with other southwest Indiana streams (Stefanavage, 1993).

Considering the Patoka River's low dissolved oxygen levels, muddy brown/green water, and limited in-stream structure (habitat), it is not surprising that common carp was found to be the most abundant species. Gizzard shad, an important food source for more desirable predatory fish, was the second most abundant. Third in number was smallmouth buffalo, an edible species frequently sought by anglers. It is interesting to note that the smallmouth buffalo population appears large enough to support commercial fishing. Of the more popular game fish, channel and flathead catfish probably provide the best sport fishing opportunities in this section of the river. Largemouth bass, bluegill and crappie, while present, do not have populations large enough, or do not grow at a sufficient rate, to offer substantial fishing opportunities.

As a result of the U.S. Army Corps of Engineers channel clearing project in the early 1980s, and ongoing, similar activities by the Upper and Lower Conservancy Districts, fish habitat in terms of in-stream cover ranges from none to very little. Few log jams, brush piles and root-wads are found in the river within the proposed Project area. Consequently, species requiring in-stream cover (largemouth bass, bluegill, crappie) are limited by available habitat. Riffle/pool habitat is also scarce. In general, the stretch of river within the proposed Project is classified glide/run, and is characterized by a mud and silt bottom. Species diversity in the channelized portion of the river (downstream from Winslow) is lower than in the natural, meandering channel. Diversity at sampling sites averaged 14 species in the channelized river while the natural river supported an average of 19 species. Fish of interest to commercial and sport fishermen (buffalo, drum, channel and flathead catfish and spotted bass) were more abundant in the unchannelized section.

In addition to inadequate in-stream habitat, non-point source pollution, particularly acidic waters from abandoned coal mines and illegal releases of salt brine produced from oil wells, has been a limiting factor for the Patoka River fisheries. Decreases in fish numbers and species diversity immediately below Mill Creek and the South Fork Patoka River, both of which have carried high levels of acid mine waters, attest to the deleterious impacts associated with this pollutant. Fish kills associated with acid drainage were not uncommon in the South Fork at the time of the Refuge's establishment. One of these occurred on September 1, 1991, when heavy rain fell after two months of dry weather. Dead bluegill, bowfin, common carp, gar, and largemouth bass were observed. It appears that fish species from the Patoka River would recolonize the lower portion of the South Fork during drought periods. Then, as described above, fish populations in the South Fork would be wiped out when major storm events occurred which flushed acidic water into the stream from abandoned mine areas. This acid water flush-out problem of the South Fork has been largely eliminated in the past 10 years due to the efforts of the Indiana Division of Reclamation's Abandoned Mine Land Reclamation Program and local citizen efforts associated with the Appalachian Clean Stream Initiative of the U.S. Office of Surface Mining. Illegal releases of salt brine from oil wells while documented as being common practice in the 1960s,

Patoka River, Patoka River NWR & MA. Photo credit: USFWS

Chapter 3: Refuge Environment and Management

Pied-billed Grebe, Patoka River NWR & MA. Photo credit: USFWS

1970's and 1980's has largely been eliminated thanks to enforcement efforts by the Indiana Division of Oil and Gas.

One clear sign that water quality in the main stream Patoka River is improving as a result of improved enforcement actions and millions of dollars of reclamation efforts in the watershed are the increasing reports of paddlefish. (Polyodon spathula) since the late 1990s. Known to spawn in the Wabash River, part of the life cycle needs for these gill feeders includes rich feeding grounds found in flooded bottomland hardwoods. As the water quality of the Patoka River has improved, paddlefish have returned to this ancestral feeding area during spring floods to build up their body fats for successful egg production. Fishermen now report seeing paddlefish on a regular basis in the Patoka River and associated tributaries, oxbows and marshes. Recent contaminant surveys by Bloomington Ecological Services in the early 2000s also saw the return of harlequin darters which hadn't been found in the Patoka River since the late 1800s.

Invertebrates

The wetlands associated with the riparian ecosystem along the Patoka River support good invertebrate populations in their nutrient-rich waters. Nesting waterfowl, waterfowl broods and shorebirds are highly dependent on these protein-rich food sources for successful reproduction and healthy growth. Invertebrates associated with wetlands in the area include protozoa, crustaceans, mollusks, snails and insects. Contaminant studies to evaluate the impact of salt brines on freshwater shrimp and crayfish were conducted on the Patoka River between 2000-2002 by Tom Simon of the Bloomington Ecological Services Office. One result of this study was the discovery of a new species of burrower crayfish identified now as the painted-hand mudbug (Cambarus nov.sp.diogenes) named because of the red tips on its claws. It turns out that this new crayfish species is the most common species on the Patoka River NWR.

Insects

By far the most obvious (and obnoxious) insects in the area are mosquitoes. Of the 51 species known to occur in Indiana, 30 could be expected to inhabit the southwestern portion of the state (Siverly, 1972). The majority of these species are considered pests whose biting activities often thwart otherwise enjoyable outdoor living and recreational activities, but do not pose any substantial human health risk. The most common nuisance mosquitoes found in local floodplains are *Psorophora ciliata* and *Aedes vexans*, the latter being perhaps the number one pest species in the area. These floodwater species are not significant vectors(carriers) of human diseases in southern Indiana.

Molluscs

Historically, the Patoka River supported a rich diversity of freshwater mussels that were utilized by Native Americans and wildlife alike. One early survey documented 21 species occurring in the river with other historical records showing an additional 12 species. Most of these mussels are relatively common in Indiana's larger creeks. The ring pink and hickory nut are big river species and probably lived near the confluence with the Wabash River. The ring pink is on the federal list of endangered species, but is believed to be extirpated from Indiana. The clubshell, and fat pocketbook, both federally endangered species, are reported in historical records. A more recent survey of the Patoka River found no live specimens of these species, but did turn up a weathered fat pocketbook shell, although not within the portion of the river flowing through the Refuge.

A survey of freshwater mussels conducted in 2000 along the entire length of the Patoka River and portions of its tributaries found 28 mussel species (Ecological Specialists, Inc. 2001). This is fewer than the 33 species reported in historic records. The segment of the Patoka River flowing through the Refuge contained 17 mussel species. No species were found in the channelized portion of the river probably because the habitat in this stretch has been altered so as to render it unsuitable.

The diversity of freshwater mussels within the Patoka River has declined from historic levels, a trend that is similar for freshwater mussels across North America. Human activities during the past 90 years have greatly reduced the river's capability to support the once large assortment of bottom-dwelling mollusks. River channelization, erosion-related sedimentation, pesticide and fertilizer runoff, pollutants from oil and coal extraction, improperly treated sewage, and toxic industrial discharges have combined to degrade bottom substrates, water quality, and the riverine ecosystem in general. The diversity and numbers of mussels present in a river serves as an excellent barometer of river water quality. The more species and the higher the number of mussels found indicate the higher the water quality and stream bottom health. Future mussel surveys will be used to compare back to the initial surveys conducted when the Patoka River NWR was established to verify improvements resulting from management practices.

Threatened and Endangered Species

Threatened and Endangered Flora

The Indiana Natural Heritage Data Center is a continuously updated data management system which contains locations of all rare plant species in Indiana. Based on this information, which includes both historical collections and recent discoveries, the Indiana Division of Nature Preserves (IDNP) compiled a list of 55 potential rare plants that could occur within the proposed Wetlands Project. IDNP personnel then conducted field investigations to confirm the presence of any of these rare plant species. In 1991, 17 individual areas within the Project area were inventoried. A total of 20 state-listed plant species were verified during the survey (Homoya, et al., 1992). No federally-listed threatened or endangered plants are known to occur within the NWR/MA. The vast majority of rare plants found during IDNP'S survey are associated with forested and emergent wetlands.

Two of the 20 state-listed plant species are particularly noteworthy. The discovery of sickle pod (*Cassis obtusifolia*) was the first documented occurrence of this species in the state. Also, three populations of buttonweed (*Diodia virginiana*) were found in what is now the Refuge & MA. These finds were the second, third and fourth occurrences of this species documented in Indiana.

More current data on endangered, threatened and rare plants in Gibson and Pike counties are available from the Indiana Department of Nature Preserves (IDNP) within Indiana DNR (IDNP, 2005a; IDNP, 2005b). Table 2 shows those vascular plants listed by IDNP expected to occur in either Gibson or Pike counties, or both, as of 2005. (Table 2)

In addition to these species and subspecies/varieties of wild plants, IDNP lists four "high quality natural communities" found in Gibson and/or Pike counties, including Forest – floodplain wet-mesic, Forest – upland dry-mesic, Forest – upland mesic, and Wetland – swamp shrub. Each of these communities occurs on the Refuge & MA.

Threatened and Endangered Fauna

Whooping Crane (*Grus Americana*)

In 2001, the U.S. Fish and Wildlife Service initiated a reintroduction of a Nonessential Experimental Population of Whooping Cranes in the Eastern United States. The intent was to establish a migratory flock that would summer and breed in Wisconsin and winter in west-central Florida which was historical habitat. Since the migration route is a learned rather than an innate behavior, captive-reared Whooping Cranes released in Wisconsin were led by ultralight aircraft to establish their historical flight path to suitable wintering areas in Florida. Five Whooping Crane yearlings were led over 1,200-miles in 2001, followed by 16 in 2002, 15 in 2003, 17 in 2004, 21 in 2005 and 18 in 2006. The first record of these introduced Whooping Cranes visiting the Patoka River NWR was on November 17, 2003, when a pair (2-02-F and 13-02-M) spent several days in the Patoka River bottoms near the Francisco Mine within the Refuge acquisition area. On March 27, 28 and 29, 2005, No. 2-01-F and No. 8-02-M spent their time in corn field stubble at Patoka River NWR in Pike County near Line Road. Annual stop overs on the Refuge are expected to occur every spring and fall once a viable flock is established.

Bald Eagle (*Haliaeetus leucocephalus*)

An increase in abundance and distribution of the Bald Eagle across the United States led to its reclassification from endangered to threatened in

Table 2: Endangered, Threatened, or Rare Vascular Plants in Gibson and Pike Counties, Indiana, as of 2005

Scientific Name	Common Name	Gibson County	Pike County	FED	STATE	GRANK	SRANK
Acalypha deamii	Mercury	✓			SR	G4?	S2
Armoracia aquatica	Lake Cress	✓			SE	G4?	S1
Azolla caroliniana	Carolina Mosquito-fern	✓			ST	G5	S2
Calycocarpum lyonii	Cup-seed	✓			ST	G5	S2
Carex socialis	Social Sedge	✓			SR	G4	S2
Carex straminea	Straw Sedge	✓			ST	G5	S2
Catalpa speciosa	Northern Catalpa	✓			SR	G4?	S2
Chelone obliqua var. speciosa	Rose Turtlehead	✓	✓		WL	G4T3	S3
Clematis pitcheri	Pitcher Leather-flower	✓			SR	G4G5	S2
Crataegus grandis	Grand Hawthorn	✓			SE	G3G5Q	S1
Crataegus viridis	Green Hawthorn	✓			ST	G5	S2
Cyperus pseudovegetus	Green Flatsedge	✓	✓		SR	G5	S2
Didiplis diandra	Water-purslane	✓	✓		SE	G5	S2
Diodia virginiana	Buttonweed	✓	✓		WL	G5	S2
Gleditsia aquatica	Water-locust	✓			SE	G5	S1
Hibiscus moscheutos ssp. lasiocarpos	Hairy-fruited Hibiscus	✓			SE	G5T4	S1
Hottonia inflata	Featherfoil		✓		ST	G4	S2
Iresine rhizomatosa	Eastern Bloodleaf	✓			SR	G5	S2
Itea virginica	Virginia Willow		✓		SE	G4	S1
Juglans cinerea	Butternut	✓			WL	G3G4	S3
Linum striatum	Ridged Yellow Flax	✓			WL	G5	S3
Ludwigia decurrens	Primrose Willow	✓	✓		WL	G5	S2
Mikania scandens	Climbing Hempweed		✓		SE	G5	S1
Orobanche ludoviciana	Louisiana Broomrape	✓			SE	G5	S2
Phacelia ranunculacea	Blue Scorpion-weed		✓		SE	G4	S1
Platanthera flava var. flava	Southern Rein Orchid	✓			SE	G4T4?Q	S1
Potamogeton pusillus	Slender Pondweed	✓	✓		WL	G5	S2
Rhexia mariana var. mariana	Maryland Meadow Beauty		✓		ST	G5T5	S1
Sagittaria australis	Longbeak Arrowhead		✓		SR	G5	S2
Selaginella apoda	Meadow Spike-moss		✓		WL	G5	S1
Senna obtusifolia	Blunt-leaf Senna		✓		SR	G5	S2
Sparganium androcladum	Branching Bur-reed	✓			ST	G4G5	S2

Table 2: Endangered, Threatened, or Rare Vascular Plants in Gibson and Pike Counties, Indiana, as of 2005 (Continued)

Scientific Name	Common Name	Gibson County	Pike County	FED	STATE	GRANK	SRANK
Styrax americanus	American Snowbell	✓	✓		WL	G5	S3
Taxodium distichum	Bald Cypress	✓			ST	G5	S2
Trachelospermum difforme	Climbing Dogbane	✓	✓		SR	G4G5	S2
Vitis palmata	Catbird Grape	✓	✓		SR	G4	S2
Wisteria macrostachya	Kentucky Wisteria		✓		SR	G5	S2

Sources: IDNP, 2005a and IDNP, 2005b
FED: LE = Endangered; LT = Threatened; C = candidate; PDL = proposed for delisting
STATE: SE = state endangered; ST = state threatened; SR = state rare; SSC = state species of special concern; SX = state extirpated; SG = state significant; WL = watch list
GRANK: Global Heritage Rank: G1 = critically imperiled globally; G2 = imperiled globally; G3 = rare or uncommon globally; G4 = widespread and abundant globally but with long term concerns; G5 = widespread and abundant globally; G? = unranked; GX = extinct; Q = uncertain rank; T = taxonomic subunit rank
SRANK: State Heritage Rank: S1 = critically imperiled in state; S2 = imperiled in state; S3 = rare or uncommon in state; G4 = widespread and abundant in state but with long term concern; SG = state significant; SH = historical in state; SX = state extirpated; B = breeding status; S? = unranked; SNR = unranked; SNA = nonbreeding status unranked

1995. It also led to a 1999 proposal to remove the Bald Eagle from the endangered species list. The Bald Eagle was removed from the list of threatened and endangered species in July 2007. The species became endangered because of habitat loss and reproductive failure brought on by the accumulation of the pesticide DDT and other organochlorine insecticides. Today, the DDT threat is largely gone. Efforts focus on maintaining sites eagles depend on for nesting, feeding, migration, and wintering. On the Refuge, the Bald Eagle occurs as a winter migrant and a summer breeder. Absent as a nesting species for many years, a chick was produced in spring 2002. A pair of Bald Eagles began nesting near the Snakey Point Marsh adjacent to the South Fork Patoka River in 2001. Unsuccessful that first year, one eaglet was raised in 2002, one in 2003, two out of three in 2004, one killed by falling tree in 2005, two lost from wind storm in 2006, and two fledged in 2007.

Least Tern (*Sterna antillarum*) (Interior Population)

The historic breeding range of the federally listed endangered Least Tern extended from Texas to Montana and from eastern Colorado and New Mexico to southern Indiana. It included large rivers of the Red, Missouri, Arkansas, Mississippi, Ohio, and Rio Grande River systems. It nests on sand and gravel bars and protected beach areas of large rivers, and winters in coastal Central and South America. The species is endangered because human disturbance and alteration of river systems have rendered much of its nesting habitat unusable.

The 488-acre Cane Ridge Wildlife Management Area lies 24 miles west of the Refuge headquarters includes 193 acres of moist soil wetlands in four management units, 180 acres of reforested bottomland hardwoods, and a 59-acre deep water impoundment with nesting islands that provide habitat for the Least Tern. The terns have used the nesting islands for that purpose fledging 52 young in 2005 and 42 young in 2006.

Fat Pocketbook (*Potamilus capax*)

Designated as federally endangered in 1976, this mussel is found in slow flowing waters of large rivers with mud or sand bottoms. The primary contributors to its decline are activities related to navigation and flood control such as impounded waters or dredging. The fat pocketbook has been found in the Wabash and White Rivers in Indiana. Its specific occurrence and distribution within the Refuge/MA is unknown at this time.

Indiana Bat (*Myotis sodalist*)

The Indiana bat was listed as federally endangered in 1967 under the Endangered Species Conservation Act, a precursor to the Endangered Species Act of 1973. Primarily the bats declined in number because of loss or disturbance of caves or other hibernacula. The bats hibernate communally in large numbers. Disruption or destruction of a single site can dramatically affect the population. It occurs in several locations across Indiana. A maternity colony containing more than 100 adults in a large dead tree was first documented on the Refuge in 2005.

Copperbelly Water Snake (Nerodia erythrogaster neglecta)

The copperbelly water snake was proposed for listing as a threatened species in 1993 because of habitat loss and fragmentation largely associated with coal mining. The listing was never finalized. Instead, the Service entered into conservation agreements with mining regulatory agencies and coal industry representatives in Indiana, Kentucky, and Illinois. The agreements greatly reduced existing threats to the species, especially those posed by mining operations, precluding the need to list the southern population of the snake under the Endangered Species Act. Research conducted on the Patoka River NWR in 1994, 1995 and 1996 showed the Refuge area contained a significant viable population of copperbelly water snakes in suitable habitat which centered around buttonbush swamps associated closely with beaver impoundments. A large area of the Refuge bottomlands were designated Core Conservation Habitat in the Copperbelly Conservation Agreement with coal companies. This designation placed those lands off limits to any future surface coal mining efforts to protect some the highest quality copperbelly habitat remaining in its national range.

In addition to these federally listed species, a number of animal species are listed by the Indiana Department of Nature Preserves on their database of endangered, threatened and rare wildlife in the state (IDNP, 2005a; IDNP, 2005b). Table 3 shows those wild animal species and subspecies listed by IDNP expected to occur in either Gibson or Pike Counties, or both, as of 2005.

Threats to Resources

There are two main kinds of threats to environmental quality and plant and animal communities at Patoka River National Wildlife Refuge and Management Area: invasive species and contaminants. These are now considered in turn.

Current coal mine reclamation, Patoka River NWR & MA. Photo credit: USFWS

Invasive Species

Invasive species are plants or animals that are often (but not always) non-native or exotic to a given habitat. They are capable of spreading, sometimes quickly, to the detriment of native flora and fauna, which may be displaced, reduced in population, or even extirpated. In pursuing its mission to conserve America's native biodiversity, the Service contributes to nationwide efforts to control the unchecked expansion of invasive plant and animal species.

Some exotic (non-native) plants may substantially alter the plant communities of more natural, undisturbed areas while others more commonly affect disturbed or agricultural areas. Left unchecked, these invasive plant species can seriously degrade the productivity and natural value of invaded sites.

Most of the Refuge's wetlands are relatively free of noxious plants. Those in the area possessing the greatest potential for serious impacts include common reed grass (*Phragmites communis*), reed canary grass (*Phalaris arundinacea*) and moneywort (*Lysimachia nummularia*). The first two are a greater threat in open wetland sites, whereas money wart can carpet large areas of floodplain forests (as well as open areas). A plant not yet noted, but certainly expanding its range toward the area, is purple loosestrife (*Lythrum salicaria*). This species and common reed grass have been observed to completely overrun wetlands to the exclusion of almost all other plant species.

In uplands the most troublesome invasive is Johnson grass (*Sorghum halepense*). Due to its hardiness, growth and reproductive mechanisms, and its close relationship to domestic corn, this introduced species is widespread and difficult to control in both Pike and Gibson counties. As a result of seed

Table 3: Endangered, Threatened, or Rare Fauna in Gibson and Pike Counties, Indiana, as of 2005

Scientific Name	Common Name	Gibson County	Pike County	FED	STATE	GRANK	SRANK
Crustacean: Malacostraca							
Orconectes indianensis	Indiana Crayfish	✓			SR	G2G3	S2
Mollusk: Bivalvia (Mussels)							
Cumberlandia monodonta	Spectaclecase	✓		C	SX	G2G3	SX
Cyprogenia stegaria	Eastern Fanshell Pearlymussel	✓	✓	LE	SE	G1	S1
Epioblasma flexuosa	Leafshell	✓			SX	GX	SX
Epioblasma propinqua	Tennessee Riffleshell	✓			SX	GX	SX
Epioblasma torulosa torulosa	Tubercled Blossom	✓	✓	LE	SE	G2TX	SH
Fusconaia subrotunda	Longsolid	✓	✓		SE	G3	S1
Lampsilis ovata	Pocketbook	✓				G5	S2
Lampsilis teres	Yellow Sandshell	✓	✓			G5	S2
Ligumia recta	Black Sandshell	✓				G5	S2
Obovaria retusa	Ring Pink	✓		LE	SX	G1	SX
Obovaria subrotunda	Round Hickorynut	✓	✓		SSC	G4	S2
Plethobasus cooperianus	Orangefoot Pimpleback	✓		LE	SE	G1	S1
Plethobasus cyphyus	Sheepnose	✓		C	SE	G3	S1
Pleurobema clava	Clubshell	✓	✓	LE	SE	G2	S1
Pleurobema cordatum	Ohio Pigtoe	✓	✓		SSC	G3	S2
Pleurobema pyramidatum	Pyramid Pigtoe	✓	✓		SE	G2	S1
Potamilus capax	Fat Pocketbook	✓	✓	LE	SE	G1	S1
Ptychobranchus fasciolaris	Kidneyshell		✓		SSC	G4G5	S2
Quadrula cylindrica cylindrica	Rabbitsfoot	✓	✓		SE	G3T3	S1
Simpsonaias ambigua	Salamander Mussel		✓		SSC	G3	S2
Insect: Ephemeroptera (Mayflies)							
Homoeoneuria ammophila	A Sand-filtering Mayfly	✓			SE	G4	S1
Pseudiron centralis	A Mayfly	✓	✓		SE	G5	S1
Insect: Lepidoptera (Butterflies & Moths)							
Euphyes dukesi	Scarce Swamp Skipper	✓			ST	G3	S1S2
Fish							
Ammocrypta clara	Western Sand Darter		✓		SSC	G3	S3
Ammocrypta pellucida	Eastern Sand Darter		✓			G3	S2
Cycleptus elongatus	Blue Sucker	✓	✓		G3	G4	S2
Etheostoma camurum	Bluebreast Darter		✓			G4	S1

Table 3: Endangered, Threatened, or Rare Fauna in Gibson and Pike Counties, Indiana, as of 2005

Scientific Name	Common Name	Gibson County	Pike County	FED	STATE	GRANK	SRANK
Etheostoma histrio	Harlequin Darter	✓	✓			G5	S1
Etheostoma squamiceps	Spottail Darter	✓			G4	G5	S1
Etheostoma tippecanoe	Tippecanoe Darter		✓		SSC	G3G4	S1
Amphibian							
Rana areolata circulose	Northern Crawfish Frog		✓		SE	G4T4	S2
Reptile							
Kinosternon subrubrum	Eastern Mud Turtle	✓			SE	G5	S2
Nerodia erythrogaster neglecta	Copperbelly Water Snake	✓	✓	PS:LT	SE	G5T2T3	S2
Opheodrys aestivus	Rough Green Snake	✓			SSC	G5	S3
Pseudemys concinna hieroglyphica	Hieroglyphic River Cooter	✓			SE	G5T4	S1
Bird							
Ammodramus henslowii	Henslow's Sparrow	✓			SE	G4	S3B
Ardea herodias	Great Blue Heron	✓	✓			G5	S4B
Asio flammeus	Short-eared Owl		✓		SE	G5	S2
Botaurus lentiginosus	American Bittern	✓			SE	G4	S2B
Buteo lineatus	Red-shouldered Hawk	✓	✓		SSC	G5	S3
Buteo platypterus	Broad-winged Hawk		✓	No Status	SSC	G5	S3B
Circus cyaneus	Northern Harrier	✓	✓		SE	G5	S2
Cistothorus platensis	Sedge Wren	✓			SE	G5	S3B
Falco peregrinus	Peregrine Falcon	✓		No Status	SE	G4	S2B
Haliaeetus leucocephalus	Bald Eagle	✓		Delisted 2007	SE	G5	S2
Ixobrychus exilis	Least Bittern	✓			SE	G5	S3B
Lanius ludovicianus	Loggerhead Shrike		✓	No Status	SE	G4	S3B
Nyctanassa violacea	Yellow-crowned Night-heron	✓	✓		SE	G5	S2B
Nycticorax nycticorax	Black-crowned Night-heron		✓		SE G5 S1B	G5	S1B
Phalaropus tricolor	Wilson's Phalarope	✓			SX	G5	SHB
Rallus elegans	King Rail	✓	✓		SE	G4	S1B
Sterna antillarum athalassos	Interior Least Tern		✓	LE	SE	G4T2Q	S1B
Thryomanes bewickii	Bewick's Wren	✓				G5	S1B
Tyto alba	Barn Owl	✓	✓		SE	G5	S2
Mammal							
Lutra canadensis	Northern River Otter	✓	✓			G5	S2
Lynx rufus	Bobcat		✓	No Status		G5	S1
Mustela nivalis	Least Weasel	✓			SSC	G5	S2?

Table 3: Endangered, Threatened, or Rare Fauna in Gibson and Pike Counties, Indiana, as of 2005

Scientific Name	Common Name	Gibson County	Pike County	FED	STATE	GRANK	SRANK
Myotis sodalis	Indiana Bat or Social Myotis	✓	✓	LE	SE	G2	S1
Sylvilagus aquaticus	Swamp Rabbit	✓			SE	G5	S1
Taxidea taxus	American Badger	✓	✓			G5	S2

Sources: IDNP, 2005a and IDNP, 2005b
FED: LE = Endangered; LT = Threatened; C = candidate; PDL = proposed for delisting
STATE: SE = state endangered; ST = state threatened; SR = state rare; SSC = state species of special concern; SX = state extirpated; SG = state significant; WL = watch list
GRANK: Global Heritage Rank: G1 = critically imperiled globally; G2 = imperiled globally; G3 = rare or uncommon globally; G4 = widespread and abundant globally but with long term concerns; G5 = widespread and abundant globally; G? = unranked; GX = extinct; Q = uncertain rank; T = taxonomic subunit rank
SRANK: State Heritage Rank: S1 = critically imperiled in state; S2 = imperiled in state; S3 = rare or uncommon in state; G4 = widespread and abundant in state but with long term concern; SG = state significant; SH = historical in state; SX = state extirpated; B = breeding status; S? = unranked; SNR = unranked; SNA = nonbreeding status unranked

dispersal during flood events, bottomland agricultural fields are particularly prone to infestation, making it common to see this plant in those areas.

Other plants classified as noxious weeds in the Refuge & MA include Canadian thistle, bur cucumber and shatter cane. Although locally significant, these species do not represent as pervasive a problem as Johnson grass.

Aquatic resources at Patoka River National Wildlife Refuge are also at risk from non-native invasive animals, such as zebra mussels, common carp, grass carp, bighead carp, and silver carp. Although most of these species have not been documented in the Patoka River, all have been documented in the Ohio and Wabash Rivers, many have been documented in other tributaries to the Wabash River in Indiana, and all have the potential to expand their range into the Patoka River. These nuisance aquatic animals may substantially alter habitats and food web dynamics that native aquatic communities are dependant upon for sustainability.

Common carp are established within waters of the Patoka River National Wildlife Refuge and are troublesome in rivers, streams, and wetlands due to their ability to alter aquatic habitats by uprooting vegetation, reducing water transparency, and reducing aquatic plant growth. Grass carp, which are established in the Ohio and Wabash Rivers, consume aquatic vegetation and also have the potential to alter aquatic habitats and their native communities. Bighead and silver carps are established in the Ohio and Wabash Rivers and are rapidly dispersing throughout many interior smaller order streams throughout the Midwest. It is likely that these fish will disperse into the Patoka River. Bighead and silver carp feed on plankton and have the potential to alter aquatic food webs. Zebra mussels primarily consume phytoplankton, but also filter other suspended materials from the water column and can substantially alter ecosystems that they invade. Zebra mussels have extirpated native unionid mussels after colonizing new waters.

Table 4 lists key invasive species at Patoka River NWR & MA.

Contaminants

The principal contaminants present in the Patoka River area are those associated with surface coal mining and crude oil extraction. Present-day surface mining (post-1977 and SMCRA) is tightly regulated and closely monitored to assure water quality in downstream areas is not substantially impacted by mining refuse or erosion-related sediments. Although occasional accidental discharges of deleterious materials such as slurry from wash plants or equipment-related petroleum products adversely affect aquatic resources in portions of the watershed, for the most part current surface mining contributes little contamination to the Patoka River.

Before SMCRA, however, coal mining, both underground and surface, produced coal refuse piles and slurry ponds containing waste material such as pyrite, shale and clay, which were separated from the usable coal during cleaning operations. In Pike County, at the time of the Refuge's establishment in the early 1990s, there were at least 186 acres of refuse piles, 129 acres of slurry ponds, and 3,113 acres of mined land with less than 75 percent vege-

Table 4: Invasive Plants and Animals at Patoka NWR/MA

Species Name	Summary
Common Carp	Originating in Asia, common carp were introduced to North America in 1877, first in Maryland and subsequently throughout the United States. They spread rapidly and became naturalized in all waters into which they were introduced. They are adapted to relatively low-oxygen, polluted, turbid waters. Due to their habit of grubbing through bottom sediments for food and alteration of their environment, they destroy, uproot and disturb submerged vegetation, causing serious damage to native duck and fish populations.
Phragmities or Common Reed Grass	*Phragmites* or common reed is a widely distributed, highly aggressive wetland plant whose origin is unclear, although both native and non-native genotypes or lineages have been documented. It can grow up to 6 meters high in dense stands and is long-lived. *Phragmites* is capable of reproduction by seeds, but primarily does so asexually by means of rhizomes.
Johnson Grass	Originally native to the Mediterranean, this tall, coarse grass with stout rhizomes now occurs in all warm-temperate regions of the world. Johnson grass invades riverbanks and disturbed sites crowding out native species and slowing succession. Rhizome cuttings commonly form new plants, making it very difficult to eradicate. It spreads rapidly and is not affected by many of the agricultural herbicides.
Moneywort or Creeping Jenny	Originally from Europe, this attractive but weedy herb, a member of the Primrose family, has escaped from lawns and gardens and now occurs in many states in the East and West. Moneywort is reported from many counties in Indiana, where it can be found growing in a variety of different habitat types. Preferring moist, rich, shaded soils, it flourishes best and poses the biggest threat in wetter areas such as wet meadows, swamps, floodplain forests, stream banks, bottoms, ditches, roadsides and along the banks of small water bodies.
Japanese Knotweed	Introduced from Asia in the late 1800s as an ornamental and for erosion control, this weed can tolerate a variety of adverse conditions, including deep shade, high temperatures, high salinity and drought. Knotweed is commonly found near water sources, such as streams and rivers, in low-lying areas, waste places and utility rights-of-way and around old home sites. It spreads quickly to form dense thickets that exclude native vegetation and greatly alter natural ecosystems. Japanese knotweed poses a significant threat to riparian areas, where it can survive severe floods and rapidly colonize scoured shores and islands. Once established, populations are extremely persistent.
Reed Canary Grass	This grass is native to lowland areas of the Midwest and has escaped from cultivation in other regions. Various strains of reed canary grass are found throughout the world except Antarctica and Greenland. It is a major threat to marshes and natural wetlands because its hardiness, aggressive nature, and rapid growth allow it to displace native wetland plant species. This species occurs in wetlands, including marshes, wet prairies, wet meadows, fens, stream banks, and swales. It has been planted widely for forage and for erosion control.
Autumn Olive	This deciduous shrub is native to China and Japan and can range from 3 to 20 feet in height. It is easily recognized by the silvery, dotted underside of the leaves. Small, yellowish flowers or red, juicy fruits are abundant and occur on clusters near the stems. Autumn olive invades old fields, woodland edges, and other disturbed areas. It can form a dense shrub layer which displaces native species and closes open areas. Since its introduction in 1830, it has been widely planted for wildlife habitat, mine reclamation, and shelterbelts.

Table 4: Invasive Plants and Animals at Patoka NWR/MA (Continued)

Species Name	Summary
Japanese Honeysuckle	This species is native to eastern Asia and was first introduced into America in 1806 at Long Island, NY. It is an evergreen to semi-evergreen vine that can be found either trailing or climbing to heights of over 80 feet. It has opposite, oval shaped leaves that are 1 to 2.5 inches long and showy, fragrant, tubular flowers that are whitish-pink to yellow in color. Japanese honeysuckle invades a variety of habitats, including forest floors and canopies, roadsides, wetlands, and disturbed areas. It can girdle small saplings by twining around them and can form dense mats in the canopies of trees, shading everything below. Japanese honeysuckle has been planted widely throughout the United States as an ornamental, for erosion control, and for wildlife habitat.
Bush Honeysuckle	The four species of bush honeysuckle that cause most invasive problems (Amur, Morrow's, Tartarian, and Belle) are all referred to as "bush honeysuckle." Native to Asia and western Europe, these shrubs were introduced to North America in the 1700s and 1800s and are frequently used for landscaping and to improve wildlife habitats; they have become naturalized in many areas of the Northeast and Midwest. The bush honeysuckles are tolerant of a variety of edaphic (soil) and environmental conditions. Typical habitats include disturbed successional communities, wetlands, prairie, woodland edges, and partially closed forests.

tation cover (haul roads, railroad grades, etc.) (Allen et al., 1978). Most of these areas were located off the refuge but contributing to runoff in the watershed.

Surface mining also created pyrite-laced cast overburden ridges which act as unconsolidated aquifers easily transporting water through the spoils. Pyrite is the most common sulfide mineral, and its oxidation is one of the most acidic of all weathering actions. In the presence of oxygen and water, sulfuric acid is formed, and results in what is commonly called acid mine drainage (Kolankiewicz, 1982). This runoff water contains high concentrations of acid, calcium, magnesium, iron, aluminum, manganese, sulfate and coal fines, and contributes to the degradation of many of the area's streams and lakes. In some instances, such as Augusta Lake on Sugar Ridge Fish and Wildlife Area 4, acid concentrations are so high that most aquatic organisms, including fish, cannot survive. Although little of this land is within the Refuge, drainage from off-site adversely impacts aquatic resources in several tributaries to the Patoka River as well as the river itself. Mill Creek, Stone Coe Creek, Barren Creek and the South Fork Patoka River have carried heavy loads of acidic water into the Patoka, particularly following heavy rains.

The Abandoned Mine Land Reclamation program, funded by a tax on current coal production, has been active in the watershed starting in the late 1980's remediating barren, acid-producing spoil and refuse sites. Initial efforts of this reclamation program focused on revegetating numerous barren sites, de-watering low-pH lakes and eliminating safety hazards including steep highwalls. Efforts to control acid mine drainage seeps and to minimize downstream flowage to mingle with higher quality fresh waters, increased as a result of theAppalalachian Clean Stream Initiative began in 1994. This special program made water quality improvement to enhance the general welfare of local communities an equal priority with safety considerations for the Abandoned Mine Land Program. Since then, much headway has been made in reducing the volume of acid mine drainage. Water quality studies completed by the Service in 1992 indicated that acidity levels in affected waterways were as high then as they were in a comprehensive study completed in 1968 (Corbett, 1969). Where there were few if any fish or invertebrates in the South Fork Patoka River in 1992, there are now sufficient quantities to attract nesting Bald Eagles and sport fishermen.

Oil production operations in the area have also affected water quality in the Patoka River and its tributaries. Inadequate storage tank containment, open pits of oil, and irresponsible spills or overflowages of crude oil from some of the 82 operating wells/storage tanks within or adjacent to the Refuge have contaminated surface waters and adversely impacted the area's plant and wildlife resources in the past. While not a continuous phenomenon, spills of one sort or another have occurred regularly enough to be of concern. For example, during 1992, at least three spill events were documented to have directly impacted the South Fork Patoka River. The last spill involving approximately 4,000 gallons of crude oil resulted when a storage tank was struck by lightning. Inadequate earthen berms failed to contain the spill which flowed into the South Fork and had to be contained and removed with soaker booms and pumps. Abandoned orphan oil wells resulting from bankrupt or dead operators remain in place until the Indiana Division of Oil and Gas has funds to clean them up. Cooperative efforts and cost sharing between the refuge and the Division of Oil and Gas have resulted in the removal of at least 10 abandoned oil wells within the refuge area. Presently, there are no abandoned oil wells within the refuge acquisition area.

An additional, and perhaps more insidious, oil production-related pollutant is the salt water often discharged at oil wells. A 1969 study found that at some sites on the Patoka, chlorides from oil well brine waste was a greater threat to water quality than acid mine drainage (Corbett, 1969). Salt water not only impairs water quality, but also sterilizes upland spill areas to the point of eliminating plant life. Stricter regulations, improved enforcement efforts and the increased use of salt water injection wells have reduced the magnitude of this problem in the last decade. Occasional accidents, and, in some cases, deliberate discharges continue to pose the threat of contamination in the watershed.

Being located in a watershed with a substantial amount of agriculture, the Refuge & MA's resources may be exposed to an assortment of agriculture-related contaminants. Erosion of farmland soils as well as direct rainfall runoff can introduce fertilizers and a variety of pesticides, mainly organochlorine or organophosphate products, into the bottomland ecosystem. These substances may be toxic both through direct exposure as well as through bioaccumulation in the food chain with secondary effects on reproduction and behavior. In a 1989 Indiana Department of Environmental Management (IDEM) monitoring study, tissue analysis of fish from Patoka River confirmed the presence of numerous metals, including mercury, and several pesticides, most notably chlordane, nonachlor and dieldrin. Similar findings have been documented in other bottomland systems in this region of the country (U.S. Fish and Wildlife Service, 1992).

According to files maintained by the IDEM Office of Solid and Hazardous Waste, there are 41 sites in Pike and Gibson counties that are identified under the Comprehensive Environmental Response and Compensation Liability Inventory System (CERCLIS, 1991). Of the total sites, 10 are located within or close to Patoka River NWR & MA. Nine of these were placed on the CERCLIS list because Surface Impoundment Assessments (SIA) had been completed for these sites. These small surface impoundments were created and used to store and dispose of brine and oil well drilling wastes before this practice was banned. The conclusion of "no further remedial action planned" was made regarding these sites. The remaining site on the CERCLIS list is a railroad tie treatment plant located southwest of Winslow. The site was reviewed under authority of the Resource Conservation and Recovery Act (RCRA) by IDEM and EPA for past improper waste disposal in surface impoundments. Subsequent upgrading of the facility corrected those problems.

Interstate 69

In 1999 the Indiana Department of Transportation (INDOT) initiated an Environmental Impact Statement (USDOT and INDOT 2003) for the Federal Highway Administration (FHWA) that considered a range of possible highway corridors to link Evansville and Indianapolis, including one that would cross an area within the Refuge acquisition boundary. In March 2004, after extensive public involvement and analysis, the FHWA issued a Record of Decision (USDOT 2004) that selected an alternative that included the Refuge crossing (Figure 8).

After the Record of Decision (ROD) was issued, INDOT began secondary analyses for each of six sections of the highway corridor. These secondary

Refuge entrance sign, Patoka River NWR & MA. Photo credit: USFWS

Figure 8: Projected Route of Interstate 69

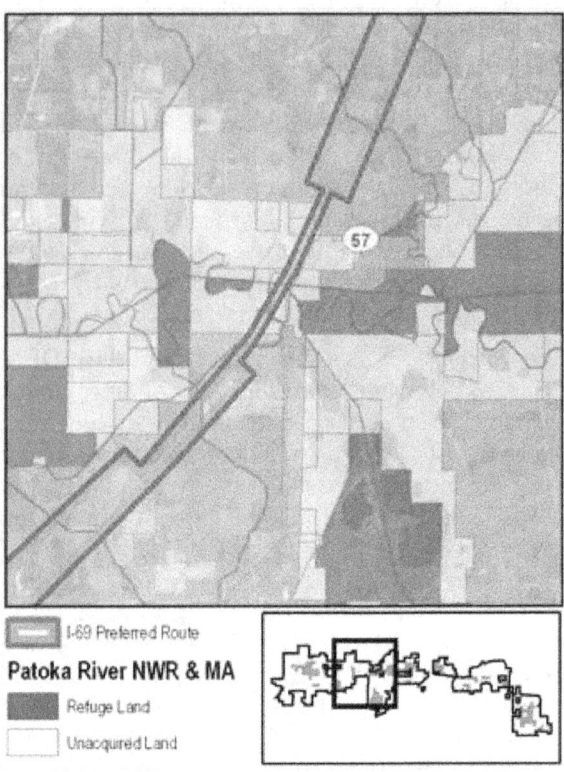

analyses, which include additional public involvement, help determine the final alignment of the 350-foot wide highway within the 2,000-foot wide approved corridor. The impacts of the highway crossing on Refuge resources will be considered in the secondary analysis. Each of the six secondary analyses will culminate with a Record of Decision by the FHWA. Once the ROD is issued for a section, final design, land acquisition, and construction can commence. The Refuge Manager continues to work closely with INDOT officials concerning the design and placement of the highway. Although the highway would cross an area within the Refuge acquisition boundary, none of the lands within the highway corridor are presently part of the Refuge and there are no plans to acquire lands within the highway corridor.

As part of a concerted effort to minimize impacts to the fish and wildlife resources of the Refuge, the highway planners agreed to bridge the entire floodplain crossing of the Patoka River NWR & MA. The bridge, approximately one mile long, will be as high as 30 feet above the floodplain floor to allow safe wildlife passage and minimize construction and placement of fill in this wetland environment. This would greatly reduce the hydrologic impacts in the watershed by minimizing upstream flooding and, thereby, reducing the need for additional mitigation action.

Administrative Facilities

The Refuge utilizes GSA leased space in Oakland City for its headquarters. The office building was newly constructed in 1993. Renovation and expansion occurred in 2003 when the GSA lease was renewed. Currently the office has nine rooms (offices and storage) which encompass approximately 1,900 square feet. The Refuge will continue to pursue opportunities to acquire facilities and move out of leased space.

Through the same GSA lease, the Refuge has access to a 30-foot by 50-foot heated pole barn (1,500 square feet) that is utilized for equipment storage and minor maintenance needs.

Through its land acquisition program, the Refuge owns another pole barn which measures approximately 50 feet by 100 feet (5,000 square feet), and is used to store supplies and equipment.

Archeological and Cultural Values

Responding to the requirement that these plans include "the archaeological and cultural values of the planning unit," the Service contracted for a cultural resources overview and management direction study. This short section of the CCP derives in part from this source as well as others.

The earliest generally accepted human culture in North America is termed PaleoIndian, commencing approximately 13,000 years ago in Indiana. Evidence of these people is relatively extensive in southern Indiana, and at least 16 PaleoIndian sites are reported in Gibson County. The Refuge, however, is outside the known geological concentrations of PaleoIndian sites.

The next cultural group is termed Archaic, and its origins dated to 10,000 years ago. The Archaic culture is quite evident in southern Indiana. The warm and dry period known as the Hypsithermal (or Altithermal) occurred during the Middle Archaic period when many sources of water disappeared. Archaic period sites occur on the Refuge.

Pottery, constructed burial and other mounds, gardening, and eventually the bow and arrow are among the distinguishing characteristics of the Woodland period that commenced about 2,600 years ago. A variety of sites from the Woodland period are found and more are anticipated within the Refuge.

The Middle Mississippian culture commenced about 950 years ago and continued into the early historic people. Sites from this period are found within the Refuge boundaries and more, especially in buried contexts, can be anticipated in the Refuge area.

The connection between prehistoric cultures and recognized Indian tribes in southwest Indiana has not been established. Treaties at Vincennes included the Shawnee, Potawatomi, Eel River, Kickapoo, Kaskaskia (later Peoria), Delaware, Piankashaw, Wea, and Miami; only the last four plus the Fox having an apparent connection to the Refuge area.

The French moved into southern Indiana, especially Vincennes, in the late 17th century. They were replaced by the British in 1763. In turn, British claims gave way to the United States whose possession was confirmed in 1794. The Refuge area was settled by farmers from the upland South (Appalachia) whose cultural patterns continue into the 21st century; also by Germans and Irish who came to build the Wabash and Erie Canal and stayed as farmers; and by southern and eastern Europeans and African-Americans.

Early transportation routes included the mid-19th century Wabash and Erie Canal.

Following the Civil War, coal mining became the major industry in the area and continues into the 21st century. At least 10 per cent of Pike County has been strip mined.

Current Management

Habitat Management

Forested Wetlands (Bottomland Forest)

Wetland management at Patoka River NWR & MA consists primarily of restoring forested wetlands, that is bottomland forests (Figure 10 and Figure 9). In 2007, the total acreage of forested wetlands on the Refuge & MA was 8,647 acres, of which 3,056 acres were owned by the Service. With the aim of maximizing species diversity within the restored wetland, we are trying to reintroduce the mast component of the forested wetland communities, plant-

Bald Eagle pair, Patoka River NWR & MA. Photo credit: USFWS

ing seedlings at 500 per acre. Trees are planted with a mechanical planter, in rows, and the priority sites are those that will complement our objective to restore a forested border along the river.

We are also engaged in restoration on prior converted wetland, areas that were in agricultural production when they are purchased. Typically we obtain a field that is planted right up to the edge of the River. We then plant seedlings a couple of hundred feet wide parallel to the River. The management of these, once planted, is passive. We just "walk away," allow competition to encroach, and permit these sites to remain brushy and thick. It does not affect seedling survival, but the thick habitat benefits wildlife. Patoka River wetlands are flooded annually naturally.

Under current management, over the long term (100-200 years), we would like to achieve approximately 12,000 to 13,000 acres of bottomland hardwood stands with a mosaic of age and structural classes distributed across a narrow elevation gradient. Lower elevations would be dominated by black willow, sweetgum, silver maple, and river birch. Pin oak, Shumard oak, swamp chestnut oak, swamp white oak, red maple, green ash, sycamore, and cottonwood would dominate mid-elevations, while upper elevations would be dominated by cherry bark oak, other oaks, hickory, and pecan. Over the coming 10-15 years, the Refuge will maintain existing bottomland forest area of 3,056 acres. We will

Chapter 3: Refuge Environment and Management

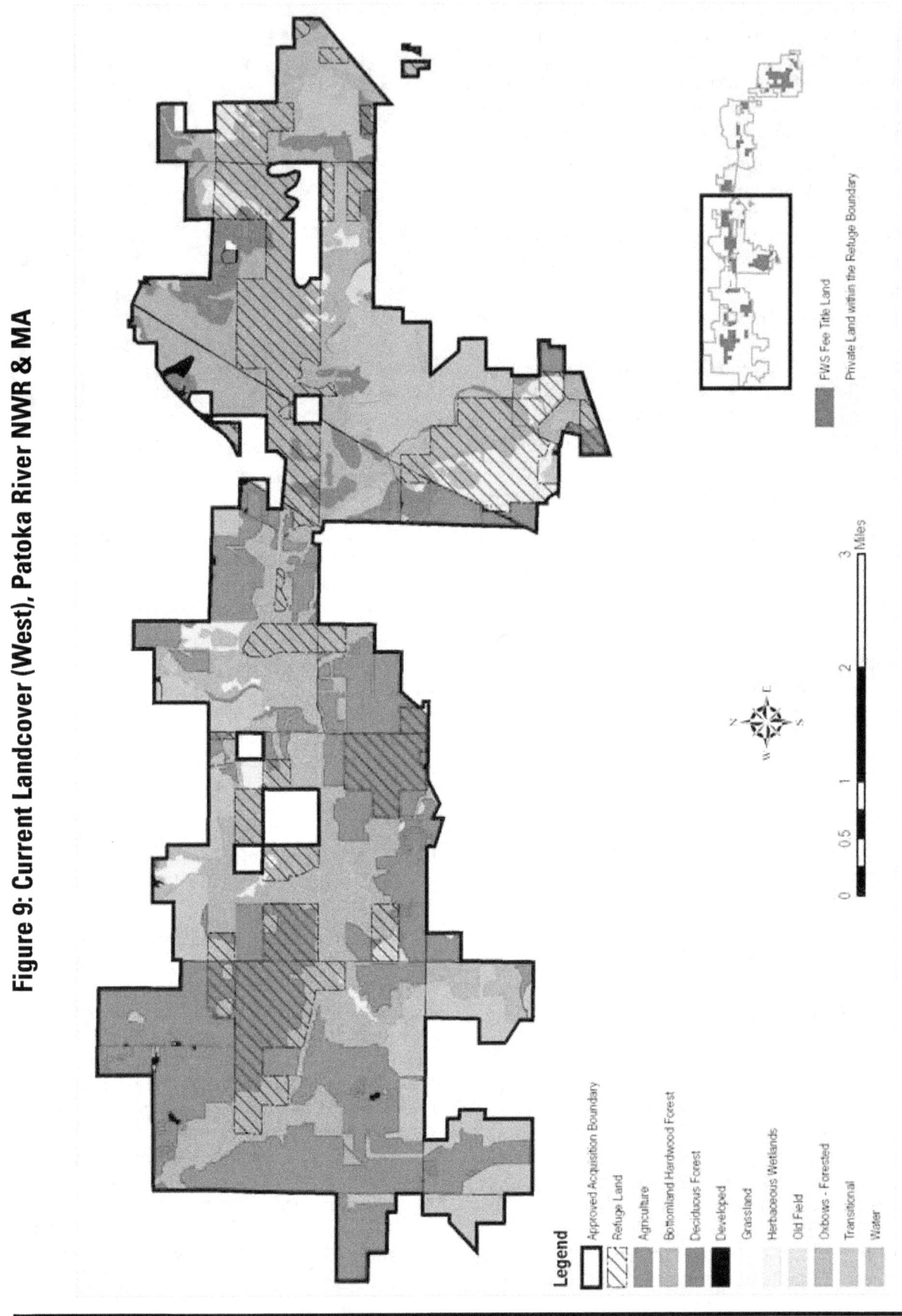

Figure 9: Current Landcover (West), Patoka River NWR & MA

Chapter 3: Refuge Environment and Management

Figure 10: Current Landcover (East), Patoka River NWR & MA

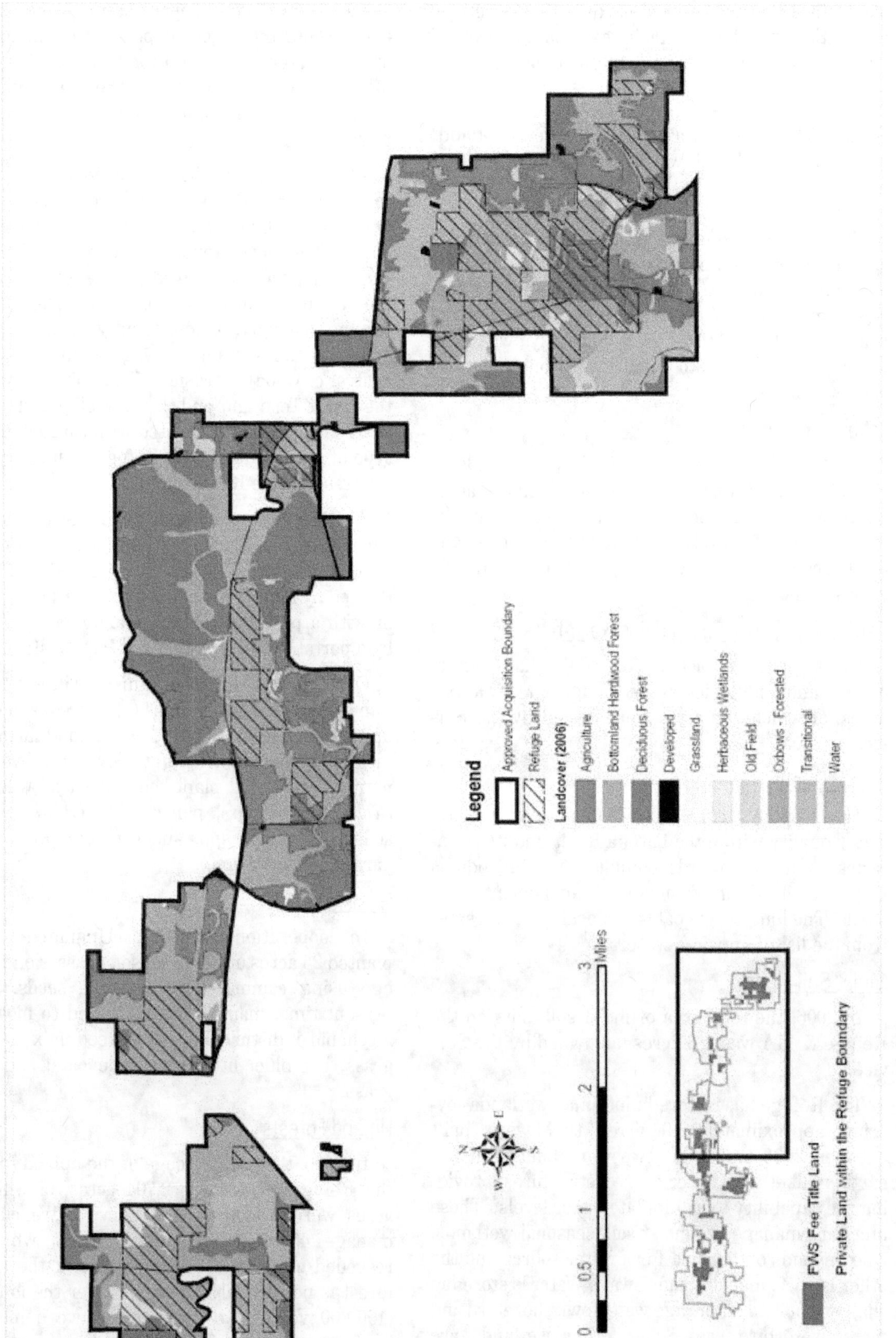

Patoka River National Wildlife Refuge and Management Area / Comprehensive Conservation Plan

also reforest to bottomland hardwoods future land acquisitions that have suitable soils and that are outside of areas managed as non-forested habitat.

Emergent Wetlands

In 2006, the total acreage of emergent wetlands on the Refuge & MA was 775 acres, of which 465 acres were owned by the Service. Our current objective is to maintain presently owned emergent wetlands (465 acres) in a mixture of vegetation such as cattail, bulrush, sedges, spatterdock, water lily and smartweeds. We will allow the amount and species composition of emergent wetlands across the remainder of the Refuge (both currently owned and future acquisitions) to fluctuate through natural succession.

Lakes and Ponds

In 2006, the total acreage of lakes and ponds on the Refuge & MA was 885 acres, of which 345 acres were owned by the Service. Our objective over the medium term future is to maintain the number and total surface area of lakes and ponds at or above the current amount.

Patoka River, Oxbows, and Patoka Tributaries

In 2006, the total acreage of the Patoka River, its oxbows and tributaries on the Refuge & MA was 534 acres, of which 200 acres were owned by the Service.

Water Quality

The Refuge's current objective is to improve water quality within the Patoka River and its tributaries to move towards compliance with Indiana Department of Environmental Management standards. The long-term goal is removal of the streams from the list of impaired waters.

Moist Soil Units

In 2006, the total area of moist soil units on the Refuge & MA was 265 acres, all owned by the Service.

The Refuge has restored nine small wetlands covering approximately 19 acres that were built between 2000 and 2006. Two were built with low earthen dikes with water control structures, providing the capability to manipulate water levels. These units are managed as moist soil, seasonal wetlands. One depends on flooding for a water source and the other is on a small drainage swale. Water is stored in shallow pools to encourage waterfowl, shorebird and marsh/waterbird use. Seven other wetlands are referred to as macrotopography wetlands which are shallow scrapes no deeper than two feet in floodplain cropfield locations dependent on annual flooding for water supply. Bottomland hardwood trees have been planted all around these wetlands. They are set up for passive management to resemble old river oxbows.

At Cane Ridge we have four moist soil units that total 193 acres. These are managed to achieve shallow fall flooding, and are slowly drained in the spring. They are intended to benefit waterfowl and shorebirds and are allowed to revegete and grow in the summer with moist soil plants. The four units can be managed independently with occassional needs of manipulating the vegetation to ensure the control of woody intrusion. The units are fed from the Least Tern unit and they are all gravity flow, so there are no costs associated with this low-intensity type of management. The Refuge maintains 6 miles of dikes at Cane Ridge.

At Dillin Bottoms, Ducks Unlimited designed and supervised construction of two moist soil units covering 62 acres. These units are designed to be flooded by reverse flow flap gates during high water or with a permanent station auger pump operated by a portable diesel engine and PTO shaft.

Over the medium term future, we intend to maintain existing moist soil areas (265 acres) and convert up to a total of 700 acres of bottomland farmland to moist soil management that provides a diversity of native herbaceous plant foods such as wild millet (*Echinochloa* spp.), panic grass (*Panicum* spp.), sedges (*Cyperus* spp. and *Carex* spp.), and beggarticks (*Bidens* spp.).

Grasslands

In cooperation with Quail Unlimited we have planted 25 acres of warm season grasses on the Refuge using commercially available seeds. At the present time, maintainace is limited to mowing or mechanical disturbance. The seed mix is Indian grass, big blue, little blue, side oats, and switch grass.

Upland Forests

In 2006, the total acreage of the upland forest on the Refuge & MA was 2,704 acres, of which 183 acres were owned by the Service. We currently manage 40 acres of upland forest, which was reseeded cropland. The remainder of the upland forest is not actively managed. Over the long term (100-200 years), we hope to achieve a mosaic of hardwood stands of different age and structural classes distributed on upland areas. These forests

Wabash and Erie Canal (left), Patoka River NWR & MA. Photo credit: USFWS

would be dominated by white oaks, black oaks, hickory, and blackgum on drier sites, and by red oaks, yellow poplar, beech, sugar maple, walnut, hickory, and cherry on wetter sites. In the coming years, we intend to maintain upland forest on presently owned areas (183 acres) and for future acquisitions maintain existing upland forest and restore upland forest on non-forested upland sites with suitable soils.

Cropland

In 2006, the total acreage of bottomland farmland on the Refuge & MA was 4,507 acres, of which 1,059 acres were owned by the Service. For the most part, land acquired as cropland is being maintained as cropland until we have the money and ability to convert them to moist soil units or bottomland forests. The continued farming is being done by the original farmer, or a tenant farmer, through an annual cooperative farming agreement. One-quarter of the crop is left standing in the field as our share. Frequently these fields are not planted at all due to flooding. In those cases, the farmer will plant a mix of wildlife friendly plants (millet, buckwheat, milo) for waterfowl on our fourth of the acreage. Over time, we intend to convert bottomland cropland areas into bottomland forest and moist soil units.

Upland Openings

In 2006, the total acreage of upland openings on the Refuge & MA was 2,139 acres, of which 98 acres were owned by the Service. Over the coming 10-15 years, our objective is to maintain existing owned upland openings and those existing upland openings on future acquisitions of reclaimed minelands.

Invasive Plant Species

Our aim now and over the medium-term future (10-15 years) is to slow the spread of invasive plant species (of present interest are Japanese honeysuckle, reed canary grass, autumn olive, Johnson grass, and Japanese knotweed) through monitoring and control measures.

Interior Least Tern Nesting Habitat

The Refuge provides six acres of nesting habitat for Interior Least Terns at Cane Ridge Wildlife Management Area. This area is kept free of vegetation and is fenced to prevent predation by mammals.

Private Lands and Watershed Management

Patoka River staff work with surrounding private landowners on conservation projects that benefit us jointly. Over the coming 10-15 years, our aim is to increase wildlife habitat and reduce sedimentation on 150 acres of private lands within the Patoka River and surrounding watersheds.

Farm Services Administration Conservation Easements

The Farm Services Agency, formerly known as the Farm Services Administration, is an agency within the U. S. Department of Agriculture. FSA makes loans to farmers and ranchers temporarily unable to obtain credit from commercial lending institutions. FSA sometimes obtains title to real property when a borrower defaults on a loan secured by the property. FSA holds such properties in inventory until sale or other disposal.

The Service is involved in the inventory disposal program because some FSA inventory properties contain or support significant fish and wildlife resources or have healthy restorable wetlands or other unique habitats. Some qualifying properties are transferred to the Service and become part of the National Wildlife Refuge System. Others are sold, with restrictions known as conservation easements that protect wetlands or other habitats. In most cases, the Service is responsible for the management and administration of properties with conservation easements.

Since the late 1980s and early 1990s, the Refuge has managed habitat on six Farm Services Administration Conservation Easements in five different Indiana counties:

- 90 acres with 24.5 acres of riparian habitat in Vermillion County;
- 40 acres of forested wetland in Gibson County;

- 35.8 acres of forested wetland and ripairan area in Vermillion County;
- 55 acres of riparian and forested wetlands in Sullivan County;
- 14 acres of riparian habitat in Fountain County;
- 365 acres with eight easements in Martin County.

Land Acquisition

We continue to acquire lands from willing sellers within the acquisition boundary as a means of managing and conserving a diversity of habitats.

Wildlife Management

Threatened and Endangered Species

At present, the only threatened and endangered species on the Refuge that is actively managed is the Interior Least Tern. As noted elsewhere, at the Cane Ridge Wildlife Management Area 24 miles west of the Refuge, the Service is providing a protected nesting area, where a bare sandy substrate on two 3-acre islands is maintained for nesting and fencing provides some protection from disturbance). While other T & E species like the Indiana bat occur at Patoka River NWR & MA, no active measures are underway at this time to conserve their populations. In the near term we intend to implement a monitoring program to track abundance, population trends, and/or habitat associations of listed species.

Migratory and Resident Birds

Currently, there is active management of 62-acres in Dillin Bottoms for migratory and resident birds at Patoka River NWR & MA and 193 acres of moist soil management units at Cane Ridge WMA. Over the next 5 years, we intend to implement a monitoring program to track abundance, population trends, and/or habitat associations of selected migratory and resident bird species or groups of species (e.g. waterfowl, migrating land birds, shorebirds, marsh birds).

Native Resident Wildlife

Currently, there is no active management of native resident wildlife at Patoka River NWR & MA. It is our intent to implement a monitoring program to track abundance, population trends, and/or habitat associations of selected native resident wildlife species in the coming years.

Fish and Other Aquatic Species

At present, Patoka River NWR & MA does not have an active fisheries management program. Management's aim over the next decade and a half is to create or maintain diverse, self-sustaining fisheries in Refuge lakes, ponds, and streams.

Interior Least Terns

We actively manage a nesting population of Interior Least Terns at Cane Ridge Wildlife Management Area. Our objective is to support 100 nesting adult terns producing 75 fledglings annually.

Pest Management

On occasion it is necessary for us to remove beaver dams when their activities impact a neighbor's property or structures.

Fish and Wildlife Monitoring

Except for waterfowl, at present, Patoka River management conducts no standardized monitoring or surveying that results in weekly entries into a database. Instead, we make opportunistic observations. For waterfowl, there are weekly surveys at the Cane Ridge Area. When the Refuge grounds are flooded, we make a circuit to those areas that are accessible to conduct waterfowl counts.

River otter were released on the Refuge in 1996. In the winter when there is snow, the Refuge wildlife biologist walks and drives transects on the Refuge looking for otter sign and thus gauge trends in their activity. Activity that is decreasing, constant, or increasing from one year to the next is a good indication of whether the area's otter population is decreasing, stable, or increasing.

South Fork birding trail, Patoka River NWR & MA. Photo credit: USFWS

Visitor Services

As a relatively new refuge with a small staff and an initial priority on land acquisition, habitat restoration, and environmental remediation (reduction of contaminants), Patoka River has had a smaller visitor services program than other more established national wildlife refuges. Nevertheless, each of the "Big Six" public uses emphasized in the National Wildlife Refuge System Improvement Act of 1997 – hunting, fishing, wildlife observation, wildlife photography, environmental education and interpretation – those uses traditionally supported and encouraged on the National Wildlife Refuge System, occurs at Patoka River National Wildlife Refuge and Management Area.

Visitation has grown since the Refuge's establishment in 1994, increasing to 21,221 visits in 2005. Visitor services have increased commensurately. There are multiple access points to the Refuge and with approximately 75 percent of the land within the Refuge acquisition boundary not yet acquired, Refuge lands are intermingled with private holdings. This intermingling requires clear signing and visitor information. Refuge management plans on placing new entrance signs and kiosks at existing boat ramps, Snakey Point, and along Highway 57 over the next 5 years.

There is not currently a visitor center on the Refuge and there are no plans for one in the foreseeable future. The Refuge headquarters on SR 64 (West Morton) in Oakland City is an administrative site that offers visitor information.

Hunting

There were 8,873 hunting visits (waterfowl 4,093, other migratory birds 466, upland game 1,399, big game 2,915) in 2006. This use is likely to increase over the life of the CCP because of the impending closure of mine company lands and the loss of public hunting opportunities on lands elsewhere in the area. Hunting on the Refuge is in accordance with applicable State regulations.

Migratory birds hunted at Patoka River NWR include ducks, geese, coots, Sora Rails, Common Snipes, Woodcocks, and Mourning Doves. Game birds sought by hunters on the Refuge include Quail and Wild Turkey. Small game at Patoka River NWR & MA includes cottontail rabbits, gray and fox squirrels. Furbearers pursued include red and gray fox, coyote, raccoon, and opossum. The only big game hunting on the Refuge is for white-tailed deer.

Shotgun hunters using scattershot may possess and use only approved non-toxic shot. Use or possession of lead shot is prohibited while hunting all species except Wild Turkey on the Refuge. Firearms, archery equipment and crossbows meeting State requirements are permitted on the Refuge only during the designated hunting season.

All motor vehicles must remain on maintained roads and be parked so as not to interfere with other traffic. Off-road vehicles are not permitted on Refuge lands. Hunters with disabilities must possess the required State permit; State regulations and access conditions apply.

Dogs are allowed for hunting according to State regulations during designated seasons only. Dog training or running in the off-season is prohibited.

For waterfowl hunting, pits or permanent blinds may not be constructed on the Refuge. Only portable blinds or structures constructed of native plant materials are permitted and blinds must be removed or dismantled at the end of each day's hunt. Decoys must also be removed at the end of each day's hunt. Likewise, permanent turkey or deer stands may not be erected or used on the Refuge. Portable tree stands may be used for turkey or deer hunting following the same guidelines established for State-owned lands.

Fishing

There were 7,346 fishing visits to Patoka River NWR in 2006. The Refuge provides both bank and boat fishing opportunities on the Patoka River, its oxbows and tributaries, and at Snakey Point Marsh, in accordance with State seasons and regulations and the Refuge fishing plan. Access to some reaches of the river is limited. Refuge staff works cooperatively with the Indiana Department of Natural Resources on fisheries management.

Of the more popular game fish, channel and flathead catfish probably provide the best sport fishing opportunities in the section of the river running through the Refuge. Largemouth bass, bluegill and crappie, offer outstanding fishing opportunities at Snakey Point Marsh.

As a result of channel clearing along the Patoka River, fish habitat structure is poor; there is little in-stream cover, that is, few log jams, brush piles and root-wads. Thus, those species requiring in-stream cover (largemouth bass, bluegill, crappie) are limited by available habitat. Riffle/pool habitat is also scarce. Species diversity in the channelized portion of the river (downstream from Winslow) is lower

Chapter 3: *Refuge Environment and Management*

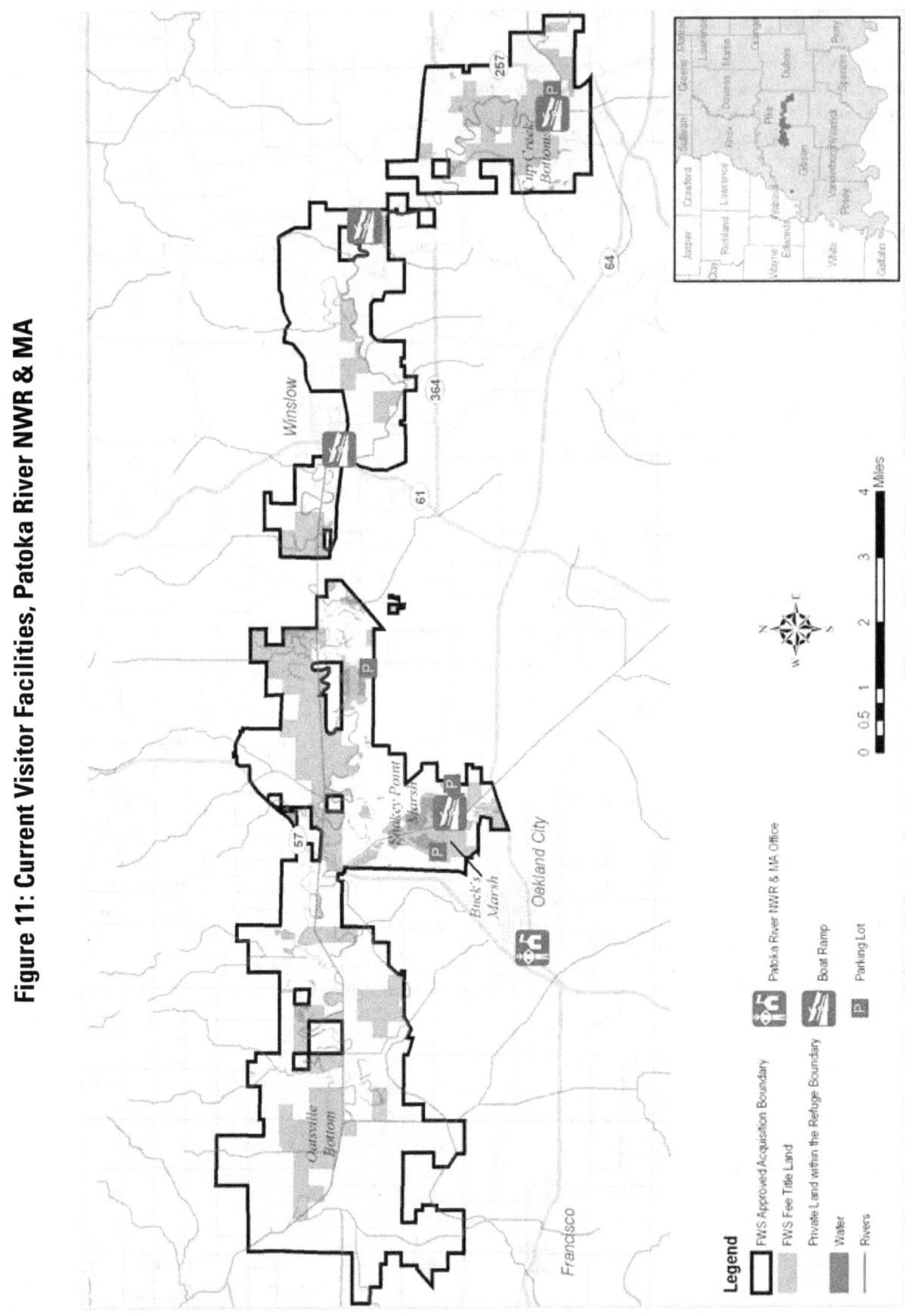

Figure 11: Current Visitor Facilities, Patoka River NWR & MA

than in the natural, meandering channel. Fish of interest to recreational anglers, including buffalo, drum, channel and flathead catfish and spotted bass, are more abundant in the unchannelized section of the Patoka River.

Wildlife Observation and Photography

There were 6,063 wildlife observation visits and 106 photography visits in 2006. Photography and observation visits are projected to increase to 500 in 2007 because of the new observation platform at Cane Ridge. The Refuge provides opportunities for wildlife observation and photography throughout, but Cane Ridge and Snakey Point in particular have facilities such as trails, docks or observation platforms that facilitate these two activities. The Refuge intends to enhance opportunities for observation and photography by building an observation platform at Cane Ridge and trails at Snakey Point and South Fork.

Interpretation

The Refuge Manager and Assistant Refuge Manager provide guided tours and programs upon request and maintain a monument on the McClure Tract. In the near term, they plan to provide interpretive elements in proposed kiosks and other selected sites as well as increase opportunities for interpreted trails, walks, and programs.

Environmental Education

The Refuge Manager and Assistant Refuge Manager provide environmental education upon request typically less than five times annually. In the near future, their intent is to develop capacity to provide Environmental Education materials and programs to teachers and others upon request.

Friends and Volunteers

Volunteers donated 403 hours of their time to the Refuge in 2006. Staff hopes to help convert this enthusiasm into a more formal Friends group in the coming years.

Outreach

Refuge staff speaks to local civic and sportsmen's groups upon request approximately 12-15 times per year. We also provide information and interviews for local news media and outdoors writers as well as distribute news releases 2-3 times annually. In the coming years, we will be exploring how to establish off-site facilities and opportunities.

Archeological and Cultural Values

Cultural resources are important parts of the nation's heritage. The Service is committed to protecting valuable evidence of human interactions with each other and the landscape. Protection is accomplished in conjunction with the Service's mandate to protect fish, wildlife, and plant resources.

Cultural resources management in the USFWS is the responsibility of the Regional Director and is not delegated for the Section 106 process when historic properties could be affected by Service undertakings, for issuing archeological permits, and for Indian tribal involvement. The Regional Historic Preservation Officer (RHPO) advises the Regional Director about procedures, compliance, and implementation of the several cultural resources laws. The Refuge Manager assists the RHPO by early and timely notification of the RHPO about USFWS undertakings, by protecting archeological sites and historic properties on USFWS managed and administered lands, by monitoring archeological investigations by contractors and permittees, and by reporting violations.

Special Management Areas

There are no designated Special Management Areas on the Refuge.

Wilderness Review

As part of the CCP process, lands within the acquisition boundary of Patoka River National Wildlife Refuge and Management Area were reviewed for wilderness suitability. No lands were considered suitable at this time for Congressional designation as wilderness as defined by the Wilderness Act of 1964. Patoka River NMR/MA does not contain 5,000 contiguous acres of roadless, natural lands. Nor does the Refuge possess any units of sufficient size to make their preservation practicable as wilderness. Refuge lands and waters have been substantially altered by humans, especially by agriculture, river channelization, road-building, and coal mining. As a result of both extensive modification of natural habitats and ongoing manipulation of natural processes, adopting a "hands-off" approach to management at the Refuge would not facilitate the restoration of a pristine or pre-settlement condition, which is the goal of wilderness designation.

Chapter 4: Management Direction

Goals, Objectives and Strategies

The Environmental Assessment in Appendix A describes and analyzes three management alternatives for Patoka River NWR. The Service identifies one as its preferred alternative and it is described in the following chapter as the proposed future management direction that would guide activities on the Refuge for the next 15 years. In some cases the proposed future management direction describes initial steps of a long-term vision that may take 100 years or more to achieve.

Figure 14 and Figure 13 depict the long-term vision (100 years or more in the future) for habitat distribution within the Refuge & MA. It was derived using soils data to determine potential vegetation and by reviewing historical maps and photos. The bottomland forest shown to cover much of the Refuge would be a patchy mosaic with a variety of wetland habitats as well as open areas created by dead and dying trees. Over time, disturbances from wind, water, and wildlife would shift the amount and distribution of these habitats. Lands reclaimed after strip mining may eventually revert to forest or remain as grassy upland openings. A meandering Patoka River is also part of the long-term vision. Channel restoration that includes reconnecting oxbows would add many miles to the straightened portion of the river (Figure 14). The management direction that follows describes steps that move towards the long-term vision, but that are practical and attainable within the 15-year timeframe of this plan.

Goals, objectives, and strategies comprise the proposed future management direction. Goals are descriptive broad statements of desired future con-

Patoka River NWR & MA. Photo credit: USFWS

ditions that convey a purpose. There are three goals for Patoka River NWR. Goals are followed by objectives, specific statements that describe management intent. Objectives provide detail and are supported by rationale statements that describe background, history, assumptions, and technical details to help understand how the objective was formulated. Finally, beneath each objective there is a list of strategies – specific actions, tools, and techniques required to fulfill the objective.

Goal 1: Habitat

Manage a diversity of habitats to benefit threatened and endangered species, waterfowl, other migratory birds, and indigenous species in the Patoka River and associated watersheds.

Objective 1.1: Forested Wetlands (Bottomland Forest)

Total Acres: 8,647; 2007 Owned Acres: 3,056

Over the long-term (100-200 years), achieve approximately 12,000 to 13,000 acres of bottomland hardwood stands with a mosaic of age and structural classes distributed across a narrow elevation gradient with lower elevations domi-

Chapter 4: Management Direction

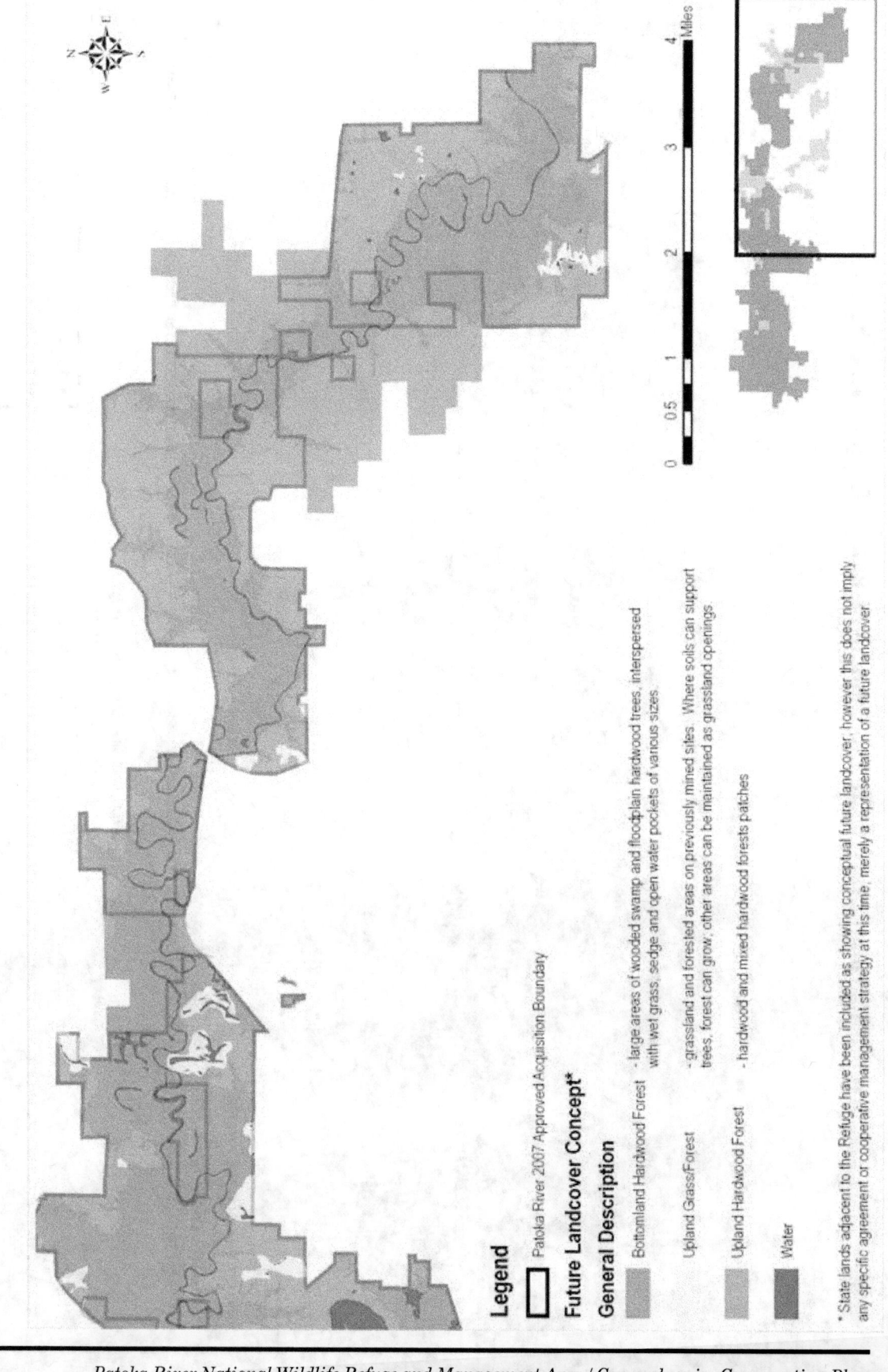

Figure 12: Long-term (100 Years) Landcover, Patoka River NWR & MA (East)

Chapter 4: Management Direction

Figure 13: Long-term (100 Years) Landcover, Patoka River NWR & MA (West)

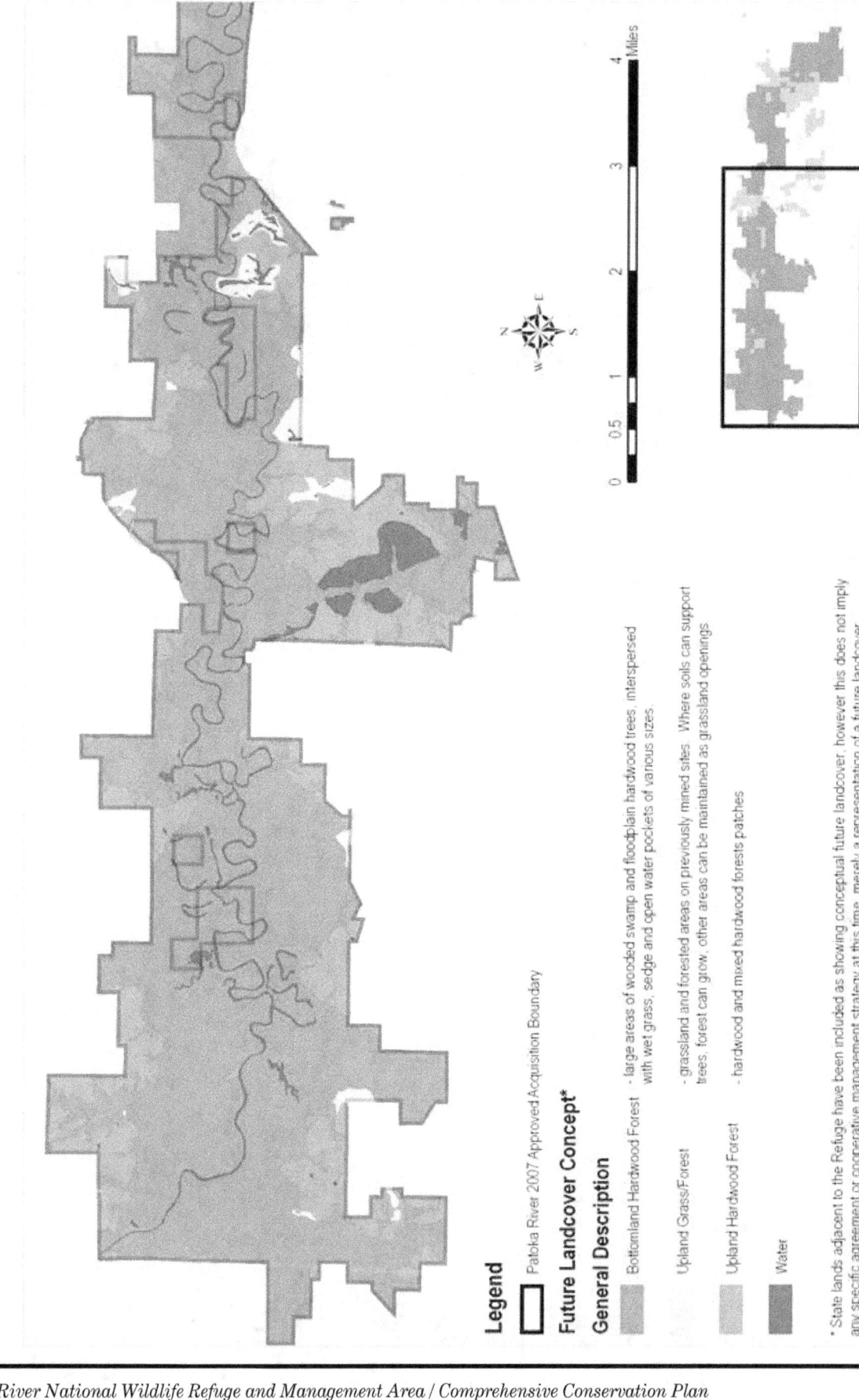

Figure 14: Current and Future Concept of Patoka River Channel

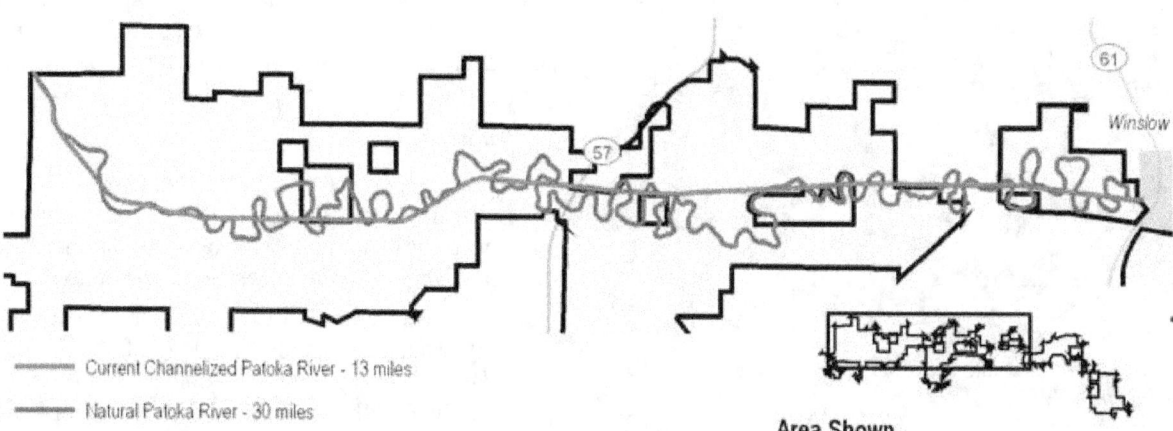

nated by black willow, sweetgum, silver maple, and river birch, mid elevations dominated by pin oak, shumard oak, swamp chestnut oak, swamp white oak, red maple, green ash, sycamore, and cottonwood, and upper elevations dominated by cherry bark oak, other oaks, hickory, and pecan. Over the life of the plan, maintain existing bottomland forest (presently 3,056 acres) and reforest to bottomland hardwoods future land acquisitions that have suitable soils and that are outside of areas managed as non-forested habitat (see Objective 1.6 Bottomland Farmland and Objective 1.7 Moist Soil Units).

Rationale: Bottomland forests are diverse wetlands with many hydrologic features including sheet or overland flow, meander scrolls or relic channels, vernal pools, habitat mounds, depressions, and ridge and swale topography (Wharton et al. 1982, Dunn and Roach 2001). Incorporating these features in wetland restoration creates a diverse wetland habitat providing areas with permanent water, semi-permanent water and seasonally flooded wetlands (Smith 2001). Bottomland forests are also characterized by a multi-tiered canopy and a shifting mosaic of age classes. Canopy gaps created by one or more fallen trees resulting from flooding, windstorms, beaver activity, or other disturbance make up 3-5 percent of bottomland forests (Heitmeyer et al. 2005). These openings in the forest canopy quickly succeed to scrub-shrub habitats and most eventually succeed to bottomland forest.

We identified 15,633 acres of bottomland soils – those on the Indiana list of hydric soils as well as other frequently flooded soils – within the Refuge boundary. Presently, 9,032 acres of these soils are covered by bottomland forest. The Natural Resources Conservation Service's Official Soil Series Descriptions (Soil Survey Staff NRCS – USDA undated) show hardwood forest as the natural vegetation suited for all but 166 acres of the remaining 6,601 acres of bottomland soils (Figure 12 and Figure 13). These potential bottomland forest sites are presently in various cover types with the majority in farmland (5,367 acres). Restoring the extent and species diversity of forested wetlands within the planning area is consistent with Refuge purposes, existing soils information, known presettlement vegetative cover (Parker and Ruffner 2004), and Service policy (U.S. Fish and Wildlife Service 2001). We derived the long-term goal of 12,000 to 13,000 acres by subtracting acreages devoted to moist soil units, and other land uses from the total acres of bottomland soils suited for bottomland forest.

Strategies

1. Plant mast producing bottomland hardwood species on sites with suitable soils.

2. Conduct forest surveys or inventories every 5 years to monitor changes in health, composition, and structure of bottomland forest.

3. Complete a Habitat Management Plan with specific management recommendations to maintain bottomland forest species and age class diversity.

4. Restore micro and macro topographic features on selected bottomland farmland and

Chapter 4: Management Direction

Habitat restoration, Patoka River NWR & MA. Photo credit: USFWS

reforest 60-80 percent of these sites with the balance (20-40 percent) remaining as scrub-shrub wetlands. See Stratman (2000) and Dunn and Roach (2001) for additional information.

5. On suitable sites enhance or restore native canebrakes.

6. Add one full-time (1.0 FTE) forester/wildlife biologist.

7. Target reforestation to minimize fragmentation, create large contiguous blocks of forest, and increase connectivity to other forested areas.

Objective 1.2: Emergent Wetlands

Total Acres: 775; 2007 Owned Acres: 465

Over the next 15 years, maintain presently owned emergent wetlands at Snakey Point and Buck's Marsh in a mixture of vegetation such as cattail, bulrush, sedges, spatterdock, water lily and smartweeds. Allow the amount and species composition of emergent wetlands across the remainder of the refuge (both currently owned and future acquisitions) to fluctuate through natural succession.

Rationale: Snakey Point and the adjoining Buck's Marsh contain much of the 775 acres of emergent wetlands within the Refuge acquisition boundary. These sites are likely wetter than before the South Fork Patoka River was channelized in the 1920s. Sediments dredged from the stream bottom and piled along either side of the channel form levees that impede drainage creating a mixture of open water and emergent vegetation. Siltation and beaver activity also played a role in creating the present condition of these wetlands. Emergent wetlands attract a variety of wildlife. In addition to providing food and resting sites for resident and migrating waterfowl, numerous wading birds, song birds, fur-bearing mammals, reptiles and amphibians, and fish and other aquatic organisms use the marshes during various seasons of the year.

Strategies

1. As part of a Habitat Management Plan, develop a management regime for emergent wetlands that maintains desired plant species and vegetation/open water interspersion.

2. Conduct a study to learn more about the hydrology and geomorphology of the Snakey Point/Buck's Marsh complex in order to determine the feasibility of future water level manipulations that may be necessary to enhance/maintain habitat conditions.

Objective 1.3: Lakes and Ponds

Total Acres: 885; 2007 Owned Acres: 345

Over the next 15 years, maintain the number of lakes and ponds at or above the amount present in 2006 and increase their aquatic habitat diversity.

Rationale: Natural and man-made lakes within the Refuge acquisition boundary provide habitat diversity, support aquatic species, and provide wildlife dependent recreation opportunities.

Strategies

1. Place structure (tree tops, boulders, etc.) in lakes and ponds to increase aquatic habitat diversity.

Objective 1.4: Patoka River, Oxbows, and Patoka Tributaries

Total Acres: 534; 2007 Owned Acres: 200

Within 5 years of plan approval, collect information necessary to evaluate stream channel restoration options for the Patoka River and its tributaries that includes restoring channelized stream to meandering stream.

Rationale:

In the 1920s there was an attempt to drain nearly 100,000 acres of forested wetlands along the Patoka River to make it suitable for farming. Known as Houchin's Ditch and beginning at the town of Winslow, the project replaced 36 miles of natural, meandering river with about 17 miles of dredged, straight ditch. Nearly 19 miles of natural river meanders

Snakey Point fishing pier, Patoka River NWR & MA. Photo credit: USFWS

were cut off and isolated from the main channel. Water exchange within these man-made oxbows is now limited to periods of high water, but heavy sediment loads carried during these periods results in increased deposition in the oxbows. Consequently, these important ecological units are becoming shallower and hold water for a shorter duration. Although this process occurs in all natural riverine systems, normally new oxbows are continually being created as river meanders are severed from the main channel. In the case of Houchins's Ditch, these oxbows are not being replaced and the associated wetland habitat is being lost. We require more information about the morphology and hydrology of the Patoka River and its tributaries before undertaking channel restoration.

Strategies

1. Develop partnership with Corps of Engineers to complete evaluation of stream restoration.

Objective 1.5: Water Quality

Within 15 years of plan approval, improve water quality within the Patoka River and its tributaries to move towards compliance with Indiana Department of Environmental Management standards with the long-term goal of removal of the streams from the list of impaired waters.

Rationale: Presently, the Patoka River and its tributaries are listed as impaired waters by the Indiana Department of Environmental Management (IDEM 2006b). Waters are considered impaired when they fail to meet one or more standards necessary to support one or more of the following uses: aquatic life support, fish consumption, drinking water supply, and recreational use. Improving water quality will help restore the biological integrity and environmental health of the Patoka River system and is consistent with current Service policy (U.S. Fish and Wildlife Service 2001).

Strategies

1. Continue working on abandoned mine land reclamation in conjunction with the IDNR Division of Mining and Reclamation and Department of Interior Office of Surface Mining and Reclamation.
2. Work with local groups to monitor and identify opportunities to improve water quality within the Patoka River watershed.
3. Attend and support watershed planning activities to enhance water quality.
4. Cooperate with Upper and Lower Patoka River Conservancy Districts to maximize wildlife benefits associated with their activities.
5. Maintain relationships with Indiana DNR Division of Oil and Gas, Indiana Department of Environmental Management to ensure proper operation of oil and gas wells in the watershed.

Objective 1.6: Bottomland Farmland

Total acres: 4,507; 2007 Owned acres: 1,059

Over the life of the plan, maintain up to 1,000 acres of bottomland farmland in two to three contiguous blocks as stopover habitat for migratory waterbirds. Convert all other bottomland farmland, both currently owned and future acquisitions, to bottomland forest (including ridge/swale macrotopography wetlands) or moist soil management units.

Rationale: Service policy calls for maintaining or restoring refuge habitats to historic conditions if doing so is feasible and does not conflict with refuge purposes (U. S. Fish and Wildlife Service 2001). Retaining up to 1,000 acres of bottomland farmland departs substantially from the bottomland forest indicated by historic conditions (Parker and Ruffner 2004) and soils (Soil Survey Staff NRCS—USDA undated) of these sites, but it helps fulfill Refuge purposes by providing stopover habitat for migrant waterbirds that favor wetlands with short vegetation (Helmers 1992). This type of stopover habitat historically occurred as sandbars, mudflats, and oxbows along the floodplains and tributaries of the Mississippi and Ohio Rivers before they were extensively altered (de Szalay et al. 2000). Migrants shifted to flooded farmland in the absence of this habitat. Presently, spring flooding inundates bottomland farmland along the Patoka River, providing stopover habitat for migrant shorebirds and some types of waterfowl. Such frequently flooded farmland is a focus of the Indiana Wetland Reserve Program (WRP). Nearly 49,000 acres are enrolled in the Indiana WRP with more than 25,000 acres occurring along the lower reaches of the Wabash and White Rivers, areas close to Patoka River NWR (USDA—NRCS website, G. Roach personal communication June 6, 2006). The majority of sites along the lower reaches of the Wabash and White River are being reforested, making them unsuitable for some migrant waterbirds. This trend is expected to continue. Given the loss of native habitat and the restoration of frequently flooded farmland to forest, it is consistent with Refuge purposes to retain one or more large open blocks of bottomland to provide habitat for open wetland dependent migratory species. Retarding succession on these sites through moist soil management, prescribed burning, or other mechanical or chemical means is not possible because of insufficient land ownership and/or it would exceed current and projected future funding and staffing levels. For the 15-year planning horizon of this CCP, farming is the most cost-effective means to prevent these sites from succeeding to forest and to maintain them as stopover foraging habitat.

Each spring thousands of waterfowl, shorebirds, and wading birds use flooded bottomland farmland within the Refuge as stopover habitat. Many of these migrant waterbirds prefer non-forested wetlands with short vegetation (Helmers 1992) and would not use these areas if they were forested. The birds prefer flooded bottomland farmland within the Refuge for several reasons. Surrounding privately owned farmland is not buffered by bottomland forest and agricultural practices on these sites do not leave residual vegetation as is done on Refuge owned farmland.

Strategies

1. Maintain cooperative agreements, which require cooperating farmers to annually leave a portion of crops as food for wildlife.
2. Where feasible, restore micro and macro topographic features on portions of bottomland farmland fields to increase the duration they provide wetland conditions. See Stratman (2000) and Dunn and Roach (2001) for additional information.

Objective 1.7: Moist Soil Units

500-700 acres

Within 15 years of plan approval, maintain existing moist soil areas (265 acres) and convert up to a total of 700 acres of bottomland farmland to moist soil management that provides a diversity of native herbaceous plant foods such as wild millet (*Echinochloa* spp.); panic grass (*Panicum* spp.); sedges (*Cyperus* spp. and *Carex* spp.); and beggarticks (*Bidens* spp.).

<u>Rationale:</u> Moist soil management is a widespread practice for producing a diverse mixture of native herbaceous plant foods and invertebrates (Frederickson and Taylor 1982). It mimics seasonal flooding that has long occurred in the lowlands of the Patoka River corridor, but moist soil units – areas impounded by levees, dikes, and structures that permit precise control of water levels – allow managers to consistently produce conditions favorable to growth of native plants. Seeds produced by these plants provide balanced nutrition for migrating waterfowl, and also provide food and habitat for other migratory birds and wildlife. The diverse mixture of native plants also creates conditions that produce abundant invertebrates, a high protein wildlife food source.

Strategies

1. Disturb (through mowing, disking, fire, etc…) an average of one third of Moist Soil Unit acreage annually to set back succession.

Bottomland forest hydrology, Patoka River NWR & MA. Photo credit: USFWS

2. Moist soil units will be maintained in early successional native plant communities for the production of annual seed crops.

3. Flood Moist Soil Units in stages beginning in October or November, initially flooding one-third and progressively flooding more of each unit as waterfowl deplete the food supply until units are entirely inundated.

4. Begin draining in March to expose mudflats by April to benefit migrating shorebirds which can feed on invertebrates.

5. Maintain pumps, dikes and water control structures in good working order.

6. Maintain units to demonstrate comparison practices for educational purposes.

Objective 1.8: Upland Forest

Total Acres: 2,704; 2007 Owned Acres: 183

Over the long-term (100-200 years), achieve a mosaic of hardwood stands of different age and structural classes distributed on upland areas and dominated by white oaks, black oaks, hickory, and blackgum on drier sites, and by red oaks, yellow poplar, beech, sugar maple, walnut, hickory, and cherry on wetter sites. Over the life of the plan, maintain upland forest on presently owned acres (183) and for future acquisitions maintain existing upland forest and restore upland forest on non-forested upland sites with suitable soils.

Rationale: We identified 6,720 acres of upland soils within the Refuge boundary. Presently, 2,704 acres of these soils are covered by upland forest. The Natural Resources Conservation Service's Official Soil Series Descriptions (Soil Survey Staff NRCS – USDA undated) shows hardwood forest as the potential natural vegetation suited for the remaining 4,016 acres of upland soils. These potential upland forest sites are presently in various cover types with the majority in farmland (3,213 acres). Restoring the extent and species diversity of upland forest within the planning area is consistent with Refuge purposes, existing soils information, known presettlement vegetative cover (Parker and Ruffner 2004), and Service policy (U.S. Fish and Wildlife Service 2001).

There is additional support for maintaining or restoring upland sites within the Refuge to oak-hickory forest. McNab and Avers (1994) identify oak-hickory forest as the potential natural vegetation for the uplands within the Central Till Plains Oak-Hickory Ecological Section where the Refuge is located. Parker and Ruffner (2004) and Fralish (1997) assert that human caused disturbance played a major role in the dominance of oak-hickory forest in this region for at least the past 400 years and likely much longer (Fralish 2004). Fire suppression within this landscape over the past century has shifted the forest composition away from oaks towards maple and beech (Ruffner and Groninger 2004). Fralish (2004) argues that oak and hickory play a keystone role in the Central Hardwood Forest and are of major importance in maintaining biodiversity. Thompson and Dessecker (1997) also note the importance of oak and early successional communities within the Central Hardwood Forest.

Strategies

1. Conduct forest surveys or inventories every 5 years to monitor changes in health, composition, and structure of forestlands.

2. Develop and implement 5-year forest management plan to promote regeneration of white and red oaks.

3. As indicated, conduct timber stand improvement, including selective harvest if necessary, to provide habitat diversity and stimulate regeneration and plant growth on the forest floor.

4. Plant tree species appropriate to upland sites with emphasis on mast producing species particularly oaks.

Objective 1.9: Upland Openings

Total Acres: 2,139; 2007 Owned Acres: 98

Over the life of the plan, maintain reclaimed minelands as early successional habitat (grasslands) and convert other upland openings to upland forest.

Rationale: Surface mining has and continues to occur on upland sites within the Refuge acquisition boundary. Since 1977 federal law requires coal operators to restore mined land to beneficial uses. Some reclamation sites were planted to grass and remain in this condition. Populations of many grassland bird species are declining in part because of loss of grassland habitat. These "mine grasslands" serve as surrogate habitat for some grassland birds including Grasshopper Sparrows, Henslow's Sparrows, Eastern Meadowlarks, and Dickcissels, which are identified as conservation priorities for the Midwest Region of the Service (Bajema et al. 2001, DeVault et al. 2002).

Service policy calls for maintaining or restoring refuge habitats to historic conditions if doing so is feasible and does not conflict with refuge purposes (U. S. Fish and Wildlife Service 2001). Available information on historic vegetation indicates hardwood forests occurred on upland sites within and surrounding the Refuge (Parker and Ruffner 2004). Hardwood forest is also listed as the potential natural vegetation for upland soils (those not classified as hydric or frequently flooded) within the Refuge (Soil Survey Staff NRCS – USDA undated). Surface mined lands may eventually revert to forest, but mining activity severely altered soil structure and properties allowing grasses to predominate. Although grasslands probably did not historically occur on surface mined areas within the Refuge the habitat is not out of place. Homoya (personal communication March 8, 2007) notes that historically grassland habitat did occur near the Refuge. This is further supported by the description of the Central Till Plains Oak-Hickory Ecological Section where the Refuge is located. It notes fire and other disturbance agents generally discouraged woody vegetation and encouraged grasslands on the flatter upland divides between forested drainages and opened the canopy in the ravines and on slopes (McNab and Avers 1994).

Habitat restoration – tree planting, Patoka River NWR & MA. Photo credit: USFWS

Strategies

1. Use prescribed burning, mechanical, or chemical methods to maintain upland openings.
2. Where feasible, place openings along perimeter of Refuge to minimize fragmentation and promote habitat diversity.

Objective 1.10: Invasive Plant Species

Within 5 years of plan approval assess the location and extent of invasive plant infestations and develop measurable annual targets to help eradicate or slow the spread of invasive plant species (of present interest are Japanese honeysuckle, reed canary grass, autumn olive, Johnson grass, and Japanese knotweed).

<u>Rationale:</u> Exotic or non-native plants are those that have been deliberately or inadvertently transported and transplanted by humans outside their native range, often found on another continent. Certain exotic plants become "invasive" if they survive and begin to spread on their own, in the absence of the population controls (e.g. diseases, parasites, environmental constraints, organisms that fed on them) that held their propagation in check in their native ranges. Invasive exotics are troublesome because they displace native vegetation on which native animal species depend.

Strategies

1. Complete a comprehensive inventory to assess the location and extent of invasive plant infestations.
2. Use mechanical, chemical and biological controls to check the spread of invasive plant species.
3. Communicate with other state and federal resource agencies, as well as non-governmental organizations, to stay current on emerging threats and effective management and control techniques related to invasive species.

Objective 1.11: Private Lands and Watershed Management

Over the life of the plan, increase wildlife habitat and reduce sedimentation on 150 acres of private lands within the Patoka River and surrounding watersheds.

<u>Rationale:</u> The Patoka River watershed extends beyond the boundaries of the Refuge. Land use and activities within the watershed affect the quality of Refuge habitats. Working with neighboring land owners to improve wildlife habitat and water quality complements conservation actions on the Refuge. The Service's Partners for Fish and Wildlife Program is devoted to providing technical and financial assistance to private landowners and Tribes who are willing to work with the Service and other partners on a voluntary basis to help meet the habitat needs of Federal Trust Species.

Strategies

1. Distribute information concerning habitat development opportunities on private lands during Refuge presentations and via local media and other agency (USDA, Indiana DNR) publications and web sites.
2. Coordinate with interested landowners on a timely basis to assess habitat development or improvement opportunities and secure voluntary agreements for appropriate projects.
3. Provide technical resource assistance to other agencies, particularly NRCS, to maximize wildlife benefits associated with programmatic conservation programs such as the Conservation Reserve Program, Wetlands Reserve Program and others.
4. Conduct annual review of Farm Services Agency easements for compliance. Reviews may be completed through a variety of methods including contact with land owners, aerial photography reconnaissance, or on-site inspection.

Objective 1.12: Interior Least Tern Nesting Habitat

Over the life of the plan, continue to provide 6 acres of nesting habitat for Interior Least Terns at Cane Ridge Wildlife Management Area capable of accommodating up to 100 nesting adult terns and producing 75 fledglings annually.

<u>Rationale:</u> The Interior Least Tern is federally listed as endangered. Cane Ridge Wildlife Management Area, a 488-acre satellite of Patoka River NWR, contains two islands created and maintained as nesting habitat for Least Terns. The site was created as part of a Habitat Conservation Agreement with Duke Energy to lure nesting terns away from sites at a neighboring power plant. The site now harbors the largest nesting colony of Interior Least Terns east of the Mississippi River.

Strategies

1. Annually inspect and repair, as necessary, predator fencing which encloses the two nesting islands.
2. Ensure adequate water depth surrounding the nesting islands to provide foraging habitat for the terns and to discourage mammalian predators.
3. Through mechanical and chemical means, ensure that the nesting substrate remains relatively free of vegetation and attractive to nesting terns.

Oxbows adjacent to the channelized river, Patoka River NWR & MA. Photo credit: USFWS

4. Ensure the Refuge has all necessary permits to allow staff to utilize whatever methods necessary to minimize avian predation on the nesting tern colony.

Objective 1.13: Land Acquisition

Within 5, 10 and 15 years of Plan approval, the Refuge will include 50 percent (11,000 acres), 70 percent (15,400 acres) and 80 percent (17,600 acres) respectively, of the lands within the acquisition boundary.

<u>Rationale:</u> Land acquisition is a critical component of fish and wildlife conservation since it permanently protects their basic need of habitat. On a narrow, linear refuge, land acquisition is a critical component of restoring the habitat connectivity needed for the health of many species. Land acquisition can also be cost-effective in the long-term due to inflation of land costs and the costs of acquiring undeveloped land versus developed land that also needs restoration. This objective represents an aggressive land acquisition program and averages 1,080-acres per year from 2007-2011, 880-acres per

year from 2012-2016 and 450-acres per year from 2017-2021 to achieve goals set in the 1994 Land Protection Plan and other approved acquisition documents.

Strategies

1. Secure land by any legal means from cooperative landowners including donations, bequeaths, purchases and land trades.
2. Secure funding from any available source including donations, bequeaths, appropriations, grants and through collaborative efforts with partners to include cost-sharing programs such as the Wetland Reserve Program, carbon sequestration trade-offs and similar programs that may become available.
3. Provide accurate and up-to-date information on land acquisition opportunities to Citizen Committees, Friends Groups, other conservation-oriented non-government organizations, Joint Venture partners and elected officials to assist in their efforts to secure adequate land acquisition funding.
4. Maintain communication with land owners within and around the Refuge of the status of the Service's land acquisition program.
5. Prioritize tracts for acquisition based on most critical wildlife needs and highest threat of loss due to other land development proposals.
6. Continue to be open to review of proposals by partners to protect other lands that may become available in the vicinity of the Refuge that provide critical habitat for threatened, endangered and other species of concern and consider all avenues of protecting that habitat including fee title purchase, conservation easements and cooperative agreements by the Service or other conservation entities.

Objective 1.14: Air Quality

Over the life of the plan, work to improve air quality within the Refuge to levels that meet or exceed Environmental Protection Agency standards.

Rationale: Maintaining air quality to protect Refuge resources is consistent with the Service policy on Biological Integrity, Diversity, and Environmental Health. In recent years, the air quality within portions of Pike and Gibson counties as well as neighboring counties Warrick, Dubois, and Vanderburgh has failed to attain the national standard for particulate matter, one of six principal pollutants that have National Ambient Air Quality Standards set by the Environmental Protection Agency. Much of Gibson and Pike counties, where the Refuge is located, are outside this "nonattainment area" most likely because no air quality data are available. In addition to primary standards intended to protect public health, the Clean Air Act sets secondary standards to protect public welfare. These secondary standards include protection for animals and vegetation, two resources that play an important role in fulfilling Refuge purposes. In 2007 there was a proposal to site an industrial facility near the Refuge that would discharge additional effluent into the atmosphere. This generated concern among Refuge staff and the local public. In 2008 the Refuge working in conjunction with the Indiana Department of Environmental Management placed an air quality monitoring station near the Refuge.

Strategies

1. Continue to work with Indian Department of Environmental Management and local citizens groups (currently Pike/Gibson Citizens for a Quality Environment).
2. Support establishment of a permanent air monitoring station in the vicinity of the Refuge.

Migrating Mallards, Patoka River NWR & MA. Photo credit: USFWS

Goal 2: Wildlife

Perpetuate listed species, waterfowl, other migratory birds, and native fish and wildlife, within the Patoka River and associated watersheds while restoring and preserving the biological integrity, diversity, and environmental health of the Refuge.

Objective 2.1: Threatened and Endangered Species

Within 5 years of plan approval, implement a monitoring program to track abundance, population trends, and/or habitat associations of listed species.

Rationale: To evaluate whether management actions are having the predicted consequences, we need to monitor actual outcomes, most often using a representative sample of sites to ensure that, on average, the effects of a particular type of treatment match expectations. Information gained through monitoring helps us learn and adapt, increasing our effectiveness in meeting conservation objectives. Established in 2005, the Service's Biological Monitoring Team is developing a series of monitoring protocols to ensure uniform data collection and analysis. Refuge monitoring activities will be compliant with the goals of the Biological Monitoring Team shown below (U. S. Fish and Wildlife Service 2005).

- Refuges will evaluate achievement of their wildlife and habitat goals, and track the management and conservation of their natural resources over time and space through systematic collection, storage, and reporting of biological data that address specific management information needs.
- Refuges will initiate management-focused research (Adaptive Management) and develop new tools and techniques to fill information gaps. Adaptive management research will be used to clarify the outcomes of specific management actions and guide future management programs.
- Refuges will contribute to regional, national, and continental conservation of trust resources as partners with other FWS Programs (Migratory Birds, Fisheries, Endangered Species, others) and the States, by collaborating with other agencies performing similar monitoring efforts to ensure that data can be easily exchanged for analyses at multiple landscape scales.

Strategies

1. Monitor Bald Eagle nest(s) to track nest success/productivity
2. Every 5 years cooperate/contract with university/Coop unit/ES endangered species specialist to determine status of Indiana bats on the Refuge.
3. Continue cooperative efforts with Indiana DNR, Duke Energy to monitor Interior Least Tern nesting colony (nesting success, production, predation)
4. Candidate species (Indiana crayfish, northern copperbelly watersnake) – survey, inventory, habitat evaluation.
5. Complete Inventory and Monitoring stepdown plan.

Objective 2.2: Migratory and Resident Birds

Within 5 years of plan approval, implement a monitoring program to track abundance, population trends, and/or habitat associations of selected migratory and resident bird species or groups of species (e.g. waterfowl, migrating land birds, shorebirds, marsh birds).

Rationale: See rationale for Objective 2-1 Threatened and Endangered Species.

Strategies:

1. In cooperation with Indiana DNR, conduct weekly waterfowl surveys at Patoka River NWR, Cane Ridge WMA, and Gibson Generating Station.
2. Develop partnership with local birding organizations and other competent birders to conduct Christmas Bird Count, Breeding Bird Survey, colonial nesters survey, and shorebird surveys in conformance with appropriate protocols
3. Develop, as appropriate, surveys designed to measure the impacts of habitat management efforts on migratory bird populations and use (reforestation, water manipulation, early successional habitat management).

Objective 2.3: Native Resident Wildlife

Over the life of the plan, track abundance, population trends, and/or habitat associations of selected native resident wildlife species.

Rationale: The Indiana Comprehensive Wildlife Strategy identifies species of greatest conservation need within the state including many that are not

Federal Trust Species. The Refuge, which includes intermingled state lands (Pike State Forest and Sugar Ridge Fish and Wildlife Area) contains habitat for many of these species. Monitoring their status in cooperation with the Indiana Department of Natural Resources supports implementation of the Indiana Comprehensive Wildlife Strategy.

Strategies

1. Cooperate with IDNR to collect monitoring information on selected native resident wildlife.

Objective 2.4: Fish and Other Aquatic Species

Over the next 15 years, create or maintain diverse, self-sustaining fisheries in Refuge lakes, ponds, and streams. Within the Patoka River and its tributaries, improve the Index of Biotic Integrity for fish and other aquatic species communities with the long term goal of meeting or exceeding the Indiana Department of Environmental Management threshold for "fully supporting".

Rationale: Presently, the Patoka River and its tributaries are listed as impaired waters by the Indiana Department of Environmental Management (IDEM 2006b). Waters are considered impaired when they fail to meet one or more standards necessary to support one or more of the following uses: aquatic life support, fish consumption, drinking water supply, and recreational use. Improving water quality will help restore the biological integrity and environmental health (U.S. Fish and Wildlife Service 2001) of the Patoka River system as measured through an increase in the Index of Biotic Integrity as monitored and reported by the Indiana Department of Environmental Management (IDEM 2006a). The Index of Biotic Integrity is a composite indicator that incorporates multiple dimensions of living systems to quantify biological conditions in aquatic environments. Such indicators have been recommended for monitoring ecological conditions on Refuges (Meretsky et al. 2006).

Strategies

1. Periodically inventory and monitor fish and aquatic species in Refuge waters.
2. See strategies under Objective 1-5 Water Quality.

Goal 3: People

Visitors, nearby residents and other stakeholders have the opportunity to enjoy wildlife-dependent recreation, understand and appreciate the natural resources, ecological processes and cultural resources of the Refuge, thereby supporting the Service's mission.

Objective 3.1: Welcoming and Orienting Visitors

Within 5 years of plan approval, improve directional signing, determine the feasibility of off-site welcoming and orientation facilities, and place new entrance signs and kiosks at existing boat ramps, Snakey Point, and along Highway 57.

Rationale: Welcoming and orienting Refuge visitors contributes to several of the criteria defining a quality wildlife dependent recreation program (U.S. Fish and Wildlife Service 2006a). The number of visitors and amount of visitor services has increased to 21,221 visits since the Refuge was established in 1994. There are multiple access points to the Refuge and with approximately 75 percent of the land within the Refuge boundary not yet acquired, Refuge lands are intermingled with other holdings requiring clear signing and visitor information.

Strategies

1. Provide online Refuge information and map of boundaries.
2. Post boundaries on lands that abut the acquisition boundary of the Refuge and along selected sites that abut county roads.
3. Develop Visitor Facility enhancement projects to provide new entrance signs and kiosks at major access points.

Trumpeter Swans, Patoka River NWR & MA. Photo credit: USFWS

4. Develop and maintain a general brochure and fact sheet.

Objective 3.2: Hunting

Over the life of the plan, provide hunting in line with State seasons and regulations except within designated sanctuary areas and according to the Refuge hunting and fishing plan.

Rationale: Hunting programs help promote understanding and appreciation of natural resources and their management on all lands and waters in the Refuge System. Hunting is a priority general public uses of the National Wildlife Refuge System, and Service policy directs us to provide hunting opportunities when compatible (U. S. Fish and Wildlife Service 2006b).

Strategies

1. Enlist assistance from the Indiana DNR and volunteers to run any additional hunts.
2. Manage hunts to minimize conflicts with other uses and resources.
3. Assist as appropriate with hunter education, youth hunts, hunts for the disabled, and a women's skill program.
4. As more land is acquired more sanctuary areas will be identified and posted closed to all hunting to provide a feeding and resting area for migratory birds. Maintaining waterfowl sanctuary areas free of all hunting serves waterfowl and hunters by keeping birds in the area thereby providing prolonged hunting opportunities in adjoining areas.
5. Maintain Cane Ridge as a sanctuary free of all hunting.

Objective 3.3: Fishing

Over the life of the plan, continue to provide fishing in line with State seasons and regulations according to the Refuge hunting and fishing plan. Continue to work cooperatively with the Indiana Department of Natural Resources on fisheries management. Within 5 years of plan approval, provide enhanced fishing access (more docks, ramps, etc…).

Rationale: Fishing programs help promote understanding and appreciation of natural resources and their management on all lands and waters in the Refuge System. Fishing is a priority general public uses of the National Wildlife Refuge System, and Service policy directs us to provide

Plant identification workshop, Patoka River NWR & MA. Photo credit: USFWS

fishing opportunities when compatible (U. S. Fish and Wildlife Service 2006c).

Strategies

1. If successful in acquiring suitable lands, install a boat ramp near Oatsville in cooperation with the IDNR.
2. Provide additional accessible facilities such as trails, boat ramps, and fishing piers along fishable waters as lands are acquired within the Refuge.
3. Provide accessible bank fishing opportunities.

Objective 3.4: Wildlife Observation and Photography

Over the life of the plan, continue to provide opportunities for wildlife observation and photography at Cane Ridge and Snakey Point. Within 5 years of plan approval, enhance observation and photography Refuge-wide as opportunities present themselves.

Rationale: Wildlife observation and photography programs can help promote understanding and appreciation of natural resources and their management on all lands and waters in the Refuge System. Wildlife observation and photography are priority general public uses of the National Wildlife Refuge System, and Service policy directs us to provide wildlife observation and photography opportunities when compatible (U. S. Fish and Wildlife Service 2006d and 2006e).

Strategies

1. Provide additional accessible wildlife observation and photography facilities such as blinds,

observation platforms, trails, etc. at selected sites as lands are acquired within the Refuge.

2. Install spotting scope at Cane Ridge Wildlife Management Area observation platform.
3. Determine the feasibility of a canoe route along the Patoka River.

Objective 3.5: Interpretation

Over the life of the plan, continue to provide guided tours and programs upon request and maintain monument on McClure Tract. Within 5 years of plan approval, provide interpretive elements in proposed kiosks and other selected sites and increase opportunities for interpreted trails, walks, and programs.

Rationale: Well-designed interpretive programs can be effective resource management tools that provide us an opportunity to influence visitor attitudes about natural resources, refuges, the Refuge System, and the Service and to influence visitor behavior when visiting units of the Refuge System. Interpretation is a priority general public use of the National Wildlife Refuge System, and Service policy directs us to provide interpretation programs when compatible (U. S. Fish and Wildlife Service 2006g).

Strategies

1. Evaluate interest and feasibility of developing an interpretive canoe/boating route along the Patoka River.
2. Place orientation kiosks at one or more of the following locations: Pikeville boat ramp, Survant boat ramp and Snakey Point.
3. Place kiosk and interpretive signs at Cane Ridge Wildlife Management Area.
4. Place interpretive signs at all observation sites.
5. Consider providing a visitor contact area within or adjoining the Refuge office to offer interpretive materials.

Objective 3.6: Environmental/Conservation Education

Over the life of the plan, continue to provide environmental education upon request at the current level of less than 5 times per year. Within 3 years of plan approval, develop capacity to provide Environmental Education materials and programs to teachers and others upon request.

Rationale: Providing and promoting environmental education helps develop a citizenry that has the awareness, knowledge, attitudes, skills, motivation, and commitment to work cooperatively towards the conservation of our Nation's environmental resources. Environmental education is a priority general public use of the National Wildlife Refuge System, and Service policy directs us to provide environmental education programs when compatible (U. S. Fish and Wildlife Service 2006f).

Strategies

1. Offer teacher workshops to introduce educators to the Refuge, Refuge System and Service provided environmental education materials.
2. Provide opportunities for scouts and 4H students to complete conservation projects on the Refuge.
3. Maintain a supply or access to a source of environmental education materials for local teachers.

Objective 3.7: Friends and Volunteers

Within 5 years of plan approval, establish a Friends group.

Rationale: A Refuge Friends Group is a grassroots organization formed by citizens who have a shared vision of supporting their local National Wildlife Refuge. They join with Service personnel in a partnership that seeks to accomplish mutually defined goals. Establishing a Friends group helps build a constituency of support for the Refuge, provides people with opportunities to assist us in the accomplishment of our mission, enhances our performance through the creativity and innovations, labor, and expertise contributed by Friends members.

Strategies

1. Continue to work with Southwest Four Rivers Project Committee of the Upper Mississippi River Joint Venture.
2. Continue to maintain a working relationship with Evansville Audubon Society and the Izaak Walton League, Ducks Unlimited, Waterfowl USA, Quail Unlimited, and other organizations.
3. Continue to solicit support from the local community for special projects.

Objective 3.8: Outreach

Over the life of the plan, continue to speak to local civic and sportsmen's groups upon request approximately 12-15 times per year. Also con-

Canoeing the Patoka River, Patoka River NWR & MA. Photo credit: USFWS

tinue to provide information and interviews for local news media and outdoors writers as well as distribute news releases 2-3 times annually. Within 5 years of CCP approval, explore opportunities to establish off-site facilities and opportunities.

<u>Rationale:</u> The Service's National Outreach Strategy (U.S. Fish and Wildlife Service, 1997) defines outreach as two-way communication between the U.S. Fish and Wildlife Service and the public to establish mutual understanding, promote involvement, and influence attitudes and actions, with the goal of improving joint stewardship of our natural resources. Providing a clear consistent message about the role of the Refuge helps build support and understanding.

Strategies

1. Work with county tourism associations to help promote the Refuge.
2. Continue with active participation and communication throughout the watershed through media articles, meeting with elected officials, representatives or other organizations such as soil and water conservation districts to promote Refuge programs.

Chapter 5: Plan Implementation

New and Existing Projects

This CCP outlines an ambitious course of action for the future management of Patoka River NWR & MA. The ability to enhance wildlife habitats on the Refuge and to maintain existing and develop additional quality public use facilities will require a significant commitment of staff and funding from the Service. The Refuge will continually need appropriate operational and maintenance funding to implement the objectives in this plan.

The following provides a brief description of the highest priority Refuge projects, as chosen by the Refuge staff and listed in the Service Asset and Maintenance Management System (SAMMS). Completion of these projects is dependent on acquiring suitable lands. A full listing of unfunded Refuge projects and operational needs can be found in Appendix J.

Construct Visitor Parking Lots

As new lands are acquired, appropriate sites will be identified to construct small gravel parking lots to provide safe parking for wildlife dependent recreation activities.

Completion of Observation Deck

Completion of this project will include an accessible boardwalk from the parking lot to the existing observation deck, an interpretive kiosk and signs, and two ADA approved spotting scopes.

Reconnect Oxbows on Patoka River

In cooperation with the Army Corps of Engineers we will select a small site along the channelized portion of the Patoka River cutoff oxbow will be

Anas platyrhynchos ova, Patoka River NWR & MA. Photo credit: USFWS

reconnected to the main channel of the Patoka River as a demonstration project and to evaluate its effectiveness in restoring bottomland hydrology.

Maintenance and Construction of Storage Facilities

When an appropriate tract of land is purchased a permanent maintenance and storage facility will be constructed to support Refuge operations.

Macrotopography Wetlands

On bottomland farmland construct a series of ridge and swale wetland complexes with depressional basins within the floodplain ranging in size from one-tenth to 5 acres with depths from 0 to 24 inches. These wetlands will be formed in a variety of shapes to provide landscape diversity. The ridges and mounds will be planted with bottomland hardwood trees.

Figure 15: Current Staffing Chart, Patoka River NWR

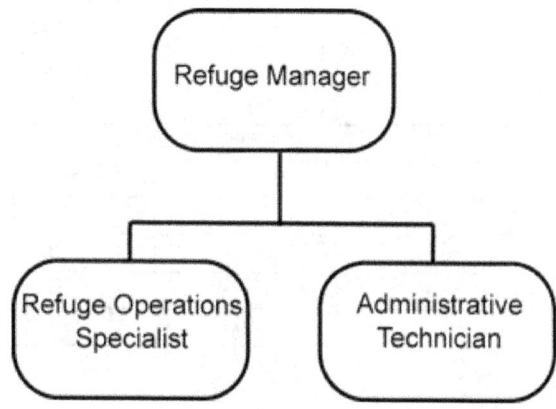

Figure 16: Staffing Required to Fully Implement Plan

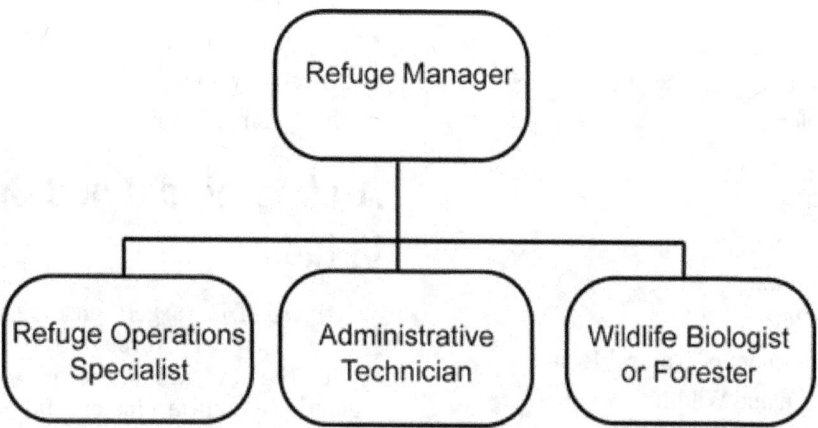

Future Staffing Requirements

Implementing the visions set forth in this CCP will require additions to the organizational structure of Patoka River National Wildlife Refuge. Existing staff will direct their time and energy in somewhat new directions and one new staff member would be added to assist in these efforts. The first organizational chart shows the existing Refuge staff as of Fiscal Year 2007. A permanent full-time wildlife biologist or forester is needed to fully implement this plan. See Figure 16.

Partnership Opportunities

Partnerships have become an essential element for the successful accomplishment of Patoka River NWR goals, objectives, and strategies. The objectives outlined in this CCP need the support and the partnerships of federal, state and local agencies, non-governmental organizations and individual citizens. This broad-based approach to managing fish and wildlife resources extends beyond social and political boundaries and requires a foundation of support from many. Patoka River NWR will continue to seek creative partnership opportunities to achieve its vision for the future.

Particularly notable partners of the Refuge include:

Table 5: Step-down Management Plan Schedule

Step-down Management Plan	Completed or Updated	Anticipated Completion or Revision
Safety	--	2008
Air Quality Management	--	2008
Hunting and Fishing	1996	2010
Wildlife Observation and Photography	--	2012
Interpretation	--	2013
Habitat Management	--	2010
Inventory and Monitoring	--	2009
Fire Management	2002	-

- Ducks Unlimited
- Duke Energy
- Waterfowl USA
- National Fish and Wildlife Foundation
- Natural Resources Conservation Service
- Audubon Society
- Izaak Walton League
- Quail Unlimited
- McCormick Farms
- Conservation Fund
- Four Rivers RC&D
- Indiana Department of Natural Resources
- Division of Fish and Wildlife
- Division of Forestry
- Division of Oil and Gas
- Division of Mining and Reclamation
- Army Corps of Engineers

Step-down Management Plans

Step-down management plans help meet the goals and objectives of the CCP. Some step-down plans are required by Service policy and others are used to specify strategies and implementation schedules beyond the detail of the CCP. The following list and Table 5 show the step-down management plans we intend to prepare or revise to realize the intent of the CCP.

- Safety
- Air Quality Management
- Hunting and Fishing
- Wildlife Observation and Photography
- Interpretation
- Habitat Management
- Inventory and Monitoring
- Fire Management

Archeological and Cultural Values

As part of its larger conservation mandate and ethic, the Service through the Refuge Manager applies the several historic preservation laws and regulations to ensure historic properties are identified and are protected to the extent possible within its established purposes and Refuge System mission.

The Refuge Manager early in project planning for all undertakings, informs the RHPO (Regional Historic Preservation Officer) to initiate the Section 106 process. Concurrent with public notification and involvement for environmental compliance and compatibility determinations if applicable, or cultural resources only if no other issues are involved, the Refuge Manager informs and requests comments from the public and local officials through presentations, meetings, and media notices; results are provided to the RHPO.

Archeological investigations and collecting are performed only in the public interest by qualified archeologists or by persons recommended by the Governor working under an Archaeological

Young white-tailed buck, Patoka River NWR & MA. Photo credit: USFWS

Resources Protection Act permit issued by the Regional Director. Refuge personnel take steps to prevent unauthorized collecting by the public, contractors, and Refuge personnel.

The Refuge Manager will, with the assistance of the RHPO, develop a step-down plan for surveying lands to identify archeological resources and for developing a preservation program to meet the requirements of Section 14 of the Archaeological Resources Protection Act and Section 110(a)(2) of the National Historic Preservation Act.

The Refuge Manager should have and implement a plan for inspecting the condition of known cultural resources on the Refuge and report to the RHPO changes in the conditions.

The Refuge Manager will initiate budget requests or otherwise obtain funding from the 1 percent O&M program base provided for the Section 106 process compliance:

1. Inventory, evaluate, and protect all significant cultural resources located on lands controlled by the FWS, including historic properties of religious and cultural significance to Indian tribes.
2. Identify and nominate to the National Register of Historic Places all historic properties including those of religious and cultural significance to Indian tribes.
3. Cooperate with Federal, state, and local agencies, Native American tribes, and the public in managing cultural resources on the Refuge.
4. Integrate historic preservation with planning and management of other resources and activities. Historic buildings are rehabilitated and adapted to reuse when feasible.
5. Recognize the rights of Native American to have access to certain religious sites and objects on Refuge lands within the limitations of the FWS mission.

Monitoring and Evaluation

The direction set forth in this CCP and specifically identified strategies and projects will be monitored throughout the life of this plan. On a periodic basis, the Regional Office will assemble a station review team whose purpose will be to visit Patoka River NWR and evaluate current Refuge activities in light of this plan. The team will review all aspects of Refuge management, including direction, accomplishments and funding. The goals and objectives presented in this CCP will provide the baseline from which this field station will be evaluated.

Plan Review and Revision

The CCP for the Refuge is meant to provide guidance to the refuge manager and staff over the next 15 years. However, the CCP is also a dynamic and flexible document and several of the strategies contained in this plan are subject to natural uncontrollable events such as windstorms and floods. Likewise, many of the strategies are dependent upon Service funding for staff and projects. Because of all these factors, the recommendations in the CCP will be reviewed periodically and, if necessary, revised to meet new circumstances. If any revisions are major, the review and revision will include the public.

Appendix A: Finding of No Significant Impact

FONSI here

and here.

Appendix B: Glossary

Appendix B: Glossary

Aquatic Species

Includes all freshwater, anadromous and estuarine fishes, freshwater mollusks, freshwater crustaceans and freshwater amphibians.

Archaeological and Cultural Values

Any material remains of past human life or activity greater than 100 years old which are of archaeological interest as defined by Section 4(a) of the Archaeological Resources Protection Act and 43 CFR Part 7.3.

Biodiversity

The variety of life and its processes, including the variety of living organisms, the genetic differences among them, and the communities and ecosystems in which they occur.

Candidate Species

Those species for which the Service has on file sufficient information on biological vulnerability and threats to propose them for listing.

Compatible Use

A wildlife-dependent recreational use or any other use of a refuge that, in the sound professional judgment of the Director or designee, will not materially interfere with or detract from the fulfillment of the mission of the System or the purposes of the refuge (PL 105-57).

Comprehensive Conservation Plan

Plan: A document, completed with public involvement, that describes the desired future condition and provides long-term (15 year planning horizon) guidance to accomplish the purposes of the refuge system and the individual refuge units.

Conservation

The management of natural resources to prevent loss or waste. Management actions may include preservation, restoration and enhancement.

Conservation (Species)

The use of all methods and procedures which are necessary to bring any species to the point at which the measures provided are no longer necessary. Such methods and procedures include, but are not limited to, all activities associated with scientific resources management such as research, census, law enforcement, habitat acquisition and maintenance, propagation, live trapping, and transplantation. Conservation is the act of managing a resource to ensure its survival and availability.

Cultural Resources

Cultural Resources: "those parts of the physical environment – natural and built – that have cultural value to some kind of sociocultural group... [and] those non-material human social institutions...." (King, p.9). Cultural resources include historic sites, archeological sites and associated artifacts, sacred sites, traditional cultural properties, cultural items (human remains, funerary objects, sacred objects, and objects of cultural patrimony) (McManamon, Francis P. DCA-NPS; letter 12-23-97 to Walla Walla District, COE), and buildings and structures.

Ecosystem

Dynamic and interrelating complex of plant and animal (including humans) communities and their associated non-living environment.

Ecosystem Approach

1) Protecting or restoring the natural function, structure, and species composition of an ecosystem, recognizing that all components are interrelated. 2) Management of natural resources using system-wide concepts to ensure that all plants and animals in ecosystems are maintained at viable levels in native habitats and that basic ecosystem processes are perpetuated indefinitely (Clark and Zaunbrecher 1987).

Endangered Species

A listed species in danger of extinction throughout all or a significant portion of its range.

Enhance (habitats)

Improves habitat through alteration, treatment, or other land management of existing habitat to increase habitat value for one or more species without bringing the habitat to a fully restored or naturally occurring condition.

Forest Fragmentation

Fragmentation may occur when a forested landscape is subdivided into patches. Fragmentation may also occur when numerous openings for such things as fields, roads, and powerlines interrupt a continuous forest canopy. The resulting landscape pattern alters habitat connectivity and edge characteristics, influencing a variety of species.

Interjurisdictional Fish

Populations of fish that are managed by two or more states or national or tribal governments because of the scope of their geographic distributions or migrations.

Invasive Species

An alien species whose introduction does or is likely to cause economic or environmental harm or harm to human health.

Migratory Nongame Birds of Management Concern

Those species of nongame birds that (a) are believed to have undergone significant population declines; (b) have small or restricted populations; or (c) are dependent upon restricted or vulnerable habitats.

Migratory Species

Species that move substantial distances to satisfy one or more biological needs, most often to reproduce or escape intolerable cyclic environmental conditions.

National Wildlife Refuge System

All lands and waters and interests therein administered by the Service as wildlife refuges, wildlife ranges, wildlife management areas, waterfowl production areas, and other areas for the protection and conservation of fish and wildlife, including those that are threatened with extinction.

Protect (habitat)

Maintain current quality or prevent degradation to habitat. The act of ensuring that habitat quantity and quality do not change, most often as a result of human activities but sometimes in response to unwelcome natural processes or phenomena.

Recovery Plans (species)

Documents developed by the Service that outline tasks necessary to stabilize and recover listed species. Recovery plans include goals for measuring species progress towards recovery, estimated costs and time frames for the recovery process, and an identification of public and private partners that can contribute to implementation of the recovery plan.

Restore (habitat)

Returns the quantity and quality of habitat to some previous naturally occurring condition, most often some baseline considered suitable and sufficient to support self-sustaining populations of fish and wildlife.

Riparian Habitats

Those lands adjacent to streams or rivers that form a transition zone between aquatic and upland systems and are typically dominated by woody vegetation that is of a noticeably different growth form than adjacent vegetation. Riparian areas may or may not meet the definition of wetlands used by Cowardin *et al.* (1979).

Rotation

The period during which a single generation is allowed to grow.

Species of Concern

A species not on the federal list of threatened or endangered species, but a species for which the Service or one of its partners has concerns.

Stakeholders

State, tribal, and local government agencies, academic institutions, the scientific community, non-governmental entities including environmental, agricultural, and conservation organizations, trade groups, commercial interests, and private landowners.

Threatened Species

A listed species which is likely to become an endangered species within the foreseeable future throughout all or a significant portion of its range.

Undertaking

A project, activity, or program funded in whole or in part under the direct or indirect jurisdiction of a Federal agency, including those carried out by or on behalf of a Federal agency; those carried out with Federal financial assistance; those requiring a Federal permit, license or approval..." (36 CFR 800.16(y); 12-12-2000), i.e., all Federal actions.

Uplands

All lands not meeting the definition of wetlands, deepwater, or riverine.

Watershed

The area drained by a river or stream and its tributaries.

Wetlands

Lands transitional between terrestrial and aquatic systems where the water table is usually at or near the surface or the land is covered by shallow water (Cowardin et al., 1979. In layman's terms, this habitat category includes marshes, swamps and bogs.

Wildlife-dependent Recreational Use

A use of a refuge involving hunting, fishing, wildlife observation and photography, or environmental education and interpretation.

Appendix C: Species Lists

List of Bird Species / page 99
List of Mammal Species / page 106
List of Herptofauna Species / page 107
List of Fish Species / page 109
List of Fresh Water Mussel Species / page 112
List of Plant Species / page 113

Appendix C: Species Lists

Bird Species List, Patoka River NWR & MA

Common Name	Scientific Name	Patoka River	Cane Ridge WMA	Noted in Indiana Comprehensive Wildlife Strategy as Species of Greatest Conservation Need
Common loon	*Gavia immer*	✔		
Pied-billed grebe	*Podilymbus podiceps*	✔	✔	
Horned grebe	*Podiceps auritus*	✔		
American white pelican	*Pelecanus erythrorhynchos*	✔		
Double-crested cormorant	*Phalacrocorax auritus*	✔	✔	
American bittern	*Botaurus lentiginosus*	✔	✔	✔
Least bittern	*Ixobrychus exilis*	✔	✔	✔
Great blue heron	*Ardea herodias*	✔	✔	
Snowy egret	*Egretta thula*	✔	✔	
Great egret	*Casmerodius albus*	✔	✔	✔
Little blue heron	*Egretta caerulea*	✔	✔	
Cattle egret	*Bubulcus ibis*	✔	✔	
Green heron	*Butorides striatus*	✔	✔	
Black-crowned night-heron	*Nycticorax nycticorax*	✔	✔	✔
Yellow-crowned night-heron	*Nycticorax violaceus*	✔		✔
White-faced ibis	*Plegadis chihi*		✔	
Wood stork	*Mycteria americana*		✔	
Greater white-fronted goose	*Anser albifrons*	✔	✔	
Snow goose	*Chen caerulescens*	✔	✔	
Canada goose	*Branta canadensis*	✔	✔	
Tundra swan	*Cygnus columbianus*	✔	✔	
Trumpeter swan	*Cygnus buccinator*	✔		✔
Mute swan	*Cygnus olor*	✔		
Wood duck	*Aix sponsa*	✔	✔	
Gadwall	*Anas strepera*	✔	✔	
American wigeon	*Anas americana*	✔	✔	
American black duck	*Anas rubripes*	✔	✔	
Mallard	*Anas platyrhynchos*	✔	✔	
Blue-winged teal	*Anas discors*	✔	✔	
Green-winged teal	*Anas crecca*	✔	✔	
Northern shoveler	*Anas clypeata*	✔	✔	
Northern pintail	*Anas acuta*	✔	✔	
Canvasback	*Aythya valisineria*	✔	✔	
Redhead	*Aythya americana*	✔	✔	
Ring-necked duck	*Aythya collaris*	✔	✔	
Lesser scaup	*Aythya affinis*	✔	✔	
Bufflehead	*Bucephala albeola*	✔	✔	

Appendix C: Species Lists

Bird Species List, Patoka River NWR & MA (Continued)

Common Name	Scientific Name	Patoka River	Cane Ridge WMA	Noted in Indiana Comprehensive Wildlife Strategy as Species of Greatest Conservation Need
Common goldeneye	*Bucephala clangula*	✔	✔	
Hooded merganser	*Lophodytes cucullatus*	✔	✔	
Common merganser	*Mergus merganser*	✔		
Ruddy duck	*Oxyura jamaicensis*	✔	✔	
Turkey vulture	*Cathartes aura*	✔	✔	
Osprey	*Pandion haliaetus*	✔	✔	✔
Mississippi kite	*Ictinia mississippiensis*	✔		✔
Golden eagle	*Aquila chrysaetos*		✔	
Bald eagle	*Haliaeetus leucocephalus*	✔	✔	✔
Northern harrier	*Circus cyaneus*	✔	✔	✔
Sharp-shinned hawk	*Accipiter striatus*	✔	✔	✔
Cooper's hawk	*Accipiter cooperii*	✔	✔	
Red-shouldered hawk	*Buteo lineatus*	✔	✔	✔
Broad-winged hawk	*Buteo platypterus*	✔		✔
Red-tailed hawk	*Buteo jamaicensis*	✔	✔	
Rough-legged hawk	*Buteo lagopus*	✔	✔	
American kestrel	*Falco sparverius*	✔	✔	
Merlin	*Falco columbarius*	✔	✔	
Peregrine falcon	*Falco peregrinus*	✔	✔	
Wild turkey	*Meleagris gallopavo*	✔	✔	
Northern bobwhite	*Colinus virginianus*	✔	✔	
King rail	*Rallus elegans*	✔	✔	✔
Yellow rail	*Coturnicops noveboracensis*	✔		
Virginia rail	*Rallus limicola*	✔	✔	✔
Sora	*Porzana carolina*	✔	✔	
Purple gallinule	*Porphyrula martinica*	✔		
Common moorhen	*Gallinula chloropus*	✔	✔	✔
American coot	*Fulica americana*	✔	✔	
Sandhill crane	*Grus canadensis*	✔	✔	✔
Whooping crane	*Grus americana*	✔		✔
Black-bellied plover	*Pluvialis squatarola*	✔	✔	
American golden plover	*Pluvialis dominica*	✔	✔	
Semipalmated plover	*Charadrius semipalmatus*	✔	✔	
Killdeer	*Charadrius vociferus*	✔	✔	
Black-necked stilt	*Himantopus mexicanus*	✔	✔	
American avocet	*Recurvirostra americana*	✔	✔	
Greater yellowlegs	*Tringa melanoleuca*	✔	✔	
Lesser yellowlegs	*Tringa flavipes*	✔	✔	
Solitary sandpiper	*Tringa solitaria*	✔	✔	
Spotted sandpiper	*Actitis macularia*	✔	✔	

Bird Species List, Patoka River NWR & MA (Continued)

Common Name	Scientific Name	Patoka River	Cane Ridge WMA	Noted in Indiana Comprehensive Wildlife Strategy as Species of Greatest Conservation Need
Willet	*Catoptrophorus semipalmatus*		✔	
Ruddy turnstone	*Arenaria interpres*	✔	✔	
Semipalmated sandpiper	*Calidris pusilla*	✔	✔	
Least sandpiper	*Calidris minutilla*	✔	✔	
Pectoral sandpiper	*Calidris melanotos*	✔	✔	
Buff-breasted sandpiper	*Tryngites subruficollis*		✔	
Short-billed dowitcher	*Limnodromus griseus*	✔	✔	
Long-billed dowitcher	*Limnodromus scolopaceus*	✔	✔	
Stilt sandpiper	*Calidris himantopus*		✔	
Common snipe	*Gallinago gallinago*	✔	✔	
American woodcock	*Scolopax minor*	✔		
Wilson's phalarope	*Phalaropus tricolor*	✔	✔	
Bonaparte's gull	*Larus philadelphia*	✔	✔	
Ring-billed gull	*Larus delawarensis*	✔	✔	
Herring gull	*Larus argentatus*		✔	
Caspian tern	*Sterna caspia*		✔	
Common tern	*Sterna hirundo*	✔	✔	
Forster's tern	*Sterna forsteri*	✔	✔	
Least tern	*Sterna antillarum*		✔	✔
Black tern	*Chlidonias niger*	✔	✔	✔
Rock dove	*Columba livia*	✔	✔	
Mourning dove	*Zenaida macroura*	✔	✔	
Black-billed cuckoo	*Coccyzus erythropthalmus*	✔	✔	
Yellow-billed cuckoo	*Coccyzus americanus*	✔	✔	
Barn owl	*Tyto alba*	✔		✔
Eastern screech-owl	*Otus asio*	✔	✔	
Great-horned owl	*Bubo virginianus*	✔	✔	
Barred owl	*Strix varia*	✔	✔	
Short-eared owl	*Asio flammeus*	✔	✔	✔
Common nighthawk	*Cordeiles minor*	✔	✔	✔
Chuck-will's-widow	*Caprimulgus carolinensis*		✔	
Whip-poor-will	*Caprimulgus vociferus*	✔	✔	✔
Chimney swift	*Chaetura pelagica*	✔	✔	
Ruby-throated hummingbird	*Archilochus colubris*	✔	✔	
Belted kingfisher	*Ceryle alcyon*	✔	✔	
Red-headed woodpecker	*Melanerpes erythrocephalus*	✔	✔	
Red-bellied woodpecker	*Melanerpes carolinus*	✔	✔	
Yellow-bellied sapsucker	*Sphyrapicus varius*	✔	✔	
Downy woodpecker	*Picoides pubescens*	✔	✔	
Hairy woodpecker	*Picoides villosus*	✔	✔	

Bird Species List, Patoka River NWR & MA (Continued)

Common Name	Scientific Name	Patoka River	Cane Ridge WMA	Noted in Indiana Comprehensive Wildlife Strategy as Species of Greatest Conservation Need
Northern flicker	*Colaptes auratus*	✔	✔	
Pileated woodpecker	*Dryocopus pileatus*	✔	✔	
Easter wood-pewee	*Contopus virens*	✔	✔	
Yellow-bellied flycatcher	*Empidonax flaviventris*	✔		
Acadian flycatcher	*Empidonax virscens*	✔	✔	
Alder flycatcher	*Empidomax alnorum*	✔		
Willow flycatcher	*Empidomax trailii*	✔	✔	
Least flycatcher	*Empidomax minimus*	✔		
Easter phoebe	*Sayornis phoebe*	✔	✔	
Great crested flycatcher	*Myiarchus crinitus*	✔	✔	
Eastern kingbird	*Tyrannus tyrannus*	✔	✔	
Loggerhead shrike	*Lanius ludovicianus*	✔	✔	✔
White-eyed vireo	*Vireo griseus*	✔	✔	
Bell's vireo	*Vireo bellii*	✔	✔	
Yellow-throated vireo	*Vireo flavifrons*	✔	✔	
Blue-headed vireo	*Vireo solitarius*	✔		
Warbling vireo	*Vireo gilvus*	✔	✔	
Philadelphia vireo	*Vireo philadelphicus*	✔		
Red-eyed vireo	*Vireo olivaceus*	✔	✔	
Blue jay	*Cyanocitta cristata*	✔	✔	
American crow	*Corvus brachyrhynchos*	✔	✔	
Horned lark	*Eremophila alpestris*	✔	✔	
Purple martin	*Progne subis*	✔	✔	
Tree swallow	*Tachycineta bicolor*	✔	✔	
Northern rough-winged swallow	*Stelgidopteryx serripennis*	✔	✔	
Bank swallow	*Riparia riparia*	✔	✔	
Cliff swallow	*Hirundo pyrrhonota*	✔	✔	
Barn swallow	*Hirundo rustica*	✔	✔	
Carolina chickadee	*Parus carolinensis*	✔	✔	
Tufted titmouse	*Parus bicolor*	✔	✔	
Red-breasted nuthatch	*Sitta canadensis*	✔		
White-breasted nuthatch	*Sitta carolinensis*	✔	✔	
Brown creeper	*Certhia americana*	✔	✔	
Marsh wren	*Cistothorus palustris*		✔	✔
Sedge wren	*Cistothorus platensis*		✔	✔
Carolina wren	*Thryothorus ludovicianus*	✔	✔	
House wren	*Troglodytes aedon*	✔	✔	
Winter wren	*Troglodytes troglodytes*	✔	✔	
Golden-crowned kinglet	*Regulus satrapa*	✔	✔	

Bird Species List, Patoka River NWR & MA (Continued)

Common Name	Scientific Name	Patoka River	Cane Ridge WMA	Noted in Indiana Comprehensive Wildlife Strategy as Species of Greatest Conservation Need
Ruby-crowned kinglet	*Regulus calendula*	✔	✔	
Blue-gray gnatcatcher	*Polioptila caerulea*	✔	✔	
Northern wheatear	*Oenanthe oenanthe*	✔		
Eastern bluebird	*Sialia sialis*	✔	✔	
Veery	*Catharus fuscescens*	✔	✔	
Gray-cheeked thrush	*Catharus minimus*	✔	✔	
Swainson's thrush	*Catharus ustulatus*	✔	✔	
Hermit thrush	*Catharus guttatus*	✔	✔	
Wood thrush	*Hylocichla mustelina*	✔	✔	
American robin	*Turdus migratorius*	✔	✔	
Gray catbird	*Dumetella ccarolinensis*	✔	✔	
Northern mockingbird	*Mimus polyglottos*	✔	✔	
Brown thrasher	*Toxostoma rufum*	✔	✔	
European starling	*Sturnus vulgaris*	✔	✔	
American pipit	*Anthus rubescens*	✔	✔	
Cedar waxwing	*Bombycilla cedrorum*	✔	✔	
Blue-winged warbler	*Vermivora pinus*	✔		
Golden-winged warbler	*Vermivora chrysoptera*	✔		✔
Tennessee warbler	*Vermivora peregrina*	✔	✔	
Nashville warbler	*Vermivora ruficapilla*	✔		
Northern parula	*Parula americana*	✔		
Yellow warbler	*Dendroica petechia*	✔	✔	
Chestnut-sided warbler	*Dendroica pensylvanica*	✔		
Magnolia warbler	*Dendroica magnolia*	✔	✔	
Cape May warbler	*Dendroica tigrina*	✔		
Black-throated blue warbler	*Dendroica caerulescens*	✔		
Yellow-rumped warbler	*Dendroica coronata*	✔	✔	
Black-throated green warbler	*Dendroica virens*	✔	✔	
Blackburnian warbler	*Dendroica fusca*	✔		
Yellow-throated warbler	*Dendroica dominica*	✔	✔	
Pine warbler	*Dendroica pinus*	✔		
Prairie warbler	*Dendroica discolor*	✔		
Palm warbler	*Dendroica palmarum*	✔	✔	
Bay-breasted warbler	*Dendroica castanea*	✔		
Blackpoll warbler	*Dendroica striata*	✔		
Cerulean warbler	*Dendroica cerula*	✔		✔
Black-and-white warbler	*Mniotilta varia*	✔	✔	✔
American redstart	*Setophaga ruticilla*	✔	✔	
Prothonotary warbler	*Protonotaria citrea*	✔	✔	
Ovenbird	*Seiurus aurocapillus*	✔	✔	

Bird Species List, Patoka River NWR & MA (Continued)

Common Name	Scientific Name	Patoka River	Cane Ridge WMA	Noted in Indiana Comprehensive Wildlife Strategy as Species of Greatest Conservation Need
Northern waterthrush	*Seiurus noveboracensis*	✔		
Louisiana waterthrush	*Seiurus motacilla*	✔		
Kentucky warbler	*Oporornis formosus*	✔		
Connecticut warbler	*Oporornis agilis*	✔		
Mourning warbler	*Oporornis philadelphia*	✔	✔	
Common yellowthroat	*Geothylpis trichas*	✔	✔	
Hooded warbler	*Wilsonia citrina*	✔		✔
Wilson's warbler	*Wilsonia pusilla*	✔	✔	
Canada warbler	*Wilsonia canadensis*	✔		
Yellow-breasted chat	*Icteria virens*	✔	✔	
Summer tanager	*Piranga rubra*	✔	✔	
Scarlet tanager	*Piranga olivacea*	✔	✔	
Eastern towhee	*Pipilo erythrophthalmus*	✔	✔	
American tree sparrow	*Spizella arborea*	✔	✔	
Chipping sparrow	*Spizella passerina*	✔	✔	
Field sparrow	*Spizella pusilla*	✔	✔	
Vesper sparrow	*Pooecetes gramineus*	✔		
Savannah sparrow	*Passerculus sandwichensis*	✔	✔	
Grasshopper sparrow	*Ammodramus savannarum*	✔	✔	
Henslow's sparrow	*Ammodramus henslowii*	✔		✔
Fox sparrow	*Passerella iliaca*	✔		
Song sparrow	*Melospiza melodia*	✔	✔	
Lincoln's sparrow	*Melospiza lincolnii*	✔	✔	
Swamp sparrow	*Melospiza georgiana*	✔	✔	
White-throated sparrow	*Zonotrichia albicollis*	✔	✔	
White-crowned sparrow	*Zonotrichia leucophrys*	✔	✔	
Dark-eyed junco	*Junco hyemalis*	✔	✔	
Northern cardinal	*Cardinalis cardinalis*	✔	✔	
Rose-breasted grosbeak	*Pheucticus ludovicianus*	✔	✔	
Blue grosbeak	*Guiraca caerulea*	✔	✔	
Indigo bunting	*Passerina cyanea*	✔	✔	
Dickcissel	*Spiza americana*	✔	✔	
Bobolink	*Dolichonyx oryzivorus*	✔	✔	
Red-winged blackbird	*Agelaius phoeniceus*	✔	✔	
Eastern meadowlark	*Sturnella magna*	✔	✔	
Brewer's blackbird	*Euphagus cyanocephalus*	✔	✔	
Rusty blackbird	*Euphagus carolinus*	✔	✔	
Common grackle	*Quiscalus quiscula*	✔	✔	
Brown-headed cowbird	*Molothrus ater*	✔	✔	
Orchard oriole	*Icterus spurius*	✔	✔	

Bird Species List, Patoka River NWR & MA (Continued)

Common Name	Scientific Name	Patoka River	Cane Ridge WMA	Noted in Indiana Comprehensive Wildlife Strategy as Species of Greatest Conservation Need
Baltimore oriole	*Icterus galbula*	✔	✔	
Yellow-headed blackbird	*4anthocephalus xanthocephalus*		✔	✔
Purple finch	*Carpodacus purpureus*	✔	✔	
House finch	*Carpodacus mexicanus*	✔	✔	
Pine siskin	*Carduelis pinus*	✔		
American goldfinch	*Carduelis tristis*	✔	✔	
House sparrow	*Passer domesticus*	✔	✔	

Appendix C: Species Lists

Mammals Known or Expected to Occur in the Patoka River Area

Common Name	Scientific Name	Noted in Indiana Comprehensive Wildlife Strategy as Species of Greatest Conservation Need
Modified from July 1994 Patoka River National Wetlands FEIS, Appendix I		
Virginia opossum	*Didelphis virginiana*	
Southeastern shrew	*Sorest longirostris*	
Short-tailed shrew	*Blarina brevicauda*	
Least shrew	*Cryptotis parva*	
Eastern mole	*Scalopus aquaticus*	
Star-nose mole	*Condylura cristata*	✓
Little brown bat	*Myotis lucifugus*	✓
Indiana bat	*Myotis sodalis*	✓
Eastern pipistrelle	*Pipistrellus subflavus*	✓
Big brown bat	*Eptesicus fuscus*	
Red bat	*Lasiurus borealis*	✓
Hoary bat	*Lasiurus cinereus*	✓
Eastern cottontail rabbit	*Sylvilagus floridanus*	
Swamp rabbit	*Sylvilagus aquaticus*	✓
Eastern chipmunk	*Tamias striatus*	
Woodchuck	*Marmota monax*	
Gray squirrel	*Sciurus carolinensis*	
Fox squirrel	*Sciurus niger*	
Southern flying squirrel	*Glaucomys volans*	
Beaver	*Castor canadensis*	
Deer mouse	*Peromyscus maniculatus*	
White-footed mouse	*peromyscus leucopus*	
Meadow vole	*Microtus pennsylvanicus*	
Prairie vole	*Microtus ochrogaster*	
Woodland vole	*Microtus pinetorum*	
Muskrat	*Ondatra zibethicus*	
Southern bog lemming	*Synaptomys cooperi*	
Norway rat	*Rattus norvegicus*	
House mouse	*Mus musculus*	
Meadow jumping mouse	*Zapus hudsonius*	
Coyote	*Canis latrans*	
Red fox	*Vulpes vulpes*	
Gray fox	*Urocyon Cinereoargenteus*	
Raccoon	*Procyon lotor*	
Long-tailed weasel	*Mustela frenata*	
Mink	*Mustela vison*	
River Otter	*Lutra canadensis*	✓
Badger	*Taxidea taxus*	✓
Striped skunk	*Mephitis mephitis*	
Bobcat	*Felix rufus*	✓
White-tailed deer	*Odocoileus virginianus*	

Herptofauna List, Patoka River NWR & MA

Common Name	Scientific Name	Noted in Indiana Comprehensive Wildlife Strategy as Species of Greatest Conservation Need
Snakes		
Midland water snake	*Nerodia sipedon pleuralis*	
Copperbelly water snake	*Nerodia erythrogaster neglecta*	✔
Diamond-backed water snake	*Nerodia rhombifera*	
Midland brown snake	*Storeria dekayi wrightorum*	
Red-bellied snake	*Storeria occipitomaculata occipitomaculata*	
Eastern garter snake	*Thamnophis sirtalis sirtalis*	
Eastern ribbon snake	*Thamnophis sauritis sauritis*	
Western smooth earth snake	*Virginia valeriae elegans*	
Eastern hognose snake	*Heterodon platirhinos*	
Northern ringneck snake	*Diadophis punctatus edwardsi*	
Midwest worm snake	*Carphophis amoenus helenae*	
Southern black racer	*Coluber constrictor priapus*	
Rough green snake	*Opheodrys aestivus*	✔
Black rat snake	*Elaphe obsoleta obsoleta*	
Black king snake	*Lampropeltis getula niger*	
Prairie king snake	*Lampropeltis calligaster calligaster*	
Red milk snake	*Lampropeltis triangulum syspila*	
Northern copperhead	*Agkistrodon contortrix mokasen*	
Western cottonmouth	*Agkistrodon piscivorus leucostoma*	✔
Mud snake	*Farancia abaevra reinwardtii*	✔
Turtles		
Common snapping turtle	*Chelydra serpentina serpentina*	
Stinkpot	*Sternotherus odoratus*	
Eastern mud turtle	*Kinosternon subrubrum subrubrum*	✔
Map turtle	*Graptemys geographica*	
Midland painted turtle	*Chrysemys picta marginata*	
Red-eared turtle	*Pseudemys scripta elegans*	
Eastern box turtle	*Terrapene carolina carolina*	
Smooth softshell turtle	*Apalone mutica mutica*	
Eastern spiny softshell turtle	*Apalone spinifera spinifera*	
Lizards and Skinks		
Northern fence lizard	*Sceloporus undulatus hyacinthinus*	
Ground skink	*Scincella lateralis*	
Five-lined skink	*Eumeces fasciatus*	

Herptofauna List, Patoka River NWR & MA (Continued)

Common Name	Scientific Name	Noted in Indiana Comprehensive Wildlife Strategy as Species of Greatest Conservation Need
Broad-headed skink	Eumeces laticeps	
Salamanders, Newts, and Sirens		
Mudpuppy	Necturus maculosus	✔
Western lesser siren	Siren intermedia nettingi	
Central newt	Notophthalmus viridescens louisianensis	
Spotted salamander	Ambystoma maculatum	
Small-mouthed salamander	Ambystoma texanum	
Marbled salamander	Ambystoma opacum	
Eastern tiger salamander	Ambystoma tigrinum tigrinum	
Red-backed salamander	Plethodon cinereus cinereus	
Zig-zag salamander	Plethodon dorsalis dorsalis	
Slimy salamander	Plethodon glutinosus glutinosus	
Southern two-lined salamander	Eurycea bislineata bislineata	
Eastern newt	Notophthalmus viridescens viridescens	
Longtail salamander	Eurycea longicauda longicauda	
Toads and Frogs		
Eastern spadefoot	Scaphiopus holbrooki holbrooki	✔
Fowler's toad	Bufo fowleri	
Northern spring peeper	Hyla crucifer crucifer	
Eastern gray tree frog	Hyla versicolor	
Blanchard's cricket frog	Acris crepitans blanchardi	
Western chorus frog	Pseudacris triseriata triseriata	
Southern leopard frog	Rana sphenocephala utricularia	
Northern crayfish frog	Rana areolata circulosa	
Green frog	Rana clamitans melanota	
Wood frog	Rana sylvatica	
Bullfrog	Rana catesbeiana	
Cope's gray treefrog	Hyla chrysoscelis	

Fish Species Occurring in the Patoka River and Its Tributaries

Common Name	Scientific Name	Noted in Indiana Comprehensive Wildlife Strategy as Species of Greatest Conservation Need
Spotted gar	*Lepisosteus oculatus*	
Shortnose gar	*Lepisosteus platostomas*	
Longnose gar	*Lepisosteus ossus*	
Bowfin	*Amia calva*	
Paddlefish	*Polyodon spathula*	
Gizzard shad	*Dorsoma cepedianum*	
Threadfin shad	*Dorsoma petenense*	
Goldeye	*Hiodon alosoides*	
Weed shiner	*Notropis texanus*	
Spotfin shiner	*Cyprinella spiloptera*	
Steelcolor shiner	*Cyprinella whipplei*	
Ribbon shiner	*Lythrurus fumeus*	
River shiner	*Notropis blennius*	
Suckermouth minnow	*Phenocobius mirabilis*	
Bluntnose minnow	*Pimephales notatus*	
Redfin shiner	*Lythrurus umbratilis*	
Shoal chub	*Macrhybopsis hyostomus*	
Golden shiner	*Notemigonus crysoleucas*	
Central stoneroller	*Campostoma anomalum*	
Creek chub	*Semotilus atromaculatus*	
Common carp	*Cyprinus carpio*	
Emerald shiner	*Notropis atherinoides*	
Pallid shiner	*Hybopsis amnis*	✔
Sand shiner	*Notropis stramineus*	
Channel shiner	*Notropis wickliffi*	
Pugnose minnow	*Opsopoeodus emiliae*	
Bullhead minnow	*Pimephales vigilax*	
Silverjaw minnow	*Ericymba buccatta*	
Striped shiner	*Luxilus chrysocephalus*	
Blacknose dace	*Rhinichthys obtusus*	
Fathead minow	*Pimphales promelas*	
Cypress minnow	*Hybognathus hayi*	
Mississippi silvery minnow	*Hybognathus nuchalis*	
Mimic shiner	*Notropis volucellus*	
Southern redbelly dace	*Phoxinus erythrogaster*	
Spotted sucker	*Minytrema melanops*	
Golden redhorse	*Moxostoma erythrurum*	
Silver redhorse	*Moxostoma anisurum*	
Shorthead redhorse	*Moxostoma macrolepidotum*	
River carpsucker	*Carpiodes carpio*	
Quillback	*Carpiodes cyprinus*	

Appendix C: Species Lists

Fish Species Occurring in the Patoka River and Its Tributaries

Common Name	Scientific Name	Noted in Indiana Comprehensive Wildlife Strategy as Species of Greatest Conservation Need
Highfin carpsucker	*Carpiodes velifer*	
Smallmouth buffalo	*Ictiobus bubalus*	
Largemouth buffalo	*Ictiobus cyprinella*	
Black buffalo	*Ictiobus niger*	
White sucker	*Catostomus commersonii*	
Creek chubsucker	*Erimyzon oblongus*	
Lake chubsucker	*Erimyzon sucetta*	
Flathead catfish	*Pylodiotis olivaris*	
Channel catfish	*Ictalurus punctatus*	
Stonecat	*Noturus flavus*	
Tadpole madtom	*Noturus gyrinus*	
Brindled madtom	*Noturus miurus*	
Yellow bullhead	*Ameiurus natalis*	
Brown bullhead	*Ameiurus nebulosus*	
Black bullhead	*Ameiurus melas*	
Grass pickerel	*Esox americanus*	
Northern pike	*Esox lucius*	
Central mudminnow	*Umbra limi*	
Pirate perch	*Aphredoderus sayanus*	
Blackstripe topminnow	*Fundulus notatus*	
Starhead topminnow	*Fundulus dispar*	
Western mosquitofish	*Gambusia affinis*	
Brook silverside	*Labidesthes sicculus*	
Rock bass	*Ambloplites rupestris*	
Flier	*Centrarchus macropterus*	
Green sunfish	*Lepomis cyanellus*	
Longear sunfish	*Lepomis megalotis*	
Orangespotted sunfish	*Lepomis humilis*	
Bluegill	*Lepomis macrochirus*	
Redear sunfish	*Lepomis microlophus*	
Warmouth	*Lepomis gulosus*	
Redspotted sunfish	*Lepomis miniatus*	
Smallmouth bass	*Micropterus dolomieu*	
Spotted bass	*Micropterus punctulatus*	
Largemouth bass	*Micropterus salmoides*	
White crappie	*Pomoxis annularis*	
Black crappie	*Pomoxis nigromaculatus*	
White bass	*Morone chrysops*	
Yellow bass	*Morone mississippiensis*	
Mud darter	*Etheostoma asprigene*	
Rainbow darter	*Etheostoma caeruleum*	

Fish Species Occurring in the Patoka River and Its Tributaries

Common Name	Scientific Name	Noted in Indiana Comprehensive Wildlife Strategy as Species of Greatest Conservation Need
Bluntnose darter	*Etheostoma chlorosoma*	
Harlequin darter	*Etheostoma histrio*	
Slough darter	*Etheostoma gracile*	
Johnny darter	*Etheostoma nigrum*	
Orangethroat darter	*Etheostoma spectabile*	
Logperch	*Percina caprodes*	
Blackside darter	*percina maculata*	
Slenderhead darter	*Percina phoxocephala*	
Dusky darter	*Percina sciera*	
River darter	*Percina shumardi*	
Saddleback darter	*Percina vigil*	
Sauger	*Sander canadense*	
Freshwater drum	*Aplodinotus grunniens*	
Banded sculpin	*Cottus carolinae*	
Silver carp	*Hypophthalmichthys molitrix*	
Grass carp	*Ctenopharyngodon idella*	
Bighead carp	*Hypophthalmichthys nobilis*	
Blue catfish	*Ictalurus furcatus*	
Crustacean Species		
Calico crayfish	*Orconectes immunis*	
Indiana crayfish	*Orconectes indianensis*	
Northern clearwater crayfish	*Orconectes propinquus*	
Northern cave crayfish	*Orconectes inermis inermis*	
White River crayfish	*Procambarus acutus*	
Painted-hand mudbug	*Cambarus polychromatus*	
Great Plains mudbug	*Cambarus (Lacunicambarus) species A*	
Karst crsyfish	*Cambarus laevis*	
Mississippi grass shrimp	*Palaemonetes kadiakensis*	
Cavespring crayfish	*Cambarus tenebrosus*	
Digger crayfish	*Fallicambarus fodiens*	
Reproduced from July 1994 Patoka River National Wetlands FEIS, Appendix I Modified by Tom Simon (USFWS) & Dan Carnahan (Indiana DNR), April, 2007		

Appendix C: Species Lists

Fresh Water Mussels Found on Patoka River MWR/MA

Common Name	Scientific Name
Threeridge	*Amblema p. plicata*
Flat Floater	*Anodonta suborbiculata*
Rock Pocketbook	*Arcidens confragosus*
Wabash Pigtoe	*Fusconaia flava*
Fatmucket	*Lampsilis siliquoidea*
Yellow Sandshell	*Lampsilis teres*
White Heelsplitter	*Lasmigona c. complanata*
Fragile Papershell	*Leptodea fragilis*
Washboard	*Megalonaias nervosa*
Pink Heelsplitter	*Potamilus alatus*
Pink Papershell	*Potamilus ohiensis*
Giant Floater	*Pyganodon grandis*
Pimpleback	*Quadrula p. pustulosa*
Mapleleaf	*Quadrula quadrula*
Pistolgrip	*Tritogonia verrucosa*
Deertoe	*Truncilla truncata*
Pondhorn	*Uniomerus tetralasmus*

Plant List, Patoka River NWR & MA

Common Name	Scientific Name
American elm	*Ulmus americana*
Black gum	*Nyssa sylvatica*
Black haw	*Viburnum prunifolium*
Black willow	*Salix nigra*
Boneset	*Eupatorium serotinum*
Box elder	*Acer negundo*
Broadleaf uniola	*Chasmanthemum latifolium*
Bugleweed	*Lycopus rubellus*
Calico aster	*Aster lateriflorus*
Cardinal flower	*Lobelia cardinalis*
Catbird grape	*Vitis cinerea*
Catchfly grass	*Leersia lenticularis*
Cherrybark oak	*Quercus falcata var. pagodaefolia*
Clearweed	*Pilea pumila*
Common persimmon	*Diospyros virginiana*
Ditch stonecrop	*Penthorum sedoides*
Dogbane	*Trachelospermum difforme*
Eastern cottonwood	*Populus deltoides*
False nettle	*Boehmeria cylindrica*
Fleabane	*Pluchea camphorate*
Frog fruit	*Phyla lanceolata*
Green ash	*Fraxinus pennsylvanica*
Greenbrier	*Smilax hispida*
Groundnut	*Apios americana*
Hackberry	*Celtis occidentalis*
Kingnut hickory	*Carya laciniosa*
Lizard's tail	*Saururus cernuus*
Louisiana sedge	*Carex louisianica*
Mad-dog skullcap	*Scutellaria lateriflora*
Milkweed	*Asclepias perennis*
Moneywort	*Lysimachia nummularia*
Moonseed	*Menispermum canadensis*
Nettle	*Laportea canadensis*
Pecan	*Carya illinoensis*
Pin oak	*Quercus palustris*
Poison ivy	*Rhus radicans*
Purple fringeless orchid	*Platanthera peramoena*
Ragwort	*Senecio glabellus*

Plant List, Patoka River NWR & MA (Continued)

Common Name	Scientific Name
Red maple	Acer rubrum
River birch	Betula nigra
Sedge	Carex muskingumensis
Sedge	Carex squarrosa
Sedge	Carex intumescens
Sedge	Carex tribuloides
Sedge	Carex grayi
Sedge	Carex lupulina
Sensitive fern	Onoclea sensibilis
Shumard oak	Quercus shumardii
Silver maple	Acer saccharinum
Small white aster	Aster vimineus
Smooth buttonweed	Spermacoce glabra
Swamp chestnut oak	Quercus michauxii
Swamp white oak	Quercus bicolor
Sweetgum	Liquidambar styraciflua
Sycamore	Platanus occidentalis
Trumpet creeper	Campsis radicans
Virginia dayflower	Commelina virginica
Water parsnip	Sium suave
Winged monkey flower	Mimulus alatus
Woodreed	Cinna arundinacea
Emergent Wetland Communities--selected plant species	
American snowbell	Styrax americana
Barnyard grass	Echinochloa crus-galli
Beggarticks	Bidens discoidea
Beggarticks	Bidens frondosa
Beggarticks	Bidens tripartita
Blunt spikerush	Eleocharis obtusa
Buttonbush	Cephalanthus occidentalis
Cattail	Typha latifolia
Catchfly grass	Leersia lenticularis
Clammy hedge hysop	Gratiola neglecta
Clearweed	Pilea pumila
Common bladderwort	Utricularia vulgaris
Common arrowhead	Sagittaria latifolia
Creeping eragrostis	Eragrostis hypnoides

Plant List, Patoka River NWR & MA (Continued)

Common Name	Scientific Name
Cyperus	*Cyperus ferruginescens*
Cyperus	*Cyperus erythrorhizos*
Dayflower	*Commelina diffusa*
Ditch stonecrop	*Penthorum sedoides*
Duckweed	*Lemna spp.*
Fall panicum	*Panicum dichotomiflorum*
False pimpernel	*Lindernia dubia*
False nettle	*Boehmeria cylindrica*
Featherfoil	*Hottonia inflata*
Fleabane	*Pluchea camphorata*
Frog fruit	*Phyla lanceolata*
Grass-leaved arrowhead	*Sagittaria graminea*
Greater duckweed	*Spirodela polyrhiza*
Hornwort	*Ceratophyllum demersum*
Humped bladderwort	*Utricularia gibba*
India heliotrope	*Heliotropium indicum*
Lizard's tail	*Saururus cernuus*
Long beak arrowhead	*Sagittaria australis*
Loosestrife	*Rotata ramosior*
Mad-dog skullcap	*Scutellaria lateriflora*
Mermaid weed	*Proserpinaca palustris*
Mild water pepper	*Polygonum hydropiperoides*
Nodding bur marigold	*Bidens cernua*
Nodding smartweed	*Polygonum lapathifolium*
Panicum	*Panicum agrosticoides*
Paspalum	*Paspalum fluitans*
Pink knotweed	*Polygonum pennsylvanicum*
Pumpkin ash	*Fraxinus tomentosa*
Rice cutgrass	*Leersia oryzoides*
Scarlet ammannia	*Ammannia coccinea*
Short beak arrowhead	*Sagittaria brevirostra*
Small water plantain	*Alisma subcordatum*
Smooth buttonweed	*Spermacoce glabra*
Southern pond lily	*Nuphar advena*
St. John's-wort	*Hypericum mutabile*
Swamp cottonwood	*Populus heterophylla*
Swamp loosestrife	*Decodon verticillatus*
Swamp privet	*Forestiera acuminata*

Plant List, Patoka River NWR & MA (Continued)

Common Name	Scientific Name
Swamp dock	Rumex verticillatus
Virginia dayflower	Commelina virginiana
Water starwort	Callitriche heterophylla
Water-plantain	Lophotocarpus calycinus
Water-purslane	Didiplis diandra
Water-purslane	Ludwigia palustris
Whitegrass	Leersia virginica
Wolffia	Wolffia spp.
Yellow water buttercup	Ranunculus flabellaris
Yerba de tajo	Eclipta alba
Upland Forest Community--selected plant species	
American beech	Fagus grandifolia
American elm	Ulmus americana
Basswood	Tilia americana
Bitternut hickory	Carya cordiformis
Black cherry	Prunus serotina
Black oak	Quercus velutina
Black locust	Robinia pseudoacacia
Black gum	Nyssa sylvatica
Black walnut	Juglans nigra
Black ash	Fraxinus nigra
Bladdernut	Staphylea trifolia
Blue beech	Carpinus caroliniana
Butternut	Juglans cinerea
Catalpa	Catalpa speciosa
Chestnut oak	Quercus montana
Chinkapin oak	Quercus muehlenbergii
Downy serviceberry	Amelanchier arborea
Eastern red cedar	Juniperus virginiana
Flowering dogwood	Cornus florida
Hackberry	Celtis occidentalis
Hawthorne	Crataegus spp.
Honey locust	Gleditsia triacanthos
Ironwood	Ostrya virginiana
Jack pine	Pinus banksiana
Kentucky coffeetree	Gymnocladus dioicus
Mockernut hickory	Carya glabra

Plant List, Patoka River NWR & MA (Continued)

Common Name	Scientific Name
Northern red oak	*Quercus rubra*
Ohio buckeye	*Aesculus glabra*
Osage-orange	*Maclura pomifera*
Pawpaw	*Asimina triloba*
Persimmon	*Diospyros virginiana*
Pignut hickory	*Carya glabra*
Post oak	*Quercus stellata*
Red mulberry	*Morus rubra*
Red maple	*Acer rubrum*
Red pine	*Pinus resinosa*
Redbud	*Cercis canadensis*
Sassafras	*Sassafras albidum*
Scarlet oak	*Quercus coccinea*
Scotch pine	*Pinus sylvestris*
Shagbark hickory	*Carya ovata*
Shellbark hickory	*Carya laciniosa*
Shingle oak	*Quercus imbricaria*
Southern red oak	*Ouercus falcata*
Spicebush	*Lindera benzoin*
Staghorn sumac	*Rhus typhina*
Sugar maple	*Acer saccharum*
Sycamore	*Platanus occidentalis*
White pine	*Pinus strobus*
White oak	*Quercus alba*
White ash	*Fraxinus americana*
Witch-hazel	*Hamamelis virginiana*
Yellow poplar	*Liriodendron tulipifera*

Appendix D: Resource Conservation Priorities, Ohio River Valley Ecosystem

Resource Conservation Priorities, Ohio River Valley Ecosystem[1]

Common Name	Scientific Name	Documented on Refuge	Noted in Indiana Comprehensive Wildlife Strategy as Species of Greatest Conservation Need
Amphibians			
Hellbender	Cryptobranchus allenganiensis		
Arachnids			
Pseudoscorpion (no common name)	Apochthonous hobbsi		
Birds			
Acadian flycatcher	Empidonax virescens	✔	
American woodcock	Scolopax minor	✔	
Bachman's sparrow	Aimophila aestivalis		
Bald eagle	Haliaeetus leucocephalus	✔	✔
Barn owl	Tyto alba	✔	✔
Bell's vireo	Vireo bellii	✔	
Bewick's wren	Thryomanes bewickii		
Black-billed Cuckoo	Coccyzus erythropthalmus	✔	
Blue-winged warbler	Vermivora pinus	✔	
Buff-breasted sandpiper	Tryngites subruficollis	✔	
Canada goose - Giant population	Branta canadensis	✔	
Canada goose - Southern James Bay population	Branta canadensis	✔	
Canada goose - resident giants	Branta canadensis	✔	
Cerulean warbler	Dendroica cerulea	✔	✔
Chuck-will's-widow	Caprimulgus carolinensis	✔	
Common moorhen	Gallinula chloropus	✔	✔
Dickcissel	Spiza americana	✔	
Field sparrow	Spizella pusilla	✔	
Golden-winged warbler	Vermivora chrysoptera	✔	✔
Grasshopper sparrow	Ammodramus savannarum	✔	
Greater yellowlegs	Tringa melanoleuca	✔	
Henslow's sparrow	Ammodramus henslowii	✔	✔
Kentucky warbler	Oporornis formosus	✔	
King rail	Rallus elegans	✔	✔
Loggerhead shrike	Lanius ludovicianus	✔	
Long-eared owl	Asio otus	✔	
Louisiana waterthrush	Seiurus motacilla	✔	
Mallard	Anas platyrhynchos	✔	

Resource Conservation Priorities, Ohio River Valley Ecosystem[1]

Common Name	Scientific Name	Documented on Refuge	Noted in Indiana Comprehensive Wildlife Strategy as Species of Greatest Conservation Need
Northern flicker	*Colaptes auratus*	✔	
Northern harrier	*Circus cyaneus*	✔	✔
Orchard oriole	*Icterus spurius*	✔	
Peregrine Falcon	*Falco peregrinis anatum*	✔	✔
Prairie warbler	*Dendroica discolor*	✔	
Prothonotary warbler	*Protonotaria citrea*	✔	
Red-headed woodpecker	*Melanerpes erythrocephalus*	✔	
Red-shouldered hawk	*Buteo lineatus*	✔	✔
Rusty blackbird	*Euphagus carolinus*	✔	
Short-billed dowitcher	*Limnodromus griseus*	✔	
Short-eared owl	*Asio flammeus*	✔	✔
Stilt sandpiper	*Calidris himantopus*	✔	
Swainson's warbler	*Limnothylpis swainsonii*		
Upland sandpiper	*Bartramia longicauda*		✔
Whip-poor-will	*Caprimulgus vociferus*	✔	✔
Whooping crane - Eastern population	*Grus americana*	✔	
Wood duck	*Aix sponsa*	✔	
Wood thrush	*Hylocichla mustelina*	✔	
Worm-eating warbler	*Helmitheros vermivorus*		✔
Crustaceans			
Crayfish (O. illinoisensis)	*Orconectes illinoisensis*		
Crayfish (O. inermis testii)	*Orconectes inermis testii*		✔
Crayfish (O. kentuckiensis)	*Orconectes kentuckiensis*		
Crayfish (O. sloanii)	*Orconectes sloanii*		
Crayfish (O. stannardi)	*Orconectes stannardi*		
Indiana crayfish	*Orconectes indianensis*	✔	✔
Rusty crayfish	*Orconectes rusticus*		
Fish			
Bighead carp	*Hypophthalmichthys nobilis*	✔	
Blue sucker	*Cycleptus elongatus*		
Eastern sand darter	*Ammocrypta pellucida*		
Grass carp	*Ctenopharyngodon idella*	✔	
Lake sturgeon - Inland population	*Acipenser fulvescens*		✔
Logperch (P. evermanni)	*Percina evermanni*		
Logperch (P. manitou)	*Percina manitou*		

Resource Conservation Priorities, Ohio River Valley Ecosystem[1]

Common Name	Scientific Name	Documented on Refuge	Noted in Indiana Comprehensive Wildlife Strategy as Species of Greatest Conservation Need
Longhead darter	*Percina macrocephala*		
Northern cavefish	*Amblyopsis spelaea*		✔
Paddlefish	*Polyodon spathula*	✔	
Scioto madtom	*Noturus trautmani*		
Shovelnose sturgeon	*Scaphirhynchus platorynchus*		
Spotted darter	*Etheostoma maculatum*		✔
Insects			
Kramer's cave beetle	*Pseudanophthalums krameri*		
Ohio cave beetle	*Pseudanophthalums ohioensis*		
Wabash belted skimmer	*Macaromia wabashensis*		
Mammals			
Gray bat	*Myotis grisescens*		✔
Indiana Bat	*Myotis sodalis*	✔	✔
Mussels			
Asiatic clam	*Corbicula fluminea*		
Black sandshell	*Ligumia recta*		
Clubshell	*Pleurobema clava*		✔
Elktoe	*Alasmidonta marginata*		
Fanshell	*Cyprogenia stegaria*		✔
Mapleleaf	*Quadrula quadrula*	✔	
Monkeyface	*Quadrula metanevra*		
Northern riffleshell	*Epioblasma rangiana*		✔
Orange-foot pimpleback	*Plethobasus cooperianus*		✔
Pimpleback	*Quadrula pustulosa*	✔	
Pink mucket pearlymussel	*Lampsilis abrupta*		✔
Pistolgrip	*Tritogonia verrucosa*	✔	
Purple cat's paw pearlymussel	*Epioblasma obliquata obliquata*		
Rabbit's foot	*Quadrula cylindrica cylindrica*		✔
Ring pink mussel (=golf stick)	*Obovaria retusa*		
Rock pocketbook	*Arcidens confragosus*	✔	
Rough pigtoe	*Pleurobema plenum*		✔
Round pigtoe	*Pleurobema coccineum*		
Salamander mussel	*Simpsonaias ambigua*		✔
Scaleshell mussel	*Leptodea leptodon*		

Resource Conservation Priorities, Ohio River Valley Ecosystem[1]

Common Name	Scientific Name	Documented on Refuge	Noted in Indiana Comprehensive Wildlife Strategy as Species of Greatest Conservation Need
Sheepnose	*Plethobasus cyphyus*		✔
Slippershell	*Alasmidonta viridis*		
Snuffbox	*Epioblasma triquetra*		✔
Spectaclecase	*Cumberlandi mondonta*		
Threeridge	*Amblema plicata*	✔	
Tubercled-blossom pearlymussel	*Epioblasma torulosa torulosa*		✔
Washboard	*Megalonaias nervosa*	✔	
White cat's paw pearlymussel	*Epioblasma obliquata*		✔
White wartyback mussel	*Plethobasus cicatricosus*		✔
Zebra mussel	*Dreissena polymorpha*		
Plants			
Earleaf foxglove	*Agalinus auriculata*		
Eastern prairie fringed orchid	*Platanthera leucophaea*		
Glade (Darlington's) spurge	*Eurphorbia purpurea*		
Hall's bulrush	*Schoenoplectus hallii*		
Northern wild monkshood	*Aconitum noveboracense*		
Running buffalo clover	*Trifollium stoloniferum*		
Short's bladderpod	*Lesquerella globosa*		
Small whorled pagonia	*Isotria medeoloides*		
Virnigia spirea	*Spiraea virginiana*		
Reptiles			
Copperbelly watersnake - S pop.	*Nerodia erythrogaster neglecta*	✔	✔
Eastern massasauga	*Sistrurus catenatus catenatus*		
Timber rattlesnake	*Crotalus horridus*		✔

1. Source: U.S. Fish & Wildlife Service. *Fish & Wildlife Conservation Priorities, Region 3*, January 2002.

Appendix E: Compliance Requirements

Appendix E / Compliance Requirements

Rivers and Harbor Act (1899) (33 U.S.C. 403)

Section 10 of this Act requires the authorization by the U.S. Army Corps of Engineers prior to any work in, on, over, or under a navigable water of the United States.

Antiquities Act (1906)

Authorizes the scientific investigation of antiquities on Federal land and provides penalties for unauthorized removal of objects taken or collected without a permit.

Migratory Bird Treaty Act (1918)

Designates the protection of migratory birds as a Federal responsibility. This Act enables the setting of seasons, and other regulations including the closing of areas, Federal or non Federal, to the hunting of migratory birds.

Migratory Bird Conservation Act (1929)

Establishes procedures for acquisition by purchase, rental, or gift of areas approved by the Migratory Bird Conservation Commission.

Fish and Wildlife Coordination Act (1934), as amended

Requires that the Fish and Wildlife Service and State fish and wildlife agencies be consulted whenever water is to be impounded, diverted or modified under a Federal permit or license. The Service and State agency recommend measures to prevent the loss of biological resources, or to mitigate or compensate for the damage. The project proponent must take biological resource values into account and adopt justifiable protection measures to obtain maximum overall project benefits. A 1958 amendment added provisions to recognize the vital contribution of wildlife resources to the Nation and to require equal consideration and coordination of wildlife conservation with other water resources development programs. It also authorized the Secretary of Interior to provide public fishing areas and accept donations of lands and funds.

Migratory Bird Hunting and Conservation Stamp Act (1934)

Requires every waterfowl hunter 16 years of age or older to carry a stamp and earmarks proceeds of the Duck Stamps to buy or lease waterfowl habitat. A 1958 amendment authorizes the acquisition of small wetland and pothole areas to be designated as 'Waterfowl Production Areas,' which may be acquired without the limitations and requirements of the Migratory Bird Conservation Act.

Historic Sites, Buildings and Antiquities Act (1935), as amended

Declares it a national policy to preserve historic sites and objects of national significance, including those located on refuges. Provides procedures for designation, acquisition, administration, and protection of such sites.

Refuge Revenue Sharing Act (1935), as amended:

Requires revenue sharing provisions to all fee-title ownerships that are administered solely or primarily by the Secretary through the Service.

Transfer of Certain Real Property for Wildlife Conservation Purposes Act (1948)

Provides that upon a determination by the Administrator of the General Services Administration, real property no longer needed by a Federal agency can be transferred without reimbursement to the Secretary of Interior if the land has particular value for migratory birds, or to a State agency for other wildlife conservation purposes.

Federal Records Act (1950)

Directs the preservation of evidence of the government's organization, functions, policies, decisions, operations, and activities, as well as basic historical and other information.

Fish and Wildlife Act (1956)

Established a comprehensive national fish and wildlife policy and broadened the authority for acquisition and development of refuges.

Refuge Recreation Act (1962)

Allows the use of refuges for recreation when such uses are compatible with the refuge's primary purposes and when sufficient funds are available to manage the uses.

Wilderness Act (1964), as amended

Directed the Secretary of Interior, within 10 years, to review every roadless area of 5,000 or more acres and every roadless island (regardless of size) within National Wildlife Refuge and National Park Systems and to recommend to the President the suitability of each such area or island for inclusion in the National Wilderness Preservation System, with final decisions made by Congress. The Secretary of Agriculture was directed to study and recommend suitable areas in the National Forest System.

Land and Water Conservation Fund Act (1965):

Uses the receipts from the sale of surplus Federal land, outer continental shelf oil and gas sales, and other sources for land acquisition under several authorities.

National Wildlife Refuge System Administration Act (1966), as amended by the National Wildlife Refuge System Improvement Act (1997) 16 U.S.C. 668dd668ee. (Refuge Administration Act)

Defines the National Wildlife Refuge System and authorizes the Secretary to permit any use of a refuge provided such use is compatible with the major purposes for which the refuge was established. The Refuge Improvement Act clearly defines a unifying mission for the Refuge System; establishes the legitimacy and appropriateness of the six priority public uses (hunting, fishing, wildlife observation and photography, or environmental education and interpretation); establishes a formal process for determining compatibility; established the responsibilities of the Secretary of Interior for managing and protecting the System; and requires a Comprehensive Conservation Plan for each refuge by the year 2012. This Act amended portions of the Refuge Recreation Act and National Wildlife Refuge System Administration Act of 1966.

National Historic Preservation Act (1966), as amended:

Establishes as policy that the Federal Government is to provide leadership in the preservation of the nation's prehistoric and historic resources.

Architectural Barriers Act (1968)

Requires federally owned, leased, or funded buildings and facilities to be accessible to persons with disabilities.

National Environmental Policy Act (1969)

Requires the disclosure of the environmental impacts of any major Federal action significantly affecting the quality of the human environment.

Uniform Relocation and Assistance and Real Property Acquisition Policies Act (1970), as amended:

Provides for uniform and equitable treatment of persons who sell their homes, businesses, or farms to the Service. The Act requires that any purchase offer be no less than the fair market value of the property.

Endangered Species Act (1973)

Requires all Federal agencies to carry out programs for the conservation of endangered and threatened species.

Rehabilitation Act (1973)

Requires programmatic accessibility in addition to physical accessibility for all facilities and programs funded by the Federal government to ensure that anybody can participate in any program.

Archaeological and Historic Preservation Act (1974)

Directs the preservation of historic and archaeological data in Federal construction projects.

Clean Water Act (1977)

Requires consultation with the Corps of Engineers (404 permits) for major wetland modifications.

Surface Mining Control and Reclamation Act (1977) as amended (Public Law 95-87) (SMCRA)

Regulates surface mining activities and reclamation of coal-mined lands. Further regulates the coal industry by designating certain areas as unsuitable for coal mining operations.

Executive Order 11988 (1977)

Each Federal agency shall provide leadership and take action to reduce the risk of flood loss and minimize the impact of floods on human safety, and preserve the natural and beneficial values served by the floodplains.

Appendix E: Compliance Requirements

National Trails System Act

Assigns responsibility to the Secretary of Interior and thus the Service to protect the historic and recreational values of congressionally designated National Historic Trail sites.

Treasury and General Government Appropriations Act of 2001 (Public Law 106-554)

In December 2002, Congress required federal agencies to publish their own guidelines for ensuring and maximizing the quality, objectivity, utility, and integrity of information that they disseminate to the public (44 U.S.C. 3502). The amended language is included in Section 515(a). The Office of Budget and Management (OMB) directed agencies to develop their own guidelines to address the requirements of the law. The Department of the Interior instructed bureaus to prepare separate guidelines on how they would apply the Act. The U.S. Fish and Wildlife Service has developed "Information Quality Guidelines" to address the law.

Cultural Resources and Historic Preservation

The National Wildlife Refuge System Improvement Act of 1997, Section 6, requires the Service to make a determination of compatibility of existing, new and changing uses of Refuge land; and Section 7 requires the Service to identify and describe the archaeological and cultural values of the refuge.

The National Historic Preservation Act (NHPA), Section 106, requires Federal agencies to consider impacts their undertakings could have on historic properties; Section 110 requires Federal agencies to manage historic properties, e.g., to document historic properties prior to destruction or damage; Section 101 requires Federal agencies consider Indian tribal values in historic preservation programs, and requires each Federal agency to establish a program leading to inventory of all historic properties on its land.

The Archaeological Resources Protection Act of 1979 (ARPA) prohibits unauthorized disturbance of archeological resources on Federal and Indian land; and other matters. Section 10 requires establishing "a program to increase public awareness" of archeological resources. Section 14 requires plans to survey lands and a schedule for surveying lands with "the most scientifically valuable archaeological resources." This Act requires protection of all archeological sites more than 100 years old (not just sites meeting the criteria for the National Register) on Federal land, and requires archeological investigations on Federal land be performed in the public interest by qualified persons.

The Native American Graves Protection and Repatriation Act of 1990 (NAGPRA) imposes serious delays on a project when human remains or other cultural items are encountered in the absence of a plan.

The American Indian Religious Freedom Act (AIRFA) iterates the right of Native Americans to free exercise of traditional religions and use of sacred places.

EO 13007, Indian Sacred Sites (1996), directs Federal agencies to accommodate access to and ceremonial use, to avoid adverse effects and avoid blocking access, and to enter into early consultation.

Appendix F: Mailing List

- Executive Director, Pike County Chamber of Commerce
- Executive Director, Princeton Area Chamber of Commerce, Gibson County
- Executive Director, Warrick County Chamber of Commerce, Warrick County
- Executive Director, Evansville Convention & Tourism Bureau, Vanderburgh County
- Executive Director, Gibson County Visitors & Tourism Bureau, Gibson County
- Executive Director, Vincennes/Knox County Convention and Visitors, Knox County
- Jasper Chamber of Commerce
- Gibson County Commissioners
- Gibson County Council
- Oakland City Mayor
- Pike County Commissioners
- Pike County Council
- Columbia Township Fire Department
- Francisco Volunteer Fire Department
- Gibson County Courthouse
- Gibson County Visitors & Tourism Bureau
- Hoosier Environmental Council
- Huntingburg Chamber of Commerce, Dubois County
- Jefferson Township Fire Department
- Lockhart Township Fire Department
- Petersburg Volunteer Fire Department
- Pike County Commissioners
- Union Community Volunteer Fire Department

Libraries

- Petersburg, Indiana
- Huntingburg, Indiana
- Princeton, Indiana
- Oakland City, Indiana

Business

- Alliance Coal, LLC
- Americal Real Estate Inc
- American Acres Inc.
- Bernardin-Lochmueller And Associates
- Brookston Resources Inc
- Broshears Realty
- C/O Locust Street Company Inc - Attn: William Muller
- Charity Farm
- Dan's Fence Company
- Duke Energy, Environmental Services
- Four Rivers Rc&D
- Gibson County Coal, LLC
- Gilbert J Rode & Sons Inc
- Heritage Realty LLC
- Hopper Resources Inc
- Jasper Engines & Transmissions
- JDH Contracting Inc
- Jerry Aigner Construction Inc
- Landmark Archaeological & Environmental Services Inc
- Lechner's Inc
- McCormick Farms Inc
- Mesker Park Zoo & Botanic Garden
- Morgan Backhoe Service
- Multi Resource Management, Inc.
- Mulzer Crushed Stone Inc.
- Nature Preserves
- Old National Bank
- Owensville Montgomery TFP District
- Peabody Energy
- Quality Climate Control
- R&T Garage
- Ryan Kerns Excavating LLC
- Solar Sources, Inc
- Southern RR Company
- Tri State Equipment
- Triad Mining
- Triad Mining, Inc
- Velpen C&D Fill Site Inc
- Velpen Trucking & Disposal Company Inc
- Vincennes Sun-Commercial
- Wyatt Seed Company Inc.

Non-Government Organizations

- Audubon Society
- Audubon Society of the District of Columbia
- Evansville Audubon Society
- Defenders of Wildlife
- Ducks Unlimited

Appendix H: List of Preparers

Name	Title/Contribution	Degrees/Other Related Experience	Years with FWS
Indiana Department of Natural Resources			
Jeff Thompson	District Wildlife Biologist	Not Available	N/A
Mangi Environmental Group			
Leon Kolankiewicz	Biologist/Environmental Planner Direct Planning Effort, Writing	B.S., Wildlife Management, Virginia Tech, Blacksburg. M.S., Natural Resources Management & Environmental Planning, University of British Columbia, Vancouver. Other: 25 years as an a conservation professional including experience with U.S. Fish and Wildlife Service, Alaska Department of Environmental Conservation, Alaska Department of Fish and Game, University of Washington, National Marine Fisheries Service, Peace Corps, Orange County (CA) Environmental Management Agency, Carrying Capacity Network.	N/A

University of Missouri-Columbia, Gaylord Memorial Laboratory, Special Publication No. 10, Puxico, Missouri, USA.

Helmers D.L. 1992. Shorebird management manual. Western Hemisphere Shorebird Reserve Network, Manomet, Mass. 58 p.

Homoya, M.A., D.B. Abrell, J.R. Aldrich and T.W. Post. 1995. Natural Regions of Indiana. Indiana Academy of Science. Vol. 94:245-268.

Indiana Department of Environmental Management (IDEM). 2006a. Indiana Integrated Water Monitoring and Assessment Report 2006. Office of Water Quality Watershed Branch.

Indiana Department of Environmental Management (IDEM) website. 2006b.

http://www.in.gov/idem/programs/water/303d/index.html [Accessed November 14, 2006]

Indiana Department of Geology and Natural Resources. 1898. Twenty-third Annual Report.

Indiana Department of Natural Resources. No date-a. Sugar Ridge Fish & Wildlife Area. Accessed at: http://www.in.gov/dnr/fish-wild/publications/sugar.htm on the World Wide Web on 2-20-06.

Indiana Department of Natural Resources. No date-b. Glendale Fish & Wildlife Area. Accessed at: http://www.in.gov/dnr/fish-wild/publications/glendale.htm on the World Wide Web on 2-20-06.

Indiana Department of Natural Resources. 1988. Wetlands – Indiana's Endangered Natural Resource. Appendix to Indiana Outdoor Recreation 1989: An Assessment and Policy Plan. Indianapolis, Indiana.

Indiana Department of Natural Resources. 1990. Hydrogeology of Gibson County, Indiana.

Indiana Department of Natural Resources. 2005a. Division of Forestry. Pike State Forest. Accessed on the World Wide Web on 2-20-06 at: http://www.in.gov/dnr/forestry/index.html?http://www.in.gov/dnr/forestry/stateforests/pike.htm&2

Indiana Department of Natural Resources. 2005b. Division of Forestry. Ferdinand State Forest. Accessed on the World Wide Web on 2-20-06 at: http://www.in.gov/dnr/forestry/index.html?http://www.in.gov/dnr/forestry/stateforests/ferdind.htm&2

Indiana Division of Nature Preserves. 2005a. Indiana Department of Natural Resources. List of Endangered, Threatened, and Rare Species by County: Gibson County. 11-22-05. Accessed 12-13-06 on the World Wide Web at: http://www.in.gov/dnr/naturepr/species/gibson.pdf.

Indiana Division of Nature Preserves. 2005b. Indiana Department of Natural Resources. List of Endangered, Threatened, and Rare Species by County: Pike County. 11-22-05. Accessed 12-13-06 on the World Wide Web at: http://www.in.gov/dnr/naturepr/species/pike.pdf.

Indiana WETlands. 2004. Data and Information. Accessed online on 14 February 2006 at: http://www.in.gov/wetlands/data/index.html.

King, Thomas F. Cultural Resource Laws & Practice 1998: AltaMira Press, Walnut Creek, California.

Kolankiewicz, Leon. 1982. *Alaskan Coal Development: An Assessment of Potential Water Quality Impacts.* Alaska Department of Environmental Conservation, Water Quality Management Planning Program.

McNab, W. H. and P. E. Avers. 1994. Ecological Subregions of the United States: Section Descriptions. Administrative Publication WO-WSA-5. Washington, DC: U.S. Department of Agriculture, Forest Service. 267 pp.

Meretsky, V.J., R.L. Fischman, J.R. Karr, D.M. Ashe, J.M. Scott, R.F. Noss, and R.L. Schroeder. 2006. New Directions in Conservation for the National Wildlife Refuge System. BioScience: Vol. 56, No. 2 pp. 135–143.

Munson, C.A (editor). 1980. Archeological Salvage Excavations at Patoka Lake, Indiana. Glenn A. Black Laboratory of Archeology, Indiana University.

Appendix I: Literature Cited

U. S. Census Bureau. 2006. State and County QuickFacts: Indiana. Accessed on 2-21-06 at: http://quickfacts.census.gov/qfd/states/18000.html.

USDA—Natural Resources Conservation Service website http://www.nrcs.usda.gov/programs/wrp/states/in.html [accessed May 22, 2006].

U. S. Department of the Interior, National Park Service. 2006. National Register of Historic Places – Index by State and County: Indiana and Gibson and Pike counties. Accessed 12/19/06 on the World Wide Web at: http://www.nr.nps.gov/iwisapi/explorer.dll?IWS_SCHEMA=NRIS1&IWS_LOGIN=1&IWS_REPORT=100000066.

U.S. Department of Transportation Federal Highway Administration. 2004. Tier 1 Record of Decision Evansville to Indianapolis, Indiana FEIS.

U.S. Department of Transportation Federal Highway Administration and Indiana Department of Transporation. 2003. Tier 1 Final Environmental Impact Statement and Section 4(f) Evaluation. Evansville to Indianapolis, Indiana FEIS.

U. S. Fish and Wildlife Service. No date. Overview of the U.S. Shorebird Conservation Plan and Council. Accessed online 2-19-06 at http://shorebirdplan.fws.gov/USShorebird/overview.htm.

U. S. Fish and Wildlife Service. 1989. Preacquisition Contaminant Survey for the Patoka River National Wildlife Refuge. Unpublished agency report. Ecological Services, Bloomington, Indiana.

U. S. Fish and Wildlife Service. 1990. Regional Wetlands Concept Plan. Emergency Wetlands Resources Act.

U. S. Fish and Wildlife Service. 1994. Patoka River National Wetlands Project: Final Environmental Impact Statement. July.

U. S. Fish and Wildlife Service. 1997. National Outreach Strategy: a Master Plan for Communicating in the U. S. Fish and Wildlife Service. Washington D.C., USA. Available URL: http://library.fws.gov/Pubs/outreach_strategy.pdf

U. S. Fish and Wildlife Service. 1999. Strategic Plan for Conservation of Fish and Wildlife Service Trust Resources in the Ohio River Valley Ecosystem. U.S. Fish and Wildlife Service Regions 5, 4, and 3. December 1999 (Second Revision). Accessed online on 14 Feb. 2006 at: http://www.fws.gov/orve/stratplan.html.

U. S. Fish and Wildlife Service. 2001. Biological integrity, diversity, and environmental health. 601 FW 3. National Wildlife Refuge System, Department of Interior. Available URL: http://policy.fws.gov/601fw3.html

U. S. Fish and Wildlife Service. 2005. National Wildlife Refuge System Strategic Plan for Biological Monitoring and Adaptive Management: Fiscal Years 2006-2010. Biological Monitoring Team Regions 3 and 5.

U. S. Fish and Wildlife Service. 2006a. General Guidelines for Wildlife-Dependent Recreation. 605 FW 1. National Wildlife Refuge System, Department of Interior. Available URL: http://www.fws.gov/policy/605fw1.html

U. S. Fish and Wildlife Service. 2006b. Wildlife-Dependent Recreation: Hunting. 605 FW 2. National Wildlife Refuge System, Department of Interior. Available URL: http://www.fws.gov/policy/605fw2.html

U. S. Fish and Wildlife Service. 2006c. Wildlife-Dependent Recreation: Fishing. 605 FW 3. National Wildlife Refuge System, Department of Interior. Available URL: http://www.fws.gov/policy/605fw3.html

U. S. Fish and Wildlife Service. 2006d. Wildlife-Dependent Recreation: Wildlife Observation. 605 FW 4. National Wildlife Refuge System, Department of Interior. Available URL: http://www.fws.gov/policy/605fw4.html

U. S. Fish and Wildlife Service. 2006e. Wildlife-Dependent Recreation: Wildlife Photography. 605 FW 5. National Wildlife Refuge System, Department of Interior. Available URL: http://www.fws.gov/policy/605fw5.html

The Refuge has the same obligations as any other landowner and the same rights as any other landowner. Being adjacent to or surrounded by Refuge land does not impede a landowners' rights, access, or use of property.

Land Acquisition Support

Comment: *Some individuals expressed support for continued emphasis on land acquisition, calling it the "critical piece of the puzzle" in the CCP. Others noted that there are a number of willing sellers within the approved acquisition area and that the Refuge suffers from a lack of funding to pursue those properties.*

Response: Building a refuge takes time and we truly appreciate all support for Patoka River NWR & MA. We are especially grateful to the individuals who have partnered with the refuge to help secure funding grants and to those who are making the Refuge possible by selling their land to the Service.

Annual appropriations for land acquisition on National Wildlife Refuges are made by the U.S. Congress from the Land and Water Conservation Fund (LWCF). This fund receives revenue when the U.S. Government leases offshore oil development rights and collects annual royalty payments from oil production. There is stiff competition for these funds as there are many other refuges across the United States that are also growing in size and faced with severe threats of development on those lands approved for inclusion in those refuges. Friends and supporters of refuges expressing their concerns for growth of their local refuge really do make a difference.

While some may feel that Patoka River NWR (5,946 acres) has grown too slowly especially when compared to similar refuges established in the same time period such as Canaan Valley NWR (15,901 acres) in West Virginia or Cypress Creek NWR (15,395 acres) in southern Illinois, there are some bright spots. The lack of funding support has resulted in formation of partnerships with many individuals, non-profit organizations, industry and state agencies. For example, with the help of partners, the refuge has competed for and received four North American Waterfowl Management Plan grants since 1995. These grants have provided $1,144,500 for land acquisition plus $294,000 for habitat restoration.

There has always been a long list of many willing sellers. The list is growing shorter as private interests and corporations continue to take advantage of the lack of regular funding from the LWCF and buy land for personal use and development from frustrated willing sellers. Too be sure, the vision for which Patoka River NWR was established is facing a long and tedious journey which only increased public support can hope to remedy.

Support of the Refuge

Comment: Many people wrote to express support for the work of Refuge staff and management of the land to benefit wildlife and wildlife habitat. Others wrote to support Alternative 3, the preferred alternative.

Response: Refuge staff and Regional Office planners appreciate your support. Many people contributed to the Comprehensive Conservation Plan by asking good questions at public meetings, reviewing the draft CCP and offering comments on the plan. We appreciate the time you have been willing to dedicate to the planning process and we appreciate your thoughts on the plan. The Patoka River NWR and MA is a unique place and we are looking forward to implementing the plan over the next 15 years.

Timber Management

Comment: *Timber Harvest should be used as a management tool to maintain age class diversity within forested portions of the Refuge.*

Response: Strategy 3 under Objective 1.1 Forested Wetlands of the selected alternative calls for completion of a Habitat Management Plan with specific management recommendations to maintain bottomland forest species and age class diversity. The Habitat Management Plan is more site specific than the CCP and will consider various management options including timber harvesting.

Anyone familiar with the history of land use practices in the Patoka River bottoms recognizes that the timber resource has been high-graded for over a century with more valuable timber species being continuously cut and removed from the forest stand. With the past emphasis on clearing and draining to make more land available for agriculture, little effort was ever expended to manage the composition of the forest. Whatever grew back, grew back on its own. This meant that mast producing trees includ-

dix F of the Draft CCP and Environmental Assessment. Also, the selected alternative includes a strategy under *Objective 3.2 Hunting* that calls for additional sanctuary areas as more land is acquired.

Economic Concerns

Comment: *One individual wondered whether it was cost effective to plant trees in areas prone to beaver caused flooding.*

Response: Prolonged flooding whether caused by beavers or other sources is one of the challenges to restoring bottomland forest. In some cases planted trees are lost to flooding, despite this, planting is the most effective means of restoring tree species reduced or eliminated from bottomland forests by previous land use practices. Restoring native habitat is part of the National Wildlife Refuge System mission and is supported by other Service policies. Beavers are native to forested wetlands like those along the Patoka River and beaver-caused disturbance is part of the bottomland forest system. Nearly every location along the Patoka River is potentially subject to beaver activity as well as prolonged flooding caused by other factors within the Patoka River watershed. Restoring such sites sometimes results in additional costs if replanting is deemed necessary rather than relying on natural succession of vegetative communities following beaver or other flooding disturbances

Support for Alternative 3

Comment: *The Refuge received several comments supporting Alternative 3 of the Draft Environmental Assessment.*

Response: We appreciate support for the preferred alternative, and we appreciate all of the time and thought that people devoted to the CCP.

Hunting Support

Comment: *Hunting is a safe activity that should always be emphasized and expressed at every opportunity when the subject of hunting comes up in the future.*

Response: Hunting is one of the six priority wildlife-dependent public uses identified in the National Wildlife Refuge Improvement Act of 1997. Refuges evaluate whether wildlife populations are sufficient to support hunting and whether there is enough space for hunters to have a positive and safe experience. Presently, all but 606 acres of the more than 6,000 acres of Refuge lands are open to hunting consistent with Indiana DNR regulations.

Public Use

Comment: *We heard from individuals who are interested in more public access to the Refuge and the Patoka River, individuals who are concerned that the sound of traffic and conflicts with other Refuge uses are diminishing visits for birders and hikers, and an individual who would like to see a step-down plan for ATV use on the Refuge.*

Response: Public access at Patoka River NWR & MA is limited by how much land the Refuge has acquired and the location of that land. In some cases, public access isn't feasible because the land owned by the Refuge is surrounded by private land. In other cases, a tract might be too small to accommodate visitors pursuing different interests. We want visitors to have as much access to the Refuge as possible without compromising wildlife needs, and we want those visits to be satisfying. We expect public access and the overall visitor experience to improve as the Refuge grows.

The Service is developing regulations to govern Off-Road Vehicle (ORV) use on national wildlife refuges. No new ORV use is authorized until the regulations are complete and Service policy is revised. Off-Road Vehicles including All-Terrain Vehicles are prohibited on the Refuge and there are no plans to change this. Any use permitted on a National Wildlife Refuge must pass two separate tests. The first test is to determine if the use is appropriate and the second is to determine if the use is compatible with the purposes for which the refuge was established. The terms "appropriate" and "compatible" and the associated processes are defined in Service policies.

Public Use Regulations

Comment: *One individual suggested decreasing the intensity of hunting to provide wildlife relief from hunting pressure and that any such change should be done with public involvement.*

Response: Strategy 4 under Objective 3.2 Hunting of the selected alternative calls for identifying sanctuary areas – places where hunting is prohibited – once more land is acquired. This would be done as part of developing a Hunting and Fishing Plan for the Refuge and would include public review.

with the Indiana Department of Environmental Management to develop air quality monitoring near the Refuge.

Comment: *One commenter suggested the Refuge should monitor proposals for nearby industrial, commercial and residential facilities and communicate concerns regarding any actions that may disturb any of the sites identified under the Comprehensive Environmental Response and Compensation Liability Inventory System (CERCLIS) or other contaminant sites. The commenter also suggested that the Refuge identify evacuation distances for local industrial sitings to better understand the potential hazards posed by these sites, and communicate any concerns to the Indiana Department of Environmental Management.*

Response: We have and continue to monitor off site development proposals as we become aware of them. We work in conjunction with the Service's Environmental Contaminants Program which is dedicated to identifying sources of environmental contamination, assessing impacts of contaminants to fish and wildlife resources, and helping to restore contaminated habitats. If there is potential for any proposed development to affect Refuge resources we communicate our concerns to the appropriate authority or regulating body.

There are a number of methods the Service employs to identify and deal with contaminants. First, contaminant surveys are mandatory prior to the acquisition of any Refuge lands. A preacquisition survey was conducted in 1989 for the Refuge. Second, the Environmental Contaminants Program also conducts the Contaminants Assessment Process (CAP). This is a standardized and comprehensive approach used to assess potential threats posed by environmental contaminants to National Wildlife Refuges as well as other Service lands. The CAP process involves reviewing information available on the ecological and physical characteristics of the Service land and surrounding area relative to possible contaminant issues.

This review requires the primary investigator to compile and interpret information acquired from various sources. To facilitate the investigation, the Service's Division of Environmental Contaminants and the U.S. Geological Survey, Biological Resource Division's Biomonitoring of Environmental Status and Trends (BEST) Program jointly developed a data management system. The system retrieves and organizes information from contaminants-related, on-line databases maintained by the Environmental Protection Agency (EPA). In addition, the CAP requires that the Primary Investigator acquire data from other sources including interviews with refuge managers, biologists and various experts as well as scientific literature. Potential point and nonpoint contaminant sources and types are inventoried and pathways that these contaminants may follow to reach the area of concern are identified. Then, areas of potential contamination are identified and the contaminant issues described. The information summarized through the CAP can provide the basis by which land managers select options to reduce contaminant impacts on the species and lands under their stewardship. The CAP also identifies Service-managed areas located downstream or down-gradient from highways, railways, or navigation channels that may be vulnerable to hazardous substance spills. Such areas may then be targeted for baseline data collection which could support future on-Refuge investigations, natural resource damage assessments, or field work.

Finally, if a contaminant problem is suspected, the Environmental Contaminants Program can conduct further studies to help identify the cause as well as potential solutions. A number of such studies conducted on and around the Refuge have helped guide past contaminant remediation efforts related to abandoned oil wells and acid mine drainage.

Comment: *One commenter noted that pollution problems associated with farming, mining, and sewage have improved through the efforts of Refuge staff.*

Response: Thank you for the comment. We believe our efforts in conjunction with our partners have reduced pollutants within the Patoka River watershed.

Comment: *One individual supported banning Off Road Vehicles, mining, power plant development and the construction of Interstate 69 within 10 miles of the Refuge to protect sensitive habitat.*

Response: The Refuge has no authority to ban activities, including Off Road Vehicles (ORVs), mining, power plant development, and construction of Interstate 69 on lands not under Refuge ownership. Presently, Off Road Vehicles are prohibited on Patoka River NWR lands and there are no plans to change this. In March 2004, after extensive public involvement and analysis, the Federal Highway Administration issued a Record of Decision that selected an alternative that will cross within the

sive Habitat Management and Active Visitor Services, as the preferred alternative because we think it is a better route for continuing to improve habitat and contribute to healthy populations of resident and migratory wildlife.

Visitor Center

Comment: *The plan should include provisions to construct a Visitor Center for the Refuge or at least an expansion of the existing space to provide interpretive and outreach materials.*

Response: We added a strategy to Objective 3.5 Interpretation to provide for development of a visitor contact area as necessary and feasible. We did discuss the possibility of a Visitor Center for the Refuge during the planning process, but did not develop a proposal. This should have been noted in the Environmental Assessment but was not. We added this information to the section of the Environmental Assessment entitled *Alternatives Considered But Not Developed*. Visitor Centers represent substantial capital investments and require subsequent monies for maintenance and upkeep. The Service considers a number of factors before proceeding with any new facilities. Presently, the patchwork ownership pattern and visitation levels do not support the addition of a Visitor Center at Patoka River NWR. The primary focus of the CCP over the next 15 years is on acquiring additional lands which is likely to attract additional visitors.

Trespassing

Comment: *An individual commented that he or she has signed the boundaries of his or her property and since then has not experienced problems with Refuge visitors trespassing.*

Response: Refuge staff are always very pleased when visitors are not causing conflicts with neighbors, and we applaud the writer for taking the initiative to post the boundaries. We also know that the Refuge has a responsibility to do what it can to help visitors navigate the Refuge without trespassing on private property, and the CCP calls for greater emphasis on posting the boundaries.

Public Notification

Comment: *One commenter indicated that although they were affected by the plan, they were not directly contacted for comment.*

Response: We apologize for this oversight. Our intent was to notify all those interested or affected by the CCP planning effort, but unfortunately we did not make direct contact with everyone. The draft CCP/EA, a summary, and/or a compact disc was sent to 416 members of the public; organizations; local, State, and Federal agencies; elected officials; and public libraries. The draft CCP/EA was also available online at the Region 3 Conservation Planning website. The comment period began on October 17, 2007 and lasted 45 days. During the comment period we held an open house meeting that was publicized through the local media.

Paper Waste

Comment: *One writer protested the "paper wasted" and the printing costs associated with providing people with a copy of the Draft CCP.*

Response: Although the Refuge and the entire U.S. Fish & Wildlife Service would very much like to reduce both paper use and printing costs, we have an obligation to make Refuge planning as open as possible. That means providing updates on the planning process and, ultimately, a draft CCP for people to review. We distribute draft CCPs in three ways: we print copies and mail them to individuals who have indicated an interest in receiving one as well as to local libraries; we mail the CCP in electronic format on a compact disk; and we post the CCP on the Division of Comprehensive Conservation Planning website.

Planning staff regularly discuss ways we might reduce printing costs and our use of paper, and we expect that in the future we will rely less on printed copies and more on making documents available electronically and on the Web. In the time being, we believe that computer use is not convenient enough or widespread enough among all demographic groups for us to quit printing paper copies of CCPs.

CHAPTER 5 — Miscellaneous Information

5-1. Uniform Clothing
5-2. Political Activities
5-3. Publication of Articles and Public Speaking Engagements
5-4. Applicability of the Uniform Code of Military Justice
5-5. Awards
5-6. Lapel Button
5-7. Foreign Employment
5-8. Replacement of Lost Documents
5-9. Educational Opportunities and Scholarships
5-10. Appointments to the U.S. Naval Academy
5-11. Travel, Residence, Loss of Citizenship, Effects on Retired Pay
5-12. Record of Emergency Data Form
5-13. The Armed Forces Retirement Home

CHAPTER 6 — Action Required for Surviving Members

6-1. Burial Benefits
6-2. Arlington National Cemetery (Department of the Army)
6-3. Reimbursement of Burial Expenses
6-4. Burial Flags and Military Honors
6-5. Headstones or Grave Markers
6-6. Social Security Death payment
6-7. National Cemetery Administration (NCA)
6-8. Retired or Retainer Pay
6-9. Uniformed Services Identification and Privilege Card
6-10. Medical Care
6-11. VA Dependency and Indemnity Compensation
6-12. Death Due to NonService-Connected Cause
6-13. NonService-Connected Death Pension
6-14. Death Gratuity
6-15. Other Federal Benefits Available to Surviving Spouses

CHAPTER 7 — Identification Cards

7-1. Defense Enrollment Eligibility Reporting System (DEERS) and the Real-Time Automated Personnel Identification System (RAPIDS)
7-2. Your Retired Identification Card
7-3. Your Family Members' Identification Cards
7-4. Replacement of Family Members' Identification Cards
7-5. Eligibility for Identification Cards
7-6. Authorized Privileges

(Notification of Change of Address)

About DFAS…
The Defense Finance and Accounting Service is the world's largest finance and accounting operation. It provides responsive, professional finance and accounting services to the men and women who defend America. For more information about DFAS, visit http://www.dod.mil/dfas

How to avoid indebtedness to DFAS! Contact DFAS to stop retired or annuitant pay upon death at **1-800-269-5170**. If you do not, DFAS will contact the bank directly to recover any electronic payments. This rule also applies for payments from other sources such as the VA or OPM.

DFAS expands automated services for retirees and annuitants. By using the DFAS Interactive Voice Response System (IVRS), retirees and annuitants can obtain specific account information. When customers call 1-800-321-1080 or (216) 522-5955, they will hear a new menu option to use this feature. Customers choosing to use this new feature will be prompted to enter their social security number and Personal Indetification Number (PIN).

Those who have an account with **myPay** can use the same PIN to access the IVRS. By using the IVRS, customers will be able to obtain specific account information in the following areas:

- Correspondence address
- Allotments
- Certificate of Eligibility or Report of Existense
- Deductions
- Gross and net pay
- Survivor Benefit Plan coverage
- Federal and state taxes

The IVRS is available 24 hours a day, 7 days a week.

MYPAY ACCOUNT:
https://mypay.dfas.mil/mypay.aspx
MyPay is an innovative, automated system that puts you in control of processing certain discretionary pay data items without using paper forms. You can also get your pay statements, tax forms and travel advice of payment using **myPay**. **MyPay** saves time, is convenient, and reliable. You can access **myPay** nearly 24 hours a day, 7 days a week to change or review your current information, or to check your most recent pay statement.

Obtaining a PIN is very easy. On the web site select **NEW PIN** unter the **NEED A NEW PIN** option on the **myPay** home page. The process will issue a new random temporary PIN for your account, which will be mailed to your address of records currently contained in your

topics (i.e. Appeals, Applying for Benefits, Applying for a Social Security Number, Benefits, Computing your benefits, etc.) *(Chapter 4-1. Social Security)*

THE ARMED FORCES RETIREMENT HOME:
http://www.afrh.gov/DWP/afrh/afrhhome.htm
At this web site, you can get information on the eligibility criteria, resident fees, frequently asked questions section, etc.
(Chapter 5-13. The Armed Forces Retirement Home)

TRICARE SUPPORT OFFICE:
http://www.tricare.osd.mil/
At this web site, you can get information on enrollment, claims, benefits, etc.
(Chapter 8 - Medical Care)

MARINE FOR LIFE:
https://www.m4l.usmc.mil/portal/server.pt
This website provides information about transition assistance to Marines who honorably leave active service and return to civilian life and to support injured Marines and their families.

MARINE ONLINE:
https://tfas.mol.usmc.mil/TFAS/login.do
Marine OnLine (MOL) is designed for Marines with personnel records in the Marine Corps Total Force System (MCTFS). This includes Marines on Active Duty, Reserve, Active Reserve Marines, the Inactive Ready Reserve (IRR) and Retired Marines. If you fall into one of the categories just mentioned, and you want to register on MOL, visit the Marine OnLine web site and click on "*register online*".

BOARD FOR CORRECTIONS OF NAVAL RECORDS (BCNR):
http://www.hq.navy.mil/bcnr/bcnr.htm
At this web site, you can obtain information on how to contact the BCNR (telephone numbers and address); you can download and print the required application (DD Form 149) in order to submit your case to BCNR, etc. Congress created the Board for Correction of Naval Records (BCNR) in 1946 to provide a method for correction of errors or removal of injustices from current and former Navy and Marine Corps member's records without the necessity for private legislation.

PERSONNEL MANAGEMENT SUPPORT BRANCH MMSB-12:
https://www.mmsb.usmc.mil/pocs.htm
The Personnel Management Support Branch, under the Director, Personnel Management Division, directs and controls the functions necessary to create, maintain, and archive Official Military Personnel Files (OMPFs) (i.e. DD Form 214, Retirement orders, etc.).

Our phone numbers are:
    1-800-336-4649
    (703) 784-9310
Fax: (703) 784-9834

Whenever you see instructions in this guide to contact us, you can always call unless we specify a requirement to write.

SEMPER FIDELIS MEMORANDUM FOR RETIRED MARINES

The **Semper Fidelis** memorandum is a quarterly publication distributed to all retired Marines and their survivors who receive an annuity from the Marine Corps. Formerly entitled the **Newsletter for Retired Marines**, it was first issued in February 1956. Its mission then, as it is now, is to keep you abreast of current laws and regulations, which may affect your entitled benefits and privileges. The information provided in **Semper Fidelis** is furnished as an update to this guide. Remember, the information contained in the pay system files is the source for the addresses used in mailing **Semper Fidelis**, so it is vital that you keep this information current through correspondence with DFAS and CMC (MMSR-7) as mentioned on the Notification of Change of Address section.

How to access the Semper Fidelis Online…
Go to www.usmc.mil Note that it may take several seconds before eleven links will appear on yor screen. The links are located next to the slogan, *"The Few. The Proud."* Click on the link *"Career"*, then *"Retired Marines"*, which will direct you to the *"Retired Activities Home Page"*. There, you should see the link to the *"**Semper Fidelis Memorandum**"* and other retired-related information.

SECRETARY OF THE NAVY'S RETIREE COUNCIL (RC)
http://www.lifelines.navy.mil/retireecouncil
This web site contains useful links on benefits, programs, and related areas of interest for military retirees and their families, as well as for those considering retirement. *(Chapter 12 - Secretary of the Navy's Retiree Council (RC))*

NOTIFICATION OF CHANGE OF ADDRESS

Address changes are your responsibility!!

General. A dual address is kept in each **pay** account: the mailing address of your financial institution (if you are enrolled in the Direct Deposit Program) and your home address. DFAS will mail all items such as Retiree Account Statements, 1099R forms, and other correspondence to your home mailing address.

If you receive your check through the mail, you must submit a change of address request in writing. Send a

the Permanent Disability Retired List.

❑ **Permanent Disability Retired List (PDRL):** Consists of Marines who are not physically qualified for duty and according to accepted medical principles and standards are permanently disabled.

❑ **Retired List of the Marine Corps Reserve:** Consists of Reservists who have less than 20 years of active service but at least 20 years of qualifying service who are transferred to the Retired List of the Marine Corps Reserve upon request. These retired Marines do not receive retired pay until their 60th birthday.

❑ **Retirement of Reservists Not Qualified for Retired Pay:** Members previously transferred to the Retired Reserve in an honorary status will maintain their retired status per SECNAVINST 1820.2C. Reservists who possess special qualifications or critical professional skills, or are required by law to maintain status, are not eligible for non-Regular service retired pay, and are subject to mandatory removal from an active status, may be transferred to Retired Reserve status in lieu of discharge as approved by DC/S M&RA or CHNAVPERS.

1-2. MOBILIZATION CONSIDERATIONS

All retired Marines are placed in one of three categories for mobilization purposes:

❑ **Category I:** Non-disability retired Marines under age 60 who have been retired less than five years.

❑ **Category II:** Non-disability retired Marines under age 60 who have been retired five years or more.

❑ **Category III:** Non-disability retired Marines age 60 or older and all disability retired Marines.

1-3. RECALL TO ACTIVE DUTY

Retired Marines may be recalled to active duty on either a voluntary or an involuntary basis:

❑ **Voluntary:** The Secretary of the Navy may order any retired or FMCR member to voluntary active duty at any time **with** the retired member's consent.

❑ **Involuntary:** The Secretary of the Navy may order any retired or FMCR member with at least 20 years of active service to active duty at any time to perform duties deemed necessary in the interests of national defense (Title 10, Section

make this request by telephone, you will still need to submit a letter to verify your request. Stop-payment requests should properly identify the missing check(s) (e.g., the payment issued for July will be dated for the first business day of August. This represents the settlement of your account for the month of July—and is the July payment—not the August payment, even though it is dated and received in August.). **Do not** write to DFAS about lost checks you receive from other Federal agencies such as the Department of Veterans Affairs (VA) or the Social Security Administration. Contact those agencies directly.

2-5. MISSING CHECKS LOCATED

If you report your retired, retainer, or SBP annuity paycheck as lost or stolen, and it arrives later, immediately notify DFAS. Do not negotiate both the original and successor check because this will result in an overpayment to you. If necessary, the Government will take action to recover any overpayment by deductions from your pay.

2-6. DIRECT DEPOSIT PROGRAM

Electronic Funds Transfer (EFT) Program. As of July 1996, you are <u>required</u> by law to enroll in the Direct Deposit Program for your retired, retainer, or SBP annuity pay. Enrollment will ensure your money is electronically deposited into your financial account by the first business day of the following month. If for some reason that does not happen, notify DFAS. To enroll in the program, visit your financial institution (bank, credit union, or savings and loan) and complete an SF-1199A (Direct Deposit Sign-Up Form). Mail it to DFAS. The change will normally become effective within 30 days of receipt. **Helpful hint:** Do not close your old account until your next check is deposited in your new bank account.

2-7. DISCRETIONARY ALLOTMENT SYSTEM

Authorized Allotments. As of 1 October 1997, the Discretionary/Non-Discretionary Allotment System replaced the Voluntary Allotment System. You may continue or discontinue the allotments that were active when you transferred to the retired list or the FMCR. The new system limits you to a total of six (6) discretionary allotments. Examples of discretionary allotments include, but are not limited to:

❑ Payment of insurance premiums for various types of commercial insurance. This includes life, dental and health, and vehicle insurance.

CHAPTER 2 - MARINE CORPS RETIRED PAY AND TAXES

Provide your policy number whenever you request a start or change in the amount of allotments for the payment of life insurance premiums.

Effective Date of Change. If your request to start or change an allotment is received at DFAS by the 15th of the month, the first deduction will normally occur the following month. If your request to stop an allotment is received by the 15th, the stop will normally occur with the last deduction of the month when it is received. DFAS can only permit changes when they are beyond your control and are of an administrative nature dictated by events incidental to the purpose of the allotment.

2-8. FEDERAL AND STATE INCOME TAX

General. The Internal Revenue Service (IRS) requires DFAS to withhold Federal income tax from the taxable portion of retired or retainer pay. Disability retired pay based on the actual percentage of disability assigned may be excluded from gross income for Federal income tax purposes. Factors affecting exclusion of disability pay are discussed under the Tax Benefits heading of this section.

Exclusion. The monthly cost of participation in the Retired Serviceman's Family Protection Plan (RSFPP) and/or the Survivor Benefit Plan (SBP) to provide a survivor annuity to an eligible recipient(s) is also excluded from gross income for Federal income tax purposes. The excluded amounts are not included in the "gross amount" report annually on the IRS Form 1099R. Retired members and annuitants will be issued 1099R forms, which replaces the old W2-P forms. Retired members or annuitants who do not get their 1099Rs by 15 February, have questions about their 1099R forms, or need to update their mailing addresses may contact DFAS.

Withholding Tax. The monthly withholding tax deduction is computed under the percentage withholding tables prescribed by the IRS. It is based on the marital status and number of exemptions claimed on the IRS Form W-4 (Employee's Withholding Certificate) or your signed letter. For the purpose of withholding state tax, you may also have additional amounts withheld each month in multiples of $1, without regard to the number of exemptions claimed. The minimum amount is $10. The disbursing officer settling your retired or retainer pay account is merely a withholding agent and the final determination of your tax liability is a matter under the jurisdiction of the IRS.

and only delays the timely mailing of the forms to all applicable members. Requests for a duplicate W-2 issued for active-duty pay should be send directly to: **DFAS-KC (Code FLB), 1500 E. Bannister Road, Kansas City, MO 64197-0001** or call **800-449-3327**.

Tax Benefits. There are several tax benefits available to you if you were retired for disability or if you are awarded VA disability compensation. If you were:

❏ Retired for or entitled to retired for disability before 1 January 1977,

❏ On active duty or a member of the Reserves before 25 September 1975, and are retired for disability after 1 January 1997, or

❏ You entered military service after 25 September 1975, and are retired for a combat-related disability after 1 January 1977, part or all of your retired pay may be excluded from Federal income taxation.

The manner in which your retired pay is computed determines whether any of it is subject to Federal income tax. If your retired pay is computed by multiplying the percentage of disability times basic pay, all retired pay is exempt. If you chose to have your pay computed on the basis of length of service, then only that amount of your retired pay that is in excess of the amount you would have received if you had elected computation based on disability percentage is taxable. Exempted pay is not reported by DFAS on your IRS Form W-2P and you do not have to include it on your Federal income tax return. If you are awarded VA disability compensation, and waive an amount of retired pay equal to the amount of the VA award, the VA will pay such compensation directly to you. VA disability compensation payments are Federal income tax exempt (i.e., not included in your Federal tax return and the amount is not included on any IRS Form issued by the VA or DFAS). If you are in receipt of VA disability compensation, the amount of retired pay that you waive is subtracted from that portion (if any), of your retired pay that is tax exempt due to disability. If your are permanently and totally disabled (defined as being unable to engage in any substantial gainful activity by reason of any medically determinable physical or mental impairment which can be expected to result in death or which has lasted or can be expected to last for a continuous period of not less than 12 months) and are under age 65, you may qualify for Disability Income Exclusion. If you feel you may qualify for this benefit, you are

retired pay as many retired members mistakenly believe. Current rates may be obtained from your local VA office. VA compensation will reduce, dollar for dollar, the amount of retired pay you receive; however, the VA compensation is tax-free. Review your medical records thoroughly and record all the medical problems experienced during your active duty. These problems will form the basis for your medical review by the VA. After filing the proper forms, you will be contacted by the VA and directed to the nearest VA medical facility or contract medical facility for a medical review and evaluation of the medical items for which you are seeking compensation. If you served in the Persian Gulf War, ask the VA to do a Gulf War Exam in conjunction with this procedure. Forms to file your application for VA disability compensation may be obtained from your local VA office or you can also apply on line through the VA website at **http://vabenefits.vba.va.gov/vonapp/main.asp**. This procedure takes some time and effort on your part, but is extremely important. It establishes your record in the VA which can be helpful to your family or survivors, should they apply for VA benefits based on your service.

3-3. VA GUARANTEED HOME LOANS

Qualified veterans and surviving spouses may use VA-guaranteed home loan to purchase, improve, or refinance a home or condominium. VA guarantees part of the total loan, permitting the purchaser to obtain a mortgage with a competitive interest rate, even without a down payment if the lender agrees. With a VA guarantee, the lender is protected against loss up to the amount of the guarantee if the borrower fails to repay the loan. Those eligible must make their own arrangements for loans through the usual lending channels, such as banks, savings and loans associations, building and loan associations, and mortgage loan companies. A VA guaranteed home loan could be used to:

- Buy a home,
- Buy a residential condominium,
- Build a home,
- Repair, alter, or improve a home,
- Refinance an existing home loan,
- Buy a manufactured home with or without a lot,
- Buy and improve a manufactured home lot,
- Install a solar heating or cooling system or other weatherization improvements,
- Purchase and improve a home simultaneously with energy-efficient improvements,
- Refinance an existing VA loan to reduce the interest rate and make energy-efficient improvements, or

register approximately 23 million visits a year. An estimated 2.7 million individual veterans receive care annually. VA currently is affiliated with 104 medical schools, 48 dental schools, and more than 850 other schools across the country. More than half of all practicing physicians in the United States have had part of their professional education in the VA health-care system. Each year, approximately 100,000 health professionals receive training in VA medical centers.

The VA may provide hospital care covering the full range of medical services. Outpatient treatment is available for all service-connected conditions or non-service-connected conditions in certain cases. Co-payments may be required depending on your degree of disability and your ability to pay. There is no special category for treating retired members; they are treated as veterans. Medical care is based on the limits of the VA facilities in your local area. Eligibility for care is based on your status as determined by VA eligibility criteria. Your local VA office can provide specific information and will help determine your entitlements under the VA medical system. **Family members are not eligible for treatment in VA facilities unless they are also veterans**.

For more information visit the VA web site at http://www1.va.gov/healthbenefits/ .

3-7. VA DENTAL CARE

Dental care is distinct from medical care. As a result, the types and amounts of coverage are different, as noted below.

- **Before you separate**: Early in your transition process, you and your family should have routine dental checkups. You should also ensure that your family members obtain necessary treatment under the TRICARE Family Member Dental Plan prior to your expiration of eligibility for the program. If problems are found early enough, work can be completed prior to separation, at little or no cost to you. Emergencies will also be taken care of until your separation.

- **Shortly after you separate**: Within 90 days of your retirement, the VA will fix, on a space-available basis, dental conditions existing at the time of your retirement; however, if you received complete dental treatment from the military in the 90 days preceding your retirement, you will not be able to use the VA dental benefit. Your DD 214, Record of Release from Active Duty, will note whether or not you are eligible to obtain the space-available dental treatment from the VA. Once the VA provides the space-available dental treatment,

pension benefits are counted in determining income for SSI purposes, certain types or amounts of income do not count. Also, not all resources count in determining eligibility. For example, the person's home and the land it is on do not count, regardless of value. Personal effects or household goods, automobiles, and life insurance may not count, depending on their value. Information and assistance in making application for these payments may be obtained at any Social Security office or by calling the toll-free number, 1-800-772-1213.

4-2. NAVY/MARINE CORPS RELIEF SOCIETY

The purpose of the Navy-Marine Corps Relief Society is to provide emergency financial assistance to active duty and retired Navy and Marine Corps personnel and their families. NMCRS provides assistance with basic living expenses such as food, rent, utilities, assistance with emergency transportation, funerals, medical and dental bills, essential car repair, pay problems, and other emergency needs. Assistance is provided with loans or grants, depending on financial need. The following personnel are eligible for financial and other assistance provided by the Society:

❑ Active duty and retired members of the regular Navy and Marine Corps Reserves on extended active duty, and certain retired reservists.

❑ Dependents and dependent Survivors of the above members. Indigent mothers (65 years or older) of deceased service members who have limited resources and no family to provide for their welfare.

❑ Ex-spouses "20-20-20" (un-remarried former spouses) whose marriage to a service member lasted for at least 20 years while the service member was on active duty.

❑ Uniformed members of the National Oceanic and Atmospheric Administration (NOAA).

NMCRS has a full-time budget counselor to help. Three visiting nurses are available to visit new mothers, and to assist with other health problems. Education loans are available for dependent spouses and children. Some locations have thrift stores that offer second-hand merchandise, including military and civilian clothing, small appliances, household items, and baby furniture. If you wish to donate to the shop, check with your local office for details.

Educational Programs. Educational financial assistance helps Navy and

CHAPTER 4 - BENEFITS ADMINISTERED BY OTHER AGENCIES

When a disaster threatens or strikes, they provide shelter, food, and health and mental health services, which address basic human needs. In addition, they help individuals and families to resume their normal daily activities independently. This may include a referral or a way to pay for what is needed most: groceries, new clothes, rent, emergency home repairs, transportation, household items, medicines, and occupational tools.

The Red Cross may also help those needing long-term recovery assistance when all other available resources, including insurance, government, private, and community assistance, are either unavailable or inadequate to meet the needs. All assistance is based on verified disaster-caused needs and all assistance is free—literally a gift as a result of the generous support of the American people.

Many local Red Cross chapters provide transportation to and from medical appointments and other essential trips for people who cannot provide their own transportation. This service is normally provided to seniors or persons with chronic illnesses, such as dialysis patients or persons with HIV or AIDS.

For additional information contact your local Red Cross Chapter or call the Disaster Assistance information line at:
(866) GET-INFO
(866-438-4636)
 To make a donation:
(800) HELP-NOW
(800-435-7669) or
visit the Red Cross web site at http://www.redcross.org/index.html

CHAPTER 4 – BENEFITS ADMINISTERED BY OTHER AGENCIES

❑ Except when authorized by competent service authority, when participating in activities such as public speeches, interviews, picket lines, marches, rallies or any public demonstration (including those pertaining to civil rights), which may imply service sanction of the cause for which the demonstration or activity is conducted,

❑ When wearing the uniform would tend to bring discredit upon the Armed Forces, or

❑ When specifically prohibited by Department of the Navy regulations.

With the exception of the Marine Corps Junior Reserve Officers' Training Corps program, you are not allowed to wear the uniform if employed by a military school unless the Commandant of the Marine Corps specifically authorizes you. Send your requests for such authority to **Marine Corps Uniform Board, 2200 Lester Street, Quantico, VA 22134.** Include a written statement from school officials verifying the position you held and the length of employment. As long as there is not a shortage of uniforms, you may purchase any item of uniform clothing by following current directives. Articles may be purchased for your use. Prices established by the Marine Corps pricing publications will apply to all sales. Send applications for the purchase of enlisted clothing to: **Commanding General (MAU), Marine Corps Logistics Base, Albany, GA 31704-5000.**

Do not forget to include documentation to verify entitlement, such as a copy of your DD Form 214 (*Armed Forces of the United States Report of Transfer or Discharge*) or DD Form 256 (*Honorable Discharge Certificate*). Forward applications for the purchase of officer uniform items to the nearest Marine Corps Exchange. Include your name, grade, Social Security number, and home address.

5-2. POLITICAL ACTIVITIES

Unlike your active-duty counterparts, you are not subject to certain restrictions on political activities imposed by Department of Defense directives and Marine Corps regulations. The Hatch Act (5 U.S.C., secs. 7324-7327) applies to you only if an executive agency or the government of the District of Columbia employs you.

send your request to Headquarters, U.S. Marine Corps, Military Awards Branch, 3280 Russell Road, Quantico VA 22134. All request should contain full name used while in the service, Social Security number, Military Service Number (if applicable), Date of Birth, and period of service. Any request received at the Military Awards Branch from personnel whose records have been retired to the National Personnel Record Center will be readdressed to the Navy Personnel Command for appropriate action.

5-6.   **LAPEL BUTTON**

There is a single basic design for the Honorable Discharge Button, FMCR Lapel Button, and Retired Personnel Lapel Button. Only the wording has been changed to fit each category. If you were transferred to the FMCR after 4 January 1963, you are entitled to a gratuitous issue of the FMCR Button; if you were transferred before that date you are authorized to purchase the button from Marine Corps Exchanges; and if you were retired permanently on or after 1 July 1955, you are entitled to the Retired Personnel Button. The button is not issued gratuitously to honorary retired personnel but may be purchased by them. A silver button is issued to Marines with 30 years of active service; a gold button is issued to Marines with less than 30 years of active service and to those transferred to the FMCR. You can purchase duplicate or replacement buttons from the Marine Corps Exchange or authorized military shops.

5-7.   **FOREIGN EMPLOYMENT**

Article I, Section 9, Clause 8, of the Constitution prohibits any person "holding any Office of Profit or Trust" under the United States from accepting any present, office or title, "of any kind whatsoever," from a foreign government without the consent of Congress. Because you retain status as a member of the Marine Corps, thus continuing to hold an office of trust, this constitutional prohibition applies to you.
As a result, the Comptroller General has permitted DFAS to withhold retirement pay in an amount equal to the payments received from a foreign government if you accept employment from that government without the consent of Congress. The same prohibition applies if your employment by a private contractor requires you to be placed under the direction or control of a foreign government. In 37 U.S.C., sec. 908, Congress granted automatic consent to any

a course or two, contact **MCI at 1-800-MCI-USMC (800-624-8768) or visit the MCI web site at https://www.mci.usmc.mil/newmci/**
Send any correspondence to: **Marine Corps Institute, 912 Charles Poor Street SE, Washington Navy Yard, DC 20391-5680**

Many civilian educational institutions and agencies will grant academic credit for off-duty courses, tests, or in-service training completed while serving on active duty. If you plan to continue your education and want to obtain credit for your military education and training experience, you should discuss this possibility with officials of the educational institution you plan to attend. To obtain academic credit, you will need to provide evidence of successful completion of courses, tests, and military training. Ensure that a current copy of your DD Form 295 (Application for the Evaluation of Learning Experiences During Military Service) is kept in your permanent records. You can request to have official transcripts sent to educational institutions by contacting **CMC (MMSB-12)** by calling **(703) 784-3920** or by mail at **Commandant of the Marine Corps, Headquarters U.S. Marine Corps (MMSB-12), 2008 Elliot Road, Quantico, VA 22134-5030.**

To request an official transcript for high school or college courses completed through off-duty study, write to the educational institution where the courses were taken.

Under certain conditions, some states provide scholarships for veterans, their children or both. The veterans' agency of your local state government can provide additional information. If you are looking for information about available scholarships for your children, you can obtain the current college financial aid handbook, **"Need a Lift?"** The handbook is updated annually, is a complete financial aid reference guide for veterans, their dependents and members of The American Legion family. It contains information such as Federal and state veterans' benefits, possible scholarships for veterans and their dependents, possible scholarships for Legionnaires and their families, "Tips" on how to apply for admission to college and assistance with the financial aid process. Also a comprehensive listing of colleges and universities, to include: basic information on tuition, room and board cost, and admission and financial aid deadlines and information on careers and a

not eligible. For additional information, write: **Candidate Guidance Office, United States Naval Academy, 117 Decatur Road, Annapolis, MD 21402-5018** or call at **(410) 293-4361**. You can also visit the web site at http://www.usna.edu/Admissions/steps.htm

Congressional. The Vice President of the United States, each United States Senator, each Congress Representative, and the Resident Commissioner of Puerto Rico may have five appointees at the Naval Academy at any one time. The Vice President makes his appointments from the United States at large. Congressmen make their nominations from residents of the congressional district, which they represent. Send your applications for nominations directly to the Vice President, your Senators, or your Representative.

From the Regular Navy or Marine Corps. Each year, enlisted members on active duty in the regular Navy or Marine Corps are eligible to compete for 85 available appointments. Appointees must be graduates of the Naval Academy Preparatory School at Bainbridge, Maryland.

From the Naval Reserve or Marine Corps Reserve. Each year, enlisted members of the Naval and Marine Corps Reserve, whether on active or inactive duty, are eligible to compete for 85 available appointments.

From the Honor Military and Naval Schools. Each designated honor military or naval school may nominate three honor graduates or prospective honor graduates each year to compete among themselves for ten midshipmen vacancies. The school concerned and the Chief of Naval Personnel handle submission of nominations.

From the Naval Reserve Officers Training Corps Units. No more than three candidates may be nominated yearly by each of the educational institutions in which an NROTC unit is in operation to compete among themselves for vacancies at the Naval Academy.

Children of Deceased Veterans and Children of Holders of the Medal of Honor. Those applying under the law providing for the children of personnel falling in this category may write to: **Superintendent, United States Naval Academy, ATTN: Nominations and Appointments Office, 117 Decatur Road, Annapolis, MD 21402-5019.** Include the full name, grade, and organization of the deceased veteran or the holder of the Medal of Honor; the full name of the

United States Soldiers' and Airmen's Home (USSAH) under the unified management of the Armed Forces Retirement Home Board.

AFRH is considered a model retirement community complete with facilities and services conveniently located in Gulfport, MS and Washington, DC.

Veterans are eligible to become a resident of the AFRH if their active duty service in the military was at least 50 percent enlisted, warrant officer or limited duty officer and who are:

- Veterans with 20 or more years of active duty service and are at least 60 years old, or

- Veterans unable to earn a livelihood due to a service-connected disability, or

- Veterans unable to earn a livelihood due to non service-connected disability, and who served in a war theater or received hostile fire pay, or

- Female veterans who served prior to 1948.

There are two parts to the application process; an application filled out by the individual and a medical certification completed by a healthcare provider. Applicants must also provide additional documents, such as the DD Form 214, to establish their eligibility. Upon receipt of all the documents, it usually takes about one week for the admissions council to review the application.

Applicants must be free of drug, alcohol, and psychiatric problems, and never have been convicted of a felony. Married couples are welcome, but both must be eligible in their own right. At the time of admission applicants must be able to live independently. As an example of this, they must be able to take care of their own personal needs, attend a central dining facility for meals and keep all medical appointments. If increased health care is needed after being admitted, assisted living and long term care are available at both campuses.

Resident Fees for Armed Forces Retirement Home - Washington DC are as follows:

- Independent living residents, 35 percent of total current income, but not to exceed $1,063 each month.

- Assisted living residents, 40 percent of total current income, but not to exceed $1,595 each month.

including opening, closing, and marking of the grave are provided without charge. Visit the web site for more information at http://www.cem.va.gov/eligible.htm.

6-2. ARLINGTON NATIONAL CEMETERY (DEPARTMENT OF THE ARMY)

This cemetery is under the jurisdiction of the Department of the Army. Burial is limited to specific categories of military personnel and veterans except in the case of cremated remains to be placed in the columbarium. For scheduling funeral arrangements please contact the **Superintendent, Arlington National Cemetery, Arlington, VA 22211** at **(703) 607-8585.** For additional information call **(703) 607-8000.** You can also visit the web site at http://www.arlingtoncemetery.org/.

6-3. REIMBURSEMENT OF BURIAL EXPENSES

The VA will pay a burial allowance if the veteran's death is service-connected. In some instances, VA also will pay the cost of transporting the remains of a service-disabled veteran to the national cemetery nearest the home of the deceased that has available gravesites. In such cases, the person who bore the veteran's burial expenses may claim reimbursement from VA. <u>There is no time limit for filing reimbursement claims in service-connected death cases.</u>

VA will pay a burial and funeral expense allowance for veterans who, at time of death, were entitled to receive pension or compensation or would have been entitled to compensation but for receipt of military retirement pay. Eligibility also may be established when death occurs in a VA facility, a nursing home under VA contract or a state veterans nursing home. Additional costs of transportation of the remains may be paid. **In non-service-connected death cases, claims must be filed within two years after permanent burial or cremation.**

VA will pay a plot allowance when a veteran is not buried in a cemetery that is under U.S. government jurisdiction under the following circumstances:

❏ the veteran was discharged from active duty because of disability incurred or aggravated in the line of duty; or

❏ the veteran was in receipt of compensation or pension or would have been except for receiving military retired pay; or

❏ the veteran died in a VA facility.

private cemetery). The VA will also provide a headstone or marker upon request for the graves of spouses or other eligible family members buried in a military, state veteran, or national cemeteries.

An application is not required for national cemeteries. Eligibility is the same as for burial in a national cemetery. The headstone or grave marker is provided without charge and shipped at Government expense to the consignee designated. The applicant must assume the cost of placing the marker in a private cemetery.

Applicants are cautioned to ensure that all information to be placed on the marker is correct before they provide it to the VA. Headstones and markers are also available for eligible members of a veteran's family who are buried in national cemeteries, without application, and for state-owned veterans cemeteries. This benefit does not apply to family members buried in private cemeteries. If you have questions concerning a headstone or marker application you may call **1-800-697-6947** or for more information you can visit the web site at http://www.cem.va.gov/hm.htm.

Send your application (**VA Form 40-1330**) along with **veterans military discharge documents**, to request a Government-provided headstone or marker. Do not send original documents, as they will not be returned to: **Memorial Programs Service (41A1), Department of Veterans Affairs, 5109 Russell Road, Quantico, VA 22134-3903**

6-6. SOCIAL SECURITY DEATH PAYMENT

The Social Security Administration may make a lump-sum payment not to exceed $255 to the eligible spouse or child entitled to benefits. The lump-sum death benefit can be paid upon the death of the insured person even if they were not receiving retirement or disability benefits at the time of death. The person entitled to the lump-sum payment has two years after the date of burial to file a claim for payment. Contact the Social Security office about eligibility and filing procedures at **1-800-772-1213** or visit the web site at http://www.ssa.gov/ww&os2.htm

6-7. NATIONAL CEMETERY ADMINISTRATION (NCA)

The National cemetery Administration (NCA) honors Veterans with a final resting place and lasting memorials that commemorate their service to our nation.

The purpose of the National Cemetery Administration is:

❑ To provide burial space

commissary and exchange privileges.

Upon the death of a retired Marine, the surviving spouse and eligible children should take the DD Form 1172 to the nearest Realtime Automated Personnel Identification System (RAPIDS) site for reissuance. They will need to take a copy of the retired Marine's death certificate to support a change in the sponsor's status. If the nearest RAPIDS site is unknown, call CMC (MMSR-6) at **800-336-4649** for this information.

A parent or parent-in-law of a deceased member who was, at the time of the member's death, dependent on the member for over one-half of his or her support and was living in a dwelling provided or maintained by the member may request a verified application for an identification card from CMC (MMSR-6).

6-10. MEDICAL CARE

Surviving unremarried spouses and eligible children continue to be eligible for the same medical care under the Military Health System that they were receiving before the retired Marine's death.

TRICARE For Life (TFL), which became effective October 1, 2001, offers TRICARE benefits to Medicare-eligible military retirees and dependents that are enrolled in Medicare Part B.

By law, TRICARE is second payer to Medicare on all services covered by both Medicare and TRICARE. TFL is an entitlement and does not require an enrollment fee, **but you do need a valid military ID card.**

To take advantage of TFL, you and your eligible family members' personal information and Medicare Part B status must be up-to-date in the Defense Enrollment Eligibility Reporting System (DEERS).

You may update your information by phone (**1-800-538-9552**) or by visiting your nearest ID card issuing facility. Visit www.dmdc.osd.mil/rsl to locate the nearest ID card facility.

Here's how TFL works for medical services:

❏ **Covered by Medicare and TRICARE:** Medicare pays the Medicare allowable amount; TRICARE pays your Medicare cost-share, as well as your Medicare deductible.

❏ **Covered by Medicare, but not by TRICARE:** Medicare pays its normal amount, and you pay the Medicare cost-share and deductible. TRICARE makes no payment.

❏ **Covered by TRICARE, but not by Medicare:** TRICARE pays the same as it would for a retiree not covered by

❏ if separated, was not at fault for the separation, and is not currently remarried.

Note: A surviving spouse who remarries on or after December 16, 2003, and on or after attaining age 57, is entitled to continue to receive DIC.

The surviving child(ren), if he/she is:

❏ not included on the surviving spouse's DIC

❏ unmarried and

❏ under age 18, or between the ages of 18 and 23 and attending school.
(Note: Certain helpless adult children are entitled to DIC. Call toll-free 1-800-827-1000 for the eligibility requirements for those survivors).

The **surviving parent(s)** may be eligible for an income-based benefit. See our fact sheet, *Parents' DIC*, (http://www.vba.va.gov/bln/21/Milsvc/Docs/DICParents.doc) or call the toll-free **1-800-827-1000** for more information.

The basic monthly rate of DIC will vary per year for an eligible surviving spouse. The rate is increased for each dependent child, and also if the surviving spouse is housebound or in need of aid and attendance. VA also adds a transitional benefit to surviving spouse's monthly DIC if there are children under age 18.

The amount is based on a family unit, not individual children. It is paid for two years from the date that entitlement to DIC commences, but is discontinued earlier when there is no child under age 18 or no child on the surviving spouse's DIC for any reason. Benefit rate tables, including those for children alone and parents, can be found on the Internet at http://www.vba.va.gov/bln/21/Rates, or call the toll-free **1-800-827-1000**.

Claimants should complete **VA Form 21-534** (*Application for Dependency and Indemnity Compensation, Death Pension and Accrued Benefits by a Surviving Spouse or Child*), and submit it to the VA regional office serving the claimant's area. Call the toll-free **1-800-827-1000** for information about supporting materials that VA may need to process a DIC claim.

6-12. DEATH DUE TO A NONSERVICE-CONNECTED CAUSE

Dependency and Indemnity Compensation (DIC) payments also may be authorized for surviving spouses, unmarried children under 18, helpless children, and those between 18

payable to those with estates large enough to provide maintenance.

The veteran must have been discharged under conditions other than dishonorable and must have had 90 days or more of active military service, at least one day of which was during a period of war, or a service-connected disability justifying discharge for disability. If the veteran died in service not in line of duty, benefits may be payable if the veteran had completed at least two years of honorable service.

Children who became permanently incapable of self-support because of a disability before reaching age 18 may be eligible for a pension as long as the condition exists, unless the child marries or the child's income exceeds the applicable limit. A surviving spouse who is a patient in a nursing home, is in need of the regular aid and attendance of another person or is permanently housebound may be entitled to higher income limitations or additional benefits, depending upon the type of pension received.

6-14. DEATH GRATUITY

Military services provide a death gratuity payment to a deceased servicemember's spouse or children. Parents, brothers or sisters may be provided the gratuity, if designated by the deceased. This is paid as soon as possible by the last military command of the deceased. If the beneficiary has not been paid within a reasonable time, application may be made to the service concerned. The death gratuity is payable in case of any death in active service, or any death within 120 days thereafter from causes related to active service.

6-15. OTHER FEDERAL BENEFITS AVAILABLE TO SURVIVING SPOUSES

Home Loan Guarantees.
The unmarried surviving spouse of a **veteran who died on active duty or as the result of a service-connected disability** is eligible for the home loan benefit. If you wish to apply for the home loan benefit as a surviving spouse, contact one of the **VA Eligibility Centers**. In addition, a surviving spouse who obtained a VA home loan with the veteran prior to his or her death (regardless of the cause of death) **may** obtain a VA guaranteed interest rate reduction refinance loan. For more information, contact one of the **VA Eligibility Centers** at www.homeloans.va.ogv/elig.htm

active-duty ID card. If your retired ID card is lost or damaged, you may get a replacement card from the nearest RAPIDS site. If you are not shown in the DEERS, the issuing activity may request verification of your entitlement by contacting CMC (MMSR-6) at **1-800-336-4649.**

7-3. YOUR FAMILY MEMBERS' IDENTIFICATION CARDS

You and your family were enrolled in DEERS while you were on active duty, but once you retire, the ID cards must be reissued. Enrollment is accomplished by completing the DD Form 1172 and furnishing legal documents to establish proof of dependency. Failure to enroll eligible family members will result in refusal of benefits and privileges.

7-4. REPLACEMENT OF FAMILY MEMBERS' IDENTIFICATION CARDS

You may apply for renewal or replacement of the DD Form 1172 for your family members at any RAPIDS site. The DEERS representative at Headquarters Marines Corps may verify eligibility if there are any discrepancies found during the renewal or replacement process. If the family member is not listed in DEERS, you must provide sufficient documentation to show entitlement (e.g., retirement orders, DD Form 214, marriage certificate, documents dissolving prior marriages, birth certificates, etc.)

7-5. ELIGIBILITY FOR IDENTIFICATION CARDS

Those eligible to receive an identification card include:

- Spouses,

- Unremarried surviving spouses,

- Unmarried children/stepchildren under age 21,

- Unmarried children/stepchildren under age 23 who attend college full-time and receive more than 50% of their financial support from you,

- Unmarried children/stepchildren of any age, if the child is incapable of self-support because of a mental or physical incapacity which existed before reaching age 21,

- Legal wards,

- Parents, parents-in-law or stepparents-in-law who receive over 50% of their financial support from you and who live in your household or a household provided by you,

- Unremarried former spouses who meet 20 years of service/20 years of marriage/20 years overlap

CHAPTER 7 – IDENTIFICATION CARDS

8-2. RETIREE DENTAL PROGRAM

The **TRICARE Retiree Dental Program (TRDP)** is a voluntary dental benefits program first authorized in the National Defense Authorization Act of 1997. When the program began in February 1998, it offered limited basic and preventive dental coverage to Uniformed Services retirees and their family members. On October 1, 2000, the scope of coverage was enhanced to form a more comprehensive dental benefits program never before available to this population. While the basic program is still in existence today, no new enrollments are being accepted.

The TRDP benefits are enhanced under the current TRDP contract to form the most comprehensive dental benefit program available to uniformed services retirees and their family members. The TRDP contract is administered by Delta Dental Plan of California. The TRDP is separate from the TRICARE Dental Program (TDP), which is available only to active duty family members and reserve members and their family members.

The TRDP enrollment is voluntary and open to retired uniformed services members and their family members and National Guard and Reserve retirees and their family members, including "gray area" retired reservists who are entitled to retired pay but will not receive it until age 60. Enrollment is also open to certain surviving family members of deceased active duty sponsors and Medal of Honor recipients, and their immediate family members and survivors.

There is an initial 12-month commitment for new enrollees after which enrollment may be continued on a month-to-month basis. During the 30-day grace period from the coverage effective date, voluntary termination of enrollments is allowed without further enrollment obligation provided that no benefits have been used.

The TRDP offers dental coverage throughout the 50 United States, the District of Columbia, Puerto Rico, Guam, the U.S. Virgin Islands, American Samoa, the Commonwealth of the Northern Mariana Islands, and Canada. All premiums are paid by the enrollee and vary depending on where the enrollee lives. <u>Enrollees in the TRDP are advised that although they may receive dental services from any licensed dentist they choose, there are advantages to receiving treatment from a participating network dentist</u>.

Eligible retirees and their family members can find answers to their questions about the program as well as

TRICARE pays your Medicare cost-share, as well as your Medicare deductible.

Covered by Medicare, but not by TRICARE: Medicare pays its normal amount, and you pay the Medicare cost-share and deductible. TRICARE makes no payment.

Covered by TRICARE, but not by Medicare: TRICARE pays the same as it would for a retiree not covered by Medicare. You pay the TRICARE deductible — $150.00 for individuals and $300.00 for families — and a 20% cost-share of the allowable amount. The deductible is separate from, and in addition to, your cost-share. Medicare makes no payment.

For more information you can call toll-free **1-888-DOD-LIFE (1-888-363-5433)** or visit the web site at http://www.mytricare.com/internet/tric/tri/tricare.nsf/PGS/TRCRBscs Prgrms 8.

8-5. CIVILIAN HEALTH CARE/TRICARE

You, your spouse, and your eligible children are entitled to necessary medical care (both inpatient and outpatient) from civilian sources under the TRICARE umbrella. To obtain benefits, you must have a valid identification card and be entered into the DEERS database. Eligible children under age 10 must also be entered into the system, but they can be treated on the basis of your identification card or that of your spouse. To obtain claim forms, pamphlets, or other necessary information, call TRICARE's Information Toll-Free Customer Service Line at **1-888-DoD-CARE (1-888-363-2273)**.

DoD TRICARE Managed Care Program. TRICARE is the DoD regional managed care program for members of the uniformed services and their families and survivors and retired members and their families.

The main challenge for most is deciding which TRICARE option - **Prime, Extra, or Standard** - is best for them. Enrollment is only required for TRICARE Prime. Active-duty families who are assigned to a civilian Primary Care Manager (PCM) under TRICARE Prime or who use TRICARE Extra will save money compared to what they would spend if they used TRICARE Standard. There are **no enrollment fees for active-duty families**, however, **they must** complete an enrollment form to select Prime as their coverage plan. Retired military families have to consider expected savings from TRICARE Prime against the annual enrollment fees ($230 for a single retired military; $460 for a family). If you have other primary health care insurance, TRICARE Prime may not be your best option.

to make an appointment with a TRICARE network provider. TRICARE Extra, like TRICARE Standard, requires no enrollment and involves no enrollment fee.

Extra is essentially an option for <u>TRICARE Standard</u> beneficiaries who want to save on out-of-pocket expenses by making an appointment with a TRICARE Prime network provider (doctor, nurse practitioner, lab, etc.). The appointment with the in-network provider will cost 5% less than it would with a doctor who is a TRICARE <u>authorized or participating provider</u>. Also, the TRICARE Extra option-user can expect that the network provider will file all **claims** forms for him.

TRICARE Extra Advantages:

❑ Co-payment 5% less than TRICARE Standard.

❑ No balance billing.

❑ No deductible when using retail pharmacy network.

❑ No enrollment fee.

❑ No forms to file.

❑ May use TRICARE Standard if you want.

TRICARE Extra Disadvantages:

❑ No Primary Care Manager.

❑ Provider choice is limited.

❑ Patient pays deductible and co-payment.

❑ Non-availability statement required for areas surrounding MTFs.

TRICARE Standard. A new name for the traditional Standard CHAMPUS. TRICARE Standard is the basic TRICARE health care program, offering comprehensive health care coverage, for people not enrolled in TRiCARE Prime (Active duty service members are automatically enrolled in prime, and many other beneficiaries choose to enroll). TRICARE Standard does not required enrollment.

TRICARE Standard is a fee-for-service plan that gives beneficiaries the option to see any TRICARE-certified/authorized provider (doctor, nurse-practitioner, lab, clinic, etc.).

TRICARE Standard Advantages:

❑ Broadest choice of provider.

❑ Available throughout the world.

❑ No enrollment fee.

❑ May use TRICARE Extra if you want.

CHAPTER 8 - MEDICAL CARE

Active-Duty Family Members

	TRICARE Prime	TRICARE Extra	TRICARE Standard
Annual Deductible	$0	$150/individual or $300/family for E-5 & above; $50/$100 for E4 & below	$150/individual or $300/family for E-5 & above; $50/$100 for E4 & below
Civilian Outpatient Visit	$0	15% of negotiated fee	20% of allowable charges for covered service
Civilian Inpatient Admission	$0	Greater of $25 or $13.90/day	Greater of $25 or $13.90/day
Civilian Inpatient Skilled Nursing Facility Care	$0 per diem charge per admission	$11/day (25 minimum) charge per admission	$11/day (25 minimum) charge per admission
Civilian Inpatient Mental Health	$0	$20/day	$20/day

Retired Military and Family Members

	TRICARE Prime	TRICARE Extra	TRICARE Standard (Standard CHAMPUS)
Annual Deductibles	$0	$150/individual $300/family	$150/individual $300/family
Annual Enrollment Fees	$230/individual $460/family	$0	$0
Civilian copays: Outpatient Visit Emergency Care Mental Health Visit	$12 per visit $30 per visit $25 per visit	20% of negotiated fees	25% of allowed charges
Civilian Inpatient Cost Share	$11/day ($25 minimum) charge per admission	Lesser of $250/day or 25% of negotiated charges plus 20% of negotiated professional fees	Lesser of $512/day or 25% of billed charges plus 25% of allowed professional fees
Civilian Inpatient Skilled Nursing Facility Care	$11/day ($25 minimum) charge per admission	$250 per diem co-payment or 20% cost-share of total charges, whichever is less, institutional services, plus 20% cost-share of separately billed professional charges	25% cost-share of allowed charges for institutional services, plus 25% cost-share of allowable for separately billed professional charges
Civilian Inpatient Mental Health	$40 per day	20% of institutional and professional fees	Lesser of $169/day or 25% of allowable fees

filing instructions before retirement.

After you reach your selected home, be sure to immediately send a claim to the finance office who last maintained your pay account, or if applicable, paid advance separation travel and transportation allowances. <u>If you fail to file a final settlement claim within the time specified by the finance office, indebtedness collection action will be initiated against you for the total amount of the advance paid.</u> You and your family members **must** complete the travel from the point of departure to the selected home for entitlement to separation travel and transportation allowances. If you are paid an advance and fail to complete the travel or only travel to a point less distant than the advance was paid for, you will owe the Government for the unearned portion of the advance payment.

If you are moving to a foreign country, familiarize yourself with the foreign government's policy about customs requirements, allowable and restricted items, and documentation required by customs authorities for importation of personal property (e.g., household goods, privately owned vehicles). Arrangements will depend on the laws of the foreign country concerned.

You may contact the American embassy as an initial point of contact for those governments that maintain diplomatic relations with the United States. Send written inquiries to the Noncommissioned Officer in Charge (NCOIC), Marine Security Battalion of the American Embassy concerned.

9-2. AUTHORIZATIONS AND RESTRICTIONS SUMMARY FOR SHIPPING AND STORAGE OF HOUSEHOLD GOODS

AUTHORIZATIONS:

You may select a home of your choice within CONUS and have your household goods (within authorized weight allowances) shipped from your last, or any previous duty station, from a designated place in the United States, from storage, or any combination, to your selected home.

RESTRICTIONS:

❑   Once you have selected a home and received travel allowances, your selection is irrevocable as far as reimbursement for travel or shipment of household goods.

❑   See your Personal Property Transportation Officer about cost limitations if you want shipment sent to a location other than your selected home in CONUS (48 contiguous states.

<u>Include a copy of your retirement orders with these applicable statements:</u>

❏   A signed statement from a medical official indicating the inclusive date(s) of hospitalization or treatment and if applicable, the anticipated date of release from the hospital, or date the treatment will end.

❏   A signed statement from an official of the educational or training facility indicating the inclusive date(s) you attended the educational or training facility and if applicable, when the training will be completed.

AUTHORIZATIONS:

You may place all or any portion of your household goods in nontemporary storage.

RESTRICTIONS:

❏   The transportation officer will select the most economical storage facility (commercial or Government) nearest to the place the household goods are located on the date of issuance of your retirement orders.

❏   Nontemporary storage cannot exceed one year from your date of retirement.

AUTHORIZATIONS:

You may have your household goods that were placed in nontemporary storage shipped to your selected home. See your transportation officer about entitlement to temporary storage, when necessary, incident to shipment from nontemporary storage.

RESTRICTIONS:

❏   Household goods must be turned over to a carrier for shipment within one year after termination of active duty.

AUTHORIZATIONS:

You are authorized temporary storage that is cumulative and may accrue at place of origin, in transit, at destination, or any combination thereof in connection with the shipment of your household goods.

RESTRICTIONS:

❏   This type of temporary storage is limited to an initial period **not to exceed 90 days** at Government expense. Additional storage, for not more than an additional 90 days, may be authorized when household goods cannot be withdrawn because of circumstances beyond your control. For this extension, you must submit a written request including the justification for the 90-day period to the appropriate

family members (18 years or older) traveling on EML orders, DoDDS teachers or family members (accompanied or unaccompanied) in an EML status year round.

❏ **Category V – Permissive Temporary Duty (Non-House Hunting) and Students.** Students whose sponsor is stationed in Alaska or Hawaii, military personnel traveling on permissive TDY orders for other than house hunting, command sponsored dependents (18 years of age) of Uniformed Services members who are stationed overseas may travel unaccompanied from the sponsor's PCS duty location to the CONUS and return.

❏ **Category VI – Retirees.** Retired military members who are issued DD Form 2 and eligible to receive retired or retainer pay, family members (with a valid identification card) of retired members when accompanied by a sponsor, and National Guard/Reserve components/members of the Ready Reserve and members of the Standby Reserve who are on the Active Status List.

Once accepted for movement, a Space-A passenger may not be "bumped" by another space available passenger, regardless of category. Family members are permitted to travel on DoD owned or controlled aircraft to or from an overseas location when a CONUS leg segment (enroute stop) is involved. For example: Family members may travel on a mission which operates from Hickam AFB, Hawaii, to Offutt AFB, Nebraska, even though an enroute stop is made in California. They may travel on a mission that operates from Andrews AFB, Maryland, to Howard AFB, Panama, even though an enroute stop is made in Florida. Dependent travel beyond the first CONUS point is contingent on the aircraft's mission.

Members may personally report to the Space-A Passenger Service Center in the passenger terminal to register for Space-A flights or may mail or fax their travel request to the locations from which they plan to depart. The fax should provide the first names of family members traveling with them, a statement that required border clearance documents are current and a list of up to five country destinations. Travelers remain on the Space-A list up to 60 days or until their leave expires, whichever is first. A valid ID card is required for all passengers. Passports, visas, and immunization records are also required for overseas travel along with leave orders or other travel authorizations.

Once registered, the traveler must wait for notification that his/her travel category and date/time of sign up has

permit for a stay (sometimes in a "high-cost" area), while awaiting movement, Space-A travel is a good travel choice. While some travelers sign up and travel the same day, many factors could come together to make buying a commercial ticket your best or only option. Remember, Space-A travel success depends on flexibility, patience, and good timing.

Q: Who determines eligibility to fly Space A?

A: The four services jointly establish Space-A eligibility. The AMC's first responsibility is airlifting official DoD traffic. Space-A passengers are accommodated only after official duty passengers and cargo.

Q: How long does my name stay on the Space-A list?

A: All travelers remain on the register 60 days after registration, or for the duration of their travel orders authorization, or until they are selected for travel, whichever occurs first. Revalidation has been eliminated.

Q: What is "country sign-up" and how does it affect me?

A: Under this program, you may sign up for five different countries rather than five different destinations. You are also eligible for the "ALL" sign-up which makes you eligible for all other destinations served. This gives you a greater selection of destinations from which to choose.

Q: What is self sign-up?

A: Self sign-up is a program that allows passengers to sign-up at a terminal without waiting in line. Most locations now provide self sign-up counters with easy-to-follow instructions for registration. If your travel will take you a foreign country, ensure border clearance documentation is current. If you are unsure, verify it with a passenger service representative on duty.

Q: How may I find where my name is on the Space-A register?

A: Each terminal maintains a Space-A register (organized alphabetically, by priority and the date and time of registration for travel) that is updated daily. The register is conveniently located in the terminal and is directly accessible to you. Travelers may call the terminal direct to find where they stand travel wise.

Q: I am disabled. May I have a brother, sister, or friend accompany me to help me?

as a nursery, BX, or snack bar?

A: Facilities at most military terminals are generally the same as commercial facilities. Facilities include exchanges, barbershops, snack bars, pay television (free television lounge in some military terminals), traveler assistance, baggage lockers or rooms, United Services Organization lounges (USO), and nurseries (at major terminals). The type of facility available will vary according to the terminal size and location.

Q: What are the trends in the availability of Space-A travel? Does it seem as if there will be more or less Space-A travel in the coming year?

A: Although the AMC has led efforts to improve Space A travel in the past few years, movement still remains a result of unused seats. Present DoD personnel and budget trends are effecting Space-A movement opportunity. The AMC is dedicated to putting a passenger in every available seat.

Q: What is the best time of the year to travel Space A?

A: Any time other than peak travel and holidays (December-January and June-July) periods.

Q: Is it easier to go to some destinations?

A: Yes. Places where they fly often such as Germany are much easier than low frequency areas such as Australia or New Zealand.

Q: May people travel Space A to Alaska or South America?

A: Yes. Travelers may obtain Space-A travel to Alaska, South America, and other interesting locations. Travel to Alaska is relatively easy when departing from the West Coast (i.e., Travis AFB, California and McChord AFB, Washington). Travel to South America and other remote areas is much more difficult. Infrequent flights to remote areas are primarily cargo missions and have few seats available for passenger movement. Expect long waiting periods for movement.

Q: I am retired and am traveling on a passport and my flight originated overseas. Where in the continental United States (CONUS) may I fly into?

A: When traveling on a passport (family members, retired Uniform Service and Reserve members, etc.), you may return to the CONUS only through authorized ports of entry where customs and immigration clearance is available. While you may depart the CONUS literally

- **ANDREWS AFB, MD:**
(301) 981-1854, fax: (301) 981-4241 *(Europe, Caribbean, and South America)*

- **BALTIMORE-WASHINGTON IAP, MD:** (410) 918-6800 or 1-877-429-4262, fax: (410) 918-6932 *(Europe, Caribbean, and South America)*

- **CHARLESTON AFB, SC:**
(843) 963-3083, fax: (843) 963-3060 *(Caribbean and South America)*

- **CHARLESTON IAP, SC:**
(843) 963-5794/95, fax: (843) 963-3845 *(Panama and Europe)*

- **DOVER AFB, DE:**
(302) 677-4088, fax: (302) 677-2953 *(Europe)*

- **ELMENDORF AFB, AK:**
(907) 552-8588/4616, fax: (907) 552-3996 *(Pacific)*

- **HICKAM AFB, HI:**
(808) 449-1515/6833, fax: (808) 448-1503 *(Pacific)*

- **LOS ANGELES IAP:**
(310) 363-0714/0715/0716, fax: (310) 363-2790 *(Pacific)*

- **MACDILL AFB, FL:**
(813) 828-2440/2485, fax: (813) 828-7844 *(Europe)*

- **MCGUIRE AFB, NJ:**
(609) 754-5023/2864, fax: (609) 754-4621 *(Europe, Lajes Field, Greenland and Iceland)*

- **MCCHORD AFB, WA:**
(253) 982-7259, fax: (253) 982-6815 *(Alaska and the Pacific)*

- **NORFOLK NAS, VA:**
(757) 444-4148/4118, fax: (757) 445-7501 *(Europe, Caribbean, Iceland)*

- **SCOTT AFB, IL:**
(618) 256-2014/3017/4042, fax: (618) 256-1946 *(Europe/Pacific)*

10-4. WHAT TO DO IF CIRCUMSTANCES CHANGE AFTER RETIREMENT

❑   If you elected spouse coverage and your spouse dies or you are divorced, send a copy of the death certificate or the document dissolving the marriage to DFAS-CL immediately at: Defense Finance and Accounting Service, US Military Retirement Pay, PO Box 7130, London, KY 40742-7130. You can also fax the decree to (800) 469-6559. The cost reduction of your retired pay will be suspended. If you remarry, send DFAS a copy of the marriage certificate and tell them whether or not you want to cover your new spouse. If the marriage certificate and the statement are not received within one year of the remarriage, the new spouse will be automatically enrolled in the SBP at the same level of coverage you had for your previous spouse. Your new spouse will not be covered under SBP until you have been married for one year and the cost will not be deducted from your pay until the 13th month of the marriage.

❑   If you have child coverage (either child only or spouse and child) and you acquire a new child after retirement; send a copy of the birth certificate to DFAS-CL. You should also notify them when your youngest child reaches age 18 if that child is not attending college full time.

❑   If you have spouse only SBP coverage and later divorce that spouse, you must make a **deemed election** to voluntarily change the coverage from spouse to former spouse with a DD Form 2656-1, "Former Spouse Election Certificate;" or you can decline coverage altogether with a DD Form 2656-6, "Survivor Benefit Plan Election Change Certificate" by sending DFAS-CL a copy of the document dissolving the marriage. This must be done within **one year** of the date of divorce.

❑   If you have SBP coverage and are recalled to active duty for more than 30 days, the cost will be suspended until you again receive retired pay, but the coverage will remain in effect.

❑   If you have no spouse when you retire, you may cover any later acquired spouse under the SBP by sending a copy of the marriage certificate with a completely filled out DD Form 2656-6, "Survivor Benefit Plan Election Change Certificate" to DFAS-CL. The new spouse will not be eligible for an annuity until you have been married for one year and the cost will not be deducted from your pay until the 13th month of the marriage.

11-3. RETIRED ACTIVITIES PROGRAM

The Retired Activities Program (RAP) consists of four principal elements: (1) HQMC, Retired Activities Section (MMSR-6), (2) Retiree Councils, (3) Retired Activities Offices (RAO's), and (4) Retired Personnel Seminars and/or Luncheons.

❑ **HQMC, Retired Activities Section (MMSR-6).** MMSR-6 is responsible for ensuring that retired Marines, their family members, and survivors, are provided with the requisite support and assistance in matters dealing with their benefits and entitlements. MMSR-6's functions include, but are not limited to:

- Providing direct and indirect support to retired Marines, their family members, and survivors through phone calls, e-mails, personal interviews, and formal correspondence.

- Publishing quarterly, the "Semper Fidelis, Memorandum for Retired Marines", pertaining to current issues affecting retired Marines, their families, and survivors.

- Determining the eligibility of retired Marines and their family members for medical care and enrollment in the Defense Enrollment Eligibility Reporting System (DEERS); certifying applications for the Uniformed Services Identification and Privilege Cards (ID cards) for retired service members and their family members; processing requests and determining eligibility for ID cards and benefits for former spouses of Marines; serving as the focal point for military Real-Time Automated Personnel Identification System (RAPIDS) sites worldwide for the issuance of ID cards to retired service members and their family members; determining eligibility for continuance of ID card privileges for children of retired Marines who are full-time college students over age 21; serving as the liaison between the Chief, Bureau of Medicine and Surgery, Department of the Navy, and family members in the establishment of privileges for incapacitated dependent children over age 21; and serving as the liaison to the Personnel and Family Readiness Division (MR) for determination of parent's dependency affidavits for retired Marines.

- Sponsoring agency for the Navy and Marine Corps Retirement Guide (NAVMC 2642). This guide provides comprehensive information on entitlements, benefits, and privileges for retiring Marines and informs both regular and reserve component career Marines of options

efficient support for our Retired Community. Accountability and supervision are essential for the future success of this program. The following are installations that have been designated as sponsoring commands for the RAO program:

- MCAS Yuma, AZ
- MCLB Barstow, CA
- MCAGCC Twentynine Palms, CA
- MCB Camp Pendleton, CA
- MCRD San Diego, CA
- MCLB Albany, GA
- MCB Kaneohe Bay, HI
- MCB Camp SD Butler, Okinawa, JA
- MCSA Kansas City, MO
- MCB Camp Lejeune, NC
- MCAS Cherry Point, NC
- MCAS Beaufort, SC
- MCRD Parris Island, SC
- HQMC Henderson Hall VA
- MCB Quantico, VA

❏ **Retired Personnel Seminars and/or Luncheons.** The Retiree Seminars and/or Luncheons are utilized to assist in the dissemination of information and policies of concern to retired military. These seminars should be conducted semi-annual by the RAO at each Marine Corps installation. The annual Retiree Seminars provide an excellent forum for two-way communications for retired and active duty military personnel.

11-4. INSTALLATION COMMANDERS

Installation Commanders provide the necessary leadership for the establishment of the local RAO. The installation commanders will:

❏ Ensure availability of funds for the establishment/operation of the Installation's Retired Activities Office.

❏ Provide funding to meet operational requirements by ensuring each office is furnished with desks, chairs, and phones, plus suitable seating for visitors. Critical items required, such as a computer, a modem, and printer should also be installed. Additional funding support for office supplies, printing, and postal charges should also be provided.

❏ Meet quarterly (or as deemed appropriate) with the Retired Activities Program Manager (RAPM)/Retired Activities Office Director (RAOD) to discuss retired service member issues as they impact the local area.

❏ Appoint retired service members as members of advisory councils (commissary, clubs, etc.) on the recommendation of the RAPM/RAOD.

❏ Establish local retiree councils as designated.

CHAPTER 11- THE RETIRED ACTIVITIES PROGRAM

then submitted for final selection (three nominees are submitted for each vacancy). Each applicant will be notified whether or not selected as a member of the RC.

The RC meets annually in the spring of each year in the Washington, D.C. area. Members are recalled to active duty for this meeting. Civilian attire is worn.

Visit the web site for additional information as well as other useful links benefits, programs and related areas of interest for military retirees and their families
http://www.lifelines.navy.mil/retireecouncil

4. Marriage:

   To whom: _____
   (first/middle/last)

   Place and date: _____

5. Previous marriages:
   _____
   _____
   (date/place/to whom married)
   (date and place of dissolution of previous marriage)

6. Spouse's previous marriages:
   _____
   _____
   (date/place/to whom married)
   (how marriage ended: death/divorce/etc.)
   (date and place of dissolution of previous marriage)

7. Name and address of your lawyer or trusted friend who may be consulted in regard to your personal or business affairs:
   _____
   _____
   (name of lawyer or friend)
   (street/city/state/zip code)

II. FAMILY RECORDS (location):

1. Birth certificates or other proof of date of birth of yourself and of each member of immediate family *(required by insurance companies and Social Security Administration)*:
   _____
   _____
   _____
   _____

2. Naturalization (if applicable):
   _____
   (Certificate Number/Date Issued)

   _____
   (Name and location of court granting naturalization)

CHAPTER 13 - PERSONAL AFFAIRS RECORD

4. State and/or other taxes:

   a. Copies of my _____ tax returns and related papers are located at:
   _____

IV. SURVIVOR BENEFIT PLAN (SBP) AND RESERVE COMPONENT SURVIVOR BENEFIT PLAN (RCSBP):

1. Retirement/Transfer Date: _____

2. Type of election coverage: _____

3. Beneficiary Information:

   a. Name: _____

   b. Social Security Number: _____

   c. Date of Birth: _____

   d. Date of Marriage (if applicable): _____

   e. Place of Marriage (if applicable): _____

4. Level of Coverage: _____

5. Reserve Component Survivor Benefit Plan (RCSBP) Option:
   _____

6. Copy of DD Form 2656 - Data For Payment of Retired Personnel (SBP enrollment form) is located at:
   _____

V. INSURANCE:

1. My life is insured as follows:

   ❑ Government:
   _____
   (type/policy no./amount)

   ❑ Civilian:
   _____
   (company name/policy no./amount)

    d. My important papers are located at:
_____
(location of deed/abstract/mortgage/insurance/contracts and other papers)

2. Add as many other entries as may be required to complete your record as to each piece of real estate in which you have an interest.

3. Automobile Record:

    a. _____
       (make/model/year/VIN)

    b. Under _____ dated: ___/___/_____ _____
              (title no.)   *(state)*

    c. This car is now licensed for use by:
_____

    d. The automobile is insured with:
_____
       (insurance company)

        (1) Against:
_____
       (fire/theft/damage/collision/personal injury/property damage resulting from operation, etc.)

        (2) The premiums are paid to:
_____

        (3) When is the premium due:
_____
       (every 1st of the month/quarterly/semi-annually, etc.)

    e. Important papers are located at:
_____
       (location of title/mortgage/insurance and other papers)

VIII. BANK ACCOUNTS:

1. Checking account:
_____
    (account number, name of bank and location, joint or individual)

CHAPTER 13 – PERSONAL AFFAIRS RECORD

13-8

XII. MEMORANDUM:

1. Enter any additional data regarding insurance, allotments, military record, instructions to family members, etc:

_____
_____
_____

Signature: _____

Date: _____/_____/_____

2. If a copy of this statement has been given to your lawyer, trusted friend, etc., list that person's name and address:

_____
_____
(name and relationship)
(street address/city/state/zip code)

Signature: _____

Date: _____/_____/_____

CHAPTER 13 - PERSONAL AFFAIRS RECORD

NOTICE

This document is disseminated under the sponsorship of the U.S. Department of Transportation in the interest of information exchange. The United States Government assumes no liability for the contents thereof.

This publication and all Office of Aerospace Medicine technical reports are available in full-text from the Civil Aerospace Medical Institute's publications Web site: www.faa.gov/library/reports/medical/oamtechreports/index.cfm

A celebration commemorating the Institute's 50th anniversary in Oklahoma City, Oklahoma, was attended by (left-right) then-Acting Administrator Michael Huerta, Associate Administrator for Aviation Safety Peggy Gilligan, CAMI Director Melchor Antuñano, Mike Monroney Aeronautical Center Director Lindy Ritz, and Deputy Federal Air Surgeon James Fraser, reflected on highlights of medical research and the many educational programs and achievements made at CAMI over the last 50 years.

"The Institute has certainly set the gold standard in its commitment to ensure the safety of every person involved in aviation—on the flight deck, in the cabin, control tower and maintenance bay," Peggy Gilligan said. "All of us who fly are deeply grateful for their contributions."

Over the last half century, CAMI has dealt with more than 20 million medical applications and currently manages the medical certificates for roughly 400,000 U.S. pilots each year.

CAMI staff manages aerospace medicine education, scientific research, and occupational and environmental health, in addition to supporting the FAA Academy and the Transportation Safety Institute.

CAMI's contributions to aviation safety span the entire range of human involvement in aviation systems, from the identification and mitigation of medical and performance risk factors during flight to breakthroughs in crash safety design and aircraft evacuation. CAMI researchers create and apply aviation-specific medical knowledge to enhance aviation safety. CAMI's programs communicate vital aeromedical safety information to the civil aviation community.

Other contributions include drop-down oxygen masks, evacuation floor lights, and water survival techniques.

By using the latest medical technology to assess an airmen's medical fitness to fly and always putting safety first, CAMI has helped the FAA achieve the most flexible, pilot-friendly medical certification program in the world.

63-7 Tobias JV, Jeffress LA: Relation of earphone transient response to measurement of onset-duration. AD413391

63-8 McKenzie JM, Fowler PR, Lyne PJ: Calibration of an electronic counter and pulse height analyzer for plotting erythrocyte volume spectra. AD425598

63-9 Swearingen JJ, McFadden EB: Studies of air loads on man. AD602207

63-10 Gogel WC: The perception of depth from binocular disparity. AD429827

63-11 Lategola MT: In vivo measurement of total gas pressure in mammalian tissue. AD425537

63-12 Nagle FJ, Balke B, Ganslen RV, Davis AW: The mitigation of physical fatigue with Spartase. AD429001

63-13 Collins WE: Primary, secondary, and caloric nystagmus of the cat following habituation to rotation. AD428756

63-14 Collins WE: Nystagmus responses of the cat to rotation and to directionally equivalent and nonequivalent stimuli after unilateral caloric habituation. AD425565

63-15 Snyder RG: Human survivability of extreme impacts in free-fall. AD425412

63-16 Emerson TE Jr, Brake CM, Hinshaw LB: Mechanisms of action of the insecticide endrin. AD431299

63-17 Tobias JV: Application of a "relative" procedure to a problem in binaural beat perception. AD428899

63-18 Balke B: Experimental evaluation of work capacity as related to chronological and physiological aging. AD431301

63-19 Wernick JS, Tobias JV: A central factor in pure tone auditory fatigue. AD428737

63-20 Gogel WC: The visual perception of spatial extent. AD432587

63-21 Tang PC, Dille JR: In-flight loss of consciousness: A case report. AD430394

63-22 Hinshaw LB, Page BB, Brake CM, Emerson TE Jr, Masucci FD: The mechanisms of intrarenal hemodynamic changes following acute arterial occlusion. AD431302

63-23 Higgins EA, Iampietro PF, Adams T, Holmes DD: The effects of a tranquilizer on body temperature. AD432484

63-24 Dille JR, Smith PW: Central nervous system effects of chronic exposure to organophosphate insecticides. AD434090

63-25 Adams T, Funkhouser GE, Kendall WW: A method for the measurement of physiologic evaporative water loss. AD603418

63-26 Reins DA, Holmes DD, Hinshaw LB: Acute and chronic effects of the insecticide endrin on renal function and renal hemodynamics. AD602206

63-27 Dille JR, Crane CR, Pendergrass GE: The flammability of lip, face, and hair preparations in the presence of 100% oxygen. AD602204

63-28 Gogel WC: Size cues and the adjacency principle. AD602205

63-29 Collins WE: Task-control of arousal and the effects of repeated unidirectional angular acceleration on human vestibular responses. AD603419

63-30 Snyder RG, Ice J, Duncan JC, Hyde AS, Leverett S Jr: Biomedical research studies in acceleration. AD601531 Supplement-AD801793

63-31 Trites DK, Cobb BB Jr: Problems in air traffic management: IV. Comparison of preemployment, job-related experience with aptitude tests as predictors of training and job performance of air traffic control specialists. AD603416

63-32 Hinshaw LB, Emerson TE Jr, Brake CM: Mechanism of autoregulation in the intact kidney. AD603417

63-33 Dill DB, Robinson S, Balke B, Newton JL: Work tolerance: Age and altitude. AD603932

63-34 Ganslen RV, Balke B, Phillips EE, Nagle F: Effects of some tranquilizing, analeptic, and vasodilating drugs on physical work capacity and orthostatic tolerance. AD603930

63-35 Pearson RG: Human factors aspects of lightplane safety. AD603931

Tech. Pub. #1 Collins WE, Tobias JV, Capps MJ, Allen ME: Annotated bibliography of recently translated material. I. AD424640

1964

64-1 Wentz AE: Studies on aging in aviation personnel. AD456652

64-2 Naughton J, Balke B, Nagle F: The effect of physical conditioning on an individual before and after suffering a myocardial infarction. AD456653

65-17 Allen ME, Collins WE, Tobias JV, Crain RA: Aviation medicine translations: Annotated bibliography of recently translated material. III. AD617090

65-18 Collins WE: Adaptation to vestibular disorientation: I. Vertigo and nystagmus following repeated clinical stimulation. AD617091

65-19 Cobb BB Jr: Problems in air traffic management: V. Identification and potential of aptitude test measures for selection of tower air traffic controller trainees. AD620722

65-20 Swearingen JJ: Tolerances of the human face to crash impact. AD621434

65-21 Trites DK: Problems in air traffic management: VI. Interaction of training-entry age with intellectual and personality characteristics of air traffic control specialists. AD620721

65-22 Trites DK, Miller MC, Cobb BB Jr: Problems in air traffic management. VII. Job and training performance of air traffic control specialists-measurement, structure, and prediction. AD649292

65-23 Swearingen JJ, Young JW: Determination of centers of gravity of children, sitting and standing. AD661865

65-24 Collins WE: Adaptation to vestibular disorientation. II. Nystagmus and vertigo following high-velocity angular accelerations. AD621435

65-25 Feinberg R, Podolak E: Latency of pupillary reflex to light stimulation and its relationship to aging. AD689809

65-26 Snow CC, Snyder RG: Anthropometry of air traffic control trainees. N66-25185

65-27 Brake CM, Reins D, Wittmers LE, Hinshaw LB: Intrarenal hemodynamic changes following acute partial renal arterial occlusion. AD649263

65-28 Hauty GT, Adams T: Phase shifts of the human circadian system and performance deficit during the periods of transition: I, East-West flight. AD639637

65-29 Hauty GT, Adams T: Phase shifts of the human circadian system and performance deficit during the periods of transition: II. West-East flight. AD689811

65-30 Hauty GT, Adams T: Phase shifts of the human circadian system and performance deficit during the periods of transition: III. North-South flight. AD689812

65-31 Pearson RG, Hunter CE, Neal GL: Development and evaluation of a radar air traffic control research task. AD660198

65-32 Gogel WC, Mertens HW: Problems in depth perception: A method of simulating objects moving in depth. AD660171

1966

66-1 Allen ME, Mohler SR: Aviation medicine reports: An annotated catalog of Office of Aviation Medicine reports: 1961 through 1965. AD638732

66-2 Allen ME, Crain RA: Aviation medicine translations: Annotated bibliography of recently translated material. IV. AD651907

66-3 Mohler SR, Swearingen JJ: Cockpit design for impact survival. AD687411

66-4 Tobias JV: A table of intensity increments. AD642113

66-5 Clark G: Problems in aerial application: A comparison of the effects of dieldrin poisoning in cold-adapted and room-temperature mammals. N66-30197

66-6 Fiorica V: Fatigue and stress studies: An improved semiautomated procedure for fluorometric determination of plasma catecholamines. AD653748

66-7 McFadden EB: Evaluation of the physiological protective efficiency of a new prototype disposable passenger oxygen mask. AD644118

66-8 Mohler SR: The predominant causes of crashes and recommended therapy. AD639779

66-9 Young JW: Selected facial measurements of children for oxygen mask design. AD640062

66-10 O'Connor WF, Pendergrass GE: Effects of decompression on operator performance. AD675774

66-11 Hinshaw LB, Reins DA, Emerson TE Jr, Rieger JA Jr, Stavinoha WB, Fiorica V, Solomon LA, Holmes DD: Problems in aerial application: I.-V. AD660199

66-12 Swearingen JJ: Injury potentials of light-aircraft instrument panels. AD642114

66-13 McFadden EB, Simpson JM: Flotation characteristics of aircraft-passenger seat cushions. AD642349

Part I: Chronological Index

67-3 McFadden EB: Development of techniques for evaluating the physiological protective efficiency of civil aviation oxygen equipment. AD659498

67-4 McFadden EB, Reynolds HI, Funkhouser GE: A protective passenger smoke hood. AD657436

67-5 Fowler PR, McKenzie JM: Problems in aerial application: Detection of mild poisoning by organophosphorus pesticides using an automated method for cholinesterase activity. AD656211

67-6 Collins WE, Guedry FE Jr: Adaptation to vestibular disorientation. V. Eye-movement and subjective turning responses to two durations of angular acceleration. N67-38956

67-7 Guedry FE Jr, Collins WE: Adaptation to vestibular disorientation. VI. Eye-movement and subjective turning responses to varied durations of angular acceleration. AD671855

67-8 Lewis MF, Ashby FK: Diagnostic tests of color-defective vision: Annotated bibliography, 1956-1966. AD660200

67-9 McFadden EB, Harrison HF, Simpson JM: Performance characteristics of constant-flow phase dilution oxygen mask designs for general aviation. AD660201

67-10 Rowland RC Jr, Tobias JV: Interaural intensity difference limen. AD661235

67-11 Seipel JH: The biophysical basis and clinical applications of rheoencephalography. AD673082

67-12 Collins WE: Adaptation to vestibular disorientation. VII. Special effects of brief periods of visual fixation on nystagmus and sensations of turning. AD659192

67-13 Young JW: A functional comparison of basic restraint systems. AD660202

67-14 Swearingen JJ: An evaluation of potential decompression hazards in small pressurized aircraft. AD660203

67-15 Melton CE Jr, Wicks SM: In-flight physiological monitoring of student pilots. AD665660

67-16 Lewis MF: Cross-modality matching of loudness to brightness for flashes of varying luminance and duration. AD664463

67-17 Funkhouser GE, Billings SM: A portable device for the measurement of evaporative water loss. AD664465

67-18 Gogel WC: Cue-enhancement as a function of task-set. AD664466

67-19 Collins WE: Adaptation to vestibular disorientation. VIII. "Coriolis" vestibular stimulation and the influence of different visual surrounds. N68-16799

67-20 Gogel WC, Mertens HW: Perceived depth between familiar objects. AD665293

67-21 Crane CR, Sanders DC: Evaluation of a biocidal turbine-fuel-additive. AD665661

67-22 Mohler SR, Bedell RHS, Ross A, Veregge EJ: Aircraft accidents by older persons. AD663688

67-23 Veregge EJ: Type airman certification as related to accidents. AD663688

67-24 Lewis MF, Mertens HW: Reaction time as a function of flash luminance and duration. AD664464

67-25 Siegel PV: Aviation medicine, FAA-1966. AD675943

1968

68-1 Index to FAA Office of Aviation Medicine Reports: 1961 through 1967. AD673666

68-2 Collins WE: Adaptation to vestibular disorientation: IX. Influence of head position on the habituation of vertical nystagmus. AD677460

68-3 Podolak E, Kinn JB, Westura EE: Biomedical applications of a commercial capacitance transducer. AD683292

68-4 Fiorica V, Burr MJ, Moses R: Contribution of activity to the circadian rhythm in excretion of magnesium and calcium. AD674416

68-5 Booze CF Jr: Usage of combined airman certification by active airmen: An active airman population estimate. AD678947

68-6 Crosby WM, Snyder RG, Snow CC, Hanson PG: Impact injuries in pregnancy. I. Experimental studies. AD674861

68-7 Allen ME, Mertens RA: Aviation medicine translations: Annotated bibliography of recently translated material. V. AD673665

68-8 Mohler SR, Dille JR, Gibbons HL: Circadian rhythms and the effects of long-distance flights. AD672898

68-9 Siegel PV, Booze CF Jr: A retrospective analysis of aeromedical certification denial actions. January 1961-December 1967. AD675521

69-11	Booze CF Jr: Occupations of active airmen. AD704474
69-12	Melton CE Jr, Hoffmann SM, Delafield RH: The use of a tranquilizer (chlordiazepoxide) in flight training. AD703221
69-13	Snyder RG, Snow CC, Young JW, Price GT, Hanson PG: Experimental comparison of trauma in lateral (+Gy), rearwardfacing (+Gx), and forward-facing (-Gx) body orientations when restrained by lap belt only. AD707185
69-14	Chiles WD, Jennings AE: Effects of alcohol on complex performance. AD703633
69-15	Williams MJ, Collins WE: The spiral aftereffect. II. Some influences of visual angle and retinal speed on the duration and intensity of illusory motion. AD703634
69-16	Chiles WD, Bruni CB, Lewis RA: Methodology in the assessment of complex performance: The effects of signal rate on monitoring a static process. AD703635
69-17	Siegel PV, Gerathewohl SJ, Mohler SR: Time-zone effects on the long-distance air traveler. AD702443
69-18	Siegel PV, Mohler SR, Cierebiej A: The safety significance of aircraft accident post mortem findings. AD704473
69-19	Pearson DW, Clark G, Moore CM: A comparison of the behavioral effects of various levels of chronic disulfoton poisoning. AD704470
69-20	Collins WE, Updegraff BP: Adaptation to vestibular disorientation. XI. The influence of specific and nonspecific gravireceptors on nystagmic responses to angular acceleration. AD704471
69-21	Thackray RI, Touchstone RM: Recovery of motor performance following startle. AD704472
69-22	Swearingen JJ, Badgley JM, Braden GE, Wallace TF: Determination of centers of gravity of infants. AD708514
69-23	Brecher MH, Brecher GA: Motor effects from visually induced disorientation in man. AD708425
69-24	Gerathewohl SJ: Fidelity of simulation and transfer of training: A review of the problem. AD706744

1970

70-1	Index to FAA Office of Aviation Medicine Reports: 1961 through 1969. AD714027
70-2	Brecher MH, Brecher GA: Quantitative evaluation of optically induced disorientation. AD709329
70-3	Ryan LC, Endecott BR, Hanneman GD, Smith PW: Effects of an organophosphorus pesticide on reproduction in the rat. AD709327
70-4	Crane CR, Sanders DC, Abbott JK: Studies on the storage stability of human blood cholinesterases: I. AD714028
70-5	Higgins EA, Vaughan JA, Funkhouser GE: Blood alcohol concentrations as affected by combinations of alcoholic beverage dosages and altitudes. AD709328
70-6	Tobias JV: Auditory processing for speech intelligibility improvement. AD717394
70-7	Hasbrook AH, Rasmussen PG: Pilot heart rate during in-flight simulated instrument approaches in a general aviation aircraft. AD711268
70-8	Fiorica V, Higgins EA, Lategola MT, Davis AW Jr, Iampietro PF: Physiological responses of men during sleep deprivation. AD713590
70-9	Gerathewohl SJ, Morris Everett W, Sirkis JA: Anti-collision lights for the supersonic transport (SST). AD713488
70-10	Collins WE, Schroeder DJ, Rice N, Mertens RA, Kranz G: Some characteristics of optokinetic eye-movement patterns: A comparative study. AD715440
70-11	Revzin AM: Some acute and chronic effects of endrin on the brain. AD715452
70-12	Mohler SR: Physiologically tolerable decompression profiles for supersonic transport type certification. AD713055
70-13	Crane CR, Sanders DC, Abbott JK: A comparison of three serum cholinesterase methods. AD715439
70-14	Karson S, O'Dell JW: Performance ratings and personality factors in radar controllers. AD715247
70-15	Lewis MF, Mertens, HW: Two-flash thresholds as a function of comparison stimulus duration. AD716645
70-16	Snow CC, Carroll JJ, Allgood MA: Survival in emergency escape from passenger aircraft. AD735388
70-17	Collins WE: Effective approaches to disorientation familiarization for aviation personnel. AD719003
70-18	Lategola MT, Fiorica V, Booze CF Jr, Folk ED: Comparison of status variables among accident and nonaccident airmen from the active airman population. AD722148
70-19	Garner JD, Blethrow JG: Evacuation tests from an SST mockup. AD720627

71-29 Thackray RI, Touchstone RM, Jones KN: The effects of simulated sonic booms on tracking performance and autonomic response. AD729833

71-30 Smith RC, Cobb BB Jr, Collins WE: Attitudes and motivational factors in terminal area air traffic control work. AD730630

71-31 Mehling KD, Collins WE, Schroeder DJ: The spiral aftereffect: III. Some effects of perceived size, retinal size, and retinal speed on the duration of illusory motion. AD729834

71-32 Steen JA, Lewis MF: Color defective vision and day and night recognition of aviation color signal light flashes. AD730631

71-33 Mohler SR, Gerathewohl SJ: Civil aeromedical standards for general-use aerospace transportation vehicles. AD728318

71-34 Gilson RD, Schroeder DJ, Collins WE, Guedry FE Jr: Alcohol and disorientation-related responses. IV. Effects of different alcohol dosages and display illumination on tracking performance during vestibular stimulation. AD729835

71-35 Smith RC: Personality assessment in aviation: An analysis of the item ambiguity characteristics of the 16PF and MMPI. AD736266

71-36 Cobb BB Jr, Lay CD, Bourdet NM: The relationship between chronological age and aptitude test measures of advanced-level air traffic control trainees. AD733830

71-37 McFadden EB, Young JW: Evaluation of an improved flotation device for infants and small children. AD729836

71-38 Norwood GK: Senior aviation medical examiners conducting FAA first-class medical examinations. AD731849

71-39 Hill RJ, Collins WE, Schroeder DJ: Alcohol and disorientation-related responses: V. The influence of alcohol on positional, rotatory, and coriolis vestibular responses over 32-hour periods. AD735389

71-40 Cobb BB Jr: Air traffic aptitude test measures of military and FAA controller trainees. AD737871

71-41 Higgins EA, Fiorica V, Davis HV, Thomas AA: The acute toxicity of brief exposure of HF, HCl, and NO_2 and HCN singly and in combination with CO. AD735160

71-42 Mertens HW, Lewis MF: Discrimination of short-duration (two-pulse) flashes as a function of signal luminance and method of measurement. AD737872

1972

72-1 Dille JR, Grimm MH: Index to FAA Office of Aviation Medicine Reports: 1961 through 1971. AD742607

72-2 Yanowitch RE, Mohler SR, Nichols EA: The psycho-social reconstruction inventory: A postdictal instrument in aircraft accident investigation. AD738464

72-3 Sirkis JA: The benefits of the use of shoulder harness in general aviation aircraft. AD739943

72-4 Billings CE, Wick RL Jr, Gerke RJ, Chase RC: The effects of alcohol on pilot performance during instrument flight. AD740778

72-5 Chiles WD, Jennings AE, West G: Multiple-task performance as a predictor of the potential of air traffic controller trainees. AD741736

72-6 Lowrey DL, Langston ED, Reed W, Swearingen JJ: Effectiveness of restraint equipment in enclosed areas. AD739944

72-7 Langston ED, Swearingen JJ: Evaluation of a fiberglass instrument glare shield for protection against head injury. AD740732

72-8 Zeiner AR, Brecher GA: Effects of backscatter of brief high-intensity light on physiological responses of instrument-rated pilots and non-pilots. AD744234

72-9 Rasmussen PG, Hasbrook AH: Pilot tracking performance during successive in-flight simulated instrument approaches. AD743392

72-10 McFadden EB: Physiological evaluation of a modified jet transport passenger oxygen mask. AD743422

72-11 Chiles WD, Jennings AE: Effects of alcohol on a problem-solving task. AD743423

72-12 Crane CR, Sanders DC, Abbott JK: A comparison of serum cholinesterase methods: II. AD744866

72-13 Booze CF Jr: Attrition from active airman status during 1970. AD742608

72-14 Thackray RI, Jones KN, Touchstone RM: The color-word interference test and its relation to performance impairment under auditory distraction. AD743424

73-8	Booze CF Jr: Prevalence and incidence of disease among airmen medically certified during 1965. AD773544
73-9	Hasbrook AH, Rasmussen PG: In-flight performance of civilian pilots using moving-aircraft and moving-horizon attitude indicators. AD773450
73-10	Lategola MT, Lynn CA, Folk ED, Booze CF Jr, Lyne PJ: Height and weight errors in aeromedical certification data. AD773452
73-11	Thackray RI, Rylander R, Touchstone RM: Sonic boom startle effects: Report of a field study. AD773451
73-12	Lewis MF, Ferraro DP: Flying high: The aeromedical aspects of marihuana. AD775889
73-13	Tobias JV, Irons FM: Reception of distorted speech. AD777564
73-14	Thackray RI, Jones KN, Touchstone RM: Personality and physiological correlates of performance decrement on a monotonous task requiring sustained attention. AD777825
73-15	Smith RC, Melton CE Jr: Susceptibility to anxiety and shift difficulty as determinants of state anxiety in air traffic controllers. AD777565
73-16	Thackray RI, Touchstone RM, Bailey JP: A comparison of the startle effects resulting from exposure to two levels of simulated sonic booms. AD777581
73-17	Schroeder DJ, Collins WE, Elam GW: Effects of secobarbital and d-amphetamine on tracking performance during angular acceleration. AD777582
73-18	Steen JA, Collins WE, Lewis MF: Utility of several clinical tests of color-defective vision in predicting daytime and nighttime performance with the aviation signal light gun. AD777563
73-19	Constant GN, Goulden DR, Grimm EJ: Aviation medicine translations: Annotated bibliography of recently translated material. VIII. AD776136
73-20	Tobias JV, Irons FM: Ear-protector ratings. AD779552
73-21	Melton CE Jr, McKenzie JM, Polis BD, Hoffmann SM, Saldivar JT: Physiological responses in air traffic control personnel: Houston Intercontinental Tower. AD777838
73-22	Melton CE Jr, McKenzie JM, Smith RC, Polis BD, Higgins EA, Hoffmann SM, Funkhouser GE, Saldivar JT: Physiological, biochemical, and psychological responses in air traffic control personnel: Comparison of the 5-day and 2-2-1 shift rotation patterns. AD778214
73-23	Leeper RC, Hasbrook AH, Purswell JL: Study of control force limits for female pilots. AD777839

1974

74-1	Dille JR, Grimm MH: Index to FAA Office of Aviation Medicine Reports: 1961 through 1973. AD779553
74-2	Mathews JJ, Collins WE, Cobb BB: A sex comparison of reasons for attrition of nonjourneyman FAA air traffic controllers. AD780558
74-3	Collins WE: Adaptation to vestibular disorientation. XII. Habituation of vestibular responses: an overview. AD780562
74-4	Young JW, Fisher RG, Price GT, Chandler RF: Experimental trauma of occipital impacts. AD780668
74-5	Booze CF Jr: Characteristics of medically disqualified airman applicants during calendar year 1971. AD781684
74-6	Lategola MT, Layne PJ: Amplitude/frequency differences in a supine resting single-lead electrocardiogram of normal versus coronary heart diseased males. AD781685
74-7	Mathews JJ, Collins WE, Cobb BB Jr: Job-related attitudes of nonjourneyman FAA air traffic controllers and former controllers: a sex comparison. AD787238
74-8	Cobb BB Jr, Nelson PL: Aircraft-pilot and other pre-employment experience as factors in the selection of air traffic controller trainees. ADA001039
74-9	Thackray RI, Touchstone RM, Bailey JP: Behavioral, autonomic, and subjective reactions to low- and moderate-level sonic booms: A report of two experiments and a general evaluation of sonic boom startle effects. ADA002266
74-10	Chiles WD, West G: Multiple-task performance as a predictor of the potential of air traffic controller trainees: A followup study. ADA002920
74-11	Melton CE Jr, McKenzie JM, Saldivar JT, Hoffmann SM: Comparison of Opa Locka Tower with other ATC facilities by means of a biochemical stress index. ADA008378
74-12	Smith RC: A realistic view of the people in air traffic control. ADA006789

76-12 Collins WE: Some effects of sleep deprivation on tracking performance in static and dynamic environments. ADA033331/0GI

76-13 Melton CE Jr, Smith RC, McKenzie JM, Hoffmann SM, Saldivar JT: Stress in air traffic controllers: Effects of ARTS-III. ADA034752/GGI

76-14 Lentz JM, Collins WE: Three studies of motion sickness susceptibility. ADA036284/8GI

76-15 McKenzie JM: The aeromedical significance of sickle-cell trait. ADA038466/9Gl

1977

77-1 Murcko LE, Dille JR: Index to FAA Office of Aviation Medicine Reports: 1961 through 1976. ADA037234/2GI

77-2 Welsh KW, Vaughan JA, Rasmussen PG: Survey of cockpit visual problems of senior pilots. ADA037587/3GI

77-3 Lategola MT, Flux M, Lyne PJ: Spirometric assessment of potential respiratory impairment in general aviation airmen. ADA038296/0

77-4 Valdez CD: Ten-year survey of altitude chamber reactions using the FAA training chamber flight profiles. ADA03723/9GI

77-5 Saldivar JT, Hoffmann SM, Melton CE: Sleep in air traffic controllers. ADA038297/8GI

77-6 Gerathewohl SJ: Psychophysiological effects of aging: Developing a functional age index for pilots: I. A survey of the pertinent literature. ADA04032/0GI

77-7 Welsh KW, Rasmussen PG, Vaughan JA: Intermediate visual acuity of presbyopic individuals with and without distance and bifocal lens corrections. ADA038538/5GI

77-8 Hanneman GD, Higgins EA, Price GT, Funkhouser GE, Grape PM, Snyder L: A study of effects of hyperthermia on large, short-haired male dogs: A simulated air transport environmental stress. ADA040432/7GI

77-9 Crane CR, Sanders DC, Endecott BR, Abbott JK, Smith PW: Inhalation toxicology: I. Design of a small-animal test system. II. Determination of the relative toxic hazards of 75 aircraft cabin materials. ADA043646/9GI

77-10 Booze CF Jr: An epidemiologic investigation of occupation, age, and exposure in general aviation accidents. ADA040978/9GI

77-11 Blethrow JG, Garner JD, Lowrey DL, Busby DE, Chandler RF: Emergency escape of handicapped air travelers. ADA043269/0GI

77-12 Mertens HW: Perceived orientation of a runway model in nonpilots during simulated night approaches to landing. ADA044553/GGI

77-13 Welsh KW, Rasmussen PG, Vaughan JA: Readability of alphanumeric characters having various contrast levels as a function of age and illumination mode. ADA044554/4GI

77-14 Welsh KW, Rasmussen PG, Vaughan JA: Refractive error characteristics of early and advanced presbyopic individuals. ADA044555/1GI

77-15 Chiles WD: Objective methods for developing indices of pilot workload. ADA044556/9GI

77-16 Lategola MT, Flux M, Lyne PJ: Altitude tolerance of general aviation pilots with normal or partially impaired spirometric function. ADA044557/7GI

77-17 Higgins EA, Chiles WD, McKenzie JM, Davis AW Jr, Funkhouser GE, Jennings AE, Mullen SR, Fowler PR: Effects of lithium carbonate on performance and biomedical functions. ADA044824/1GI

77-18 Thackray RI, Bailey JP, Touchstone RM: The effect of increased monitoring load on vigilance performance using a simulated radar display. ADA044558/5GI

77-19 Smith PW, Robinson CP, Zelenski JD, Endecott BR: The role of monamine oxidase inhibition in the acute toxicity of chlordimeform. ADA045507/1GI

77-20 Dille JR, Booze CF: The 1975 accident experience of civilian pilots with static physical defects. ADA045429/8GI

77-21 Smith RC, Hutto GL: Job attitudes of airway facilities personnel. ADA04641/3GI

77-22 Revzin AM: Functional localization in the nucleus rotundus. ADA047717/4GI

77-23 Melton CE, Smith RC, McKenzie JM, Wicks SM, Saldivar JT: Stress in air traffic personnel: Low-density towers and flight service stations. ADA046826/4GI

78-26 Robinson CP, Beiergrohslein D, Smith PW, Crane CR: Reactions of methamidophos with mammalian cholinesterases. ADA058683/4GI

78-27 Gerathewohl SJ: Psychophysiological effects of aging: Developing a functional age index for pilots: III. Measurement of pilot performance. ADA062501/2GA

78-28 Welsh KW, Rasmussen PG, Vaughan JA: Visual performance assessment through clear and sunscreen-treated windows. ADA059750/0GA

78-29 Welsh KW, Vaughan JA, Rasmussen PG: Conspicuity assessment of selected propeller and tail rotor paint schemes. ADA061875/1GA

78-30 McKenzie JM: Assessment of factors possibly contributing to the susceptibility of sickle trait erythrocytes to mild hypoxia. ADA056200/9GI

78-31 Lacefield DJ, Roberts PA, Blossom CW: Agricultural aviation versus other general aviation: Toxicological findings in fatal accidents. ADA060110/4GA

78-32 Smith RC: As evaluation of four MTS recurrent training courses. ADA061519/5GA

78-33 Chiles WD, Jennings AE: Time-sharing ability in complex performance: An expanded replication. ADA061879/3GA

78-34 Chiles WD, Jennings AE, Alluisi EA: The measurement and scaling of workload in complex performance. ADA061725/8GA

78-35 Reighard HL, Dailey JT: Task force deterrence of air piracy-final report. ADA076457/1

78-36 Boone J0, Lewis MA: The development of the ATC selection battery: A new procedure to make maximum use of available information when correcting correlations for restriction in range due to selection. ADA066131/2GA

78-37 Jennings AE: A method to evaluate performance reliability of individual subjects in laboratory research applied to work settings. ADA063731/4GA

78-38 Eighth Bethesda Conference of the American College of Cardiology Washington D.C. April 25-26 1975: Cardiovascular problems associated with aviation safety. ADA066184/3GA

78-39 Rose RM, Jenkins CD, Hurst MW: Air traffic controller health change study. Boston University School of Medicine. ADA063709/0GA

78-40 Melton CE, McKenzie JM, Wicks SM, Saldivar JT: Stress in air traffic controllers: A restudy of 32 controllers 5 to 9 years later. ADA065767/6GA

78-41 Vaughan JA, Welsh KW, Rasmussen PG: The optical properties of smoke-protective devices. ADA064678/6GA

1979

79-1 Index to FAA Office of Aviation Medicine Reports: 1961 through 1978. ADA067983/7GA

79-2 Snow CC, Hartman S, Giles E, Young FA: Sex and race determination of crania by calipers and computer: A test of the Giles and Elliot discriminant functions in 52 forensic cases. ADA065448/36A

79-3 Lewis MA: A comparison of three models for determining test fairness. ADA066586/9GA

79-4 Lewis MF, Mertens HW: Pilot performance during simulated approaches and landings made with various computer-generated visual glidepath indicators. ADA066220/5GA

79-5 Tobias JV, Kidd GD Jr: Accoustic signals for emergency evacuation. ADA066113/2.A

79-6 Pollard DW: Injuries in air transport emergency evacuations. ADA069372/1GA

79-7 Collins WE, Chiles WD: Laboratory performance during acute intoxication and hangover. ADA069373/9GA

79-8 Lategola MT, Trent CC: A lower body negative pressure box for +Gz simulation in the upright seated position. ADA069326/7GA

79-9 Schroeder DJ, Collins WE: Effects of congener and noncongener alcoholic beverages on a clinical ataxia battery. ADA069375/4GA

79-10 Higgins EA, McKenzie JM, Funkhouser GE, Mullen SR: Effects of propranolol on time of useful function (TUF) in rats. ADA068535/4GA

79-11 Smith RC: A comparison of the job attitudes and interest patterns of air traffic and airway facility personnel. ADA067826/8GA

80-13	Rasmussen PG, Chesterfield BP, Lowrey DL: Readability of self-illuminated signs obscured by black fuel-fire smoke. ADA092529/7
80-14	Smith RC: Stress, anxiety, and the air traffic control specialist: Some conclusions from a decade of research. ADA093266/5
80-15	Boone JO, Van Buskirk L, Steen JA: The Federal Aviation Administration's radar training facility and employee selection and training. ADA093027/1
80-16	Melton CE: Effects of long-term exposure to low levels of ozone: A review. ADA094426/4
80-17	Thackray RI, Touchstone RM: An exploratory investigation of various assessment instruments as correlates of complex visual monitoring performance. ADA097276/0
80-18	deSteiguer D, Saldivar JT: Evaluation of the protective efficiency of a new oxygen mask for aircraft passenger use to 40,000 feet. ADA097046/7
80-19	Dark SJ: Characteristics of medically disqualified airman applicants in calendar years 1977 and 1978. ADA098766/9
80-20	McKenzie JM: Vocational options for those with sickle cell trait: Questions about hypoxemia and the industrial environment. ADA098706/5

1981

81-1	Dille JR, Haraway A: Index to FAA Office of Aviation Medicine Reports: 1961 through 1980. ADA106227/2
81-2	Lategola MT, Lyne PJ, Burr MJ: Cardiorespiratory assessment of 24-hour crash-diet effects on altitude, +Gz, and fatigue tolerances. ADA106379/1
81-3	Federal Aviation Administration Contract DOT-FA-77WA-4076: Neurological and neurosurgical conditions associated with aviation safety. ADA098697/6
81-4	Simpson LP, Goulden DR: Aviation medicine translations: Annotated bibliography of recently translated material. X. ADA098916/0
81-5	Hutto GL, Smith RC, Thackray RI: Methodology in the assessment of stress among air traffic control specialists (ATCS): Normative adult data for the State-Trait Anxiety Inventory from non-ATCS populations. ADA103192/1
81-6	Mertens HW, Lewis MF: Effect of different runway size on pilot performance during simulated night landing approaches. ADA103190/5
81-7	Chesterfield BP, Rasmussen PG, Dillon RD: Emergency cabin lighting installations: An analysis of ceiling- vs. lower-cabinmounted lighting during evacuation trials. ADA103191/3
81-8	Higgins EA, Mertens HM, McKenzie JW, Funkhouser GE: Physiological, biochemical, and performance responses to a 24-hour crash diet. ADA103143/4
81-9	Booze CF Jr: Prevalence of selected pathology among currently certified active airman. ADA103397/6
81-10	Kirkham WR: Improving the crashworthiness of general aviation aircraft by crash injury investigations. ADA103316/6
81-11	Hanneman GD: Factors related to the welfare of animals during transport by commercial aircraft. ADA106226/4
81-12	Thackray RI, Touchstone RM: Age-related differences in complex monitoring performance. ADA106225/6
81-13	Melton CE, McKenzie JM, Wicks SM, Saldivar JT: Fatigue in flight inspection field office (FIFO) flight crews. ADA106791/7
81-14	Dille JR, Booze CF Jr: The prevalence of visual deficiencies among 1979 general aviation accident airmen. ADA106489/8
81-15	Collins WE, Mastrullo AR, Kirkham WR, Taylor DK, Grape PM: An analysis of civil aviation propeller-to-person accidents: 1965-1979. ADA105365/1
81-16	Collins WE, Schroeder DJ, Elam GW: A comparison of some effects of three antimotion sickness drugs on nystagmic responses to angular accelerations and to optokinetic stimuli. ADA107947/4

1982

82-1	Thackray RI, Touchstone RM: Performance of air traffic control specialists (ATCS's) on a laboratory radar monitoring task: An exploratory study of complacency and a comparison of ATCS and non-ATCS performance ADA118239/3

83-10   deSteiguer D, Saldivar JT: An analysis of potential breathing devices intended for use by aircraft passengers. ADA132648/7

83-11   Pickrel EW, Convey JJ: Color perception and ATC job performance. ADA132649/5

83-12   Crane CR, Sanders DC, Endecott BR, Abbott JK: Inhalation toxicology: III. Evaluation of thermal degradation products from aircraft and automobile engine oils, aircraft hydraulic fluid, and mineral oil. ADA133221/2

83-13   Thackray RI, Touchstone RM: Rate of initial recovery and subsequent radar monitoring performance following a simulated emergency involving startle. ADA133602/3

83-14   deSteiguer D, Saldivar JT, Higgins EA, Funkhouser GE: The objective evaluation of aircrew protective breathing equipment: V. Mask/goggles combinations for female crewmembers. ADA134912

83-15   Mertens HW, Higgins EA, McKenzie JM: Age, altitude, and workload effects on complex performance. ADA133594/2

83-16   Young JW, Chandler RF, Snow CC, Robinette KM, Zehner GF, Lofberg MS: Anthropometric and mass distribution characteristics of the adult female. ADA135316

83-17   Schroeder DJ, Goulden DR: A bibliography of shift work research: 1950-1982. ADA135644

83-18   Dille JR, Booze CF, Jr: The 1980 and 1981 accident experience of civil airmen with selected visual pathology. ADA134898

1984

84-1   Pollard DW, Steen JA, Biron WJ, Cremer RL: Cabin safety subject index. ADA140409

84-2   Sells SB, Dailey JT, Pickrel EW: Selection of air traffic controllers. ADA147765

84-3   Booze CF Jr, Simcox LS: Blood pressure levels of active pilots compared with those of air traffic controllers. ADA146645

84-4   Lategola MT, Davis AW Jr, Gilcher RO, Lyne PJ, Burr MJ: Aviation-related cardiorespiratory effects of blood donation in female private pilots. ADA148045

84-5   Hanneman GD, Sershon JL: Tolerance endpoint for evaluating the effects of heat stress in dogs. ADA148104

84-6   VanDeventer AD, Collins WE, Manning CA, Taylor DK, Baxter NE: Studies of poststrike air traffic control specialist trainees: I. Age, biographic factors, and selection test performance related to Academy training success. ADA147892

84-7   Dille JR, Harris JL: Efforts to improve aviation medical examiner performance through continuing medical education and annual performance reports. ADA148078

84-8   Booze CF Jr: Health examination findings among active civil airmen. ADA148325

84-9   Dark SJ: Medically disqualified airline pilots. ADA149454

1985

85-1   Pollard DW, Steen JA, Penland T: Federal Aviation Regulations Part 135 cabin safety subject index. ADA156946

85-2   Melton CE: Physiological responses to unvarying (steady) and 2-2-1 shifts: Miami International Flight Service Station. ADA155751

85-3   Mertens HW, Collins WE: The effects of age, sleep deprivation, and altitude on complex performance. ADA156987

85-4   Crane CR, Sanders DC, Endecott BR, Abbott JK: Inhalation toxicology: IV. Times to incapacitation and death for rats exposed continuously to atmospheric hydrogen chloride gas. ADA157400

85-5   Collins WE, Mertens HW, Higgins EA: Some effects of alcohol and simulated altitude on complex performance scores and Breathalyzer readings. ADA158925

85-6   Booze CF Jr, Staggs CM: A comparison of postmortem coronary atherosclerosis findings in general aviation pilot fatalities. ADA159811

85-7   Convey JJ: Passing scores for the FAA ATCS color vision test. ADA160889

85-8   Lacefield DJ, Roberts PA, Grape PM: Drugs of abuse in aviation fatalities: 1. Marijuana. ADA161911

85-9   Dark SJ: Characteristics of medically disqualified airman applicants in calendar years 1982 and 1983. ADA162209

85-10   Higgins EA, Saldivar JT, Lyne PJ, Funkhouser GE: Evaluation of a passenger mask modified with a rebreather bag for protection from smoke and fumes. ADA162473

85-11   Rueschhoff BJ, Higgins EA, Burr MJ, Branson DM: Development and evaluation of a prototype life preserver. ADA163224

1989

89-1   Thackray RI, Touchstone RM: A comparison of detection efficiency on an air traffic control monitoring task with and without computer aiding. ADA206422

89-2   Booze CF Jr: Prevalence of disease among active civil airmen. ADA206050

89-3   Colangelo EJ, Russell JC: Injuries to seat occupants of light airplanes. ADA207579

89-4   Crane CR, Sanders DC, Endecott, BR: Inhalation toxicology: IX. Times-to-incapacitation for rats exposed to carbon monoxide alone, to hydrogen cyanide alone, to mixtures of carbon monoxide and hydrogen cyanide. ADA208195

89-5   Higgins EA, Vant JHB: Operation Workload - A study of passenger energy expenditure during an emergency evacuation. ADA209234

89-6   Manning CA, Della Rocco PS, Bryant KD: Prediction of success in FAA air traffic control field training as a function of selection and screening test performance. ADA209327

89-7   Collins WE, Schroeder DJ, Nye LG: Relationships of anxiety scores to Academy and field training performance of air traffic control specialists. ADA209326

89-8   Higgins EA, McLean GA, Lyne PJ, Funkhouser GE, Young JW: Performance evaluation of the Puritan-Bennett crewmember portable protective breathing device as prescribed by portions of FAA Action Notice A-8150.2. ADA210882

89-9   Shepherd WT, Parker JF Jr: Human factors issues in aircraft maintenance and inspection. ADA215 724

89-10   Schlegel TT, Higgins EA, McLean GA, Lyne PJ, England HM, Atocknie PA: Comparison of protective breathing equipment performance at ground level and 8,000 feet altitude using parameters prescribed by portions of FAA Action Notice A-8150.2. ADA212852

89-11   Higgins EA, McLean GA, Lyne PJ, Funkhouser GE, Young JW: Evaluation of the Scott Aviation portable protective breathing device for contaminant leakage as prescribed by FAA Action Notice A-8150.2. ADA216799

89-12   McLean GA, Higgins EA, Lyne PJ: The effects of wearing passenger protective breathing equipment on evacuation times through type III and type IV emergency aircraft exits in clear air and smoke. ADA216798

89-13   Melton CE: Airliner cabin ozone: an updated review. ADA233156.

89-14   Rasmussen PB, Chittum CG: The influence of adjacent seating configurations on egress through a type III emergency exit. ADA218393

1990

90-1   Collins WE, Wayda ME, Baxter NE: Index of FAA Office of Aviation Medicine Reports: 1961 through 1989. AD-221414

90-2   Myers JG: Management assessment: implications for development and training. ADA219178

90-3   Thackray RI, Touchstone RM: Effects of monitoring under high and low taskload on detection of flashing and colored radar targets. ADA220313

90-4   Collins WE, Nye LG, Manning CA: Studies of poststrike air traffic control specialist trainees: III. Changes in demographic characteristics of Academy entrants and biodemographic predictors of success in air traffic controller selection and Academy screening. ADA223480

90-5   Downey LE, Dark SJ: Medically disqualified airline pilots in calendar years 1987 and 1988. ADA224512

90-6   Manning CA, Schroeder DJ: Pilot views of Montgomery County, Texas automated FSS services. ADA227484

90-7   Hudson LS, Booze CF Jr Davis AW: Right bundle branch block as a risk factor for subsequent cardiac events. ADA226596

90-8   Schroeder DJ, Dollar CS, Nye LG: Correlates of two experimental tests with performance in the FAA Academy air traffic control nonradar screen program. ADA226419

90-9   Mertens HW: Evaluation of functional color vision requirements and current color vision screening tests for air traffic control specialists. ADA227436

90-10   Nakagawara VB: The use of contact lenses in the civil airman population. ADA227450

90-11   Gowdy V: Development of a crashworthy seat for commuter aircraft. ADA227486

92-7   Nye LG, Witt LA, Schroeder D: Confirmatory factor analysis of burnout dimensions: Correlations with job stressors and aspects of social support and job satisfaction ADA247699

92-8   Witt LA, Nye LG: Organizational goal congruence and job attitudes revisited. ADA247621

92-9   Witt LA, Nye LG: Gender, equity and job satisfaction. ADA246588

92-10   Nye LG, Witt LA: Dimensionality and construct validity of the Perceptions of Organizational Politics Scale (POPS). ADA247620

92-11   O'Donnell RD, Hordinsky JR, Madakasira S, Moise S, Warner D: A candidate automated test battery for neuropsychological screening of airmen: Design and preliminary validation. ADA247701

92-12   Revzin AM, Rasmussen PG: A new test of scanning and monitoring ability: Methods and initial results. ADA249123

92-13   Witt LA, Hellman C: Effects of subordinate feedback to the supervisor and participation in decision-making in the prediction of organizational support. ADA249125

92-14   Nakagawara VB, Loochan FK, Wood KJ: The prevalence of artificial lens implants in the civil airman population. ADA249125

92-15   Myers JG: Survey of aviation medical examiners: Information and attitudes about the pre-employment and pre-appointment drug testing program. ADA249124

92-16   Myers JG: A longitudinal examination of applicants to the air traffic supervisory identification and development program. ADA251879

92-17   Witt LA: Organizational politics, participation in decision-making, and job satisfaction. ADA251878

92-18   Wilcox BC, England HM Jr, McLean GA: Inward contaminant leakage tests of the S-Tron Corporation emergency escape breathing device. ADA251888

92-19   Teague SM, Hordinsky JR: Tolerance of beta blocked hypertensives during orthostatic and altitude stress. ADA249904

92-20   Gowdy V, DeWeese R: Evaluation of head impact kinematics for passengers seated behind interior walls. ADA252651

92-21   Witt LA: Procedural justice, occupational identification, and organizational commitment. ADA252493

92-22   England HM Jr, Wilcox BC Jr, McLean GA: Comparisons of molecular sieve oxygen concentrators for potential medical use aboard commercial aircraft. ADA253648

92-23   White VL, Canfield DV, Hordinsky JR: The identification and quantitation of triamterene in blood and urine from a fatal aircraft accident. ADA254550

92-24   Canfield DV, Kupiec TC, Huffine EF: Postmortem alcohol production in fatal aircraft accidents. ADA254680

92-25   Huffine EF, Canfield DV: Enhancement of drug detection and identification by use of various derivatizing reagents on GC-FTIR analysis. ADA254679

92-26   Manning CA, Broach D: Identifying ability requirements for operators of future automated air traffic control systems. ADA256615

92-27   McLean GA, Chittum CB, Funkhouser GE, Fairlie GW, Folk EW: Effects of seating configuration and number of type III exits on emergency aircraft evacuation. ADA255754

92-28   Mertens HW, Milburn NJ: Performance of color-dependent tasks of air traffic control specialists as a function of type and degree of color vision deficiency. ADA255794

92-29   Mertens HW, Milburn NJ: Validity of clinical color vision tests for air traffic control specialists. ADA258219

92-30   Della Rocco PS, Milburn N, Mertens H: Comparison of performance on the Shipley Institute of Living scale, air traffic control specialist selection test, and FAA Academy screen. ADA259249

92-31   OU Vortac, Edwards MB, Jones JP, Manning CA, Rotter AJ: En route air traffic controllers' use of flight progress strips: A graph-theoretic analysis. ADA259062

1993

93-1   Rodgers MD, Drechsler GK: Conversion of the CTA, Inc, en route operations concepts database into a formal sentence outline job task taxonomy. ADA261921

93-2   Collins WE: A review of civil aviation propeller-to-person accidents: 1980-1989. ADA260695

93-3   Antuñano MJ: Index of international publications in aerospace medicine. ADA262908

94-10	Garner RP, Wilcox BC, England HM, Nakagawara VB: Effects of cold exposure on wet aircraft passengers: A review. ADA280253
94-11	Marcus JE: A review of computer evacuation models and their data needs. ADA280707
94-12	Galaxy Scientific Corp: Human factors in aviation maintenance - Phase 3, Vol. 2 progress report. ADA283287
94-13	Nye LG, Schroeder DJ, Dollar CS: Relationships of Type A behavior with biographical characteristics and training performance of air traffic control specialists. ADA283813
94-14	Canfield DV, Flemig J, Hordinsky JR, Veronneau SJH: Unreported medications used in incapacitating medical conditions found in fatal civil aviation accidents. ADA284233
94-15	Nakagawara VB, Montgomery RW, Wood KJ: The applicability of commercial glare test devices in the aeromedical certification of pilot applicants. ADA284232
94-16	White VL, Canfield DV, Hordinsky JR: Elimination of quinine in two subjects after ingestion of tonic water: An exploratory study. ADA284760
94-17	Stern JA, Boyer D, Schroeder DJ: Blink rate as a measure of fatigue: A review. ADA284779
94-18	Endecott BR, Sanders DC, Chaturvedi AK: Simultaneous gas-chromatographic determination of four toxic gases generally present in combustion gas atmospheres. ADA285666
94-19	Gowdy V: The performance of child restraint devices in transport airplane passenger seats. ADA285624
94-20	Hilton Systems, Inc: Age 60 rule research, Part I: Bibliographic database. N95-13019
94-21	Hyland DT, Kay EJ, Deimler JD, Gurman EB: Age 60 rule research, Part II: Airline pilot age and performance: A review of the scientific literature. ADA286246
94-22	Kay EJ, Harris RM, Voros RS, Hillman DJ, Hyland DT, Deimler JD: Age 60 rule research, Part III: Consolidated database experiments final report. ADA286247
94-23	Hyland DT, Kay EJ, Deimler JD: Age 60 rule research, Part IV: Experimental evaluation of pilot performance. N95-13199
94-24	Holloway FA: Low-dose alcohol effects on human behavior and performance: An update on post-1984 studies. N95-14863
94-25	Williams KW, Ed: Summary proceedings of the joint industry-FAA conference on development and use of PC-based aviation training devices. N95-14917
94-26	Stern JA, Boyer D, Schroeder DJ, Touchstone RM, Stoliarov N: Blinks, saccades, and fixation pauses during vigilance task performance. ADA290600
94-27	Endsley M, Rodgers MD: Situation awareness information requirements analysis for en route air traffic control. ADA289649

1995

95-1	Collins WE: A review of civil aviation fatal accidents in which "lost/disoriented" was a cause/factor. ADA290944
95-2	Parker JF Jr, Shepherd WT: Development of an intervention program to encourage shoulder harness use and aircraft retrofit in general aviation: Phases I and II. ADA290966
95-3	Harris HC, Schroeder DJ, Collins WE: The effects of age and low doses of alcohol on compensatory tracking during angular acceleration. N95-23934
95-4	Edwards MB, Fuller DK, OU Vortac, Manning CA: The role of flight progress strips in en route air traffic control: A time-series analysis. ADA291152
95-5	Besco RO, Sangal SP, Nesthus TE, Veronneau SJH: A longevity and survival analysis for a cohort of retired airline pilots. ADA292060
95-6	Williams KW, Blanchard RE: Qualification guidelines for personal computer-based aviation training devices: Instrument rating. ADA292961
95-7	Schroeder DJ, Harris HC, Collins WE, Nesthus TE: Some performance effects of age and low blood alcohol levels on a computerized neuropsychological test. ADA292324
95-8	Chaturvedi AK, Sanders DC: Aircraft fires, smoke toxicity, and survival: An overview. ADA292919
95-9	OU Vortac, Edwards MB, Manning CA: Functions of external cues in prospective memory. ADA291932

96-6	Morrison JE, Fotouhi CH, Broach D: A formative evaluation of the collegiate training initiative-Air Traffic Control Specialist Program. ADA305307
96-7	Marcus J: Determination of effective thoracic mass. ADA306061
96-8	Williams KW: Qualification guidelines for personal computer-based aviation training devices: Instrument rating. ADA306206
96-9	Stern JA, Boyer D, Schroeder DJ, Touchstone RM, Stoliarov N: Blinks, saccades and fixation pauses during vigilance task performance: II. Gender and time of day. ADA307024
96-10	Kanki BG (Editor), Prinzo OV (Co-Editor): Methods and metrics of voice communications. ADA307148
96-11	Marcus JH: Dummy and injury criteria for aircraft crashworthiness. ADA308948
96-12	Nakagawara VB, Coffey JD, Montgomery RW: Ophthalmic requirements and considerations for the en route air traffic control specialist: An ergonometric analysis of the visual work environment. N96-25681
96-13	Young WC, Broach D, Farmer WL: Differential prediction of FAA Academy performance on the basis of gender and written Air Traffic Control Specialist aptitude test scores. ADA308354
96-14	Kupiec TC, Canfield DV, White VL: The analysis of benzodiazepines in forensic urine samples. ADA309377
96-15	Beringer DB: Use of off-the-shelf PC-based flight simulators for aviation human factors research. ADA309237
96-16	Beringer DB, Harris HC Jr: A comparison of the effects of navigational display formats and memory aids on pilot performance. ADA309382
96-17	Canfield D, White V, Soper J, Kupiec T: A comprehensive drug screening procedure for urine using HPLC, TLC, and mass spectroscopy. ADA309962
96-18	McLean GA, George MH, Funkhouser GE, Chittum CB: Aircraft evacuations onto escape slides and platforms I: Effects of passenger motivation. ADA311257
96-19	Kirkbride LA, Jensen RS, Chubb GP, Hunter DR: Developing the personal minimums tool for managing risk during preflight go/no-go decisions. ADA313639
96-20	Prinzo OV, Maclin O: Aviation topics speech acts taxonomy (ATSAT) pc user's guide version 2.0. ADA314179
96-21	Collins WE, Dollar CS: Fatal general aviation accidents involving spatial disorientation: 1976-1992. ADA313864
96-22	Mertens HW, Milburn NJ, Collins WE: A further validation of the practical color vision test for enroute air traffic control applicants. ADA314600
96-23	Della Rocco P, Cruz C: Shift work, age, and performance: Investigation of the 2-2-1 shift schedule used in air traffic control facilities II: Laboratory performance measures. ADA315493
96-24	Bailey L, Shaw R: Flight inspection crew resource management training needs analysis. ADA316691
96-25	Veronneau SJH, Mohler SR, Pennybaker AL, Wilcox BC, Sahiar F: Survival at high altitudes: Wheel-well passengers. ADA317375
96-26	Prinzo OV, Maclin O: An analysis of approach control/pilot voice communications. ADA317528
96-27	Nakagawara VB, Wood KJ: The use of task-specific lenses by presbyopic air traffic controllers at the en route radar console. ADA320284

1997

97-1	Collins WE, Wayda ME: Index of FAA Office of Aviation Medicine Reports: 1961 through 1996. ADA322331
97-2	DeJohn CA, Veronneau SJH, Hordinsky JR: Inflight medical care: An update. ADA322708
97-3	Driskill WE, Weissmuller JJ, Quebe J, Hand DK, Dittmar MJ, Hunter DR: The use of weather information in aeronautical decision-making. ADA323543
97-4	Young WC, Broach D, Farmer WL: The effects of video game experience on computer-based Air Traffic Control Specialist, air traffic scenario test scores. ADA322774
97-5	Gilliland K, Schlegel RE: A laboratory model of Readiness-to-Perform testing: Learning rates and reliability analyses for candidate testing measures. ADA323620
97-6	Kochan JA, Jensen RS, Chubb GP, Hunter DR: A new approach to aeronautical decision-making: The expertise method. ADA323793

98-9	Wreggit SS, Marsh DK II Cockpit integration of GPS: Initial assessment-menu formats and procedures. ADA341122
98-10	Sanders DC, Chaturvedi AK, Hordinsky JR, Aeromedical aspects of melatonin-An overview. ADA341726
98-11	Gowdy RV, DeWeese R: Evaluation of improved restraint systems for parachutists. ADA342643
98-12	Williams KW: GPS Design considerations: Displaying nearest airport information. ADA346043
98-13	Shehab RL, Schlegel RE, Palmerton DA: A human factors perspective on human external loads. ADA350729
98-14	Rodgers MD, Mogford RH, Mogford LS: The relationship of sector characteristics to operational errors. ADA350717
98-15	Mills SH: The combination of flight count and control time as a new metric of air traffic control activity. ADA350504
98-16	Gronlund SD, Ohrt DD, Dougherty MRP, Perry JL, Manning CA: Aircraft importance and its potential relevance to situation awareness. ADA350417
98-17	Prinzo OV: An analysis of voice communication in a simulated approach control environment. ADA350523
98-18	Chaturvedi AK, Vu NT, Ritter RM, Canfield DV: DNA profiling as an adjunct quality control/quality assurance in forensic toxicology. ADA379287
98-19	Cosper DK, McLean GA: Analysis of ditching and water survival training programs of major airframe manufacturers and airlines. PB99146839XSP
98-20	Prinzo OV, Lieberman P, Pickett E: An acoustic analysis of ATC communication. ADA353962
98-21	Canfield DV, Smith MD, Ritter RM, Chaturvedi AK: Preparation of carboxyhemoglobin standards and calculation of spectrophotometric quantitation constants. ADA379272
98-22	Broach D: Summative evaluation of the collegiate training initiative for air traffic control specialists program: Progress of Minnesota Air Traffic Control Training Center graduates in en route field training. ADA355085
98-23	Broach D (Editor): Recovery of the FAA Air Traffic Control specialist workforce, 1981-1992. ADA355135
98-24	Thompson RC, Bailey LL, Farmer WL: Predictors of perceived empowerment: An initial assessment. ADA355185
98-25	Nakagawara VB, Wood KJ: The aeromedical certification of photorefractive keratectomy in civil aviation: A reference guide. ADA382812
98-26	Durso FT, Truitt TR, Hackworth CA, Albright CA, Bleckley MK, Manning CA: Reduced flight progress strips in en route ATC mixed environments. ADA382818
98-27	Garner RP, Murphy RE, Hudgins CB, Mandella JG Jr: Performance of a portable oxygen breathing system at 25,000 feet altitude. ADA357729
98-28	Wickens CD, Ververs PM: Allocation of attention with head-up displays. ADA359344

1999

99-1	Collins WE, Wayda ME: Index of FAA Office of Aviation Medicine Reports: 1961 through 1998. ADA360592
99-2	Della Rocco PS, (Editor): The role of shift work and fatigue in air traffic control operational errors and incidents. ADA360730
99-3	Durso FT, Hackworth CA, Truitt TR, Crutchfield J, Nikolic D, Manning CA: Situation awareness as a predictor of performance in en route air traffic controllers. ADA360807
99-4	Garner RP: Concepts providing for physiological protection after aircraft cabin decompression in the altitude range of 60,000 to 80,000 feet above sea level. ADA360727
99-5	Gowdy V, George M, McLean GA: A comparison of buckle release timing for push-button and lift-latch belt buckles. ADA360725
99-6	Nakagawara VB, Wood KJ, Montgomery RW: Refractive surgery in the civil airman population by class of medical certificate and by aviation occupation. ADA361329
99-7	Rakovan L, Wiggins MW, Jensen RS, Hunter DR: A survey of pilots on the dissemination of safety information. ADA361233
99-8	Milburn NJ, Mertens HW: Optimizing blink parameters for highlighting an air traffic control situation display. ADA316258
99-9	Joseph K, Jahns D, Nendick M, St. George R: A usability survey of GPS avionics equipment: Some prelimary findings. ADA362193

00-8	Williams KW: Comparing text and graphics in navigation display design. ADA375445
00-9	Chaturvedi AK, Smith DR, Canfield DV: Blood carbon monoxide and cyanide concentrations in the fatalities of fire and non-fire associated civil aviation accidents. PB2001102911
00-10	Della Rocco PS, Comperatore C, Caldwell L, Cruz CE: The effects of napping on night shift performance. PB2001102912
00-11	Hynes MK: Evacuee injuries and demographics in transport airplane precautionary emergency evacuations. PB2001102913
00-12	Heil MC, Agnew BO: The effects of previous computer experience on Air Traffic-Selection and Training (AT-SAT) test performance. ADA377228
00-13	DeJohn CA, Veronneau SJH, Wolbrink AM, Larcher JG: The evaluation of in-flight medical care aboard selected U.S. air carriers: 1996 to 1997. ADA377878
00-14	Thompson RC, Joseph KM, Bailey LL, Worley JA, Williams CA: Organizational change: An assessment of trust and cynicism. PB2001102914
00-15	Russell CJ, Dean MA, Broach DM: Guidelines for bootstrapping validity coefficients in ATCS selection research. ADA379430
00-16	Vu NT, Chaturvedi AK, Canfield DV, Soper JW, Kupfer DM, Roe BA: DNA-based detection of ethanol-producing microorganisms in postmortem blood and tissues by polymerase chain reaction. ADA379226
00-17	Thompson RC, Bailey LL: Age and attitudes in the air traffic control specialist workforce: An initial investigation. ADA379286
00-18	Nakagawara VB, Veronneau SJH: A unique contact lens-related airline aircraft accident. ADA379287
00-19	Nakagawara VB, Wood KJ, Montgomery RW: Refractive surgery in aircrew members who fly for scheduled and non-scheduled civilian airlines. PB2001102915
00-20	Lewis RJ, Johnson RD, Blank CL: A novel method for the determination of sildenafil (Viagra®) and its metabolite in postmortem specimens using LC/MS/MS and LC/MS/MS. PB2001102916
00-21	Canfield DV, Hordinsky J, Millett DP, Endecott B, Smith D: Prevalence of drugs and alcohol in fatal civil aviation accidents between 1994 and 1998. ADA379272
00-22	Canfield DV, Chaturvedi AK, Boren HK, Veronneau SJH, White VL: Abnormal glucose levels found in transportation accidents. PB2001102917
00-23	Nakagawara VB, Montgomery RW: Gender differences in a refractive surgery population of civilian aviators. PB2001102918
00-24	Pfleiderer EM: Multidimensional scaling analysis of controllers' perceptions of aircraft performance characteristics. ADA382823
00-25	Bailey L, Thompson R: The effects of performance feedback on air traffic control team coordination: A simulation study. ADA382812
00-26	Schvaneveldt R, Beringer DB, Lamonica J, Tucker R, Nance C: Priorities, organization, and sources of information accessed by pilots in various phases of flight. ADA382818
00-27	Naff KC, Thompson RC: The impact of teams on the climate for diversity in government: The FAA experience. ADA382809
00-28	Bailey LL, Peterson LM, Williams KW, Thompson RC: Controlled flight into terrain: A study of pilot perspectives in Alaska. ADA382989
00-29	Lewis RJ, Southern TL, Cardona PS, Canfield DV, Garber M: Distribution of butalbital in biological fluids and tissues. PB2001102919
00-30	Mills, SH: The computerized analysis of ATC tracking data for an operational evaluation of CDTI/ADS-B technology. ADA385812
00-31	Williams K: Impact of aviation highway-in-the-sky displays on pilot situation awareness. ADA384535
00-32	Fiedler ER, Della Rocco PS, Schroeder DJ, Nguyen K: The relationship between aviators' home-based stress to work stress and self-perceived performance. ADA384889

02-5 Prinzo OV: Automatic dependent surveillance/broadcast-cockpit display of traffic information: Innovations in pilot-managed departures. PB2002107795

02-6 Nakagawara VB, Wood KJ, Montgomery RW: Contact lens use in the civil airman population. ADA404962

02-7 Beringer DB: Applying performance-controlled systems, fuzzy logic, and fly-by-wire controls to general aviation. ADA405731

02-8 Cruz C, Detwiler C, Nesthus T, Boquet A: A laboratory comparison of clockwise and counter-clockwise rapidly rotating shift schedules, Part I: Sleep. ADA402842

02-9 Broach D, Dollar C: Relationship of employee attitudes and supervisor-controller ration to en route operational error rates. ADA405141

02-10 Nakagawara VB, Montgomery RW, Wood KJ: The aviation accident experience of civilian airmen with refractive surgery. ADA428733

02-11 DeWeese R, Gowdy RV: Human factors associated with the certification of airplane seats: Seat belt adjustment and release. ADA404285

02-12 Pounds J, Isaac A: Development of an FAA-EUROCONTROL technique for the analysis of human error in ATM. ADA405379

02-13 Cruz C, Boquet A, Detwiler C, Nesthus T: A laboratory comparison of clockwise and counter-clockwise rapidly rotating shift schedules, Part II: Performance. ADA405385

02-14 Chaturvedi AK, Smith DR, Soper JW, Canfield DV: Characteristics and toxicological processing of postmortem pilot specimens from fatal civil aviation accidents. ADA405378

02-15 Lewis RJ, Johnson RD, Canfield DV: An accurate method for the determination of carbon monoxide in postmortem blood using GC/TCD. ADA408214

02-16 McLean GA, Corbett CL, Larcher KG, McDown JR, Palmerton DA, Porter KA, Shaftstall RM, Odom RS: Access-to-Egress: Interactive effects of factors that control the emergency evacuation of naïve passengers through the transport airplane Type-III overwing exit. ADA408009

02-17 Hunter D: Risk perception and risk tolerance in aircraft pilots. ADA40799

02-18 Bailey LL, Willems BF: The moderator effects of taskload on the interplay between en route intra-sector team communications, situation awareness, and mental workload. ADA408021

02-19 Roy KM, Beringer DB: General aviation pilot performance following unannounced in-flight loss of vacuum system and associated instruments in simulated instrument meteorological conditions. ADA408027

02-20 Boquet A, Cruz C, Nesthus TE, Detwiler C, Knecht W, Holcomb K: A laboratory comparison of clockwise and counter-clockwise rapidly rotating shift schedule, Part III: Effects on core body temperatures and neuroendocrine measures. ADA409994

02-21 Williams KW, Yost A, Holland J, Tyler RR: Assessment of advanced cockpit displays for GA aircraft: The Capstone Program. ADA409997

02-22 Moertl PM, Canning JM, Gronlund SD, Dougherty MRP, Johansson J, Mills SH: Aiding planning in air traffic control: An experimental investigation of the effects of perceptual information integration. ADA409992

02-23 Goldman SM, Fiedler ER, King RE: General aviation maintenance-related accidents: A review of 10 years of NTSB data. ADA409385

02-24 Heil MC, Detwiler CA, Agen RA, Williams CA, Agnew BO, King RE: The effects of practice and coaching on the Air Traffic Selection and Training Battery. ADA409734

2003

03-1 Collins WE, Wayda ME: Index of FAA Office of Aerospace Medicine Reports: 1961 through 2002. ADA410971

03-2 Joseph KM, Domino D, Battisie V, Bone RS, Olmos BO: A summary of flightdeck observer data from SafeFlight 21 OpEval-2. ADA413898

03-3 Taylor HL, Talleur DA, Bradshaw GL, Eanuel TW Jr., Rantanen E, Hulin CL, Lendrum L: Effectiveness of personal computers to meet recency of experience requirements. ADA413334

03-4 Shappell SA Wiegmann DA: A human error analysis of general aviation controlled flight into terrain accidents occurring between 1990-1998. ADA417230

04-4   Johnson RD, Lewis RJ, Angier MK, Vu NT: The formation of ethanol in postmortem tissues. ADA423300

04-5   Beringer DB, Ball JD: The effects of NEXRAD graphical data resolution and direct weather viewing on pilot's judgments of weather severity and their willingness to continue a flight. ADA423239

04-6   Nakagawara VB, Montgomery RW, Wood KJ: Demographics and vision restrictions in civilian pilots: Clinical implications. ADA423237

04-7   Garner RP, Wong KL, Ericson SC, Baker AJ, Orzechowski JA: CFD validation for contaminant transport in aircraft cabin ventilation flow fields. ADA423999

04-8   Broach D: Methodological issues in the study of airplane accident rates by pilot age: Effects of accident and pilot inclusion criteria and analytic strategy. ADA423237

04-9   Nakagawara VB, Montgomery RW, Dillard AE, McLin LN, Connor CW: The effects of laser illumination on operational and visual performance of pilots during final approach. ADA425392

04-10 Milburn NJ: A historical review of color vision standards for automated flight service station air traffic control specialists. ADA426278

04-11 Prinzo OV: Automatic Dependent Surveillance-Broadcast/Cockpit Display of Traffic Information: Innovations in aircraft navigation on the airport surface. ADA427908

04-12 McLean GA, Palmerton DA, Corbett CL, Larcher KG, McDown JR: Simulated evacuations into water. ADA427908

04-13 Johnson RD, Lewis RJ, Canfield DV, Dubowski KM, Blank CL: Accurate assignment of ethanol origin in postmortem urine: A case study. ADA427914

04-14 Milburn NJ, Mertens HW: Predictive validity of the aviation lights test for testing pilots with color vision deficiencies. ADA428358

04-15 Angier MK, Lewis RJ, Chaturvedi AK, Canfield DV: Gas chromatographic/mass spectrometric differentiation of atenolol, metoprolol, propanolol, and an interfering metabolite product of metoprolol. ADA428964

04-16 DeJohn CA, Wolbrink AM, Larcher JG: In-flight medical incapacitation and impairment of U.S. airline pilots: 1993 to 1998.

04-17 Xing J: Measures of information complexity and the implications for automation design. ADA428690

04-18 DeWeese R, Moorcroft D: Evaluation of a head injury criteria component test device. ADA428692

04-19 McLean GA, Cosper DK: Availability of passenger safety information for improved survival in aircraft accidents. ADA372580

04-20 Williams KW, Ball JD: Usability and effectiveness of advanced general aviation cockpit displays for visual flight procedures. ADA423591

04-21 Dollar CS, Schroeder DJ: A longitudinal study of Myers-Briggs personality types in air traffic controllers. PB2005103900

04-22 Hackworth CA, Cruz CE, Goldman S, Jack DG, King SJ, Twohig P: Employee attitudes within the Federal Aviation Administration. ADA460092

04-23 Hackworth CA, Cruz CE, Jack DG, Goldman S, King SJ: Employee attitudes within the air traffic organization. PB2005103902

04-24 Williams K: A summary of unmanned aircraft accident/incident data: Human factors implications. ADA460102

2005

05-1   Collins WE, Wayda ME, Wade K: Index to FAA Office of Aerospace Medicine Reports: 1961 through 2004. ADA460101

05-2   Corbett CL: Caring for precious cargo, Part II: Behavioral techniques for emergency aircraft evacuations with infants through the Type III overwing exit. ADA460057

05-3   Collins WE, Wade KJ: A milestone of aeromedical research contributions to civil aviation safety: The 1000th report in the CARI/OAM series. ADA460106

05-4   Xing J, Manning CA: Complexity and automation displays of air traffic control: Literature review and analysis. ADA460107

05-5   Bailey L, Schroeder DJ, Pounds J: The Air Traffic Control Operational Errors Severity Index: An initial evaluation. ADA460573

06-6   Xing J, Schroeder DJ: Reexamination of color vision standards, Part II. A computational method to assess the effect of color deficiencies in using ATC displays. ADA463063

06-7   Detwiler C, Hackworth C, Holcomb K, Boquet A, Pfleiderer E, Wiegmann D, Shappell, S: Beneath the tip of the iceberg: A human factors analysis of general aviation accidents in Alaska vs. the rest of the United States. ADA460891

06-8   Williams KW: Human factors implications of unmanned aircraft accidents: Flight control problems. ADA460892

06-9   Nakagarwara VB, Wood KJ, Montgomery RW: New refractive surgery procedures and their implications for aviation safety. ADA460896

06-10   Shaffstall RM, Garner RP, Bishop J, Cameron-Landis L, Eddington DL, Hau G, Spera S, Mielnik T, Thomas JA: Vaporized hydrogen peroxide (VHP®) decontamination of a section of a Boeing 747 cabin. ADA460897

06-11   Xing J: Reexamination of color vision standards, Part III: Analysis of the effect of color vision deficiencies in using ATC displays. ADA460956

06-12   Canfield DV, Salazar GJ, Lewis RJ, Whinnery JE: Comparison of pilot medical history and medications found in postmortem specimens. ADA461233

06-13   Nesthus TE, Cruz C, Hackworth C, Boquet A: An assessment of commuting risk factors for air traffic control specialists. ADA460857

06-14   Kupfer DM, Huggins M, Cassidy B, Vu N, Burian D, Canfield D: A rapid and inexpensive PCR-based STR genotyping method for identifying forensic specimens. ADA460885

06-15   Xing J: Color and visual factors in ATC displays. ADA460886

06-16   Dattel AR, King RE: Reweighing AT-SAT to mitigate group score differences. ADA461242

06-17   Johnson RD, Lewis RJ, Angier MK: The LC/MS quantitation of Vardenafil (Levitra®) in postmortem biological specimens. ADA460865

06-18   Shappell SA, Detwiler CA, Holcomb KA, Hackworth CA, Boquet AJ, Wiegmann DA: Human error and commercial aviation accidents: A comprehensive, fine-grained analysis using HFACS. ADA463865

06-19   Caldwell DC, Lewis RJ, Shaffstall RM, Johnson RD: Sublimation rate of dry ice packaged in commonly used quantities by the air cargo industry. ADA461451

06-20   Pounds J, Rodgers MD, Thompson D, Jack DG: Developing temporal markers to profile operational errors. ADA461407

06-21   Schroeder D, Bailey L, Pounds J, Manning C: A human factors review of the operational error literature. ADA461408

06-22   Xing J: Color analysis in air traffic control displays, Part I. Radar displays. ADA461409

06-23   Nakagawara VB, Wood KJ, Montgomery RW: A review of recent laser illumination events in the aviation environment. ADA461728

06-24   Shappell S, Wiegmann D: Developing a methodology for assessing safety programs targeting human error in aviation. ADA461400

06-25   Prinzo OV, Hendrix AM, Hendrix R: The outcome of ATC message complexity on pilot readback performance. ADA461355

06-26   Milburn NJ, Dobbins L, Pounds J, Goldman S: Mining for information in accident data. ADA464086

06-27   Baker AJ, Ericson SC, Orzechowski JA, Wong KL, Garner RP: Validation for CFD prediction of mass transport in an aircraft passenger cabin. ADA465914

06-28   Nakagawara VB, Montgomery RW, Wood KJ: Aircraft accidents and incidents associated with visual disturbances from bright lights during nighttime flight operations. ADA465917

06-29   Manning CM, Pfleiderer EM: Relationship of sector activity and sector complexity to air traffic controller taskload. ADA463881

06-30   Dollar C, Broach D: Comparison of intent-to-leave with actual turnover within the FAA. ADA463866

2007

07-1   Collins WE, Wayda ME: Index to FAA Office of Aerospace Medicine reports: 1961 through 2006. ADA463875

07-2   Antuñano MJ, Wade K: Index of international publications in aerospace medicine. ADA464057

2008

08-1 Peterman CL, Rogers PB, Véronneau SJH, Whinnery JE: Development of an aeromedical scientific information system for aviation safety. ADA477153

08-2 Gale WF, Gale HS, Watson J: Field evaluation of whole airliner decontamination technologies for narrow-body aircraft. ADA477159

08-3 Ball J: The impact of training on general aviation pilots' ability to make strategic weather-related decisions. ADA477162

08-4 Gale WF, Gale HS, Watson, J: Field evaluation of whole airliner decontamination technologies—wide-body aircraft with dual-use application for railcars. ADA477163

08-5 Burian D: Functional genomics group—Program description. ADA481081

08-6 Knecht WR: Use of weather information by general aviation pilots, Part I, quantitative: reported use and value of providers and products. ADA481118

08-7 Knecht WR: Use of weather information by general aviation pilots, Part II, qualitative: Exploring factors involved in weather-related decision making. ADA481119

08-8 Kupfer DM, Jenkins M, Burian D, Canfield DV: Use of alternative primers for gender discrimination in human forensic genotyping. ADA481070

08-9 Carretta TR, King RE: USAF enlisted air traffic controller selection: Examination of the predictive validity of the FAA air traffic selection and training battery versus training performance. ADA481110

08-10 Botch SR, Johnson RD: Drug usage in pilots involved in aviation accidents compared with drug usage in the general population: From 1990 to 2005. ADA481072

08-11 Botch SR, Chaturvedi AK, Canfield DV, Forster EM: Vitreous fluid and/or urine glucose concentrations in 1,335 civil aviation accident pilot fatalities. ADA482969

08-12 Detwiler C, Holcomb K, Hackworth C, Shappell S: Understanding the human factors associated with visual flight rules flight into instrument meteorological conditions. ADA482973

08-13 King RE, Schroeder DJ, Manning CA, Retzlaff PD, Williams CA: Screening air traffic control specialists for psychopathology using the Minnesota Multiphasic Personality Inventory-2. ADA482976

08-14 Nakagawara VB, Montgomery RW, Wood KJ: Laser illumination of aircraft by geographic location for a 3-year period (2004–2006). ADA482979

08-15 Nakagawara VB, Montgomery RW, Marshall WJ: Infrared radiation transmittance and pilot vision through civilian aircraft windscreens. ADA482971

08-16 Bailey L, Pounds J, Scarborough A: En route operational errors: Transfer of position responsibility as a function of time on position. ADA485496

08-17 Scarborough A, Bailey L, Pounds J: Analyzing vehicle operator deviations. ADA485664

08-18 Xing J: Designing questionnaires for controlling and managing information complexity in visual displays. ADA 488605

08-19 Prinzo OV, Campbell A: United States airline transport pilot international flight language experiences, Report 1: Background information and general/pre-flight preparation. ADA 488606

08-20 Corbett CL, McLean GA, Cosper DK: Effective presentation media for passenger safety I: Comprehension of briefing card pictorials and pictograms. ADA488828

08-21 Prinzo OV, Hendrix AM, Hendrix R: Pilot English language proficiency and the prevalence of communication problems at five U.S. air route traffic control centers. ADA488738

08-22 Botch SR, Johnson RD: Alcohol-related aviation accidents involving pilots with previous alcohol offenses. ADA 490324

08-23 Williams K: Documentation of sensory information in the operation of unmanned aircraft systems. ADA 490325

08-24 Chaturvedi AK, Craft KJ, Cardona PS, Rogers PB, Canfield DV: The second seven years of the FAA's postmortem forensic toxicology proficiency-testing program. ADA 490323

2009

09-1 Collins WE, Wayda ME: Index to FAA Office of Aerospace Medicine reports: 1961 through 2008. ADA494601

09-2 Prinzo OV, Hendrix AM, Hendrix R: The outcome of ATC message length and complexity on en route pilot readback performance. ADA494551

10-3   Williams CA, King RE: The effects of testing circumstance and education level on MMPI-2 correction scale scores. ADA518969

10-4   Johnson RD, Lewis RJ, Angier MK: False carbamazepine positives due to 10,11-dihydro-10-hydroxycarbamazepine breakdown in the GC/MS injector port. ADA518989

10-5   Loo SM, Kiepert J, Klein D, Pook M, Chou SF, Overfelt T, Watson J: Evaluation of the effects of hydrogen peroxide on common aircraft electrical materials. ADA518975

10-6   Knecht WR, Ball J, Lenz M: Effects of video weather training products, Web-based preflight weather briefing, and local vs. non-local pilots on general aviation pilot weather knowledge and flight behavior, Phase 2. ADA519023

10-7   Prinzo OV, Campbell A, Hendrix A, Hendrix R: United States airline transport pilot international flight language experiences, Report 2: Word meaning and pronunciation. ADA531040

10-8   Johnson RD: General unknown screening by ion trap LC/MS/MS. ADA530985

10-9   Prinzo OV, Campbell A, Hendrix A, Hendrix R: U.S. airline transport pilot international flight language experiences, Report 3: Language experiences in non-native english-speaking airspace/airports. ADA531087

10-10   Botch SR, Davidson MS, Ricaurte EM, Chaturvedi AK: Toxicological findings in 889 fatally injured obese pilots involved in aviation accidents. ADA531003

10-11   Botch SR, Johnson RD, Chaturvedi AK, Lewis RL: Distribution of oxycodone in postmortem fluids and tissues. ADA531004

10-12   Prinzo OV, Campbell A, Hendrix A, Hendrix R: U.S. airline transport pilot international flight language experiences, Report 4: Non-native English-speaking controllers communicating with native English-speaking pilots. ADA531041

10-13   Knecht WR, Lenz M: Causes of general aviation weather-related, non-fatal incidents: Analysis using NASA aviation safety reporting system data. ADA530988

10-14   Peterson LS, Haworth LA, Jones RC, Newman RL, McGuire RJ, Lambregts AA, McCloy T, Chidester TR: An international survey of transport airplane pilots' experiences and perspectives of lateral/directional control events and rudder issues in transport airplanes (rudder survey). ADA531000

10-15   Antuñano MJ, Wade K: Index of international publications in aerospace medicine. ADA534691

10-16   Shappell S, Hackworth C, Holcomb K, Lanicci J, Bazargan M, Baron J, Iden R, Halperin D: Developing proactive methods for general aviation data collection. ADA534693

10-17   Knecht WR, Lenz M: Effects of video weather training products, Web-based preflight weather briefing, and local vs. non-local pilots on general aviation pilot weather knowledge and flight behavior, Phase 3.

10-18   Prinzo OV, Campbell A, Hendrix A, Hendrix R: U.S. airline transport pilot international flight language experiences, Report 5: Language experiences in native English-speaking airspace/airports. ADA534673

10-19   Lewis RJ, Ritter RM, Johnson RD, Crump RW: Postmortem concentrations of tramadol and *O*-desmethyltramadol in 11 aviation accident fatalities. ADA534674

10-20   Self DA, Mandella J, Prinzo OV, Forster EM, Shaffstall RM: Physiological equivalence of normobaric and hypobaric exposures of humans to 25,000 feet. ADA534698

10-21   Nakagawara VB, Montgomery RW, Wood KJ: The illumination of aircraft at altitude by laser beams: A 5-year study period (2004-2008). ADA534694

10-22   Roma PG, Mallis MM, Hursh SR, Mead AM, Nesthus TE: Flight attendant fatigue Recommendation II: Flight attendant work/rest patterns, alertness, and performance assessment. ADA534695

2011

11-1   Collins WE, Wayda ME: Index to FAA Office of Aerospace Medicine Reports: 1961 through 2010. ADA542886

11-2   Botch S, Johnson R, Ricaurte E, Selensky M: Benzodiazepine use in pilots of civil aviation accidents: 1990-2008 toxicology and autopsy findings. ADA542726

11-3   DeWeese RL, Moorcroft DM, Taylor AM: Aviation child safety device performance standards review. ADA542733

11-4   Prinzo OV, Campbell A, Hendrix A, Hendrix R: U.S. airline transport pilot international flight language experiences, report 6: Native English-speaking controllers communicating with non-native English-speaking pilots. ADA542891

Part I: Chronological Index

12-8   Broach D: Incremental validity of biographical data in the prediction of en route air traffic control specialist technical skills. ADA566825

12-9   Ma MJ, Rankin WL: Implementation guideline for Maintenance Line Operations Safety Assessment (M-LOSA) and Ramp LOSA (R-LOSA) programs. ADA566771

12-10   Branaghan RJ, Schvaneveldt RW, Beringer DB: Baseline assessment of the use of weather information in airline systems operations centers. ADA566695

12-11   Lanicci J, Halperin D, Shappell S, Hackworth C, Holcomb K, Bazargan M, Baron J, Iden R: General aviation weather encounter case studies.

12-12   Roma PG, Hursh SR, Mead AM, Nesthus TE: Flight attendant work/rest patterns, alertness, and performance assessment: Field validation of biomathematical fatigue modeling.

12-13   Thoren TM, Thompson KS, Cardona PS, Chaturvedi AK, Canfield DV: *In vitro* absorption of atmospheric carbon monoxide and hydrogen cyanide in undisturbed pooled blood.

12-14   Roma PG, Hursh SR, Mead AM, Nesthus TE: Analysis of commute times and neurobehavioral performance capacity in aviation cabin crew.

12-15   Knecht WR: Predicting general aviation accident frequency from pilot total flight hours.

12-16   Avers KB, Johnson B, Banks J, Wenzel B: Technical documentation challenges in aviation maintenance: A proceedings report.

12-17   Lewis RJ, Angier MK, Williamson KS, Johnson RD: Analysis of sertraline in postmortem fluids and tissues in 11 aviation accident victims.

12-18   DeWeese R, Moorcroft D, Abramowitz A, Pellettiere J: Civil aircraft side-facing seat research summary.

12-19   Dean MA, Broach DM: Development, validation, and fairness of a biographical data questionnaire for the air traffic control specialist (ATCS) occupation.

Part II: Author Index

Author	Report Number
Booze CF Jr	68-5, 68-9, 69-11, 70-18, 72-13, 73-8, 73-10, 74-5, 75-5, 76-7, 77-10, 77-20, 78-21, 79-19, 80-8, 81-9, 81-14, 83-18, 84-3, 84-8, 85-6, 87-7, 89-2, 90-7
Boquet A	02-8, 02-13, 02-20, 05-24, 06-7, 06-13, 06-18, 07-27, 09-5, 09-17
Boren HK	00-22
Botch SR	07-29, 08-10, 08-11, 08-22, 09-15, 10-10, 10-11, 11-2
Bourdet NM	71-36
Boyer D	94-17, 94-26, 95-23, 96-9
Braden GE	69-22, 73-1
Bradshaw GL	03-3
Brake CM	62-18, 63-1, 63-16, 63-22, 63-32, 65-27
Branaghan RJ	12-7, 12-10
Branson DM	85-11
Brecher GA	69-23, 70-2, 71-22, 72-8
Brecher MH	69-23, 70-2, 71-22
Brecht-Clark J	94-4
Brink JD	07-22
Britton TW	93-20, 95-15
Broach DM	91-4, 91-11, 91-18, 92-26, 93-4, 94-4, 94-9, 96-6, 96-13, 97-4, 97-15, 97-19, 98-8, 98-22, 98-23, 99-16, 99-24, 00-15, 02-9, 03-14, 03-20, 04-8, 05-6, 05-22, 05-23, 11-12, 12-8, 12/19
Broadhurst JL	72-30
Bruni CB	69-6, 69-16
Bryant KD	89-6
Burian D	06-14, 07-9, 08-5, 08-8, 09-19, 09-21, 10-2
Busby DE	77-11
Buschle-Diller G	09-16
Byrne CL	12-6

C

Author	Report Number
Caldwell DC	06-19
Caldwell L	00-10
Cameron-Landis L	06-10
Campbell A	08-19, 10-7, 10-9, 10-12, 10-18, 11-4
Canfield DV	91-12, 92-23, 92-24, 92-25, 94-14, 94-16, 95-26, 95-28, 96-14, 96-17, 98-5, 98-18, 98-21, 99-14, 99-15, 99-29, 00-9, 00-16, 00-21, 00-22, 00-29, 00-34, 01-12, 02-14, 02-15, 03-18, 03-22, 03-24, 04-1, 04-13, 04-15, 05-8, 05-9, 05-20, 06-12, 06-14, 07-9, 07-12, 07-19, 07-22, 07-23, 08-8, 08-11, 08-24, 09-12, 09-19, 11-13, 12-5, 12-13
Canning JM	01-16, 02-1, 02-22
Cannon MM	11-12
Capps MJ	Tech.Pub.#1, 64-14, 65-1, 65-2
Cardona PS	00-29, 03-22, 03-24, 08-24, 12-5, 12-13
Carretta TR	08-9
Carroll JJ	70-16
Cassidy B	06-14
Chandler RF	68-24, 72-27, 74-4, 76-9, 77-11, 78-6, 78-12, 78-23, 78-24, 79-17, 80-12, 82-8, 83-16
Chang CD	07-23
Chase RC	72-4
Chaturvedi AK	91-17, 93-7, 93-8, 94-7, 94-18, 95-8, 95-26, 97-14, 98-10, 98-18, 98-21, 99-11, 99-14, 99-15, 99-29, 00-9, 00-16, 00-22, 00-34, 01-12, 02-14, 03-7, 03-22, 03-24, 04-1, 04-15, 05-9, 05-20, 07-12, 07-19, 08-11, 08-24, 09-8, 09-19, 10-10, 10-11, 11-13, 11-21, 12-5, 12-13
Chen YJ	07-23
Chidester TR	07-7, 07-16, 07-28, 10-14, 11-6, 11-8, 12-1
Chesterfield BP	80-13, 81-7
Chiles WD	69-6, 69-9, 69-10, 69-14, 69-16, 71-17, 71-28, 72-5, 72-11, 72-19, 72-21, 74-10, 75-10, 75-14, 76-1, 76-11, 77-15, 77-17, 78-19, 78-33, 78-34, 79-7
Chittum CB	89-14, 92-27, 95-22, 96-18, 98-2, 98-3, 99-10
Chou SF	09-16, 09-23, 10-5
Chubb GP	96-19, 97-6
Cierebiej A	69-18, 71-9
Clark G	66-5, 66-26, 66-34, 69-19
Clough DL	88-5
Cobb BB Jr	62-2, 62-3, 63-31, 65-19, 65-22, 67-1, 68-14, 71-30, 71-36, 71-40, 72-18, 72-22, 72-33, 73-7, 74-2, 74-7, 74-8, 75-3, 76-6
Coffey JD	96-12
Colangelo EJ	89-3
Collins WE	62-17, 63-3, 63-13, 63-14, 63-29, Tech.Pub.#1, 64-14, 64-15, 64-16, 65-1, 65-2, 65-17, 65-18, 65-24, 66-37, 67-2, 67-6, 67-7, 67-12, 67-19, 68-2, 68-10, 68-28, 69-15, 69-20, 70-10, 70-17, 71-20, 71-30, 71-31, 71-34, 71-39, 72-34, 72-35, 73-17, 73-18, 74-2, 74-3, 74-7, 75-1, 75-3, 75-4, 76-12, 76-14, 77-24, 78-13, 79-7, 79-9, 79-26, 80-7, 81-15, 81-16, 82-19, 83-6, 84-6, 85-3, 85-5, 86-9, 87-4, 88-2, 88-3, 89-7, 90-1, 90-4, 91-8, 92-1, 93-2, 94-1, 95-1, 95-3, 95-7, 95-13, 96-1, 96-21, 96-22, 97-1, 98-1, 99-1, 00-1, 01-1, 03-1, 05-1, 05-3, 07-1, 09-1, 11-1
Coltman JW	83-3
Comerford DA	02-3, 03-5

Part II: Author Index

Author	Report Number

F

Faaborg T --------- 05-24
Fairlie GW -------- 91-6, 92-27
Farmer WL-------- 96-13, 97-4, 98-24, 99-16, 00-3, 01-4
Faulkner DN ----- 78-8, 82-12, 92-2
Feinberg R -------- 65-9, 65-25
Fergus JW---------- 09-23
Ferrante A--------- 03-19
Ferraro DP -------- 73-12, 75-6
Fiedler ER--------- 00-32, 01-11, 02-23
Fineg J ------------- 68-24
Fiorica V ---------- 66-6, 66-11, 66-14, 66-41, 68-4, 68-15, 68-23, 70-8, 70-18, 71-11, 71-15, 71-23, 71-41
First MW --------- 09-7
Fisher RG --------- 74-4
Flemig JW -------- 94-14, 95-28
Flux M------------- 77-3, 77-16, 82-5
Folk ED ----------- 70-18, 72-30, 73-10, 82-8, 92-27
Forster EM-------- 06-5, 08-11, 09-9, 10-20
Fotouhi CH ------ 96-6
Fowler PR--------- 63-8, 67-5, 75-7, 77-17, 80-10, 83-2
Fox CM ----------- 01-10, 02-4
Fraser AD --------- 12-5
Freud SL ---------- 64-9, 64-10, 64-17, 66-25
Friedberg W ------ 71-26, 78-8, 80-2, 82-12, 92-2, 00-33, 03-16, 05-14, 09-6, 11-9
Fromhagen C----- 71-18
Fulk GW---------- 91-1
Fuller DK --------- 94-3, 95-4
Funkhouser GE -- 63-25, 66-14, 67-4, 67-17, 68-13, 68-15, 68-18, 70-5, 71-2, 71-17, 72-17, 73-22, 75-10, 75-14, 76-11, 77-8, 77-17, 78-19, 79-10, 80-10, 81-8, 82-10, 83-2, 83-14, 85-10, 87-2, 89-8, 89-11, 91-6, 92-27, 95-20, 95-22, 96-18, 98-3, 99-10

G

Galaxy SciCorp--- 93-5, 93-15, 94-12, 95-14, 96-2
Gale HS ----------- 08-2, 08-4, 09-16, 09-23
Gale WF----------- 08-2, 08-4, 09-16, 09-23
Galerston EM ---- 68-13, 68-18
Ganslen RV ------- 63-12, 63-34
Garber M --------- 00-29, 01-12
Garner JD--------- 62-1, 62-9, 65-7, 66-42, 70-19, 72-30, 77-11, 78-3, 78-23, 79-22, 80-12, 94-10, 95-17, 95-29, 96-4, 97-7, 98-4, 98-27, 99-4, 00-6, 04-3, 04-7, 05-18, 06-10, 06-27

Garner R ---------- 94-10, 95-17, 95-29, 96-4, 97-7, 98-4, 98-27, 99-4, 00-6, 04-3, 04-7, 05-18, 06-10, 06-27
Gay DJ ------------ 77-24
Geiwitz KL-------- 00-6
George MH------- 91-2, 91-3, 95-20, 95-22, 95-25, 96-18, 98-3, 99-5, 99-10
Gerathewohl SJ--- 69-17, 69-24, 70-9, 71-10, 71-33, 75-5, 77-6, 78-16, 78-27
Gerke RJ ---------- 72-4
Gibbons HL ------ 68-8, 69-9, 69-10, 71-18
Gilcher RO ------- 84-4
Gildea K---------- 11-15
Giles E ------------- 79-2
Gilliland K-------- 93-13, 97-5, 97-25, 99-20
Gilson RD -------- 71-20, 71-34, 72-34
Glaser S ----------- 09-17
Gogel WC -------- 62-15, 63-10, 63-20, 63-28, 64-13, 65-11, 65-32, 66-22, 66-24, 67-18, 67-20
Goldman RF ----- 62-5
Goldman SM ----- 02-23, 04-22, 04-23, 06-4, 06-26, 07-11, 07-25, 07-28
Good GW -------- 05-21
Goulden DR------ 71-5, 72-16, 73-19, 76-4, 81-4, 83-17
Gowdy RV -------- 90-11, 92-20, 93-14, 94-19, 98-11, 99-5, 02-11, 03-9
Grape PM --------- 77-8, 78-13, 80-3, 81-15, 82-15, 85-8
Green T ----------- 07-13
Grimm EJ--------- 72-16, 73-19, 75-4, 76-4
Grimm MH ------ 72-1, 74-1, 87-1
Gronlund SD----- 97-22, 98-16, 01-16, 02-1, 02-22
Guedry FE Jr ----- 67-6, 67-7, 71-20, 71-34, 72-34
Guilkey JE -------- 98-6
Gurman EB------- 94-21
Guzman L--------- 09-21

H

Hackworth CA--- 98-26, 99-3, 03-10, 03-11, 04-22, 04-23, 05-13, 06-7, 06-13, 06-18, 07-16, 07-17, 07-25, 08-12, 10-16, 11-15, 12-11
Halperin D ------- 10-16, 12-11
Hand DK --------- 97-3, 97-23, 98-7
Hanneman GD -- 70-3, 77-8, 78-8, 81-11, 84-5, 87-3, 87-8
Hanson PG ------- 68-6, 68-24, 69-5, 69-13
Hansrote RW----- 97-21
Haraway A -------- 81-1, 83-1
Harper CR-------- 66-30
Harris HC Jr------ 95-3, 95-7, 96-16, 97-24, 99-22, 05-7, 05-12

Author	Report Number
Johnson R	11-2, 12-3
Johnson RD	00-20, 02-15, 03-18, 03-23, 04-4, 04-13, 05-11, 06-3, 06-5, 06-17, 06-19, 07-15, 07-22, 07-29, 08-10, 08-22, 09-3, 09-15, 10-4, 10-8, 10-11, 10-19, 11-17, 12-16, 12-17
Johnson WB	07-25, 91-16, 11-11, 11-19
Jones B	09-18
Jones D	06-1
Jones JP	92-31
Jones KN	71-5, 71-7, 71-29, 72-14, 72-16, 72-25, 73-14, 75-1
Jones RC	10-14
Jordan JL	82-14, 06-1
Josenhans WKT	65-8
Joseph KM	99-9, 99-17, 99-25, 99-27, 00-4, 00-14, 03-2

K

Author	Report Number
Kanki BG	96-10
Karim B	72-27
Karson S	70-14
Kay EJ	94-21, 94-22, 94-23
Keen FR	66-31
Kegg PS	88-3
Kendall WW	63-25
Kendra A	07-30
Key OR	97-21
Kidd GD Jr	79-5
Kiepert J	09-18, 10-5
King JS	11-16
King RE	02-23, 02-24, 03-20, 06-16, 07-14, 08-9, 08-13, 10-3
King SJ	03-11, 04-22, 04-23, 05-13, 07-17, 09-24
Kinn JB	68-3
Kirkbride LA	96-19
Kirkham WR	78-13, 80-3, 80-6, 81-10, 81-15, 82-7, 82-13, 83-8
Klein D	09-18, 10-5
Knecht W	02-20, 05-7, 05-15, 07-16, 08-6, 08-7, 10-1, 10-6, 10-13, 10-17, 11-5, 12-15
Knowlan DM	64-11
Kochan JA	97-6
Korty P	62-10, 63-4
Kot PA	64-11
Kranz G	70-10
Kuntz DJ	12-5
Kupfer DM	00-16, 06-14, 07-9, 08-8, 09-19, 09-21, 10-2
Kupiec TC	92-24, 96-14, 96-17, 97-14

L

Author	Report Number
Lacefield DJ	78-31, 82-15, 85-8
Lacey DE	62-10, 63-4
Lacy CD	71-5
LaJonchere CM	99-28
Lamb MW	96-3
Lambregts AA	10-14
Lambrou P	99-22
Lamonica J	00-26, 12-7
Langston ED	72-6, 72-7
Lanicci J	10-16, 12-11
Larcher JG	00-13, 02-16, 04-12, 04-16
Lategola MT	63-11, 66-16, 66-17, 66-20, 66-21, 70-8, 70-18, 70-21, 71-8, 71-19, 72-20, 72-26, 73-10, 74-6, 77-3, 77-16, 78-5, 78-20, 79-8, 79-20, 80-9, 81-2, 82-3, 82-4, 82-5, 84-4
Lay CD	71-36, 72-22, (see also Dollar CS)
Layne PJ	74-6
Layton CF	95-31
Leeper RC	73-23
Leland R	09-17
Lendrum L	03-3
Lennon AO	75-4, 77-24
Lentz JM	76-14
Lenz M	10-1, 10-6, 10-13, 10-17
Lester LF	87-6
Leverett S Jr	63-30
Lewis MA	78-7, 78-36, 79-3, 79-14
Lewis MF	67-8, 67-16, 67-24, 68-20, 68-27, 70-15, 71-27, 71-32, 71-42, 72-29, 73-6, 73-12, 73-18, 75-6, 79-4, 81-6, 82-6
Lewis RA	69-6, 69-16
Lewis RJ	99-15, 00-20, 00-29, 02-15, 03-18, 03-23, 04-4, 04-13, 04-15, 05-8, 05-10, 05-11, 06-3, 06-5, 06-12, 06-17, 06-19, 07-15, 07-22, 09-3, 09-12, 10-4, 10-11, 10-19, 11-17, 12-17
Leyva MJ	12-5
Li G	96-3
Lieberman P	98-20
Linder MK	80-11
Ling C	09-14
Lintern G	97-11
Linville JG	07-23
Lio TL	05-8
Liu RH	07-23
Loewenfeld I	65-9

Part II: Author Index

Author	Report Number
Moorcroft D	04-18, 07-13, 11-3, 12-18
Moore CM	69-19
Moore R	07-17
Morgan JC	68-26
Morris Edward W	66-27
Morris Everett W	70-9
Morrison JE	96-6
Morrow DG	99-21
Moser E	83-2
Moser KM	64-5, 64-7, 64-8
Moses R	66-14, 68-4, 71-11, 71-15, 80-10
Mullen SR	77-17, 78-19, 79-10
Murcko LE	76-4, 77-1
Murphy RE	98-4, 98-27, 00-6
Myers JG	90-2, 91-5, 91-10, 92-15, 92-16, 95-10

N

Author	Report Number
Nadler E	07-30
Naff KC	00-27
Nagle FJ	63-12, 63-34, 64-2, 66-36
Nakagawara VB	90-10, 91-1, 91-14, 92-14, 93-11, 93-21, 94-10, 94-15, 95-11, 96-12, 96-27, 98-25, 99-6, 00-18, 00-19, 00-23, 01-7, 01-14, 02-6, 02-10, 03-6, 03-12, 04-6, 04-9, 05-21, 06-9, 06-23, 06-28, 07-20, 08-14, 08-15, 09-13, 10-21, 11-7, 11-14
Nance C	00-26
Naughton J	64-2, 66-17, 66-21, 66-36
Neal GL	65-31
Neas BR	78-8, 80-2
Neddick M	99-9
Nei D	11-11, 11-16, 11-19
Nelson JM	71-26
Nelson PL	72-33, 73-7, 74-8
Nepal S	11-17
Nesthus TE	95-5, 95-7, 97-7, 97-9, 97-25, 99-20, 02-8, 02-13, 02-20, 06-13, 07-21, 09-20, 09-22, 09-24, 09-25, 10-22, 11-16, 12-12, 12-14
Newman RL	10-14
Newton JL	63-33
Newton NL	62-12
Nguyen K	0032
Nicholas J	00-33
Nichols EA	72-2
Nikolic D	99-3
Norris A	12-3
Norwood GK	71-25, 71-38, 82-14

Author	Report Number
Nye LG	89-7, 90-4, 90-8, 91-8, 92-7, 92-8, 92-9, 92-10, 94-13

O

Author	Report Number
O'Brien K	00-33
O'Connor WF	65-10, 66-10, 66-15
O'Dell JW	70-14
O'Doherty DS	65-4
Odom RS	02-16
O'Donnell RD	92-11, 95-24
Ohrt DD	97-22, 98-16
Olmos BO	03-2
Orme DR	01-11
Orzechowski JA	04-7, 06-27
OU Vortac	92-31, 94-3, 95-4, 95-9, 96-5
Overfelt RA	09-16, 09-23
Overfelt T	10-5
Owen M	09-18
Owuor ED	04-1
Ozur H	82-11

P

Author	Report Number
Packingham KD	99-28
Page BB	63-22
Palmerton DA	98-3, 98-13, 02-16, 04-12, 05-17
Parker JF Jr	89-9, 90-14, 95-2
Patterson JC	01-11
Pearson DW	68-17, 69-7, 69-19
Pearson RG	63-35, 65-10, 65-31, 66-19
Pedigo M	11-15
Pellettiere J	12-18
Pendergrass GE	63-27, 66-10, 66-15
Penland T	85-1
Pennybaker AL	96-25
Perloff JK	64-19
Perry JL	98-16
Perry RB	64-8
Peterman CL	08-1, 09-9
Peterson LM	00-28, 01-19, 01-20, 03-10, 11-8
Peterson LS	10-14
Pfleiderer EM	00-24, 01-10, 02-2, 02-4, 03-8, 05-16, 06-4, 06-7, 07-11, 07-18, 07-28, 09-4, 11-6, 12-1
Phillippens MMGM	07-13
Phillips EE	63-34
Phillips S	97-11

Part II: Author Index

Author	Report Number
Sauer HH	05-14, 09-6
Scarborough A	05-25, 08-16, 08-17
Scarborough WR	64-12, 65-8, 65-15
Scarpa P	06-1
Schlegel RE	93-13, 97-5, 97-25, 98-13, 99-20
Schlegel TT	89-10
Schroeder DJ	68-10, 70-10, 71-6, 71-16, 71-20, 71-31, 71-34, 71-39, 72-34, 73-17, 79-9, 81-16, 82-19, 83-7, 83-17, 87-4, 89-7, 90-6, 90-8, 92-7, 93-4, 94-6, 94-13, 94-17, 94-26, 95-3, 95-7, 95-32, 96-9, 97-17, 99-17, 99-22, 00-32, 03-14, 03-20, 04-21, 05-5, 05-22, 06-2, 06-6, 06-21, 07-21, 07-25, 08-13
Schvaneveldt R	00-26, 12-7, 12-10
Scow J	66-15
Scroggins CL	09-4
Seipel JH	64-6, 65-4, 67-11
Selensky M	11-2
Self DA	10-20
Sells SB	84-2
Sen A	07-12, 07-19
Sershon JL	84-5, 87-3, 87-8, 12-5
Shaffstall RM	02-16, 06-10, 06-19, 10-20
Shanbour K	66-17, 66-21
Shannon CG	09-16, 09-23
Shappell SA	00-7, 01-3, 03-4, 05-7, 05-24, 06-7, 06-18, 06-24, 08-12, 10-16, 12-11
Shaw RV	96-24
Shehab RL	98-13
Shepherd WT	89-9, 90-14, 91-16, 95-2, 95-14, 95-31, 96-2
Siegel PV	67-25, 68-9, 69-2, 69-17, 69-18, 71-10
Silberman WS	06-1
Simcox LS	84-3
Simpson JM	66-13, 67-9, 78-13, 80-3
Simpson LP	81-4
Sirevaag EJ	99-28
Sirkis JA	70-9, 72-3
Sk MH	09-23
Skaggs VJ	12-3
Smith DR	00-9, 00-21, 02-14, 00-34
Smith LT	93-19
Smith MD	98-5, 98-21
Smith PW	62-8, 63-24, 69-9, 70-3, 77-9, 77-19, 78-26
Smith RC	70-20, 71-14, 71-21, 71-28, 71-30, 71-35, 72-23, 72-24, 73-2, 73-15, 73-22, 74-12, 75-7, 75-9, 76-2, 76-13, 77-21, 77-23, 78-32, 79-11, 80-14, 81-5
Snow CC	62-9, 65-14, 65-26, 68-6, 68-19, 68-24, 69-3, 69-4, 69-5, 69-13, 70-16, 72-27, 75-2, 79-2, 82-9
Snyder L	77-8, 82-12, 92-2
Snyder RG	62-13, 62-19, 63-15, 63-30, 65-12, 65-26, 68-6, 68-19, 68-24, 69-3, 69-4, 69-5, 69-13, 76-9
Sofyan NI	09-23
Solomon LA	66-11
Soper JW	96-17, 99-29, 00-16, 02-14, 03-22, 03-24, 11-21, 12-5
Southern TL	00-29
Spengler JD	09-7
Spera S	06-10
Spieth W	64-4
St George R	99-9
Staggs CM	85-6
Stavinoha WB	66-11
Stedman VG	71-9
Steen JA	71-27, 71-32, 72-29, 73-18, 75-1, 75-6, 80-5, 80-15, 84-1, 85-1
Stern JA	94-6, 94-17, 94-26, 96-9, 99-28
Stoliarov N	94-6, 94-26, 96-9
Stutzman TM	91-5
Swearingen JJ	62-1, 62-4, 62-13, 62-14, 63-9, 65-7, 65-20, 65-23, 66-3, 66-12, 66-18, 66-40, 67-14, 69-22, 71-3, 71-12, 71-13, 72-6, 72-7, 72-15, 73-1

T

Author	Report Number
Taite S	05-23
Talleur DA	97-11, 03-3
Tang PC	63-21
Taylor AM	11-3
Taylor DK	75-9, 81-15, 83-6, 84-6
Taylor HL	97-11, 03-3
Taylor JC	91-16
Teague SM	92-19
Thackray RI	68-17, 69-7, 69-8, 69-21, 71-7, 71-29, 72-14, 72-25, 73-11, 73-14, 73-16, 74-9, 75-8, 77-18, 78-11, 79-12, 79-24, 80-1, 80-17, 81-5, 81-12, 82-1, 82-16, 83-13, 85-13, 86-4, 88-1, 88-4, 89-1, 90-3, 92-3, 92-6, 94-6
Thomas AA	71-41
Thomas JA	06-10
Thomas S	05-8, 07-17, 09-24, 11-16
Thomson GL	97-22
Thompson AC	09-10
Thompson D	06-20

Part II: Author Index

Author	Report Number
Winget CM	75-10
Wise RA	97-7
Witt LA	91-10, 91-11, 91-15, 92-7, 92-8, 92-9, 92-10, 92-13, 92-17, 92-21, 93-18, 94-2, 95-32, 97-8
Wittmers LE	65-27
Wolbrink AM	00-13, 04-16
Wolf MB	98-4
Wong KL	04-7, 06-27
Wood KJ	91-14, 92-14, 93-11, 93-21, 94-15, 95-11, 96-27, 98-25, 99-6, 00-19, 01-14, 02-6, 02-10, 03-6, 04-6, 06-9, 06-23, 06-28, 08-14, 09-13, 10-21, 11-7
Worley JA	99-17, 99-25, 99-27, 00-14
Wreggit S	97-9, 98-9
Wright JE	12-5
Wu CH	07-23

X

Author	Report Number
Xing J	04-17, 05-4, 06-2, 06-6, 06-11, 06-15, 06-22, 07-5, 07-10, 07-24, 07-26, 08-18, 09-14

Y

Author	Report Number
Yanowitch EA	73-5
Yanowitch RE	72-2, 73-5
Yost A	02-21, 07-30
Young CL	76-6
Young FA	79-2
Young JW	62-21, 65-23, 66-9, 66-33, 67-13, 69-3, 69-4, 69-5, 69-13, 71-37, 74-4, 76-9, 78-14, 82-9, 83-16, 89-8, 89-11, 93-10
Young PE	68-11, 68-12
Young WC	93-4, 96-13, 97-4

Z

Author	Report Number
Zehner GF	83-16
Zeiner AR	72-8
Zelenski JD	77-19
Zhu H	04-1
Ziemnowicz SAR	65-4

Contents (continued)

Neurology	22
Noise	22
Nystagmus	22
Orthostatic tolerance	22
Oxygen	22
Oxygen masks	22
Ozone	23
Passengers	23
Patients	23
Perception	23
Performance (also see: Human Factors)	23
Personnel, FAA (see also, Air Traffic Controllers)	26
Pesticides	26
Physical fitness	26
Physiology	26
Pilots	27
Pregnancy	28
Propellers	28
Protective breathing equipment	28
Psychology	28
Pulmonary	29
Radiation	29
Renal function	30
Research, aeromedical	30
Restraint	30
Seat	31
Seatbelts	31
Shiftwork and shift rotations	31
Shoulder harness	31
Sickle cell trait	31
Simulation	31
Skin	32
Sleep	32
Smoke	32
Smoking	32
Sonic booms	32
Stalls	32
Standards	32
Stress	32
Suicide	33
Supersonic transport	33
Temperature	33
Tests	33
Tobacco	34
Tolerance	34
Toxicology	34
Training	35
Translations	36
Turbulence	36
Vertigo	36
Vestibular function	36
Vibration	36
Video games	36
Vigilance	36
Vision	36
Warning signals	37
Water survival	37
Weather	37
Work	37

...lapbelt-restraint injuries to pregnant females, 68-24
...lost/disoriented, 95-1
...obese pilots, 10-10
...occupation of pilots, 77-10
...older pilots, 67-22, 70-18, 04-8
...padding for crash protection, 66-40
...Part 135 pilots, toxicological findings, 09-15
...physician pilots, 66-25, 71-9
...pilots with static physical defects, 76-7, 77-20, 79-19, 81-14, 83-18, 93-11, 11-14
   –prior alcohol offenses, 08-22
...post mortem findings, 69-18, 92-23, 92-24, 92-25, 94-14, 95-28, 97-14, 98-18, 00-9, 00-16, 00-29, 03-4, 03-22, 03-24, 04-13, 05-9, 05-10, 05-11, 05-20, 06-3, 06-14, 06-17, 07-12, 07-15, 07-19, 07-22, 08-8, 08-10, 08-11, 08-22, 09-3, 09-15, 09-21, 10-10, 10-11, 10-19, 11-2, 11-13, 11-21, 12-13
   –in relation to medical history, 06-12, 07-19
   –quality assurance of forensic analyses, 99-11, 99-14, 99-15, 99-29, 03-18, 04-1, 04-4, 04-13, 04-15, 06-14, 07-23, 08-24, 09-19, 09-21, 10-4, 10-8, 10-11, 12-13
...predicting GA frequency from pilot total flight hours, 12-15
...predisposition, 72-2, 73-5, 93-9
...prevention with blind flight instrument, 66-32
...propeller-to-person, 81-15, 93-2
...railroad, 73-1
...risk factors, for controlled flight into terrain (Alaska), 00-28
   –for marginal weather take-offs by general aviation pilots, 05-7, 05-15, 08-12, 10-16
...rotorcraft, rollover and injury/fatality rates, 05-17
...safety information for improved survival, 04-19
...seat cushions for flotation, 66-13, 98-19
...shoulder harnesses to increase survival, 72-3, 83-8, 89-3
...spatial disorientation, 78-13, 95-1, 96-21
...stall warning, 66-31
...suicide, 72-2, 73-5, 06-5
...survivability, fire/smoke, 95-8, 05-17
   –free-fall impacts, 63-15
   –water impacts, 65-12, 68-19
...triamterene in blood, identification of, 92-23
...unmanned aircraft, accidents and incidents, 04-24
   –flight-control problems, 06-8
...visual acuity of pilots, 75-5, 81-14, 83-18, 00-18, 11-14
...water spray systems, 98-4

...water survival, analysis of training programs, 98-19
   –frequency of occurrence, 98-19
...WinMine analytic tool applied to accident data, 06-26

Aerial application
...accidents, 66-27, 66-30, 68-16, 72-15, 78-31, 80-3
...biochemical effects of lindane and dieldrin, 62-10, 63-4
...chlordimeform toxicity, 77-19
...cholinesterase determination, 67-5
...comparison of serum cholinesterase methods, 70-13, 72-12
...dieldrin effects on liver, 66-5, 66-26
...endrin effects, 66-11, 66-26, 66-34, 70-11
...mechanisms of endrin action, 63-16, 63-26
...organophosphate insecticides effects, 63-24, 69-19, 70-3
...Phosdrin effects on performance, 72-29, 73-3
...Phosdrin effects on vision, 73-4
...storage stability of human blood cholinesterase, 70-4
...toxic hazards, 62-8, 68-16, 78-31
...treatment of methamidophos poisoning, 78-26

Aerobatics
...blood donation effects, 84-4
...G effects on pilots, 72-28, 82-13

Aerospace
...index of international publications, 93-3, 07-2, 10-15
...medical screening guidance for commercial aerospace passengers, 06-1
...toxicology, overview, 09-8

Age
...age 60 rule, 94-20, 94-21, 94-22, 94-23, 04-8
...air traffic controller, health, 65-6, 71-8, 71-19, 72-20
   –performance, 61-1, 62-3, 65-21, 67-1, 71-36, 73-7, 84-6, 90-4
   –retirement age, 05-6, 05-22
...aircraft accident survival, 70-16
...aircraft accidents, pilots involved, 67-22, 70-18, 77-10, 95-11
...alcohol and altitude interaction, 88-2
...alcohol effects on performance, 95-3, 95-7
...aviation personnel, 64-1, 94-20, 94-21, 94-22, 94-23
...binocular fusion time effects, 66-35
...cardiovascular disease and performance, 64-4
...cardiovascular health changes in airmen, 72-26

Part III: Subject Index

...vigilance of men and women on simulated radar task, 78-11, 80-17
...visual displays, cognitive complexity, 05-4, 07-26, 08-18
...visual taskload effects, on CFF change during complex monitoring, 85-13
 –on complex monitoring, 88-1, 90-3
...voice communications from, 93-20, 98-17, 98-20, 05-19
...workload production models, 07-6

Air traffic controllers

...age and retirement, 05-6
...age effects on performance, 61-1, 62-3, 65-21, 67-1, 71-36, 73-7, 81-12, 82-16, 84-6, 90-4, 96-23, 99-18, 99-23, 05-6, 05-22
...aircraft mix and complexity ratings, 05-16
...anthropometry, 65-26
...anxiety with training, 89-7, 91-8
...anxiety with workload, 73-15, 80-14, 81-5
...aptitude tests for selection, 65-19, 68-14, 71-28, 71-36, 71-40, 72-18, 89-6, 90-8, 97-15, 98-23, 99-16, 00-2, 06-16, 07-14, 08-9
 –reweighting AT-SAT scores to reduce adverse impact, 06-16, 07-14
...attitudes, 74-7, 74-12, 75-3, 79-11, 91-10, 00-17, 04-23
...attrition, 72-33, 74-2, 74-7, 75-3
...biochemical stress index, 74-11, 75-7, 77-23, 78-5, 78-40
...biodynamic evaluation, 71-8
...biographical factors, associated with training success, 83-6, 84-6, 90-4, 94-13
 –in predicting en route ATCS technical skills, 12-8, 12-19
 –in recruitment, 11-12, 12-8, 12-19
...biomedical survey, 65-5, 65-6
...collegiate training initiative, 98-22
...color deficiency in a workforce sample, 06-1
...color perception and job performance, 83-11, 90-9, 92-6, 92-28, 92-29, 96-22, 06-2, 06-6, 06-11, 06-15, 06-22, 07-10, 07-24
...color vision tests, 85-7, 90-9, 92-28, 92-29, 95-13, 96-22, 04-10, 04-14, 06-2, 06-6, 06-11
...communication, 93-20, 95-15, 96-10, 96-20, 96-26, 98-17, 98-20, 99-21, 01-8, 01-9, 05-19, 06-25, 08-19, 08-21, 09-2, 09-10, 10-7, 10-9, 10-12, 10-18, 11-4
...commuting (driving) risks before and after shifts, 06-13

...Composite Mood Adjective Check Lists to measure fatigue, 71-21
...disease incidence and prevalence, 78-21, 84-3
...education as selection factor, 76-6, 90-4
...experience as selection criterion, 63-31, 71-36, 74-8, 00-12
...fatigue and shiftwork, 99-2
 –and commuting risk factors before and after shifts, 06-13
...flight progress strips, use of, 92-31, 94-3, 95-4, 95-9, 96-5, 98-26, 00-5
...flight service station, training, 86-6, 91-4
 –organizational climate, 97-12
 –weather briefings, 07-4
...generational comparisons of reasons for choosing the ATC occupation, 11-12
...headset interference tones, 92-4
...health changes, 71-19, 72-20, 78-39, 84-3
...height and weight data, errors in, 73-10
...incident reporting, 65-10, 03-19
...memory, 97-22, 98-16
...military ATC students, performance on AT-SAT, 08-9
...military experience and selection, 92-5
...Minnesota Multiphasic Personality Inventory-2, for screening, 08-13, 10-3
...motivational factors, 71-30, 73-2, 11-12
...Multiple Task Performance Battery for selection, 72-5, 74-10
...Myers-Briggs personality types, 04-21
...napping and night shift performance, 00-10
...NEO Personality Inventory-Revised, compared with 16 PF test, 03-20
...occupational vision, 96-12, 96-27
...operational errors, evaluation of the Severity Index, 05-5
 –HFACS and other models to describe causes, 05-25
 –static sector characteristics, influence on, 06-4, 07-11, 07-18, 09-4
 –time on position and transfer of position responsibility, 08-16
...operational errors/deviations, 99-2, 03-19, 03-21, 05-22, 06-21
...perceptions of aircraft performance, 00-24, 03-8, 05-16
...performance evaluation, 61-1, 65-22, 73-7, 93-12, 98-14, 00-2
...performance on radar monitoring tasks, 82-1, 83-13, 86-4, 88-1, 88-4, 90-3, 94-26, 95-23, 97-10, 98-16, 99-8

Part III: Subject Index

...cockpit visual problems, 77-2, 77-7, 77-13, 77-14, 78-17, 03-12, 07-20, 08-15
...communication in light aircraft, 72-31
...computational fluid dynamics (CFD) in predicting pathogen distribution in a passenger cabin, 06-27
...contaminant distribution prediction in a passenger cabin, 06-27
...control forces and female pilots, 72-27, 73-23
...crew smoke-protective devices, 76-5, 78-4, 83-14, 89-5, 89-8, 89-11
...decompression hazards, 67-14, 70-12, 99-4
...decontamination, of passenger cabin, 06-10, 08-2, 08-4, 09-7, 09-16, 09-23
  –of avionics, 10-5
...design changes to reduce injuries, 71-3, 72-7, 83-8
...displays, 98-9, 98-12, 03-2, 03-5, 03-13, 04-5, 05-23, 07-30
...ditching studies, 78-1, 91-6, 98-19, 04-12
...emergency signs, readability in smoke, 79-22
...escape slides, studies of, 98-3, 99-10
...evacuation, 62-9, 65-7, 66-42, 70-16, 70-19, 72-30, 77-11, 78-3, 78-23, 79-5, 79-6, 80-12, 81-7, 89-5, 89-12, 92-27, 95-22, 95-25, 96-18, 98-19, 99-10, 99-30, 00-11, 01-18, 03-15, 04-2, 04-12, 05-2
...exits, size of in evacuation, 99-10, 04-12
...evacuation models, 94-11, 97-20
...fire, smoke protection after accidents, 67-4, 70-16, 70-20, 78-4, 83-10, 85-10, 89-5, 89-8, 89-11, 89-12
...fire vs. no fire on rotorcraft accidents, 05-17
...fires, toxicity of combustion products, 71-41, 77-9, 85-5, 86-1, 86-3, 86-5, 89-4, 91-17, 95-8
...flight inspection, evaluation, 95-18
...flight manuals, 91-7
...flight training devices, 94-25, 95-6
...floor proximity marking systems, 98-2
...GPS displays, 98-9, 98-12, 99-9, 99-13, 99-26, 00-4, 03-17
...head impact kinematics, 92-20
...Highway-in-the Sky (HITS) display, 00-31
...influenza viruses on aircraft surfaces, inactivation of, 09-7
...information sharing, safety reports, 07-7
...inspection, 89-9, 94-12, 95-14
  –visual standards used for inspectors, 05-21
...instrument display, 75-12, 98-28, 00-8, 00-31
...interior wall padding and neck injury potential, 93-14

...landing, simulated night approaches, 77-12, 78-15, 79-4, 81-6
...lateral/directional control events, 10-14
...life preserver retrieval, 03-9
...maintenance, 89-9, 90-14, 91-16, 92-3, 93-5, 93-15, 94-12, 95-14, 95-31, 96-2, 05-21, 07-25
...medical incidents inflight, 00-13
...neck injury potential, 93-14
...NEXRAD display, 04-5
...noise effects measurement, 71-1, 72-32
...noise effects on birds, 62-4
...noise levels, 68-21, 68-25, 70-6
  –and pilot hearing thresholds, 05-21
...nongyropscopic blind flight instrument, 66-32
...oxygen system design, 78-9, 04-3
...ozone concentrations and effects, 79-20, 80-9, 89-13
...padding for crash protection, 66-40
...passenger safety information, 04-19, 08-20
...performance characteristics, perceived by ATCSs, 00-24, 03-8
...propeller paint schemes conspicuity, 78-29
...radioactive material shipments, 82-12
...readability of emergency signs in smoke, 79-22
...restraint installation, 66-33, 67-13, 72-15
...restraint system evaluation, 69-3, 69-4, 69-5, 71-12, 72-3, 72-6, 78-6, 78-12, 78-24, 79-17, 80-3, 81-10, 82-7, 94-19, 95-2, 95-30, 98-11, 99-5, 11-3
  –inflatable restraint, 07-13
  –rudder issues, 10-14
...seat cushion flotation, 66-13, 98-19
...seat evaluation, 78-6, 78-24, 79-17, 80-3, 81-10, 82-7, 83-3, 90-11
  –side facing, 69-13, 07-13, 12-18
...seat impact injuries, 66-18, 72-15, 89-3
...simulator operation using drugs, 64-18
...SST anticollision lights, 70-9, 70-15, 71-42
...stall warning device, 66-31
...standards for advanced aerospace systems, 71-33
...sunscreen-treated windows, 78-28
...toxicity of engine oil thermal degradation, 83-12
...unmanned aircraft, 04-24, 06-8, 07-3, 07-8, 08-23, 12-4
...warning signals and pilot hearing thresholds, 05-12
...water spray system, 98-4
...weather information systems, in cockpit for Next Gen environment, 12-7
  –use in airline systems operations centers, 12-10
...wheel-well passengers, 96-25

...flight attendants, 75-2, 75-13
...flight inspection pilots and technicians, 95-18
...head and face of adults, 93-10
...human pelvis, 82-9
...shoulder slope, 65-14
...weight distribution when sitting, 62-1

Anthropomorphic dummies
...criteria for crashworthiness, 96-11
...design, 82-9, 83-16
...evaluation, 78-6, 78-24, 79-17, 83-3
...3- and 6-year-old dummies, 76-9
...thoracic mass, determination, 96-7

Anticollision lights
...effects of backscatter, 72-8
...exposure effects under simulated IFR conditions, 66-39
...SST, 70-9, 70-15, 71-42

Aphakia
...accident risk assessment, 95-11
...incidence in airmen, 91-14, 92-14

Arousal
...by distracting stimuli, 71-7
...nystagmus effects, 62-17
...simulated radar control task, 75-8, 77-18, 81-12, 88-1
...vestibular responses effects, 63-29

Attention
...anticollision observing responses, 73-6
...auditory distraction effects, 72-14
...conspicuity of flashing and color targets, 90-3
  –target blink amplitude, 97-10, 99-8
...personality and physiological correlates, 73-14
...self-estimates of distractibility, 72-25
...psychophysiological indices, 99-28
...simulated radar task, 77-18, 78-11, 79-12, 80-17, 81-12, 82-1, 82-16, 86-4, 88-1, 89-1
...switching in readiness to perform, 95-24
...time-sharing ability, 76-1, 78-33
...visual taskload effects on CFF change during complex monitoring, 85-13
...visual taskload effects on complex monitoring, 88-1, 90-3, 94-26, 95-23, 96-9, 99-28

Audiology
...advanced and ATC selection, 90-13
...auditory fatigue, 63-19, 65-1, 65-2
...binaural beat perception, 63-17
...cockpit noise intensities, 68-21, 68-25
...ear-protector ratings, 73-20, 75-11
...earphone transient response, 63-7
...hearing threshold, pilots vs. non-pilots, 05-12
...interaural intensity difference limen, 67-10
...noise audiometry, 71-1
...noise effects on aircrew personnel, 72-32
...speech intelligibility improvement, 70-6, 72-31, 73-13, 76-3
...table of intensity increments, 66-4
...temporary threshold shift, 79-16

Automation
...advanced, and ATCS selection, 90-13, 92-26, 97-19, 98-23
...boredom and monotony as stressors, 80-1
...complacency on radar monitoring task, 82-1
...complex monitoring performance predictors, 80-17, 86-4
...flight progress strips, 92-31, 94-3, 95-8, 96-5
...general aviation, pilot responses to autopilot malfunctions, 97-24
...information complexity measures and design implications, 04-17, 07-26, 08-18
...physiological stress in controllers, 82-17
...radar performance with and without computer aiding, 89-1
...recovery of radar monitoring performance following startle, 83-13
...visual taskload effects on CFF change during complex monitoring, 85-13
...visual taskload effects on complex monitoring, 88-1

Aviation maintenance
...fatigue risk management, 11-10, 11-19
...fatigue solutions identified, 11-19
...human factors, 89-9, 90-14, 91-16, 92-3, 93-5, 93-15, 94-12, 95-31, 96-2, 07-25, 11-11
...implementation guidelines for safety assessment programs, 12-9
...maintenance documentation isssues, 12-16
...visual standards and tests used for inspectors, 05-21

Aviation medical examiners
...demographics, 12-3, 12-20
...and drug testing program, 92-15
...exams of first-class certificate holders by senior AMEs, 71-38
...performance, 84-7

Ballistocardiography
...bibliography, 65-15
...research and current status, 64-12
...stroke volume relationship, 65-8

...post mortem findings after accidents, 69-18, 80-8, 85-6
...prediction of heart rates under stress, 69-7
...prevalence among civil airmen, 89-2
...problems associated with aviation safety, 78-38
...recognition of posterior infarction, 64-19
...rehabilitation after infarction, 64-2, 66-17, 66-21
...responses to hyperpyrexia, 64-8
...rheoencephalography and cerebrovascular disease, 65-4, 67-11
...risk factors, 90-7
...startle effects on heart rates, 69-21
...stress effects on heart rates, 68-17
...thromboembolic disease treatment, 64-5
...transducer for heart sounds, 68-3

Case reports
...ethanol origin in postmortem urine, 04-13, 07-22, 08-22
...in-flight loss of consciousness, 63-21
...insecticide exposure, 63-24
...macular degeneration in a pilot fatality, 11-14
...methamphetamine involvement in a pilot fatality, 03-22
...physical conditioning after infarction, 66-21
...pulmonary thromboembolism, 64-7
...quinine elimination, 94-16
...rheoencephalography in cerebrovascular disease detection, 65-4
...seizures inflight, 64-6

Center of gravity
...adults, 62-14
...children, 65-23
...infants, 69-22

Certification, aeromedical
...Aeromedical Scientific Information System, 08-1
  –and effects of regulatory change, 09-9
...airmen attrition, 72-13, 73-8
...alcoholic airline pilots rehabilitation, 85-12
...analysis of denial actions, 68-9, 74-5, 76-10, 78-25, 80-19, 83-5, 84-9, 85-9, 86-7, 90-5
...aphakia, 91-14, 92-14, 93-11, 95-11
...aviation medical examiner, demographics, 12-3, 12-20
  –performance, 84-7
...color vision, tests, 67-8, 83-11, 85-7, 90-9, 93-17, 95-13, 96-22, 09-11, 09-13, 11-8
  –X-Chrom lens, 78-22
...contact lens use, 90-10, 00-18
...diabetic conditions, glucose concentrations in transportation accidents, 00-22
...disease prevalence and incidence, 73-8, 81-9, 84-8, 89-2, 90-7
...errors in height and weight data, 73-10
...estimate of active airmen, 68-5
...exams of first-class certificate holders by senior AMEs, 71-38
...gender differences in refractive surgery, 00-23
...glare, 94-15
...glaucoma, 91-1
...intraocular implants, 92-14, 93-11
...macular degeneration, undiagnosed in pilot fatality, 11-14
...medications found in postmortem and medical history, 06-12
...neuropsychological screening of airmen, 92-11
...photorefractive keratectomy, 98-25
...pilot demographics, 12-3, 12-20
...procedures, 71-25, 82-14
...refractive surgery, 00-19, 00-23, 06-9
  –gender differences, 00-23
  –radial keratectomy, 98-25, 00-19, 06-9
  –radial keratotomy, 99-6, 00-19, 06-9
...rheoencephalography and cerebrovascular disease, 65-4, 67-11
...sickle cell disease and trait, 76-15, 80-20
...statistical handbook (2010), 12-3
...suicides, aircraft-assisted in general aviation pilots, drug involvement, 06-5
...tests for alcohol abuse, 83-2
...unmanned aircraft pilots, 07-3
...vision restrictions and pilot demographics, 04-6
...vision standards and screening tests used with aircraft maintenance personnel, 05-21
...vision testers, next generation, evaluation of, 09-13

Charts
...readability, 77-13, 78-17

Circadian periodicity
...bibliography of shiftwork research, 83-17
...disruption of intercontinental flights, 65-16, 65-28, 65-29, 65-30, 68-8, 69-17
...effects of shifts in wake-sleep cycle, 75-10, 76-11, 86-2
...excretion of magnesium and calcium, 68-4
...rotating shiftwork, 86-2, 99-2

Civil Aerospace Medical Institute (CAMI)
...Aeromedical Scientific Information System for Aviation Safety, 08-1

...weather information, use of, 97-3, 97-23, 04-5, 08-3, 08-6, 08-7, 08-12, 10-1, 10-6, 10-13, 10-17
...willingness to take off into marginal weather, 05-7, 05-15, 07-4, 08-12, 10-13

Decompression
...altitude chamber experience, 77-4, 90-12, 10-20
...effects on performance, 66-10
...effects of propranolol on TUF, 79-10, 80-10
...need for civilian training, 91-13, 03-10
...oxygen mask evaluation, 66-20, 67-3, 72-10, 79-13, 80-18, 96-4, 98-27, 00-6
...pressurized small aircraft, 67-14
...supersonic transports, 99-4
...tolerable profiles for SST, 70-12

Depth perception
...general, 62-15, 63-10, 63-20, 63-28, 64-13, 65-11, 65-32, 66-22, 66-24, 67-18, 67-20
...light adaptation device, 66-38
...monovision contact lenses in airline accident, 00-18

Diet
...human tolerance, effects, 81-2
...performance, effects, 81-8

Disorientation
...accidents due to, 78-13, 95-1, 96-21
...adaptation, 65-18, 65-24, 66-37, 67-2, 67-6, 67-7, 67-12, 67-19, 68-2, 68-28, 69-20, 74-3
...alcohol effects, 71-6, 71-16, 71-20, 71-34, 71-39, 72-34
...familiarization techniques, 70-17, 77-24
...visually induced, 69-23, 70-2, 71-22

Distraction
...auditory distraction and performance, 72-14
...laser illumination, 03-12, 04-9, 06-23, 08-14, 10-21
...susceptibility, measurement of, 72-25

Ditching
...flotation and survival equipment studies, 78-1, 85-11, 03-9, 04-12
...frequency of occurrence, 98-19
...infant flotation device, 71-37, 91-6
...seat cushion flotation, 66-13, 95-20
...water survival training programs, 98-19

DNA
...detection of postmortem alcohol-producing microorganisms, 00-16
...forensic genotyping, 09-21
 –gender discrimination, 08-8
...functional genomics, 08-5
...identification of forensic specimens, 06-14
...MiniSTR primers, testing, 09-21
...profiling for quality assurance, 98-18, 99-14
 –for resolving forensic toxicology issues, 09-19

Drugs
...aircraft accidents, role of, 68-16, 78-31, 85-8, 92-23, 94-14, 95-28, 96-14, 97-14, 98-10, 98-18, 99-29, 00-20, 00-21, 03-7, 05-20, 07-12, 08-10, 09-15, 11-2, 11-13, 11-21
 –quality assurance of forensic findings, 99-11, 99-15, 04-15, 07-23
...antiemetics, interaction with sedatives, 07-29
...antihistamine effects, at altitude, 68-15, 78-19, 78-20
 –on cognitive performance, 99-20
 –on shiftwork performance, 97-25
...antimotion sickness, 81-16, 82-19
...atropine, and performance, 93-19
 –and Phosdrin effects on vision, 73-4
...benzodiazepines, forensic analysis, 96-14, 11-2
...butalbital, forensic analysis, 00-29
...cannabinoids, presence in accidents, 09-12
...cocaine, forensic analysis, 03-23, 03-24
...chlordimeform toxicity, 77-19
...chlorpheniramine, forensic analysis, 99-29
...citalopram, distribution in postmortem tissues and fluids, 11-17
...complex performance effects, 69-9
...detection and identification, 92-25, 96-17, 97-14, 98-18, 04-15, 05-8, 05-10, 05-11, 05-20, 06-3, 06-12, 06-17, 09-3, 11-17, 12-17
...dextroamphetamine, effects during angular acceleration, 73-17, 76-12
 –effects during sleep loss, 75-14
...diphenhydramine, in pilot fatalities, 11-13
...enantiomeric analysis of ephedrines and norephedrines, 05-8
...etomidate in postmortem samples, 09-3
...fatigue, and use, 63-12, 75-14
...fluoxetine (Prozac), distribution in postmortem samples, 07-15
...glyceryl trinitrate effects on pulmonary vasculature, 64-11
...internal standard intensity, negative vs. inconclusive specimen reports, 07-23
...lithium carbonate effects on performance, 77-17
...marihuana, 73-12, 85-8, 09-12
...marihuana and altitude effects on performance, 75-6

...head injury criteria (HIC) test component test device, evaluation, 04-18
...head-up displays, 98-28
...Highway-in-the-Sky (HITS) display, 00-31
...infant flotation device, 71-37, 91-6
...instrument readability by senior pilots, 77-2, 77-7
...lapbelt restraint in pregnancy, 68-24
...lateral/directional control events, 10-14
...life preserver retrieval, 03-9
...light adaptation device, 66-38
...medical kits, 91-2, 91-3, 00-13, 00-13
...NEXRAD display, 04-5
...nongyroscopic blind flight instrument, 66-32
...oxygen, 62-21, 66-7, 66-9, 66-10, 66-20, 67-3, 67-9, 72-10, 78-4, 79-13, 80-18, 83-10, 85-10, 89-5, 89-10, 93-6, 95-17, 96-4, 98-27, 00-6, 04-3
...padding for crash protection, 66-40
...performance testing, 66-19
...personnel lifting devices, rotorcraft, 98-13
...protective, for aircraft accidents, 65-7, 66-3, 66-12
...restraint systems, 67-13, 69-3, 69-4, 69-5, 72-3, 72-6, 83-8, 94-19, 99-5
  –inflatable, 07-13
...rudder issues in transport aircraft, 10-14
...seat cushion flotation, 66-13
...secondary container alternative for transportation of infectious substances, 95-29
...stall warning, 66-31
...transducer, 68-3
...upper torso restraint acceptance, 71-12
...visual displays, methods to assess complexity in air traffic control, 05-4

Evacuation, passenger emergency
...acoustic signals for exit location, 79-5
...air carrier accidents, 62-9, 65-7, 70-16
...bibliography, 63-30
...blind passengers, 80-12
...briefing cards (safety) comprehension of, 08-20
...cabin simulator, experimental, 97-18
...children, 66-42, 01-18
...computer models, 94-11
...ditching (evacuation into water), simulated, 04-12
...Emergency Escape Breathing Device, 92-18
...emergency lighting, aisle seat arm rests, 81-7
  –exit signs, 79-22, 80-13, 81-7
  –floor, 98-2
...escape slides and platforms, 96-18, 98-3
...handicapped passengers, 77-11
...history of smoke/fume protective breathing equipment, 87-5
...human external loads, 98-13
...infants, 66-42, 01-18, 05-2
...injuries, 79-6, 79-23, 82-8, 99-30, 03-15
...motivation of passengers, 96-18, 04-2
...passenger flow rates between compartments, 78-3
...passenger safety information, availability, 04-19
  –comprehension of, 08-20
...passenger workload and protective breathing, 87-2, 89-5
...precautionary, 99-30, 00-11
...railroad accident, 73-1
...readability of emergency signs in smoke, 79-22, 80-13, 81-7
...seating configuration, 89-14, 92-27, 95-22, 03-15
...simulation by computer models, 72-30, 78-23, 94-11, 97-20
  –experimental cabin, 97-18
...SST mockup tests, 70-19
...size of exits in evacuation, 99-10, 04-12
...tests using L-1649, 66-42
...tests using protective smoke hood, 70-20, 89-12, 05-18
...type III exits, 92-27, 95-22, 95-25, 03-15, 04-2
...water survival training programs analysis, 98-19

Exercise
...auscultatory and intra-aortic pressures, 66-36
...human tolerances, effects on, 82-4, 82-10
...magnesium and calcium excretion, effects on, 68-4
...myocardial infarction, before and after, 64-2
  –effects after, 66-17, 66-21
...tolerance at altitude, 63-33
...treadmill work, energy cost of, 62-5
...air traffic controller selection, 63-31, 74-8, 78-7, 83-6
...ATCS, correlation with age and performance, 67-1, 73-7
...pilots in general aviation accidents, 77-10
...relation to reported symptoms of ATCSs, 65-6

Eye
...age and binocular fusion time, 66-35
...airman visual acuity, midair collisions, 75-5
...alcohol effects on eye movements, 72-34
...anticollision lights, 66-39, 70-9, 70-15, 71-42, 72-8
...aphakia, prevalence in civil airmen, 91-14, 92-14, 93-11
...bifocal effects on radar monitoring, 82-16
...bright lights and visual disturbances during night-time flight operations, 06-28
...contact lenses, 90-10, 00-18

Federal Air Surgeon
…review of 1966 program, 67-25
…review of 1976 program, 76-8

Fire
…crew smoke-protective devices, 76-5, 78-4, 78-14, 78-41, 83-14, 05-18
…effects in air carrier accidents, 62-9, 65-7, 70-16
…flammability of toiletries in oxygen, 63-27
…passenger protective breathing devices, 67-4, 70-20, 83-10, 85-10, 87-2, 87-5, 89-5, 89-8, 89-11, 89-12, 05-18
…smoke effects on identifying emergency signs, 79-22, 80-13, 81-7
…toxicity of products in aircraft fires, 71-41, 77-9, 85-5, 86-1, 86-3, 86-5, 89-4, 90-15, 90-16
…toxicity of seat fire-blocking materials, 86-1
…vs. non-fire, forensics, 00-9, 05-9
  –in rotorcraft accidents, 05-17

Flight attendants
…anthropometry, 75-2
…commute times and neurobehavioral performance, 12-15
…fatigue, 07-21, 09-22, 09-24, 09-25, 10-22, 10-25, 11-16, 12-12
  –countermeasures training, 09-20, 11-18
…functional strength, 75-13
…injuries, cabin safety data bank, 79-23, 82-8
…ozone effects, 79-20
…survey of field operations (2008), 11-16
…water survival training programs, 98-19

Flotation devices
…infant, 91-6
…life preserver retrieval, 03-9
…methods of seat cushion use, 95-20
…personal devices, 98-19

Forensics (see Toxicology)

Fuel
…biocidal additive, 67-21

G forces
…aerobatics effects, 72-28, 82-13
…simulation with lower body pressure box, 79-8, 82-3, 82-4
…tolerance after crash diet, 81-2
…tolerance effects of antihistamine-decongestant preparations, 78-20

Galactic cosmic radiation
…effect on air carrier crewmembers, 80-2, 80-12, 92-2, 00-33, 03-16, 05-14, 09-6
…source book on ionizing radiation exposure, 11-9

Global positioning system (GPS)
…design considerations, 98-9, 98-12, 99-13, 99-26, 00-4
…effectiveness, 03-17

Handicapped persons
…blind passengers, 80-12
…pilot positions in radar training, 80-5

Heat
…altitude effects on performance, 71-17
…complex performance effects, 69-10, 72-17
…dogs shipped by air transport, 77-8, 81-11, 84-5, 87-8
…human tolerances, 70-22, 71-4
…maintenance of thermal balance, 66-23
…manual performance effects, 68-13
…measurement of evaporative water loss, 63-25
…tolerance limits for rats and mice, 86-8
…tranquilizer effects on loss and conservation, 63-23, 66-14

Hearing
…acoustic signals for emergency evacuation, 79-5
…auditory fatigue, 63-19, 65-1, 65-2
…binaural beat perception, 63-17
…cockpit noise intensities, 68-21, 68-25
…conservation with earplugs, 73-20, 75-11
…earphone transient response, 63-7
…engine noise effects, pilots vs. non-pilots, 05-12
…headset interference tones, 92-4
…interaural intensity difference limen, 67-10
…noise audiometry, 71-1
…noise effects on aircrew personnel, 72-32
…pilots vs. non-pilots, 95-12
…speech intelligibility improvement, 70-6, 72-31, 73-13, 76-3
…table of intensity increments, 66-4
…temporary threshold shift, 79-16, 92-4

Hijacking
…deterrence, 78-35

History (CARI/CAMI)
…historical vignettes, prefaces to 87-1, 97-1, 98-1, 01-1, 03-1, 05-1, 07-1
…history of aeromedical research contributions, 05-3

...JANUS technique applied to ATC operational errors, 03-21, 06-21
...job task taxonomy, 93-1, 95-16
...NEXRAD display use, 04-5
...operational demonstration of flight inspection aircraft, 95-18
...photic stimulation responses, 66-39
...rotorcraft personnel lifting devices, 98-13
...SATORI, 93-12, 97-13, 98-14
...safety data communication via Voluntary Aviation Safety Information-Sharing Process (VASIP), 07-7
...severe weather flying, 66-41, 97-3, 97-23, 04-5, 05-7, 05-15, 07-4, 08-12, 10-16
...situation awareness and performance in air traffic control, 99-3
...target blink amplitude, attention-getting value, 97-10, 99-8
...unmanned aircraft, accident/incident data, 04-24
 –automation and piloting experience effects on pilot performance, 12-4
 –flight-control problems, 06-8, 07-8
 –pilot medical certification, 07-3
 –reduced sensory information, 08-23
...workstation design, flight inspection aircraft, 95-18
...vehicle operator deviations and runway incursions, 08-17
...visual displays, methods to assess information and cognitive complexities, 05-4, 08-18
...WinMine analytic tool applied to accident data, 06-26

Hypothermia
...passengers, 94-10, 95-20
...wheel-well stowaways, 96-25

Hypoxia
...and beta-blocked hypertensives, 92-19
...blood donation effects, 84-4
...civilian training need, 91-13, 03-10, 10-20
...human tolerance, 62-6, 63-33
...interaction with marihuana, 75-6
...normobaric and hypobaric exposure, physiological equivalence, 10-20
...oxygen need, 66-28, 04-3
...performance decrement, 66-10, 66-15, 71-11, 71-17, 97-9
...propranolol effects, 79-10, 80-10
...sickle cell trait susceptibility, 76-15, 78-30, 80-20
...supersonic transport, decompression in, 99-4
...visual field and glaucoma, 91-1
...wheel-well stowaways, 96-25

Identification
...DNA, profiling of accident victims, 98-18, 99-14
 –identification of forensic postmortem specimens, 06-14
 –resolving forensic toxicology issues, 09-19
...enantiomeric compositions of compounds in cold remedies, 05-8
...forensic genotyping and gender, 08-8
...sex and race diagnosis from cranial measurements, 79-2

In-flight health care
...medical emergencies, 97-2, 00-13
...medical kits, 91-2, 91-3, 97-2, 00-13

Illusions
...spiral aftereffect, 64-9, 64-10, 64-17, 68-10, 69-15, 71-31
...visual, 70-2, 71-22, 77-12

Injuries
...agricultural aircraft accidents, 72-15, 80-3
...analysis in railroad accident, 73-1
...brain tolerances to concussion, 71-13, 74-4
...cabin safety data bank, 79-23, 82-8
...cockpit delethalization, 66-3, 66-12, 71-3, 72-7, 81-10, 82-7
...correlation with kinematic behavior, 62-13
...criteria for aircraft crashworthiness, 96-11
...decompression of small aircraft, 67-14
...emergency and precautionary evacuations, 79-6, 79-23, 82-8, 99-30, 00-11, 03-15
...eye, 62-12
...facial tolerances to impacts, 65-20
...head impacts while wearing restraint systems, 72-6, 92-20
...head injury criteria (HIC) component test device, evaluation, 04-18
...impact in pregnancy, 68-6, 68-24
...in free falls, 63-15
...neck, 93-14
...padding for crash protection, 66-40
...precautionary evacuations, 99-30
...prevention in aircraft accidents, 71-3, 94-19, 11-3
...produced by restraint systems, 69-5, 89-3
...rearward-facing seats, 62-7, 69-13
...restraint systems to prevent, 67-13, 69-3, 69-4, 69-5, 69-13, 72-3, 82-7, 83-8, 98-11
...seat impacts, 66-18
...side-facing seats, 69-13, 07-13, 12-18
...smoke and fire, 62-9, 70-16
...vertical crash forces, 62-1

...voluntary safety programs, 07-7, 11-6, 11-15, 12-1, 12-9
...workplace safety behaviors, influence on, 97-8
—employee safety perceptions, 99-19

Medical kits
...used in flight, 91-2, 91-3, 97-2, 00-13

Motion sickness
...susceptibility, 76-14
...treatment effects, 81-16, 82-19

Motivation
...airway facilities personnel, 77-21
...factors in ATC work, 71-30, 74-12
...passengers, in aircraft evacuations, 96-18, 03-15, 04-2

Neurology
...alcohol effects on ataxia test battery, 79-9
...alcohol effects on visual functions, 78-2, 79-15
...brain tolerances to concussion, 71-13, 74-4
...central factor in auditory fatigue, 63-19
...chlordimeform toxicity, 77-19
...conditions associated with aviation safety, 81-3
...drug effects on performance, 64-18
...endrin effects, 63-16, 70-11
...GCRI studies, 64-1
...in-flight vertigo and unconsciousness, 63-21
...neuropsychological test battery, 92-11, 95-7
...nucleus rotundus, 77-22
...organophosphate insecticide effects, 63-24, 72-29, 73-3, 73-4, 79-15
...photic stimulation, 66-38
...pupillary movement, 65-9, 65-25
...rheoencephalography in cerebrovascular disease detection, 65-4, 67-11
...seizures in flight, 64-6
...spiral aftereffect test, 64-9, 64-10, 64-17, 68-10, 69-15, 71-31
...vestibular tests, 75-4

Noise
...aircrew personnel effects, 72-32
...auditory fatigue, 63-19, 65-1, 65-2
...birds, effects on, 62-4
...ear-protector ratings, 73-20, 75-11
...engine, and pilot vs. non-pilot hearing thresholds, 05-12
...intensity in aircraft cockpits, 68-21, 68-25, 95-18
...performance effects of simulated radar task, 79-24, 83-13
...performance impairment, 72-14

...simulated sonic boom effects, 71-29, 72-19, 72-24, 72-35, 73-16, 74-9
...sonic boom startle effects in field study, 73-11
...speech intelligibility improvement, 70-6, 72-31, 73-13, 76-3
...temporary threshold shift, 79-16

Nystagmus
...adaptation effects, 66-37, 67-6, 67-7, 67-12, 67-19, 69-20
...alcohol effects, 71-6, 71-16, 71-20, 71-34, 71-39, 72-34
...antimotion sickness drug effects, 81-16
...arousal effects, 62-17, 63-29
...caloric habituation, 63-14, 64-14, 65-18, 67-2
...dextroamphetamine and secobarbital effects, 73-17
...habituation to rotation, 63-13, 65-24, 68-2
...illumination effects during angular deceleration, 68-28
...optokinetic stimulation, 70-2, 70-10, 71-22
...secondary, elicitation by irrigation, 63-3
...sleep deprivation, during, 86-9
...translations of reports, Tech. Pub. #1, 64-16, 65-17, 66-2
...vertical, 68-2

Orthostatic tolerance
...alcohol effects at altitude, 82-3
...and beta blocked hypertensives, 92-19
...physical exertion effects, 82-4

Oxygen
...equipment studies, 79-13, 80-18, 89-10, 92-18, 92-22, 95-17, 98-27, 00-6, 04-3, 05-18
...flammability of toiletries, 63-27
...need at altitude, 66-28, 97-9
...need for training among civilians, 91-13, 03-10, 10-20
...normobaric and hypobaric exposures, physiological equivalence, 10-20
...system design, 78-9

Oxygen masks
...crew smoke-protective devices, 76-5, 78-4, 78-14, 78-41, 83-14, 89-8, 89-11, 05-18
...design for children, 66-9
...disposable, 66-7
...donning time after decompression, 66-10
...evaluation, 62-21, 66-7, 66-20, 67-3, 67-9, 72-10, 78-4, 79-13, 80-18, 83-10, 85-10, 87-5, 89-5, 93-6, 96-4, 98-27, 00-6, 04-3, 05-18

Part III: Subject Index

–color displays and color defect, 06-2, 06-6, 06-11, 06-15, 06-22
–color perception effects, 83-11, 90-3, 07-5, 07-10, 07-24
–communication, ATC/pilot, 93-20, 95-15, 96-10, 96-20, 96-26, 98-17, 98-20, 99-21, 01-8, 01-9, 05-19, 06-25, 07-4, 08-19, 08-21, 09-2, 09-10, 11-4
–commuter (driving) risk factor before and after shifts, 06-13
–computer experience and AT-SAT performance, 00-2
–development of temporal markers to profile, 06-20
–English language issues, 08-19, 08-21, 09-10, 10-7, 10-9, 10-12, 10-18, 11-4
–evaluation, 61-1, 65-22, 98-23
–experience as predictor, 63-31
–flight service station training, 86-6
–flashing target effects, 90-3, 97-10, 99-8
–human factors literature review, operational errors, 06-21
–incident reporting, 65-10
–information complexity, measures in automation design, 04-17, 07-26, 08-18, 09-14
–information and cognitive complexity assessment methods, 05-4
–job task taxonomy for en route, 93-1
–measurement in air traffic selection and training (AT-SAT) simulation, 00-2, 00-12
–memory in air traffic control, 97-22, 98-16
–military ATC students and AT-SAT performance, 08-9
–navigation displays, 00-8, 04-20
–Multiple Task Performance Battery for selection, 72-5, 74-10
–napping and night shift performance, 00-10
–operational errors, development of temporal markers to profile, 06-20
–operational errors, en route, no relation to age, 05-22
–operational errors, human factors literature review, 06-21
–operational errors, JANUS technique applied to causal factors, 03-21, 08-17
–operational errors/deviations, role of shiftwork and fatigue, 99-2
–operational errors, sector characteristics, 87-15, 06-4, 07-11, 07-18

–operational errors, time on position/transfer of position responsibility, 08-16
–pass-fail in FSS training program, 79-18
–personality factors, relation to, 70-14, 89-7, 03-20, 04-21
–radar simulator, 65-31, 75-8, 77-18, 78-11, 80-15, 80-17, 82-1, 82-16, 83-9, 83-13, 86-4, 88-4, 89-1, 90-3, 95-23
–sector characteristics, activity and complexity, 06-29
–sector characteristics and operational errors, 87-15, 06-4, 07-11, 07-18, 09-4
–sex differences, 72-22
–situation awareness, 94-27, 98-16, 99-3
–strategies for reducing causal factors, 03-19
–video game experience as a predictor, 97-4
–workload ratings, subjective, 07-6
…airworthiness inspectors, 87-4
…alcohol effects, 66-29, 69-14, 71-20, 71-34, 72-4, 72-11, 72-34, 78-2, 79-7, 79-26, 82-3, 83-2, 85-5, 88-2, 94-24, 95-3, 95-7, 95-24
…antihistamine effects, at altitude, 68-15, 78-19
  –on performance, 97-25, 99-20
…attitude indicators (flight instrument), 73-9, 05-23
…attitude questionnaires to predict under stress, 69-7
…aural glide slope cues for instrument approaches, 71-24
…aviation maintenance, fatigue risk management, 11-10
  –technical documentation issues, 12-16
…aviation medical examiners, 84-7
…aviation safety inspectors, 07-16
…biomathmatical fatigue modeling, 12-12
…chronic disulfoton poisoning effects, 69-19
…cockpit instrument display, compact, 75-12
  –Cockpit Display of Traffic Information (CDTI), 03-2, 03-5, 03-13, 04-11, 04-20
  –Electronic Attitude Direction Indicator (EADI), equivalence tests, 05-23
  –GPS, 98-9, 98-12, 99-9, 99-13, 00-4, 03-19
  –head-up, 98-28
  –Highway-in-the-Sky (HITS), 00-31
  –NEXRAD weather, 04-5
…cognitive appraisal of stress effects, 68-17
…cognitive style and learning, 99-12
…commuting times and performance, 06-13, 12-4
…computer-based training for airplane upset-recovery, 07-27, 09-5, 09-17
…crash diet effects, 81-8
…decompression effects, 66-10

...weather information, (NEXRAD) and simulator performance, 04-5
 –preflight, 07-4, 08-3, 08-6, 08-7, 08-12, 10-1, 10-6, 10-13, 10-17, 11-5
...work in heat and cold, 66-23, 68-13

Personnel, FAA (see also, Air Traffic Controllers)

...airway facilities personnel, job attitudes, 77-21, 79-11, 83-7
...Airway Science Curriculum Demonstration Project, evaluation of, 88-5
...airworthiness inspectors, job performance ratings of, 87-4
...aviation maintenance, 89-9, 90-14, 91-16, 92-3, 93-5, 93-15, 94-12, 95-14, 95-31, 96-2, 05-21, 11-10, 11-11
...aviation safety inspectors training, 07-16
...biological rhythms and rotating shiftwork considerations, 86-2
...correlates of satisfaction with training, 91-9
...decision making, equity, and job satisfaction, 91-10
...effectiveness of management training, 75-9, 78-32, 92-16
...electronics technicians, 97-19
...employee attitude survey, year 2000, process feedback, 03-11
 –year 2003 agency-wide work attitudes, 04-22
 –year 2003 Air Traffic Organization work attitudes, 04-23
 –year 2003 analysis of employee comments, 05-12
...empowerment, predictors of perceived, 98-24
...ergonomic interventions to reduce work stress, 99-17
...flight inspection aircrews, crew resource management, 96-24
...flight service station, organizational climate, 97-12
...health awareness programs, survey evaluation, 00-3
...intent to leave job, and active turnover, 06-30
 –job satisfaction, 91-15
...identification of management training needs, 90-2, 92-16
...identification with occupation, 92-21
...job task analysis for FAA supervisors, 91-5
...job task taxonomy, en route, 93-1
...matrix teams, 93-18
...organizational change, and cynicism, 99-27, 00-14
...organizational commitment, 92-21
...organizational communication, and technology change, 99-25
...organizational support, perceptions of, 92-13

...safety perceptions following safety awareness program, 99-19
...team implementation and diversity climate, 00-27
...technical operations services operations control center, organizational development survey and analyses, 12-6
...test fairness for selection, 79-3, 96-13, 99-16

Pesticides

...aerial application aircraft accidents, 66-27, 66-30, 68-16, 78-31, 80-3
...biochemical effects of lindane and dieldrin, 62-10, 63-4
...chlordimeform toxicity, 77-19
...cholinesterase determination, 67-5
...CNS, effects of organophosphates, 63-24, 69-19, 79-15
...comparison of serum cholinesterase methods, 70-13, 72-12
...dieldrin effects on liver, 66-5, 66-26
...endrin effects, 66-11, 66-26, 66-34, 70-11
...endrin, mechanisms of action, 63-16, 63-26
...methamidophos toxicity, 78-26
...organophosphates effects on reproduction, 70-3
...Phosdrin effects on performance, 72-29, 73-3
...Phosdrin effects on vision, 73-4
...storage stability of human blood cholinesterase, 70-4
...symptoms and treatment of poisoning, 62-8

Physical fitness

...aerospace, commercial passengers, guidance for medical screening, 06-1
...age relationship, 63-18
...ATC students, 71-8
...field test for, 63-6
...myocardial infarction, 64-2, 66-17, 66-21
...neuropsychological screening, 92-11

Physiology

...autonomic and performance, 93-19
...backscatter, responses to, 72-8
...blood donation effects, 84-4
...cabin water spray, effects on thermal behavior, 98-4
...crash diet effects, 81-2, 81-8
...evaporative water loss device, 67-17
...gas pressure in tissue, 63-11
...high altitude training, need for, 91-13
...hydrogen ion concentration, conversion table from pH, 68-23
...index of international publications in aerospace medicine, 93-3, 07-2, 10-15

...medications found postmortem and in medical history, 06-12, 07-19
...navigation displays, moving map, 04-20
 –using text and graphics, 00-8
...neuropsychological screening, 92-11
...noise effects on hearing, 72-32, 05-12
...obese pilots, toxicological findings, 10-10
...occupations, 69-11, 77-10
...ozone effects, 80-9, 89-13
...Part 135 pilots and drug use, forensics, 09-15
...perceptions of flight operations quality assurance programs, 11-6, 12-1
...performance, on glidepath indicator systems, 79-4, 79-25, 81-6, 82-6
 –electronic attitude-direction indicator (EADI), 05-23
 –GPS displays, 98-9, 98-12, 99-9, 99-13, 99-26, 03-17
 –head-up displays, 98-28
 –Highway-in-the Sky (HITS) display, 00-31
 –NEXRAD weather display, 04-5
 –simulated autopilot malfunctions, 97-24
 –two attitude indicators, 73-9
...peripheral visual cue response, 68-11, 68-12, 68-22
...physician accidents, 66-25, 71-9
...physiological responses on cross-country flights, 71-23
...physiological studies in air tankers, 68-26
...prior alcohol offenses and aviation accidents, 08-22
...pulmonary function, 77-3
...risk factors for cardiac events, 90-7
...safety climate, pilot perception of, 00-28
...safety programs, voluntary, 11-6, 12-1
...safety training, evaluation, 97-16, 98-6, 99-7, 03-10, 07-17
...satisfaction with ATC services, 90-6
...severe weather flying, 66-41, 05-7, 05-15, 08-3, 08-6, 08-7, 08-12, 11-5, 12-7, 12-11
...shoulder harness, use of, 95-2
...smoking effects on performance, 80-11, 83-4
...status variables with accidents, 70-18
... stress, domestic-based and perceived performance, 00-32
...stress in student pilots, 67-15, 69-12, 76-2
...suicide, 72-2, 73-5, 06-5
...tracking performance during successive approaches, 72-9
...transport airplane pilots, rudder use and lateral/directional control events, 10-14
...type airman certificate related to accidents, 67-23

...unmanned aircraft, 04-24, 06-8, 07-3, 07-8, 08-23
...upset recovery training, 07-27, 09-5, 09-17, 10-14
...vertigo, 67-19
...vision and optical radiation transmission of windscreens, 07-20
...visual acuity, midair collisions, 75-5
...voice communication, 93-20, 06-25
...weather encounters, case studies, 12-11
...workload, 77-15, 81-13

Pregnancy
...crewmember radiation exposure, 92-2, 00-33, 03-16
...emergency air transport, 82-5
...impact injuries, 68-6, 68-24
...organophosphate pesticide effects in rats, 70-3

Propellers
...paint schemes conspicuity, 78-29
...propeller-to-person accidents, 81-15, 93-2

Protective breathing equipment
...evaluation, 62-21, 66-7, 66-20, 67-3, 67-9, 72-10, 78-4, 79-13, 80-18, 83-10, 85-10, 87-5, 89-5, 93-6, 96-4, 98-27, 00-6, 04-3, 05-18

Psychology
...accident frequency prediction modeled from GA pilot total flight hours, 12-15
...accident proneness, 93-9
...aircraft mix and traffic complexity ratings, 05-16
...automation and pilot performance, 97-24, 00-8
...aviation maintenance survey, 07-25
...biodata in ATCS selection, 12-8, 12-19
...biomathmatical fatigue modeling, 12-12
...CogScreen, neuropsychological test, age effects, 99-22
...cognitive complexity in an air traffic control displays, 05-4, 07-26, 08-18, 09-14
...cognitive style and learning, 99-12
...commuting times and neurobehavioral performance, 12-14
...Composite Mood Adjective Check List to measure stress effects, 71-14, 71-21, 73-22
...cultural diversity awareness training, 95-10
...Designated Pilot Examiners, evaluations, 07-17
...disability retirement, and ATC personality factors, 03-14
...diversity climate, 00-26
...empowerment, predictors of perceived, 98-24
...expertise method in aeronautical decision-making, 97-6

...measurements at SST altitudes, 71-26, 80-2
...optical, transmittance through aircraft windscreens, 07-20, 08-15
...RBE of fast neutrons, 78-8
...transport limits for radioactive material, 82-12

Renal function
...acute arterial occlusion effects, 63-22, 65-27
...autoregulation mechanism, 63-32
...insecticide effects, 63-26
...venous pressure effects, increase of, 62-18, 63-1

Research, aeromedical
...aerospace toxicology overview, 09-8
...Aeromedical Scientific Information System, 08-1
  –and effects of regulatory change, 09-9
...aging studies at GCRI, 64-1
...aims and accomplishments, 62-20, 67-25
...alcohol effects review, low dose, 94-24
...ballistocardiography, 64-12, 65-8, 65-15
...beta blockers, analysis and differentiation, 04-15, 05-10
...bibliography of acceleration studies, 63-30
...bibliography of shiftwork research, 83-17
...butalbital, distribution of fluids and tissues, 00-29
...carboxyhemoglobin standard, 98-21
...color vision, 67-8, 71-27, 71-32, 73-18, 75-1, 83-11, 85-7, 92-6, 92-28, 92-29, 93-16, 93-17, 95-13, 96-22, 04-10, 04-14, 06-2, 06-6, 06-11, 06-15, 06-22, 11-8
...commuting risk factors, before and after work shifts, 06-13
...decontamination of aircraft, narrow-body aircraft, 08-2
  –with hydrogen peroxide, 09-7, 09-16, 09-23, 10-5
...DNA, detection of postmortem ethanol-producing microorganisms, 00-16
  –identification of forensic samples, 06-14
...DNA profiling, 98-18, 99-14, 06-14, 09-19, 09-21
...enantiomeric analysis of ephedrines and norephedrines, 05-8
...exercise, 64-2, 66-36
...forensic genotyping, gender discrimination, 08-8
...functional genomics, 08-5
...galactic radiation exposure, 92-2, 00-33, 03-16, 05-14, 09-6
...glucose concentration in pilot fatalities, 08-11
...hearing, conservation with earplugs, 73-20, 75-11
...history, CAMI, prefaces to 87-1, 97-1, 98-1, 01-1, 03-1, 05-1, 07-1

  –CAMI research contributions from 1,000 technical reports, 05-3
...index of international publications, 93-3, 07-2, 10-15
...index of OAM reports, 63-2, 64-20, 66-1, 68-1, 70-1, 72-1, 74-1, 77-1, 79-1, 81-1, 83-1, 87-1, 90-1, 92-1, 94-1, 96-1, 97-1, 98-1, 99-1, 00-1, 01-1, 03-1, 05-1, 07-1, 09-1, 11-1
...interpretation of carboxyhemoglobin and cyanide concentrations, 05-9
...medical care, inflight, 00-13
...medical incapacitation and impairment of pilots inflight, 04-16
...medical incidents inflight, 00-13
...needs, 63-35, 71-10
...noise effects on aircrew personnel, 72-32
...obese pilots, toxicological findings, 10-10
...opiates vs. poppy seed use, postmortem determinations, 05-11
...postmortem, cocaine analysis, 03-23, 03-24
  –accurate assignment of ethanol origin, 04-13, 07-22
  –distribution of fluoxetine, 07-25
  –ethanol analysis, internal standard, 98-5
  –H1 amphetamines, first generation, 07-12
  –identification of forensic specimens, 06-14
...plans, for NAS operator selection, 97-19
...quality assurance, forensic toxicology proficiency testing program, 99-11, 08-24, 09-19
...radiation, galactic, 92-2, 00-33, 03-16, 05-14, 09-6, 11-9
...RNA, isolation from peripheral blood cells, protocol validation, 04-1
  –globin-RNA reduction protocol, comparison of methods, 07-9
...quinine elimination, 94-16
...stain test for dieldrin and endrin, 66-26
...standard for reporting test specimens as negative or inconclusive, 07-23
...translated material, Tech. Pub. #1, 64-16, 65-17, 66-2, 68-7, 71-5, 76-4, 81-4
...vision testers, next generation, evaluation of, 09-13
...visual standards and tests used with aircraft maintenance personnel, 05-21

Restraint
...acceptance of upper torso restraint, 71-12
...bibliography, 63-30
...center of gravity, 62-14, 65-23, 69-22
...child, 94-19, 95-30
...cockpit delethalization, 66-3, 71-3, 72-6, 81-10

...head-up displays, 98-28
...Highway-in-the Sky (HITS) display, 00-31
...laser illumination effects on pilot responses, 03-12, 04-9
...movement of objects in depth, 65-32
...navigation display formats, 96-16
...NEXRAD weather displays and flight performance, 04-5
...night approaches to landing, 77-12, 78-15, 79-4, 81-6, 82-6
...operator skills research, 66-19
...pilot workload, 77-15, 82-10, 83-15
...sonic booms, 71-29, 72-19, 72-24, 72-35, 73-16
...stress in ground trainer use, 76-2
...transfer of training, 69-24, 09-5
...upset-recovery training, 07-27, 09-5, 09-17
...visual glidepath indicator systems, 79-4, 79-25, 81-6, 82-6

Skin
...conductance with sonic booms, 71-29
...evaporative water loss, 63-25
...flammability of toiletries, 63-27
...galvanic skin response, 64-18
...tactile communication, 62-11, 62-16
...temperature to predict tolerances to heat and cold, 71-4
...thermal stress following cabin water spray, 98-4

Sleep
...air traffic controllers, 77-5, 95-12, 95-19, 00-10, 06-13
...deprivation, 70-8, 85-3
...dextroamphetamine effects during sleep loss, 75-14
...flight attendants, 07-21
...loss, and performance, 93-19
   –and vestibular response, 86-9
...shiftwork effects in sleep-wake cycle, 75-10, 76-11
...sonic boom effects, 72-19, 72-24, 72-35
...work schedule effects, 95-32, 99-2, 00-10

Smoke
...air carrier accidents, 62-9, 65-7, 70-16
...crew protective devices, 76-5, 78-4, 78-14, 78-41, 83-14, 89-8, 89-11
...emergency signs, effects on reading, 79-22, 80-13, 81-7
...passenger protective breathing devices, 67-4, 70-20, 83-10, 85-10, 87-2, 87-5, 89-5, 89-12, 05-18
...toxicity, 95-8
...toxicity of thermal degradation products of engine oils, 83-12

Smoking
...aviation safety, effects on, 80-11, 97-7
...smoking/withdrawal effects, 83-4

Sonic booms
...autonomic responses, 71-29, 72-35, 73-16, 74-9
...sleep, effects during, 72-19, 72-24, 72-35
...startle effects, 73-11, 73-16, 74-9
...tracking performance effects, 71-29

Stalls
...warning device, 66-31

Standards
...advanced aerospace systems, 71-33
...aeromedical, 71-25, 71-33, 82-14, 00-19
...carboxyhemoglobin, 98-21
...color vision for air traffic controllers, 83-11, 90-9, 04-10, 04-14, 06-2, 06-6, 06-11, 06-15, 06-22, 11-8
...color vision requirements, recommendations for, 09-11
...escape slides, inflatable, 98-3
...floor proximity marking systems, 98-2
...head injury criteria (HIC) component test device, evaluation, 04-18
...internal standard in toxicology for negative vs. inconclusive findings, 07-23
...neurological and neurosurgical conditions, 81-3
...postmortem ethanol analysis, internal standard, 98-5
   –accurate assignment of ethanol origin, 04-13
...quality assurance in forensic toxicology, 99-11, 99-15, 03-18, 04-15, 08-24

Stress
...air tanker pilots, 68-26
...air traffic controllers, 71-2, 71-21, 73-15, 73-21, 73-22, 74-11, 75-7, 76-13, 77-23, 78-5, 78-18, 78-40, 80-14, 82-17, 05-7
...assessment with State-Trait Anxiety Inventory, 72-23, 81-5, 91-8
...aviation stress protocol—simulation, 78-5
...Composite Mood Adjective Check List, to measure, 71-14, 71-21
...domestic-based and pilots' perceived performance, 00-32
...ergonomic interventions, 99-17
...evaporative water loss device, 67-17
...flight inspection crews, 81-13
...+Gz, 79-8
...heart rate and performance effects, 68-17, 69-21

–post decompression, 66-10
–with hypoxia, 66-15, 71-11, 82-10, 83-15
…personality assessment, 71-35, 93-4, 03-20, 04-21, 08-13
…physical fitness, 63-6, 63-18, 63-33, 64-3, 66-17
…practical flight test, evaluations, 07-17
…proficiency in post mortem forensic toxicology, 99-11, 08-24
…pupillary movement, 65-9, 65-25
…readiness to perform, 93-13, 95-24
…scanning and monitoring, 92-12, 94-8
…Shipley Institute of Living Scale, 92-30
…Sixteen Personality Factors test, with ATCSs, 97-17, 03-14, 03-20
…spiral aftereffect, 64-9, 64-10, 64-17, 68-10, 69-15, 71-31
…stain for dieldrin and endrin, 66-26
…State Trait Anxiety Inventory, 72-23, 76-13, 80-14, 81-5, 89-7, 91-8
…Stroop test, 71-7, 72-14
…supervisory, air traffic control, 92-16
…system for combustion toxicology, 77-9
…urine tests, specimen validity, 12-5
…vestibular during physical exams, 75-4
…video game experience, 97-4
…visual display complexity, questionnaire assessment, 08-18

Tobacco
…effects on aviation safety, 80-11, 83-4

Tolerance
…brain, to concussion, 71-13, 74-4
…cold stress in dogs, 87-8
…decompression for SST, 70-12
…face, to impact, 65-20, 66-12, 66-40
…flight stresses, 62-6, 81-2
…free-fall impacts, 63-15
…heat for rats and mice, 86-8
…heat stress in dogs, 77-8, 81-11, 84-5, 87-8
…hot environments, 70-22
…hypoxia, propranolol effects, 79-10, 80-10
…impacts in water, 65-12, 68-19
…intercontinental flights, 65-16, 65-28, 65-29, 65-30
…orthostatic, 63-34, 82-3, 82-4., 92-19
….+Gz, 79-8, 81-2
…prediction for thermal environments, 71-4
…vertical impact, 62-19
…work at altitudes, 82-3

Toxicology
…aerospace toxicology overview, 09-8
…Aeromedical Scientific Information System, 08-1
…antiemetics and sedatives, interactions, 07-29
…atmospheric carbon monoxide and hydrogen cyanide in pooled blood, 12-13
…beta blocker, forensic analyses and differentiation, 04-15, 05-10
…butalbital, forensic analysis, 00-29
…citalopram and desmethylcitalopram distribution in postmortem fluids and tissues, 11-17
…cocaine and its metabolites, post mortem analyses, 03-23, 03-24
…carbon monoxide, 89-4, 93-7, 94-7, 94-18, 98-21, 00-9, 05-9, 12-13
…combustion products of cabin materials, 77-9, 85-5, 86-1, 86-3, 86-5, 89-4, 90-15, 90-16, 91-17, 93-7, 93-8
…comparison 2004 vs. 2008 drugs and alcohol in civil pilot fatalities, 11-13
…decontamination of cabin, 06-10, 08-2, 08-4, 09-7, 09-16, 09-23
… diphenhydramine in pilot fatal accidents, 11-13
…DNA, detection of ethanol-producing microorganisms in postmortem samples, 00-16
–forensic genotyping, gender discrimination, 08-8
–functional genomics, 08-5, 09-21
–identification of forensic specimens, 06-14
–profiling, quality assurance in forensic, 98-18, 99-14, 09-19
…drug usage in pilots, prescription and illicit, 08-10
…enantiomeric analysis of ephedrines and norephedrines, 05-8
…etomidate concentration, postmortem, 09-3
…fatal aircraft accident findings, 78-31, 80-11, 82-15, 92-23, 92-24, 94-14, 97-14, 98-5, 99-29, 03-7, 03-22, 03-23, 05-9, 05-20, 06-3, 06-5, 06-12, 07-12, 07-22, 07-29, 08-22, 09-3, 09-12, 10-10, 10-19, 11-13, 11-21
…fluoxetine (Prozac) distribution in postmortem samples, 07-15
…forensic urine drug testing, effects of subject's height, weight, body fat, and resting metabolic rate on dilution, 12-5
…gene expression profiles, maintenance after blood storage, 04-1
…glucose levels, abnormal, 00-22, 08-11
…hydrogen cyanide, 93-8, 94-7, 94-18, 05-9, 12-13
…hydrogen sulfide, 00-34

Translations

...aviation medicine, general, 64-16, 65-17, 66-2, 68-7, 71-5, 72-16, 73-19, 76-4, 81-4
...color vision tests, 67-8
...nystagmus and vestibular function, Tech. Pub. #1, 1963

Turbulence

...effects of severe weather flying, 66-41
...injuries, cabin safety data bank, 79-23, 82-8

Vertigo

...Coriolis stimulation, 67-19
...flicker, 66-39
...illumination during angular deceleration, 68-28
...in-flight case with unconsciousness, 63-21
...production by spiral aftereffect, 64-9, 64-10, 64-17

Vestibular function

...adaptation, 66-37, 67-6, 67-7, 67-12, 67-19, 69-20, 74-3
...alcohol effects, 71-6, 71-16, 71-20, 71-34, 71-39, 72-34, 79-9
...arousal effects, 62-17, 63-29
...caloric habituation, 63-14, 64-14, 65-18, 67-2
...dextroamphetamine and secobarbital effects, 73-17
...habituation to rotation, 63-13, 65-24, 68-2
...motion sickness susceptibility, 76-14
...rotation device, 64-15
...secondary, tertiary, and inverted primary nystagmus, 63-3
...sleep loss effects, 86-9
...tests during physical examinations, 75-4
...translation of reports, Tech. Pub. #1, 64-16, 65-17, 66-2, 72-16, 73-19

Vibration

...bibliography, 63-30

Video games

...experience and air traffic scenario test score, 97-4

Vigilance

...eye blink rate and fatigue, 94-17, 94-26, 96-9, 99-28
...hypoxia effects, 71-11
...napping and ATC performance, 00-10
...psychophysiological indices, 99-28
...simulated ATC tasks, 77-18, 78-11, 80-17, 94-6, 94-26, 95-23

Vision

...acuity, pilots in midair collisions, 75-5
...age and binocular fusion time, 66-35
...aircraft maintenance inspectors, visual standards and tests, 05-21
...alcohol effects, 78-2, 79-15
...anticollision lights, 66-39, 70-9, 70-15, 71-42, 72-8
...aphakia, accident risk assessment, 95-11
  –incidence in airmen, 91-14, 92-14, 93-11
...artificial lens implants, 92-14, 93-11
...atropine and Phosdrin effects, 73-4
...bifocal effects on radar monitoring, 82-16
...bright lights and visual disturbances during nighttime flight operations, 06-28
...Broca-Sulzer phenomenon, 68-27
...chart readability, 77-13, 78-17
...color, diagnostic tests, 67-8, 71-27, 71-32, 73-18, 75-1, 93-16, 93-17, 95-13, 96-22, 04-10, 04-14, 09-13, 11-8
...color perception and ATCS job performance, 83-11, 85-7, 90-3, 92-6, 92-28, 92-29, 04-10, 04-14, 06-2, 06-6, 06-11, 06-15, 06-22, 07-5, 07-10, 07-24
...contact lenses in an airline accident, 00-18
  –in certification, 90-10, 00-18
...cues for approach and landing, 79-4, 79-25, 81-6, 82-6
...deficiencies in accident airmen, 81-14, 83-18, 93-11
...disorientation, 69-23, 70-2
...drug and pesticide effects on visual reflexes, 79-15
...evaluation of Optec 5000 and Titmus i400 testers, 09-13
...fatigue effects on binocular fusion time, 69-1
...fixation effects on nystagmus, 67-12
...gender differences in refractive surgery, 00-23
...glare, 94-15, 03-6, 07-20
...glaucoma, visual field and altitude, 91-1
...illusions, 70-2, 71-22, 77-12, 78-15
...instrument readability by senior pilots, 77-2, 77-7
...laser illumination effects, 03-12, 04-9, 06-23, 08-14, 10-21, 11-7
...light adaptation device, 66-38
...macular degeneration, case report, 11-14
...matching flash loudness and brightness, 67-16
...monitoring performance on simulated radar task, 80-17, 81-12, 82-16, 90-3, 94-17, 94-26, 96-9
...occupational vision, 96-12, 96-27
...ophthalmic lenses for air traffic controllers, 96-12, 96-27
...perception of depth, 63-10, 63-28, 67-20
...perception of size and distance, 62-15, 64-13, 65-11, 66-22, 66-24, 67-18

...strength and endurance of female pilots, 72-27, 73-23
...strength of flight attendants, 75-13
...thermal balance in heat and cold, 66-23, 68-13
...workload effects, on complex performance, 83-15
 —flight progress strips, 98-26
...workload subjective ratings, models, 07-6

www.ingramcontent.com/pod-product-compliance
Lightning Source LLC
Chambersburg PA
CBHW081113290526
45795CB00006B/2108